For DPM and EBM

The Gentleman from New York

BOOKS BY GODFREY HODGSON

An American Melodrama
(*with Lewis Chester and Bruce Page*)

America in Our Time: From World War II to Nixon

All Things to All Men

The United States
(editor, 3 volumes, *Handbooks to the Modern World* series)

The Colonel: The Life and Wars of Henry Stimson, 1867–1950

A New Grand Tour: How Europe's Great Cities
Made Our World

The People's Century

The World Turned Right Side Up: A History of the
Conservative Ascendancy in America

The Gentleman from New York:
Daniel Patrick Moynihan, A Biography

The Gentleman from New York

Daniel Patrick Moynihan

A BIOGRAPHY

Godfrey Hodgson

HOUGHTON MIFFLIN COMPANY

BOSTON · NEW YORK 2000

Copyright © 2000 by Godfrey Hodgson

For information about permission to reproduce selections
from this book, write to Permissions, Houghton Mifflin Company,
215 Park Avenue South, New York, New York 10003.

Visit our Web site: www.hmco.com/trade.

Library of Congress Cataloging-in-Publication Data
Hodgson, Godfrey.
    The gentleman from New York : Daniel Patrick Moynihan :
a biography / Godfrey Hodgson.
        p.   cm.
    Includes index.
    ISBN 0-395-86042-3
    1. Moynihan, Daniel P. (Daniel Patrick), 1927 — Bio
2. Legislators — United States — Biography. 3. United States.
Congress. Senate — Biography. 4. Ambassadors — United States —
Biography. I. Title: Daniel Patrick Moynihan. II. Title.
E840.8.M68 H63 2000
973.92'092 — dc21 [B] 00-038921

Printed in the United States of America

Book design by Robert Overholtzer

QUM 10 9 8 7 6 5 4 3 2 1

Lines from the A. E. Housman poem are from *The Collected Poems of A. E. Housman*,
© 1964 by Robert E. Symons, copyright 1936 by Barclays Bank Ltd., © 1965 by
Henry Holt and Co. Reprinted by permission of Henry Holt and Company, LLC.

"Parnell" by William Butler Yeats reprinted with permission of Scribner, a Division
of Simon & Schuster, from *The Collected Poems of W. B. Yeats*, Revised Second Edition,
edited by Richard J. Finneran. Copyright 1940 by Georgie Yeats; copyright renewed
© 1968 by Bertha Georgie Yeats, Michael Butler Yeats, and Anne Yeats.

Contents

Preface and Acknowledgments

It was in January 1995 that I wrote to Senator Daniel Patrick Moynihan, springing on him the news that for many years I had wanted to write his biography and that there was a possibility that I might be commissioned to do it. He wrote back, cautiously, that he was hesitant "about what might be learned." He quoted Shakespeare: "use every man after his desert, and who should 'scape whipping." To his surprise, he added, his wife, Liz, often the more cautious of the two, was "quite enthusiastic." Later, in a little garden looking out over their farm at Pindars Corners, New York, I explained to Pat that I was primarily interested in his ideas, that I wanted to write the biography of a mind, but that I could not write about his ideas unless I showed where they came from.

Technically, then, this biography is not "authorized." I was commissioned, and paid, to write it by a commercial publisher. Yet of course I could not possibly have undertaken the book if I had not had Pat and Liz Moynihan's active and generous help. To take only the most obvious example, the Library of Congress would not have given me access to the papers of a living person without that person's express permission. Nor would I have had access, as I have had, to the papers in Senator Moynihan's Capitol Hill office. I would not have been able to listen, as I have done, to his and his wife's explanation, in conversation, of how they felt about many matters, personal and political.

Perhaps most important of all, I would not have been privileged to receive a long and rich flood of Pat Moynihan's letters. I often found it more useful to ask him a question, especially on a sensitive topic, and wait for him to answer, in his own good time, by letter, rather than press him in person on subjects where his instinct might have been to put me off with a quip or to change the subject. So, as will be obvious to the reader, while both writer and subject understood the advantages of the writer's independence, the book could nevertheless not have been written without the subject's generosity with his overburdened time, without his astonishing memory or without his sometimes devastating candor.

Still, it is not easy to write the biography of a living person. It is even harder to write truthfully about a friend. With considerable effort, you learn less about your subject than he has forgotten about himself. The danger is that he will think you an imbecile for not understanding the context of the things you were proud to have learned at all. With the best will in the world on both sides, one is constantly aware that the friendship is always at risk. And it should be said that Pat and Liz Moynihan and I have been friends since 1962. Pat came to my wedding in 1970. We met when we were close neighbors in Washington. He was an official in the Labor Department; I was the Washington correspondent of the *London Observer,* a venerable Sunday paper, then owned and edited by David Astor, which encouraged its correspondents to dig below the surface of subjects they thought important. After five years of digging on this project, I have no reason to change the judgment I offered in that first letter: there is still no one in political life in the United States, or anywhere else, whom on balance I admire more, or who has thought more penetratingly or with deeper understanding into the problems of democracy. Which is not to say, as the reader will discover, that I necessarily share every attitude or every position Senator Moynihan has taken.

My reason for coming to write this book, however, was not simply admiration. I had written a book, published in 1976, on the decline of liberalism in the United States.[1] Much more recently, I had tried to understand the reasons for the rise of conservatism.[2] I was struck by the way these two processes had operated simultaneously, not as a "zero sum game," but almost in isolation, the one from the other. Comparatively few people, it seemed to me, have lived and felt the liberal impulse, and at the same time understood the emotions behind the new conservatism. One of them was Pat Moynihan. For some reason I saw him in my mind's eye like the horizontal stone of a trilith, like those at Stonehenge. In contact with both liberalism and conservatism, he belongs to neither. Supported by both, he seems to link them, and to transcend them.

———

This book, then, could not have been written without countless acts of kindness from both Pat and Liz Moynihan. But my indebtedness does not end with them. I am especially grateful to the senator's staff, and in particular to three members: Tony Bullock, Senator Moynihan's chief of staff; Vicki Bear Dodson, his personal assistant; and Matt Cloud, his chief researcher.

I must thank the literally dozens of busy people in Washington and elsewhere who agreed to be interviewed, and I have acknowledged their help in the Notes.

The book would have been almost impossible to write without the welcome I received from the late Charles Blitzer and his colleagues at the Woodrow Wilson International Center for Scholars; or without the help I have been given by the staff of the manuscript division of the Library of Congress, the Rhodes House Library in Oxford, and the Lyndon Baines Johnson Library at the University of Texas in Austin. I cannot adequately thank all the friends in Washington who housed, fed and listened to me. My debt as always is deepest to those incomparable friends, Harry and Tricia McPherson.

I was fortunate in the sagacity, patience and Internet skills of my principal research assistant, Daniel Liam Singer of St. Cross College, Oxford.

Steve Fraser, then of Houghton Mifflin, encouraged me to undertake the book. Jayne Yaffe Kemp was a model manuscript editor, meticulous and encouraging.

Any such project also makes demands on others who are affected less directly. Here I am thinking especially of the journalists from all over the world who take part in the Reuters Foundation Programme at Oxford University (my "day job"), who respected a door closed from midafternoon on; of the Fellows of Green College, Oxford; and particularly of my colleague Rosemary Allan, the administrator of the Reuters Programme, whose administrative skills and human intuition would have enabled her to run anything from a hospital to an army far better than most hospitals or armies are run. I am aware that there were times when I made all of their lives more difficult, and when the very mention of the name Moynihan must have made them blench inwardly.

Lastly, of course, I would not have been able to carry the job through to the end without the unfailing understanding of my family, and especially of my beloved wife, Hilary.

Oxford, January 2000

BOOK I

I

The Prophet

AN INTRODUCTION

> God save thee, ancient Mariner!
> From the fiends that plague thee thus! —
> Why lookst thou so? — With my cross-bow
> I shot the Albatross.
>
> — Samuel Taylor Coleridge,
> *The Rime of the Ancient Mariner*, Part I

OVER THE PAST quarter century, Ginny Van Horn has often walked up McDougall Road to Pindars Corners. It is an idyllic walk through a bowl of wooded hills, with a stream bubbling under tall shade trees alongside. But when Mrs. Van Horn strolled up the gentle slope on the morning of July 8, 1999, she turned the corner by her neighbor's house, and was suddenly confronted by some three hundred reporters, cameramen and photographers. "There sure is a lot of commotion," she said. In twenty-five years, she'd never seen anything like it. No wonder; for what she had walked into was that late-twentieth-century political phenomenon, a full-blooded media feeding frenzy.

The commotion was understandable. It is not every day that the First Lady of the United States, or FLOTUS, as she is known to the Secret Service, decides to run, or to think seriously about running, for senator from New York. And even when she did make that momentous decision, not every candidate would think of launching her campaign from a hayfield at Pindars Corners in Delaware County.

The hayfield belongs to Senator Daniel Patrick Moynihan, whose farm lies just at the bend of McDougall Road. The hay bales had been tidied away, and when Elizabeth Moynihan, the senator's wife, looked out her window she thought the farm had been visited by space invaders. There were, she calculated, thirty satellite trucks on the hill. The barn was full of portable restrooms, and children prepared iced lemonade for the perspiring reporters in the stable.

A long chain of events had conspired to make that innocent upstate hayfield for a few brief hours the vortex of media attention and political calculation. Hillary Rodham Clinton was contemplating a campaign to succeed Moynihan as one of New York's senators. Liz Moynihan had counseled her that if she was to have any chance of success she must make a strong showing upstate. Mrs. Clinton was pleased to take that advice and had traveled to the rustic southern tier of New York State in search of the photo opportunity that might establish her in the voters' minds as a serious candidate for the whole state, and not just New York City.

At 10:30 the First Lady arrived with her team at the Binghamton airport. They drove to the white schoolhouse just up the hill from the Moynihan farm. It is a simple wooden building, warmed in winter by a Victorian cast-iron stove, where the senator has written eighteen books. After half an hour's chat there, the First Lady, in a navy pants suit, and the senator, in white chino pants and a button-down blue shirt, waving a white baseball cap to emphasize the points of his discourse, emerged from the schoolhouse and sauntered down the lane to face the media, by now installed on a large wooden stand.

The senator introduced his guest. As a tease, he pretended to forget what the reporters had come to hear. "My God," he said, beaming serenely, "I almost forgot. I'm here to say that I hope she will go all the way. I mean to go all the way with her. I think she's going to win."

The not-yet-declared candidate began by paying tribute to her host. She said she was embarking on a "listening tour" of New York, and how better to begin it than by "listening to probably the wisest New Yorker." The questions on everyone's mind, she acknowledged, were "why the Senate, and why New York and why me." Without dealing specifically with the question why she was not running in Illinois, her native state, or in Arkansas, where she had lived for years, she explained that she cared deeply about the issues that mattered to New York. She promised that if she did run and if she were elected, she would be "strong and effective for the people of New York."

In a jovial mood, the veteran senator fielded questions for his guest from the New York press. Almost the very first came from an old friend, Gabe Pressman, of WNBC. What did Mrs. Clinton say, Pressman asked, to those who say that "it takes a lot of chutzpah to come to a state you're not from and run for the Senate?"

"Gabe," said the senator. "We're in Delaware County. Now what was that word?"

When the laughter had subsided, Mrs. Clinton said that she, too, thought it was a strange idea when people first suggested that she might run for the Senate from New York, but that chutzpah was not always a bad thing. After a few more such bantering exchanges, she left, in a simple eight-car motorcade, to continue her listening in a barbecue restaurant, a junior high school, the Baseball Hall of Fame at Cooperstown and other locations carefully selected by some of the sharpest minds in politics for their cultural distance from the twin summits of the political and media ziggurats in Washington and Manhattan.

Behind this benign, if bizarre, encounter, there were rich layers of irony and meaning. Hillary Clinton, for one thing, had not always been on the best of terms with either Pat or Liz Moynihan. Publicly, the senator had spoken slightingly of her cherished plans for health care reform. Privately, the senator's wife had not hidden her impression that Hillary Clinton "didn't get it," meaning that she didn't understand how either the Senate or the senator worked. When Clinton began to consider running for the Senate from New York, she met several times with both Moynihans. They were impressed by her intelligence and candor. Yet, as late as the eve of the great Pindars Corners love-in, Liz Moynihan had her doubts about the wisdom of allowing Clinton to use her home as the launch pad for a Senate campaign. She drew the line at some of the suggestions made by the First Lady's overly enthusiastic handlers. They wanted a rope line to keep the media at a distance. "No rope line," Liz said with finality, and disappeared into the house, ostensibly to telephone her husband. She emerged, quoting him as saying, "You'll have to find another farm!" Liz went on, "I've never made a circus for Pat, and I'm not going to make a circus for her." Besides, she added shrewdly, you don't want to dilute the image. "It's worth a million votes upstate."

Pat Moynihan has the reputation of standing far above the manipulative calculations of media politics. The hayfield photo op showed that he and his political manager, who is also his wife, know a thing or two about how to stage-manage a media event.

The sun shone. The reporters were like pussycats, and the Moynihans and the First Lady had a happy dinner together in the best restaurant for miles around. And it was indeed a great picture, the veteran senator at his most avuncular, the young contender at her most earnest and aspiring.

This strange political epithalamium, this laying on of political hands, was an end and a beginning. It was, so far as anyone could see at the time, the beginning of what promised to be an extraordinary political career for Mrs. Clinton, one that could take her from the humiliations inflicted by her husband's indiscretions, to the United States Senate, and perhaps, as some hoped and others dreaded, to the White House. But that was all speculation, and for the future. It was also, barring the unlikely, the effective end of one of the most interesting political careers in twentieth-century America, a record of controversy and achievement that stretched back almost five decades. The senator would serve out his term, and there would be battles to fight in which he would play his allotted part. But at seventy-two, recovering from major back surgery in the baking summer of 1999, Pat Moynihan had essentially completed a voyage that had brought him from the most unpromising beginnings, in spite of near shipwreck on more than one occasion, to a safe haven as one of the most admired politicians of his time and certainly the most creative and original thinker among them.

Early on Friday morning, November 6, 1998, Liz Moynihan dialed Tony Bullock, Senator Daniel Patrick Moynihan's chief of staff, at home.[1] A phone call had alerted her to the fact that the AP wire was carrying a story that Carl McCall, comptroller of New York State, was "not ruling out" a run for the Senate against her husband.[2] McCall had just been reelected with a 64 percent margin. Bullock's assignment from Mrs. Moynihan was simple: "Get McCall to say he would not run."

Bullock, a cheerful extrovert with considerable political experience and a last-ditch Moynihan loyalist, was convinced that McCall would be "squished like a bug" if he did run against Moynihan.[3] Furthermore, he thought McCall, whom he liked, would do himself real damage in New York politics if he went on making noises about a run for the Senate. Within the hour he had completed his assignment, extracting a statement from McCall, for public release, that he would not run against Moynihan. "I will not challenge Pat," McCall's statement said. "[He is] a true conscience for Democrats in New York and across this great country — if he decides to seek a fifth term. I will, however, in the coming weeks and months sit down with family, friends and advisers and think about my future."[4]

At about 10:30 A.M., Liz Moynihan called again. This time the news was shattering, both in substance and manner. "You should know that Pat is going to tell Gabe Pressman that he will not run again." Gabe Pressman had been covering Moynihan and New York politics for decades as the chief political reporter for the NBC television affiliate in New York City; in fact Moynihan had known him since Averell Harriman's campaign for governor in 1954. Pressman's show would be taped on Friday and aired on Sunday. The senator would hold a press conference to explain in his office in Washington, but not until Monday morning. Liz was emphatic. No one must know until Pressman's show aired, and Bullock mustn't try to talk them out of this because their minds were made up.

Tony Bullock made a brief effort to do just that. If the senator was determined not to run again in the year 2000, then he should at all costs hold off until later in 1999. It was far too early to be turned into a lame duck, and, besides, major political earthquakes of this kind had to be planned and handled. Liz Moynihan shuns the limelight. But she has run four successful statewide elections as her husband's campaign manager, two of them victories by record margins. She knows her own mind. "We're doing it," she said, "and that's that." At which she and Pat raced off to the taping. Would they at least commit to a press conference or a statement later in the day? Again, the answer was no.

Moynihan taped the interview. Yes, he was going. No, it was not his health. (There had been various rumors, stimulated by the fact that at a local campaign event a few days earlier he felt dizzy, apparently from flu.) After twenty-four years, it was time to move on. This was a good moment, after the Democratic successes in the midterm elections.

After the taping, Liz set off for an archeological event at the New York Botanical Gardens in the Bronx. (She is an expert on Mughal India in general, and ancient Indian gardens in particular.) The senator was on the way down in the elevator at 30 Rockefeller Plaza, home of the NBC studios. As he entered the elevator, a man said, "I heard you're not running." As they hit the ground floor, some kid came up, and said, "So, senator, you really made some news on Gabe's show today!"

News, and rumor, travel fast in this age. Before he left the building,

Tony Bullock in Washington had calls from the Associated Press in Albany, from a TV station in Buffalo, from Fox News and from Moynihan's former press secretary Tim Russert, now with NBC, all on the line at the same moment. And they were just the first of several dozen calls. The reporters tried out one hypothesis after another, each more fantastic than the one before. Some asked whether Moynihan hated Chuck Schumer (Charles E. Schumer, newly elected to the other New York Senate seat) and was quitting in protest. Or was he scared that Alfonse D'Amato might run for his seat? Had he, perhaps, *fainted* on the Pressman show?

In the new age of American media, Bullock reflected, the age of CNN, MSNBC, Rupert Murdoch's Fox News, the Internet, NY 1, Geraldo and the rest of them, the pace was getting crazy. If they couldn't get a quote, in Bullock's rueful experience, they would be happy to make things up, or fill the endless hours of airtime with speculation from pundits, including enemies who would not hesitate to use the opportunity to do as much damage as they could to the senator's reputation. He wondered whether the senator and the senator's wife, both bred to politics before this circus atmosphere had taken hold, fully understood how nasty and angry the media were getting now that they were feeling bounced by a major story without warning.

Gabe Pressman got his scoop, but only just. At 6:04 P.M., an hour after Moynihan's news broke, it was announced that Newt Gingrich, Speaker of the House, was resigning. That bumped Moynihan's retirement from the lead in the *New York Times*, and the editorial commenting on it into second place. Nationally, Moynihan's departure had been largely upstaged by that of Gingrich. "No matter," Moynihan commented. "Everyone has been wonderfully kind, and it's over."

The faithful Bullock was left alone with his cell phone, trying to keep the stories going in the right direction. Somehow at the end of a day of chaos and panic it seemed that Liz had been right all along, that this was a much better way to do it. "No managed event, thank you kindly. They did it on impulse and gut feeling. In all their political decisions they seem to know instinctively what will work and what will not." In retrospect he felt what they did was masterly. They had caught the press asleep at the switch and slipped a pivotal decision through in the aftermath of the surprise Democratic victories in the midterm elections.

Actually, the Moynihans had decided after the 1994 election that it would be time to go in 2000. A whole web of subtle calculations and feelings went into that decision. One was Liz's wish to see more of a husband who had been bound on the wheel of politics and public service since they married more than forty years before. There were indeed health problems, though they were not in themselves enough to precipitate a decision to quit. The crucial question was not whether Moynihan would run for a fifth term in 2000. That they had decided he would not do. The all-important decision was about timing. The Democratic victories in the midterms, and especially the fact there would still be a Democratic senior senator from New York in the shape of Charles Schumer, were satisfying and invigorating for a New York Democratic party that had been divided and demoralized for years. But it is impossible to avoid the suspicion that even the possibility of having to run in a primary against Carl McCall, an African American, was a deciding factor.

For a McCall-versus-Moynihan clash in the New York Democratic primary would have unleashed the demons of race, those demons Moynihan feared more than anything for his beloved city. They were demons that had also pursued him personally through the two most traumatic political experiences of his life. One was the reception of the so-called "Moynihan Report" on the crisis of the African American family, the other was the rage that had greeted the leaking of a memorandum he had written to President Nixon, saying that what the issue of race in America needed was a period of "benign neglect." As Moynihan saw it, he had been pursued by the Furies after those episodes in 1965 and 1970. He bitterly resented the way he had been accused of racism. A primary campaign against an African American, even a distinguished man whom he personally liked and respected, was bound to summon up the never wholly dormant issues of racial hostility in New York. Moynihan himself commented merely that a McCall run in the primary "would have been the beginning of Lord knows how many months of people saying, 'Will he run?' 'Should he run?' which would gradually turn into, 'Hasn't he been there too long?' "[5]

The timing of his extrication from New York politics having been thus managed with inspired opportunism, the tributes duly flowed richly in from media and politicos alike. "A Giant Still Walks Among Us," the *Daily News* had headlined a column a few months earlier about whether Moynihan might retire.[6] "For all the talk about his cerebral skills," said the *New York Post* now, "nobody did more to bring home the bacon for New York."[7] "A true statesman," said Republican Governor George Pataki,[8] and Republican New York Mayor Rudolph Giuliani echoed him: "New Yorkers will lose a great public servant and a loyal friend."[9] Few people in our history, save Thomas Jefferson, said Moynihan's close friend in the Senate, Bob Kerrey of Nebraska, have had as much impact on our nation and on our government as Daniel Patrick Moynihan.[10] One of the half dozen most brilliant men ever to sit in the United States Senate, said someone. Vice President Al Gore responded promptly, calling Moynihan "both an extraordinary public servant as well as a visionary thinker . . . More than anyone, Senator Moynihan has been consistently ahead of the curve."[11] From Highfill, Arkansas, the president of the United States, whom Moynihan had attacked almost contemptuously on health care in 1993 and 1994 and angrily savaged on welfare in 1996, felt moved to issue a statement saying that Moynihan's life story could have been written by Horatio Alger. "His rise from a poor childhood in New York City's Hell's Kitchen to his place as the most popular elected statewide official in New York during four Senate terms is an inspirational life story."[12]

Leaving aside the detail that Moynihan did not spend his childhood in Hell's Kitchen, the substance of Clinton's tribute is true. The odds were surely stacked high against a boy with his start in life making it to the United States Senate as "the gentleman from New York." Disaster befell his mother and her three children when Moynihan's father, a talented journalist and publicist, but also a gambler and drinker, abandoned them. When young Moynihan was at Benjamin Franklin High School in East Harlem, or even when he was sitting in Governor Averell Harriman's outer office in Albany, entertaining supplicants with his rich repertoire of jokes and anecdotes, no one would have given a cent for his chances of climbing to the top. He himself sees his career as a series of serendipitous "chance encounters and random walks." One such chance encounter led him to study at City College of New York, and a random walk took him into a navy recruiting office that opened the highway of advancement.

A better metaphor, perhaps, might be to say that a political career is not like the steady, powered impetus of a locomotive. It is more like a sailboat. To keep afloat on the mighty, unpredictable waters of public opinion, the political navigator must know how to avoid the most dangerous storms, tack against adverse winds, and when the wind drops to a calm, catch the lightest breeze that will keep him on course.

A superficial reading of Daniel Patrick Moynihan's half century in politics would see him tacking broadly from left to right and then to the left again. He started out as something pretty close to the ideal type of New Deal Democrat of the two decades after the death of Franklin Delano Roosevelt. The word *liberal* has fallen into some disrepute. But the young man who returned from London, where he had instinctively felt at home in the social democratic Labour party of the postwar years, to work for Averell Harriman in New York started with political beliefs pretty typical of the Cold War liberals of his generation. He never had any sympathy with communism, perhaps in part because he was brought up in a world of fierce Catholic anticommunism, in part because, unlike some of his friends and intellectually gifted contemporaries, he never felt the slightest temptation to embrace Marxist ideas. And perhaps because of the Irish influences of his childhood, he instinctively felt more at home with the "regulars" in Democratic politics, as opposed to the "reformers," who when he was growing up in New York were more apt to be Jews or Wasps. He felt perfectly comfortable working for Governor Averell Harriman, a patrician with a penchant for reform. From Albany, or rather from Syracuse, where he risked being becalmed by a contract to write the history of Harriman's administration, it was inevitable that Moynihan would trim every sail to catch the breeze that would waft him to work for John F. Kennedy.

Moynihan made good use of his time in the Kennedy administration. Dropped almost by chance into a job at the Labor Department which put him in charge of research, Moynihan exploited not expertise as a social scientist, for at that stage his knowledge was limited and not particularly specialized, but an instinct for understanding the way social science could illuminate the issues in politics. A few years later, steered by chance into the Education Department at Harvard (he later succeeded in moving to the Government Department), he duly transferred his attention to education. Before long he had contrived to turn a seminar on education into a powerful tool for criticizing many of the liberal assumptions of social science generally.

The liberalism of the 1950s and 1960s — and it spread broadly in those days across the Republican as well as the Democratic party — saw political action as almost the executive arm of social science. Capitalism works, the liberals (as opposed to the Left) accepted. By increasing productivity, it generated economic growth. This in turn made it possible to meet people's needs, and a surprising number of their dreams, out of incremental resources; thus the class conflicts predicted by Marx were unnecessary. So social problems, like industrial problems, could be solved. The problems must be identified — poverty, ignorance, disease, inequality, teenage delinquency, racial injustice, it made no difference. Programs could be, must be, designed to solve them, by government leaders informed and enlightened by social science. Money and other skilled resources, such as trained social scientists, would be applied to the problems as "inputs." The "outputs" would be predictable. The problems would be solved.

Later, indeed not much later, Moynihan and his friends, especially those associated with the journal *The Public Interest,* developed a powerful critique of the way politicians in the Age of Liberalism had exaggerated what social science could do for them. They came to believe that social science had no business proposing policy; its proper role was limited to monitoring government action, not designing it. But for a time, in the Kennedy and Johnson administrations, Moynihan did share the general assumptions of optimistic, "can-do" liberalism. That was the style, as well as the philosophy, of those two Democratic administrations.

Moynihan played a significant part in three rather typical political enterprises of that period. He produced, and wrapped in a typically Rooseveltian phrase, "One Third of a Nation," a report on why so many young men failed the physical and mental tests for selective service. He threw himself into the Johnson administration's War on Poverty, setting himself, with some courage, against those who were carried away by the contemporary social science craze for "community action." With the practicality of someone who had actually experienced poverty, he argued instead that what the poor needed was simply money. He wrote what came to be known as the "Moynihan Report," but whose real title was "The Negro Family: The Case for National Action." Nothing could be more representative of the liberal way of thinking. Social science data showed that African American families were in crisis because, even when the economy picked up and black men no longer lost their jobs, they still left their children and the children's mothers. Very well: *the data constituted a case for national action.*

Yet the report was to be tied around Moynihan's neck like the ancient mariner's albatross. "The man hath penance done . . ." In the complicated way in which events are always shaped by chance, Moynihan, having succeeded in inserting into the Johnson administration's thinking his ideas about what was happening to the demographics of the black family, left the country, not as it happens for a pointless junket or a well-deserved rest, but an official trip to what was then Yugoslavia. What he learned there powerfully influenced one of the strongest strands of his thinking, his belief in the supremacy of ethnicity over class in determining political loyalties. "Blood," he came to believe, "is stronger than class."[13] While he was out of the country, he became drawn into the bitter rivalries of the New York Democratic party. His name was floated for mayor; then that possibility evaporated. Instead, he found himself on the losing side in a primary race for president of the New York City Council.

To run for office, he had to quit his job in the Johnson administration and somehow the manner of his quitting aroused the powerful, if often irrational, resentment of President Johnson. So Moynihan found himself without a job, either in Washington or New York. Worse was to come. Savage, racially motivated rioting broke out in Watts, in South Central Los Angeles. It was not the first of the racial riots of the 1960s, but it was the first on a scale that alerted the national government and the whole country to how badly, even as things were improving for Southern blacks, they were going wrong in the big cities outside the South. Journalists cottoned to the idea that a "secret" document called the "Moynihan Report" contained the administration's assessment of what had gone wrong. (It was not in fact secret, though it had not been given wide circulation.) They either read and misunderstood the Report, or — more often — read the inaccurate interpretations of others. Moynihan became a celebrity, but in a way that threatened to be disastrous for his political career. The albatross had been firmly tied around the mariner's neck.

Most of the press coverage was in fact respectful. Moynihan found himself regarded by both academia and by NBC as an expert on "the cities," a phrase that had become the new euphemism for racial conflict. But there were two segments of society who did not like the implication they read in the Report, that the unemployment, poverty and family breakdown that afflicted individual black men and women in urban ghettos were somehow "caused" by a generic phenomenon, specific to African Americans and caused by their history, called "the crisis of the Negro family." That is not what Moynihan had written. Indeed it came close to being the opposite of what he said. But many black people, or at least in the first instance many black intellectuals, felt that he had displayed insensitivity, bordering on racism. And at least some white intellectuals on the liberal Left agreed. They accused Moynihan of "blaming the victim." And some openly charged him with racism.

The effect on Moynihan was profound. The bright hopes of 1963 had been ripped away. The president with whom he identified to some degree, and in whom he had reposed his political hopes, both for the country and for himself, was dead. He had tried, and in the end failed, to win the trust of his successor. Suddenly he found himself without a job in the executive branch, his political career in New York apparently over before it had begun and now unjustly reviled for a serious attempt to understand a profound social problem. It was a bitter time, and he was bitter. He went through a crisis of depression, a dark night of the soul.

It is also true that, seen from the outside, nothing terribly disastrous happened. The very day that Moynihan learned he had lost in the New York primary, he had a very pleasant offer of a year at the Center for Advanced Studies at Wesleyan University, a delightful place, where, to every external eye, he and Liz were as happy as could be. And before the academic year was over, he had received what many academics would kill for, an invitation to join the faculty at Harvard. He moved to Cambridge. He became the director of the Joint Center for Urban Studies, run by Harvard and the Massachusetts Institute of Technology. Before long he led a faculty seminar, on education and equality, that attracted more attention than anything of its kind in Cambridge since Henry Kissinger's disarmament seminars in the 1950s.

Yet within himself, Moynihan did go through a crisis in the late 1960s, and so did the country. His generation, that of those just old enough to have been actively involved in World War II, were filled with a bursting optimism — all the more so if, like Pat Moynihan, they had not actually been exposed to the blood and the dirt, the fear and the emotional trauma of combat. The country seemed to be on a roll. The war ended the Depression, and tens of millions found themselves better off than their parents had ever dreamed they could be.

For those who had been in the service, the GI Bill and other forms of educational opportunity made a college education something they could all expect. Not that the 1950s were a serene decade. They were years of conformity, of repressive attitudes to sex and family, political intolerance. But they were also, especially for a bright young man like Pat Moynihan, from a middle-class family that had fallen on hard times, a time of hope and unprecedented opportunity.

The only cloud, it seemed at first, lay overseas, in the menacing shape of the Soviet Union and its communist and fellow-traveling allies. In retrospect it is remarkable that in his eloquent inaugural address, President John Kennedy did not so much as mention any domestic problems in American society; he called on Americans to gird themselves for an epic struggle against the dark forces of communism. It was a speech Ronald Reagan might have given. Within three years the national self-perception had changed diametrically. President Kennedy himself had been assassinated. If, more than a third of a century later, no plausible alternative explanation has appeared, and it looks as if his murder was really the random act of a deranged individual, few were content with that interpretation at the time. The assassination, and more specifically Kennedy's replacement by Lyndon Johnson, came — illogically but unmistakably — to symbolize a crisis of authority.

The Cold War intensified. If Kennedy successfully negotiated a satisfactory resolution of the threat posed by the Cuban missile crisis, he plunged the country deeper and deeper into disastrous courses in his handling of Southeast Asia. By 1963 the country was heading toward a great quarrel over the ethics and expediency of intervention in Vietnam.

Perhaps more damaging still, by the middle of the decade the successful crusade for civil rights for black Americans in the South had given way to rioting and bitter racial conflict in the North. All the nation's largest and most important cities, New York, Chicago, Los Angeles, Washington and Detroit, among others, were loud with riot and anger.

The consensus politics of the 1950s were replaced by a new politics of confrontation. The war not only divided Americans over the ethics of their foreign policy; for many it seemed that the country had abandoned its deepest anticolonial traditions, or exposed itself to humiliation. The racial crisis in the North was shocking, even frightening, for those who had assumed that race prejudice and inequality were residual problems, essentially for the South. All three crises — of authority, over the war and about race — were especially acute for those, like Moynihan from 1966, 1967 and onward, who were involved in teaching college students, and in researching into the sociology and politics of race.

There were many among his contemporaries and peers who allowed their faith in the decency and efficacy of American political institutions to be shaken by this triple barrage. Not Moynihan. His anger was directed, not against "the System," but against those who gave up on traditional American beliefs. He was bitterly scornful of what he saw as cowardly or opportunistic liberals. So much so that he never has ceased to denounce what he felt was the hypocritical stance of those who railed against a system that had guaranteed them a comfortable upper-middle-class lifestyle. For a time he even identified publicly with those, conservatives and neoconservatives, who shared his dislike for what they saw as liberal hypocrisy. But, and this point is absolutely crucial to unraveling the apparently strange meandering of his political course, while he criticized the inconsistencies and failures of liberalism, he never wholeheartedly went over and joined its enemies. Many see him as having sailed on a great circle from classic liberalism, by way of neoconservatism, back to a contemporary version of a traditional Democratic liberal position. Moynihan himself insists that it has not been he who has moved.

True, he did startle his friends and even shocked his wife in 1968 by deciding to work for Richard Nixon. This was not entirely an opportunistic career move; nor was it motivated solely by what he saw as the unfair treatment he had received at the hands of his former liberal allies. He hoped that Nixon would give him the scope to do what the Johnson administration had not allowed him to do, namely to eliminate poverty in America and in so doing to save the American family. More than that, he actually admired Richard Nixon, even though he instinctively distrusted him and many of his lieutenants. When Nixon's loyalists were heading for the penitentiary or out the door, Moynihan, in a quixotic gesture, risked his whole career by volunteering to go back to work for a man by then almost past saving.[14]

Although Moynihan could not quite bring himself to admit it, Nixon had already let him down. Although the president was persuaded to send Moynihan's visionary bid to end poverty, the Family Assistance Plan, to Congress, in the end he was not willing to fight for it. Although he enjoyed Moynihan's company and appreciated the gloss of literary culture and the intellectual weight he lent, Nixon did not seriously attempt to save Moynihan from his opponents within the White House. Even before the first anniversary of his going to work for Nixon in November 1968, Moynihan had been outmaneuvered by the dour stalwarts of Nixon's palace guard.

By the time those same loyalists were being exposed on national television by Senator Sam Ervin's hearings in 1973, Moynihan was out of Washington as the U.S. ambassador to India. Marooned in the heat and dust of New Delhi's political aviary, he had time to reflect on the crumbling of Nixon's and his hopes, and in the end to rescue his fortunes with a knight's move. He was shaken by the disintegration of the American position in the world as a result of Watergate and of the energy crisis, of the imminent loss of the Vietnam War and the cool aggression with which the Soviet Union, under Leonid Brezhnev, was taking every advantage that showed itself on the world chess board. He determined to hazard his career for a new fortune by doing what he could to stiffen America's stance in a hostile world.

Moynihan's move was to write a long article portraying the United States as being "in opposition," meaning almost "in eclipse."[15] He shocked those who saw the United States as the popular hero of the developing world by suggesting that the dominant ideology in the countries emerging from colonialism was neither Soviet communism nor the American version of democracy, but a kind of statist social democracy derived more from the London School of Economics than from either Moscow or Washington. The thesis was in some respects simplistic. It owed something to memories of arguments with Indian students in London twenty years before, something to the irritations of an ambassador isolated in Indira Gandhi's leftish Delhi, but more to the demands of the author's own tricky political situation. It met those demands brilliantly. On the strength of it, and of the way it caught the wind of a new, irritable American attitude toward the outside world, Moynihan found himself on his way, not back to Harvard to teach Government 251 ("Ethnicity in American Politics"), but to confront the massed diplomatic champions of the Third World and their bid, egged on by the Soviet Union, to destroy the legitimacy and ultimately the security of Israel by declaring that Zionism must be equated with racism.

Moynihan's time at the United Nations as U.S. ambassador during the Ford administration was stormy and frenetic. His deep instincts were aroused by the Zionism resolution. He had lived among Jews all his life, of course, and some of the people closest to him, including Nathan Glazer, Irving Kristol, Suzanne Weaver (later Garment) and many others, were Jewish. His lifelong antipathy to communism was at bay too. He felt there was something indecent, in human terms, about the attempt to equate Zionism, the survival instinct of a noble people that had come close to being persecuted out of existence, with racism, the vulgar prejudice that had been, precisely, the cause of the Jewish people's catastrophe.

He also saw more clearly than most people in Washington that there was something threatening in political terms about the campaign behind the resolution. It was a peculiarly crass example of what had been the Soviet strategy since the leadership in Moscow realized, in Khrushchev's time, that frontal assault on the West was futile. The Kremlin's best hope of spreading the influence of communism would be to convert or subvert the Third World. So Moynihan waded into the battle in a strange mood: the berserker warrior, swinging his battle-ax round his head, but at the same time constantly looking suspiciously over his shoulder for fear that someone, probably Henry Kissinger, was out to get him.

Kissinger did get him, in the sense that he was eventually forced out of the United Nations job; but not before he had snatched a kind of victory from defeat on the resolution itself. He had also recouped his political career. In 1976, after a desperately close and bitter primary race against Congresswoman Bella Abzug, he was elected to the Senate. Eleven and a half years after his decision to leave the Johnson administration, and after eight years working for Republican presidents, he was back in Washington, as a Democratic senator from New York.

It is worth noticing just how fast he moved. He was less than a year at Wesleyan. He was at Harvard for two periods of two years, with an added orphan semester. Three years in the White House, with the period of his significant influence on policy over in less than a year. Roughly two years in India. Under one year at the United Nations. It is a record that suggests impatience, dissatisfaction, persistent difficulty in getting on with superiors and the troubled emotions that afflict a man of immense ability and energy who cannot quite find the right task and is afraid that his time will run out before he does; and something of all this was true of his mood from 1965 to 1975. Contrast that tumultuous decade with four terms in the Senate as a figure of growing influence, and — in spite of many frustrations — increasing serenity.

The explanation, it is plain, lies in the way his personal crisis, which was intellectual as well as emotional, tracked and meshed with a crisis in the life of the country and, if it is legitimate to personify a great nation, of its successive moods.

A child of the Depression and the war, rescued from poverty and afforded boundless opportunity by the postwar revolution in educational opportunity, Moynihan grew up sharing the national confidence of the 1950s. Then the national crisis of confidence of the 1960s hit him more painfully than most.

He was identified to some on college campuses as an enemy of the New Left, and so in general he was, though he could show great understanding and insight into what made gifted young people rebel.[16] He was targeted as a dissenter from the ideas of the New Left and as "blaming the victim." He was a teacher, and university academics were more likely than most to experience student rebellion as a threat to cherished institutions. He was the target of a more or less serious threat to destroy his house in 1969.[17] He was an expert on "urban affairs," and as such had seen for himself how ill-conceived and ineffective were the fashionable nostrums proposed by liberal social scientists. Once again, therefore, he put his head above the parapet to be shot at by all those who wanted either to defend traditional liberal assumptions or find scapegoats for their failure. After he went to work for Richard Nixon, he inherited, and fully reciprocated, the fierce liberal hatred of Nixon.

In all these respects he experienced in exaggerated form what the country as a whole was experiencing. Moynihan and his friends felt an active commitment to the proposition that American society, contrary to what the radicals were proclaiming, was for all its faults fundamentally healthy. It was for him, therefore, a duty to try to correct error, denounce what he saw as lying and persuade doubters of the underlying strength and decency of America.

When he first arrived in the Senate, there was a danger that he would become the captive of a small group of neoconservative intellectuals, on his staff and off. To some extent he had been taken up by this group after the collapse of Senator Henry "Scoop" Jackson's unsuccessful campaign for the presidency in 1976. Some of these people dreamed of replacing Jackson with Moynihan as the Democratic presidential nominee, seeing him as a centrist who could rescue the party from liberal heresies in domestic politics and soft-boiled attitudes in foreign policy alike. As any successful first-term senator does, Moynihan flirted briefly with the idea of a presidential campaign, but only in his own mind and in guarded conversation with a few friends. Certainly there was no "overt act," no political initiative, to launch a presidential bid.

By 1981, therefore, all unawares, Ronald Reagan had done Moynihan two big favors. He had cured him of any lingering temptation to run for president; after the shooting attempt on Reagan's life in March 1981 it was plain that any attempt to unseat him would be futility itself. And he had reconfirmed the senator in his lifelong loyalty to the Democratic party. (He was, he once said, "baptized a Catholic and born a Democrat.") The similarities between Moynihan and Reagan, though superficial, are intriguing. Both had family backgrounds in the Middle West (Reagan in Illinois, Moynihan in Indiana), though Moynihan was taken to New York as a child and soon ceased even to spend family vacations in Indiana. Both had fathers who were Irish Democrats and alcoholics. Both started out as active New Deal liberals; indeed both were on the board of Americans for Democratic Action, the liberal high command. Both were shocked by the political revival of the Left in the 1960s, and by the cultural upheaval that accompanied and ultimately buried it. Both were especially angry with student radicalism.

But there the similarities end. Beginning when he was president of the Screen Actors Guild, but at an accelerating pace after he went to work for General Electric, Reagan soon became an icon of the new conservatism that had emerged from the debacle of Barry Goldwater's 1964 campaign for the White House. Moynihan worked for Richard Nixon in the White House. But he never missed an opportunity to make it plain that he was not one of the president's men, that he remained a Democrat, and an opponent of the Vietnam War.[18] As a lifelong anticommunist, Moynihan had no difficulty in representing first Nixon, then Gerald Ford, as ambassador, first in New Delhi, then at the United Nations.

He campaigned for the Democratic nomination in New York with the welcome help of conservative Democrats, and as an avowed opponent of the brand of New York liberalism embodied by Bella Abzug. But that was as far to the Right as he would go. Once arrived on Capitol Hill, he understood that his first duty was to New York State.

His political interest lay in getting the utmost for his constituents from the only source capable of delivering resources on the requisite scale: the federal government. He quickly saw through the Reagan administration's strategic plans for destroying the American welfare state by running up a deficit so huge that only deep cuts in social expenditure could prevent federal bankruptcy. At the same time he also saw that the Reagan administration's serious foreign policy, which involved challenging and at the same time negotiating with the Soviet Union, was being put at risk by ignorant wild men who were out of control. Moynihan took the behavior of the CIA in Central America and the way in which its agents tried to conceal what they were doing from the Senate Intelligence Committee, of which he was vice chairman, as a personal insult. And he came to see the attempt to circumvent the will of Congress in the Iran-contra affair as little short of a coup d'état against constitutional government.

Long before Reagan left the White House in 1988, in short, Moynihan had returned to the political allegiance of his youth, if he had ever left it. In the process he had become one of the most reliable, as well as one of the most eloquent, opponents of the Reagan administration and the conservative Republicans in Congress. As an increasingly influential member, and briefly as chairman, of the Senate Finance Committee, he concerned himself with many aspects of public finance. His special interests were — as his past experience would have predicted — in taxation, social security, welfare and education. He tried, and failed, to put together a health reform package that could attract broad bipartisan support, then managed to extricate from the ruins of the Clinton health care project massive resources for health care research, which is after all one of New York's major industries. As a ranking member, and for a time chairman, of the Environment and Public Works Committee, he left behind an impressive record. He helped to craft, and to steer through Congress, a massively ambitious transportation bill that reversed more than a generation of discrimination in favor of highways and against mass transit.

For all the high praise lavished on Moynihan when he announced that he would leave the Senate, however, the Washington insiders' view of his performance there was less flattering. It was conceded that he was an ornament, "the kind of person," one friend-turned-opponent says,[19] "the Founding Fathers would have wanted in the Senate: urbane, witty, scholarly, wise, eloquent. But what will he leave behind?"

Two knowledgeable and influential groups of people, in particular, take a poor view of Moynihan's performance as a legislator: the neoconservative intellectuals, and some of his fellow senators and, especially, their staffs. Irving Kristol, his old comrade-in-arms at *The Public Interest* and even before that his editor on *The Reporter*, speaks for the neoconservatives generally. To Kristol, Moynihan is "a highly intelligent man" and a "significant" but not an "important" man. (He didn't elaborate on the distinction.)[20]

It is revealing, Kristol went on, that there is no "Moynihan bill" that he will be known by. There could have been. Fellowship or scholarship funds, something like the Fulbright scholarships. The reason, according to Kristol, is that Moynihan is not interested in legislation. He likes to use the Senate as a place to influence debate. He is a "pussycat," says Kristol. He has always avoided hard issues because he doesn't want people to dislike him.

Kristol is right that there are many, both senators and especially their staff, who do not hold an extravagantly high view of Moynihan's qualities. Some talk about the difficulty he has had in getting and especially in keeping good staff. "Treats them like shit," one man who has dealt with Moynihan in the Clinton White House said bluntly. "In the general scheme of things," a veteran journalist observer of Congress told me, "I think he is a great man. But he can be vindictive. He is a pedant, and that annoys many of his colleagues. He enunciates the exact word with every sign of great inner satisfaction. That antagonizes his colleagues. He is not hail-fellow-well-met. There is an emotional moat around him. He can be obsequious, but he is not approachable."[21]

Others are even more critical, even contemptuous. Politics is a rough game, and some of them have gone against Moynihan and lost. One man who held "the Moynihan portfolio" in the Clinton White House professes to admire Moynihan's intelligence and the range of ideas he can address. But he calls him "a gadfly." He has led a charmed life with the press, this man told me. "The reporters go light on his ineffectiveness as a legislator." In fact, he said, Moynihan has "an inability to act as a legislator at all. It is not in his character to make the friendships, to write the chits." This judgment, of course, proceeds from a certain preconception of what it is that a legislator does.

A former Moynihan staffer, however, who has gone on to a career of considerable influence in Washington, acknowledges some of these criticisms. "He thinks anecdotally," he said. "He thinks in narrative. He cares a lot about what intellectuals think of him. He is an intellectual himself, but he is not an academic. He doesn't think with the precision of a first-rate academic." This same witness flatly denies criticisms of the way Moynihan treats his staff, saying that on the contrary he may push his staff hard, but he backs them up, even when they make mistakes.

"I'm not one of those who thinks he was an ineffective legislator," says former Republican Chairman of the Senate Finance Committee Bob Packwood of Oregon. "And boy! Was he looking out for the interests of New York!"[22] And former Majority Leader Bob Dole says, "Pat was always perceived as the intellectual of the Senate, but he was obviously effective in a different way. At the committee level he was very protective of the interests of New York. He was known for his candor and fairness. But Pat can count. He always understood where the votes were." But he wasn't a conventional legislative craftsman? I asked. "No, but he was a big-picture craftsman."[23]

"He is the most successful intellectual in electoral politics," said Rob Shapiro, who worked for Moynihan from 1981 to 1986.[24] "He is often lampooned as a figure out of the Victorian Raj. But he has a great intuitive grasp of popular politics. He always manages to position himself as a critic of the conventional wisdom. He sees what other people don't see. But his great political art is to point it out. The liberals saw him as a deserter in a period of liberal politics, then the conservatives saw him as a deserter in a period of conservative politics." He is *not* interested in power, Shapiro judges, he is more interested in reputation. "That's why the appeal of the Senate has been so great. He likes the sense of personal dignity, the way it allows him to be a gentleman."

Daniel Patrick Moynihan is a prophet, in the Greek or Old Testament meaning of the word. Not just in the sense that he can foretell the future, though on a rather impressive range of issues, from the welfare crisis in the inner cities, to the impending collapse of the Soviet Union, to the danger of ethnic conflict in the Balkans, he has shown an almost uncanny flair for seeing the importance of questions that had not yet come up on other people's screens.

The Greek word *prophetes*, from which we derive our word *prophet*, means one who speaks out. Moynihan speaks out. He dares to think for himself, and to say what he thinks, even if it hurts himself or others. He has done it up and down the East Coast, from New York to Washington and Cambridge and back to New York and Washington again, these nearly fifty years. He is in reality the modern equivalent of a prophet, which is to say that he is at heart a journalist.

If he had not been a professor or a politician, I like to think that he would have been the greatest columnist of his day. His greatest gift is to handicap the intellectual horses. He picks up tips about their form, decides which ones will run and run and sticks his intellectual and political wad on the ones he thinks will be winners. There have been some slow coaches and some fallers. But the record of his form book is truly imposing.

At the same time there has been a core of principle and consistency. Moynihan, one of his staff told me, has his "permanent agenda." At the heart of it is a double credo. Charles de Gaulle began his great war memoirs by saying that, from the start, he had a certain idea of France, and that France would not be France unless it was great.[25] Pat Moynihan has always set before himself an image of the United States that would deserve its own greatness through magnanimity to its own citizens and to the world. Second, he has always understood that, however important private enterprise and voluntary associations might be — churches, universities, political parties — greatness could not be achieved by the uncoordinated actions of individual citizens alone, still less as a by-product of maximizing the shareholder value of corporations.

Moynihan is not primarily a liberal, still less a conservative. His friend John Kenneth Galbraith says, "You will never understand Pat in terms of commitment to Left or Right. He has a mind wholly free from ideological commitments. His long-term commitment is to cities, to the poor and especially to poor children."[26] Some would say he is a Progressive. But these adjectives are only labels. What even his fiercest critics would agree with is that Moynihan has been as prolific of political ideas as any practicing politician of his generation.

This book will be a parade of those ideas and their evolution. But first we will have to turn over the soil of experience in which they grew, in a clouded childhood, a youth of gradually opening opportunity in and out of the city of New York, and formative years in London.

2

Growing Pains

NEW YORK AND LONDON

Bildungsroman: [German] A novel dealing with one
person's formative years or spiritual education.
— *Oxford English Dictionary*

THIS IS NOT a psychobiography. Its main focus is on the inter-
play between ideas and action in the life of a man who has
been called "the nation's best thinker among politicians since
Lincoln, and its best politician among thinkers since Jefferson."[1] Still,
to understand the ideas, it helps to know something of the life. All bi-
ographies of thinking men and women are the history of a mind. In
Pat Moynihan's case, an account of his early life is specially relevant.
To an unusual extent, his ideas have been the product of early experience. He has been fitted, and has from time to time fitted himself,
into a classic American myth: the story of a boy's rise from bootblack
and longshoreman in the mean streets of Hell's Kitchen, on the West
Side of Manhattan, to a professor's chair at Harvard and a desk in the
United States Senate.

The story is true, as far as it goes. The young Pat Moynihan *was*
poor. He did shine shoes. He did work on the docks. He did attend
Benjamin Franklin High School on the fringes of Harlem. But it also
oversimplifies. The truth of his upbringing is more complicated and
more interesting than the rags-to-riches tales of Horatio Alger. When
it endorsed him as candidate for the U.S. Senate in 1976, for example,
the *New York Times* called him "that rambunctious child of the sidewalks of New York,"[2] with sonorous echoes of Al Smith. But he was
born, not in Hell's Kitchen, but in Tulsa, Oklahoma; he grew up as
a young child, not in Manhattan, but in Bluffton and Jeffersonville,

Indiana. His mother's family were Protestants. And he didn't sleep a night in Hell's Kitchen until he had a college degree and a commission in the United States Navy.

The obstacles in the way of a young man with his early experience of life on the way to Harvard, the White House and the Senate were awesome. But, to a far greater extent than the simple tintype of the Irish kid from Hell's Kitchen would suggest, they were internal and psychological, rather than external and palpable. There were times, between the ages of ten and seventeen, when life for the young Moynihan was genuinely tough, and there were periods when he experienced real poverty. When I asked him if his mother had ever been on welfare, he answered, "Of course," and then went on to guess that his mother would have collected food, not money. More influential for his later development and thinking, perhaps, was the much longer portion of his youth when he experienced constant uncertainty, the fear of poverty, the vague shame of a family that has fallen through the safety nets of middle-class security, and the memory of a childhood that was by comparison an idyll of small-town America. If Pat Moynihan grew up in real poverty at times, the trauma was not the usual story of a working-class family that never had a chance. It was the more complex predicament of a middle-class family whose status and prospects were dramatically affected when the father left home. The wonder is that, while the black dog of pessimism has sometimes followed him, his general approach to life has been so positive and confident.

Pat Moynihan is a second-generation American on his father's side, but his mother's family were long settled in northern Kentucky. Although he has come to be the epitome of a New Yorker, and sees himself as one, his American roots lie in the Middle West. His paternal great-grandfather farmed and bred horses, especially steeplechasers, at Headford Junction, in County Kerry, in the far west of Ireland. (Moynihan means "man from Munster," the southwestern of the four ancient Irish kingdoms.) Cornelius Moynihan married Norah Connors, by whom he had two sons. In the classic Irish pattern, the older brother, Daniel, inherited the farm and stayed to work it, and the younger son, John C. Moynihan, known as Jack, emigrated to the United States in 1886 at the age of nineteen.

He worked at laying oil and gas lines in Pennsylvania, Ohio, Indiana and Michigan for the Standard Oil Company, and then as superintendent of construction for a firm of contractors called Kerwin Brothers in Toledo. For more than twenty years, his work took him all over the Midwest and as far as New Orleans; but in 1908 when the Fort Wayne Gas Company changed its name to the Northern Indiana Public Service Company, J. C. Moynihan was appointed as manager of its Bluffton division. He held the job until he retired. His grandson says he "quite literally dug his way" to Bluffton from Jamestown, in western New York State, where he first stayed with relatives after he landed in America. Altogether he worked for the gas company for fifty years. In 1895, he married Mary Fitzpatrick, by whom he had three sons, one of whom was Pat Moynihan's father. Mary died in 1905 of tuberculosis. In 1908, Jack settled for good in Bluffton, on the Wabash River near Fort Wayne, Indiana, and in 1910 he married again. His second wife, Elizabeth Effinger, had one daughter who lived at home.[3]

Jack Moynihan was "one of Bluffton's most prominent and public-spirited citizens," a Moose, an honorary (because he was Catholic) Rotarian and an active Democrat. He attended St. Joseph's Catholic Church and belonged to the Holy Name Society. He was also by all accounts a very nice man, well liked by the men who worked for him and by everyone else in Bluffton, a town of five thousand people, where as late as 1900 there were no more than three Roman Catholic families.

John H. Moynihan, Pat's father, was from the start "bright, but naughty."[4] He attended Notre Dame but didn't graduate. He worked for a while on the *Evening Banner* in Bluffton, but it was too small to hold him. So was Jeffersonville, where he worked on the *Bulletin,* but spent much of his time gambling, in bars, and in houses of ill repute. A colleague introduced him to Margaret Phipps, the lively daughter of Harry Willard Phipps, a successful lawyer in Jeffersonville, across the Ohio River from Louisville, who came from old Kentucky families on both sides. Harry's father, Jeremiah Phipps, was a famous card player on the Ohio riverboats. Margaret's mother was a German Protestant (her maiden name was Bickel) who converted to Roman Catholicism upon her marriage.[5]

Margaret Phipps and John Moynihan were married in 1925 and went to Florida followed by John's great friend H. Allen Smith, later a well-known writer. They hoped to make their fortune in the Florida land boom, but the boom inconveniently collapsed just as they got there. So John Moynihan moved to Tulsa, Oklahoma, and got a job on the *Tulsa Tribune*. It was in Tulsa, on March 16, 1927, the day before St. Patrick's Day, that Pat was born.

He was only briefly an Oklahoman. Later in 1927, John Moynihan moved to New York, where he got a job as an advertising copywriter for RKO, which Joseph P. Kennedy had just bought.[6] At first the Moynihans lived in Greenwich Village, where they saw a good deal of Dean Reynolds, from Bluffton, whose girlfriend, Winnie Winckler, became a close friend and later an invaluable ally for Margaret Moynihan. By 1928, the family was able to move to the suburban comfort of Ridgefield Park, New Jersey, where Pat's brother, Michael, was born, and, in 1931, after a sister, Ellen, came along, they moved again to Stewart Manor, in Nassau County, Long Island.

Life in those first years was a very long way from Hell's Kitchen. The Moynihans had a comfortable family home, charge accounts at local stores and vacations spent half in Indiana, half at Far Rockaway. In 1933 an AP reporter in search of a light feature wrote about six-year-old Pat traveling alone from New York to Indiana on the train with his banjo. Later Pat and his brother, Mike, had golden memories of life in Bluffton, a kindly grandfather and long summer days spent outside with a dog.

Life in New York was soon less idyllic. The novels of John O'Hara, among others, record that press agents and the boys who wrote copy for the movie companies were hard-drinking and hard-living. John Moynihan, it seems, was of their tribe. And then there was his friend, H. Allen Smith. When Smith died, forty years later, Pat wrote to the widow, Nelle Simpson Smith, "I have few memories of my own childhood, almost all of them involve H. Allen Smith, who graced his age."[7]

He did. But he was also a reckless drinker, prankster and hell-raiser whose influence on Pat's father was great and disastrous. Smith arrived in New York in 1929 and worked as a feature writer on the now long-defunct *World Telegram* in the 1930s. In 1941, he achieved what the *New York Times* hailed as "instant stardom" with a book called *Low Man on a Totem Pole*. Generally billed as a humorist, Smith always denied the charge. "I am funny," he insisted, "only in the sense that the world is funny." He was celebrated as "a ready carouser who amazed his friends by his ability to overcome sobriety with a single glass of beer." He won celebrity for putting down the first legal drink after the end of Prohibition, as well as for addressing the Olympian J. P. Morgan with "Hiya, toots!"[8]

By the middle 1930s, Margaret and her three children were living in Crystal Gardens, a comfortable neighborhood in Queens. In 1936, Pat and Mike, aged nine and eight, distributed FDR fliers, presumably Pat's first political activity.[9] Meanwhile, John Moynihan's life was going over the rapids. He spent late nights, then whole nights, in speakeasies with Dean Reynolds and H. Allen Smith. He started "seeing another woman." There were gambling debts, loan sharks, and once he was badly beaten by gangsters for not paying up. In 1937 he left home for good, as they say. "Marriage broke up," says Moynihan laconically, "and down we went."[10]

His father's departure, he recalled more than sixty years later, was "intensely painful: so much so that I don't really remember much of anything in my life until I was about six or seven." It was, he thinks, even more hurtful for his younger brother, Mike, and his still younger sister, Ellen, was "pretty much disabled." He believes that the catastrophe had two consequences for his life, beyond the more obvious ones.

First, "almost everything that has happened to me has taken place by chance." He cites the accident that brought his friend Bob Tenenbaum to Pier 48, where he was working, one August evening in 1943 to tell him about City College entrance exams. Again by chance, he saw a poster advertising exams for the U.S. Navy's officer training program. And it was luck that brought him a job working for Jonathan Bingham, which led to a job on Averell Harriman's gubernatorial campaign. "Next thing I am carrying the briefcase, literally, of one of the central world figures of the mid-twentieth century."[11] Moynihan acknowledges having always had "a larger sense of the fragility of things" than those who aspire to be nothing more than they are. This he attributes partly to the breakup of his parents' marriage, partly to the world in which he came of age, the world of the Depression, the war and the atom bomb. Asked about such matters, he quotes the English poet A. E. Housman:

> I to my perils
> of cheat and charmer
> Came clad in armour
> by stars benign;
> Hope lies to mortals
> and most believe her;
> But man's deceiver
> was never mine.[12]

It is hard to think of any other member of the United States Senate who could quote such lines from memory in answer to a question about his adolescence.

The other consequence of his father's departure was that it transformed the Moynihan family's social status, very much for the worse. His mother's father, he points out, was a respectable small-town lawyer. "My grandfather from Kerry started out digging trenches for the newfangled gas lines, but ended up managing the utility's office in Bluffton, Indiana." His father "seems never to have been without work," Moynihan points out; but without a male head, the family automatically lost both income and status — a point the son never forgot. Eventually John Moynihan got a job in San Jose, California, on a local paper. He remarried. Interestingly, he was allowed to marry in church. One of his sons became a priest.[13] He never saw Pat again. One of Pat's friends believes that Pat made an attempt to contact his father in 1949, but if he did it was unsuccessful.[14]

In April 1953, Mike, in the Bay Area on his way back from completing a Fulbright scholarship at the University of Rangoon in Burma, now Myanmar, did find his father. The letter he wrote Pat about the encounter reveals a good deal about the profound feelings of both brothers toward their dad. The letter leaves no doubt that the whole experience was deeply emotional for Mike, and there is no reason to believe it wouldn't have been the same for Pat. When Mike telephoned, his father suggested that he come on out to the house, which was "nothing special . . . needs paint, but is nice and petit bourgeois."

The "bursting thing" in the son's mind was that the whole family saga appeared utterly different to the father from the way the brothers had been taught to see it. "For very good reasons" — Michael Moynihan, aged twenty-four, wrote with some subtlety — "for years we had it drummed into our minds (as if we were the guilty ones) that he 'deserted his kids.' He didn't. He merely didn't support them." He had been the Sunday editor of the *San Jose Mercury News* until an ulcer made him give it up, and he still had a good job at the paper. "We had a picture of him as a sort of romantic person who mulcted his friends with neither qualm nor effort, traveled from woman to woman and backed them up at the bar before leaving." It was not like that, Mike observed. "The most shocking thing," he added, "was the depth of his Catholicism. He actually believes that the Masons and the Franciscans are engaged in a sort of Armageddon for the control of California," and the eldest son of his second marriage, Cornelius, named for the bloodstock breeder from Headford Junction, was preparing for the priesthood at a Jesuit school.[15]

For Margaret Moynihan and her three children, aged ten, eight, and six, of course, the all-absorbing question for two and a bit years was not status, but survival, financial and physical. Misfortunes, as Shakespeare knew, come "not single spies, but in battalions." Margaret Moynihan's father died in 1935. In 1937, the family home in Jeffersonville — "Jeff," the children called it — was destroyed in a flood. Before that, life changed several times in a bewildering way for the Moynihan children. For several months, from the winter of 1939 to the summer of 1940, they were looked after by their mother's sister, Julia Noe, in Louisville. Their mother married Henry Stapelfield, a friend of Winnie Winckler's mother. "An older man with a small income," Moynihan calls him, and adds bluntly, "me hating him." Stapelfield was a relatively rich man. He owned a large block of stock in Standard Brands and a fourteen-room house on thirteen acres in Kitchewan, then a rural section of Westchester County. Pat and Mike, not surprisingly, perhaps, didn't like their stepfather, who was stingy and reneged on his promise to support his new wife's children.[16] Jack Moynihan, "Grandpa," sent what money he could. But essentially, until she met Stapelfield, Margaret was on her own. She got a job teaching English at the Women's House of Detention in Manhattan. She took on work as a nurse. The family moved first from Queens to a cold-water flat on East 88th Street, then to a succession of rent-free apartments on the Upper West Side. (In those Depression years, it was hard to rent apartments, and agents sometimes offered a first month rent-free as an incentive.)

However difficult life was, Margaret Moynihan kept her children in a good Catholic school, Holy Name, at West 97th Street and Amsterdam Avenue. Sometimes both Pat and Mike shined shoes in Times Square, and not just for pocket money. Mike told a reporter[17] that once, coming home without even a dime to buy milk for supper, he sat on the floor and cried. Sometimes, according to the same source, Pat was jumped by the tough kids in the neighborhood, who would steal his earnings.

After his mother married Stapelfield, Pat went to Yorktown Heights High School in Westchester for ninth and tenth grade. He was bullied at school, partly it seems on class grounds, partly because, though tall for his age, he was awkward. (In view of his later taste for good clothes it is interesting that he was the only boy who showed up for the junior prom wearing a tuxedo.) However, Pat also made a number of friends. The closest of them was Harry Hall, who later went to Andover.

Margaret Moynihan's second marriage was not a success. In the spring of 1941, she separated from Stapelfield, though that same summer she had his son, Tommy. She moved in to stay with her sister Julia, whose husband was a golf pro in Indiana. That fall she moved to an apartment on West 92nd Street, and Pat started eleventh grade at Benjamin Franklin High School on 116th Street in East Harlem. It was a fairly new school, founded in the early 1930s, and not a bad one, even if — as Pat rather ungenerously said years later — "It was no Bronx High School of Science." In fact its grade point average was one of the lowest, if not the lowest, in the city. At the time he said, "The teachers are swell." (The principal was Leonard Covello, a prominent educator and a strong supporter of the New Deal. He had quashed student unrest in 1935, at the time of Mussolini's invasion of Ethiopia, when the Italian students, who accounted for 60 percent of Benjamin Franklin's student body, celebrated a little too raucously for the liking of the black students, the second biggest group. They tended to identify with Haile Selassie I, the emperor of Ethiopia, which Italy had just invaded with no little brutality.[18]) While Pat was at Benjamin Franklin, Mayor Fiorello H. La Guardia visited the school. Pat interviewed him, and the mayor told him, "Take the lessons seriously, but never forget to have fun."[19]

Pat went back to his pre-Westchester trade, shining shoes in different locations. Sometimes he worked a new turf, opposite the Old Paramount Theater on West 43rd Street. But it was on Central Park West, next to the planetarium, that he heard about Pearl Harbor from a customer. "I was fourteen, war meant little to me, and I went on working until I had accumulated the usual one dollar, and then went home. My mother had the radio on; there were occasional announcements, but mostly military music interspersed with football songs. I distinctly remember:

> "Hail! Men of Fordham, hail!
> On to the fray!
> Once more our foes assail in strong array."[20]

From an early stage, he and his best friend, Bob Tenenbaum, were involved in high school journalism, and Pat did well academically, outstandingly well for a boy whose life and education had been messed around as much as his had. In 1942, he was elected to the Arista honor society. He was valedictorian and class secretary. On the strength of his Benjamin Franklin grades and an entrance examination he was admitted to the City College of New York.[21]

A few years earlier, Moynihan would have met an extraordinary galaxy of talent at City College, including his later friends Irving Kristol, the political scientist Daniel Bell, and the sociologist Seymour Martin Lipset, as well as the actor Zero Mostel, the historian Irving Howe, and the literary critic Alfred Kazin. The *numerus clausus*, limiting the numbers of Jewish students, officially or unofficially adopted by most Ivy League schools in the 1930s, was City College's opportunity to recruit the highly motivated third generation of late-nineteenth-century Jewish immigration. But Moynihan's time there was relatively undistinguished, no doubt because he was doing a full college load in half the usual time. He got A's in European history and economics, C's in trigonometry and D's in French and Spanish.[22] His French and Spanish have remained modest, but he has come a long way in public speaking.

If Moynihan had been at City College a few years earlier, in the depths of the Depression, he might have been exposed to a stronger socialist influence. As it was, he was exposed in adolescence to the ideas of both the extreme Right and the extreme Left as he would never have been in Bluffton. "Among my teachers at Benjamin Franklin," he remembers, "there were nothing but Mensheviks. They would bring Kerensky to lecture on behalf of Russian war aid." The Mensheviks lost out to the Bolsheviks, who took over the Communist party of the Soviet Union. Even though Kerensky, the last prime minister of Russia before the October Revolution, was the victim of Lenin, he was himself very much on the Left.

The boy who listened to Kerensky and the Mensheviks during the week was well exposed to Catholic anticommunism on weekends. The brothers at Holy Name were obsessed by the threat of communism. The young Pat Moynihan spent Sundays in Far Rockaway, when the priests would celebrate ten twenty-minute masses in the morning, and he would earn a quarter by selling fifty copies of Father Coughlin's weekly newspaper, *Social Justice*, outside the church. No wonder he now remembers that he was "blurry" about ideology in those days.

Growing up in the thirties on the sidewalks of New York, Moynihan did learn a number of things he would not have learned in Bluffton. He acquired an instinctive understanding of the roots of New York's ethnic tensions in the ancient quarrels between the Irish and the English, Russian Jews and German Jews, Abyssinians and Italians, Bolsheviks and Mensheviks, communists and social democrats. It was knowledge he would put to good use, and it also introduced him to one of the master themes of his life: ethnicity. Moynihan likes to point out that in most parts of the country, people have difficulty distinguishing between a social democrat and a communist: not in New York, where they have always known that the democratic socialists were the worst enemies of the communists.

It was the war, not the New Deal, that got the U.S. economy back to work after a decade of Depression. And for the Moynihans, too, World War II was a saver. Margaret Moynihan got a good job as chief nurse in a war production plant. She rented a large apartment in a converted mansion, the Mary Blackwell house, on 27th Avenue in Queens. Suddenly there were jobs galore. Pat worked as a stock boy at Gimbels and sold newspapers in bars in Far Rockaway, where cousins were in the liquor business. It was during this period that Pat laid the foundation for the Moynihan legend and also for his extraordinary knowledge of, and love of, New York City.

"The West Side piers began working seven days a week," he wrote almost fifty years later. "This meant I could go to City College three days a week, work three days, and have plenty of time and money left over."[23] In the summer of 1943 he worked on Piers 48 and 49 at the end of West 11th Street in Manhattan. He was a stevedore, earning 78 cents an hour. On an "Officer Qualifications Questionnaire" for the navy, he indicated that he worked on the piers from July 1943 until June 1944 for the National Carloading Company.[24] His job, he said, involved "loading and unloading barges and freight cars [with] some experience with deep sea ships" and "limited authority over three men." They called him "Young Blood" because he worked so hard.[25] On the other hand, he was once fired for falling asleep reading Thomas Wolfe's *You Can't Go Home Again*. He had probably been up half the night in Greenwich Village, listening to Leadbelly at Nick's or jazz at the Village Gate.

This was an extraordinary period in New York, the overture to perhaps the most glorious in the city's history, the years following 1945. London and Paris, not to mention the great cities of central Europe, were dark. Los Angeles, Atlanta and Seattle had not begun to challenge New York's monopoly of the most profitable businesses, and Boston had not begun to revive. Tokyo and Berlin were in ruins, Sydney and Hong Kong still provincial. New York financiers had a monopoly as never before or since. New York publishers, newspapers, magazines, ad agencies, were expanding and flourishing when such businesses were almost invisible elsewhere. Refugees from Europe poured in to enrich the theater, the opera, music, cabaret. Between the end of Prohibition and the Depression, and the social and racial crisis that began in the sixties, New York was the *dolce vita* capital of the world. You could order a fifth of Scotch and a carton of cigarettes to be brought up to your apartment at any hour of the day or night. The Third Avenue bars never closed. The waiters just asked you to lift your feet while they swabbed the floor at four in the morning, and New Yorkers were still friendly. "We had half a million people on relief in 1935," Moynihan pointed out in 1993. "By 1943, we were down to 73,000 of which the city reported 93 were claimed as employable . . . In that time, the city began that ascent to the incomparable heights that followed just after the war."

The city, Moynihan went on, "already had a social structure, an infrastructure: the best subway system in the world, the finest housing stock, the best urban school system, and"—he added—"in many ways the best behaved citizens." Oh, yes, he knew people made a fuss about "Hell's Kitchen and a street warrior caste." But in truth, "The neighborhood was in a way idyllic." And there were only forty-four murders in the whole city in 1943.[26]

Indeed, it is worth pointing out that, while in certain respects Pat Moynihan grew up in tough circumstances, in other respects he was rather lucky. Unlike young men half a generation older, whose development was stunted by the Depression or ended by the war, Moynihan was given the opportunity to get a bachelor's, a master's and a doctoral degree, not to mention three years at the London School of Economics, virtually at public expense, thanks to World War II, the U.S. Navy and the Fulbright Bill. Moreover, he was able to take advantage of all of these opportunities without having to pay the often destructive price of "middle class guilt," which distorted the political and social reflexes of many of his contemporaries.[27]

Certainly, with the United States still expanding the army, the navy and the civilian war machine in a smooth accelerating curve, even as victory became more and more certain, opportunities for bright, energetic young men had never been better. Not only machinists, nurses and infantrymen were in demand. So too, as never before, were army and navy officers.

In March 1944, Pat Moynihan walked into the Baruch Center on 23rd Street and saw an announcement that officer training tests would be given the following week. "On July 1 I entered into an association with the United States Navy which lasted until I was discharged from the Reserves 22 years later."[28] Fifty-four years later, at a band concert at the navy memorial in Washington, Moynihan stood proudly to attention when the musicians played "Anchors Aweigh." Joining the navy was one of the decisive moves of his life. It opened the way to recouping the opportunities, and the status, he lost when his father walked out seven years earlier.

The navy inducted Cadet Daniel P. Moynihan and sent him for officer training under the V-12 program for emergency training of naval officers, first at Middlebury College in Vermont, then as an ROTC student at Tufts University, just outside Boston. The instruction prepared the cadets for an A.B. degree in Naval Science, which Pat duly acquired. It is a little-known fact that he earned not only his first degree, but a substantial proportion of the credits for his master's in this pragmatic field of social science. Altogether, according to his naval records, he clocked thirty semester hours at CCNY, fifty-one at Middlebury and fifty-three at Tufts, of which twenty-four were in naval science and twenty-four in history.[29]

At Middlebury, and again at Tufts, he was thrown in for the first time in his life with genuine, unmistakable members of the established upper middle class. As a child in Jeffersonville and Bluffton, he had grown up in a companionable small-town Middle Western elite of lawyers, managers and newspapermen. In New York, before the fall, he had lived as a child in comfortable suburbs, and after the two nightmare years, he had experienced affluent Westchester before returning to Queens. But nowhere before had he encountered the effortless superiority of the white shoe, trust fund world. Many of his fellow naval cadets came from more or less wealthy upper-middle-class backgrounds. They had names like Emmett Van Allen Murray III. "We didn't see Moynihan as a poor boy from New York among rich prep school boys," says one of them, Joe Reisler,[30] who later married one of Moynihan's serious girlfriends; but that is exactly what he was. And his attitude toward them, as one would expect, was ambivalent. As he wrote to his friend — his upper-middle-class friend from Westchester and Andover — Harry Hall: "They get my ass by the way they sit there and wallow in every kind of economic and social advantage our society has to offer and remain completely spiritually and mentally mediocre."

He was in fact ambivalent about the privileged, as he was to remain all his life. He couldn't help feeling that they "needed a good swift kick in their blue blood asses." Yet as he found them good company, and realistically, indeed cynically, "if I abstained from having anything to do with anyone who I thought could do with a kick in the ass, I wouldn't have many drinking companions."

In June 1945, the V-12 program at Middlebury and the equivalent course at Williams were both closed down. "They sent us all to Tufts," says Richard Meryman, who had been at Williams. "I went into this room and there was this lanky figure sprawled in a chair."[31] Meryman and Moynihan became fast friends, though later in life their friendship cooled somewhat for a time. Meryman, the son of an artist from Dublin, New Hampshire, grew up in an upper-middle-class family with little or no money; he was a shrewd assessor of his friend Moynihan's status. "I always felt," he said, "that Pat knew he belonged to a higher social class than where he was." Once Moynihan hitchhiked up to Dublin. Meryman was playing tennis when he arrived, and came back to find Pat having a long talk with his mother. Moynihan made it clear that he was very determined to be successful in life. Once, too, Meryman stayed in the Moynihan apartment over the tavern on West 42nd Street. The whole atmosphere, he recalled, was, "This is not where we belong."

Ensign Moynihan's first ship was the USS *Quirinus*, based in Norfolk, Virginia. Ensign Meryman was sent to a sister ship. Both were ARLs, repair ships, originally built to be LSTs, but with a huge repair shop in place of the tank decks. Meryman found his friend the best company. He also admired him. "He is unflinching," says Meryman. "It is not just courage, though he has plenty of that. It is that willingness to dare anything."

At that stage of Moynihan's life, some of the daring was plain adolescent foolishness. The two would row around Norfolk in a tiny sailboat, with huge freighters going by, nipping away at a whiskey bottle on the thwart. Norfolk was a dry city, as the navy was dry. But one could join a club for ten dollars, and raise as much hell as he liked, and both Meryman and Moynihan liked to raise a fair amount.

That fall, Moynihan went to sea as communications officer on the *Quirinus* on a cruise through the Caribbean as far as Trinidad. Before leaving, he had an accident that was to have consequences for the rest of his life. He went aboard a supply ship in Narragansett Bay, Rhode Island, to load stores. He described what happened in a letter more than fifty years later: he got on deck, wandered about, tripped on a cowling and down he went. He did not get back to the United States until the spring of 1947. That July he went to stay with his mother and so for the first time — at the age of twenty, as a naval officer about to enter graduate school — went to live in Hell's Kitchen.

For a while his mother had run a chicken concession in the bar in Far Rockaway owned by her first husband's cousin, another John Moynihan. The business didn't make money, but *another* cousin, Dan O'Riordan, offered to lend Margaret Moynihan $10,000 to buy the lease on a saloon on West 42nd Street. At about this time she also married again. Her third husband was a truck driver called Scotty Dolan, whom Pat Moynihan remembers simply as "hapless." Pat got back from the navy to find that the bar was not going well. When the bartender quit, he took over for a while.

In the fall of 1947, he went back to Tufts, where he wrote the *Cerberus* column in the college newspaper. It was not an easy time. There was trouble at Moynihan's Bar. Pat had to commute between Boston and New York to help his mother and sort things out. After officer's pay, he found himself short of money. He also developed back pains resulting from his fall into the freighter's hold, diagnosed as resulting from a herniated intervertebral lumbar disc. And it was at this point that an incident occurred that troubled him for some time. He had too much to drink one night in the working-class neighborhood in Medford, Massachusetts, where the Tufts campus is located. There was a brawl, and the police were sent for. Pat seems to have argued with a cop who beat him, and he spent the night in jail. Now he dismisses the incident as a youthful prank. "Hadn't thought of it for on to half a century. No great thing. No fist fighting. Few cracks on the knee with a nightstick. Night in jail. Out in morning."[32]

But for a few years, the Medford episode seems to have been rather more traumatic than he now remembers. Four years later he described it to his psychoanalyst in London, who tried to persuade him that the police were father substitutes: "authority — Irish — drunk etc.," as he summarized the argument.[33] "Now I was playing tough to them — suddenly they would not play back and started beating me up — result? The illusion that I was tough & independent was shattered and once more I was a child *vis à vis* father?" Moynihan noted the analyst's theory in his journal, but added a skeptical "Maybe!"[34]

In the summer of 1948, Pat did two weeks' reserve duty, which involved a cruise to Bermuda on the USS *McDougall,* and in the fall he went back to Tufts to work on an M.A. In the presidential election, he was a strong supporter of mainstream, anticommunist Harry Truman, a strong opponent of leftist Henry Wallace. He was also short of money, and troubled by back pains, as well as worried about his mother and the bar.

Dick Meryman had gone on to Harvard, and in the spring of 1949 he invited Pat to set off with him and two Harvard friends to earn some money mining gold in Alaska, where the pickings were rumored to be spectacular.[35] Meryman had gotten hold of a 1935 Packard hearse, christened the "Pleasure Dome," and off they all set. The boys slept in the hearse. Everything went well until they reached Canada and were not allowed to cross the border. The fabled gold of Alaska was not for them. Dick and Pat wound up somewhere called Hungry Horse, Montana. There was supposed to be a lot of dam-building work, but our heroes couldn't get any of it. Eventually they went to the union office, and had jobs the same day. Meryman lasted four days. He was hired as an electrician, and when he blew a main fuse, all the men on site hooted with derision. The worst of it was that the foreman didn't know how to fix it. Pat didn't last much longer. He was regularly awakened by the sound of his fellow lumberjacks slapping their spikes to clean them. All the other men on the job were French Canadians or Native Americans, and they were tough. A long line of men ran on the logs with their spikes biting into the bark, and a man behind them yelled at them to go faster. Pat was not up to this and was given the task of clearing brush. He might have worked on the piers, but Meryman recalls that he was clumsy.

It wasn't long before they were both out of a job. The Packard gave up the ghost, and the boys made their way to Chicago riding in freight cars. Those were the days when every book had a note on the dust jacket saying, "The author has worked as a lumberjack, roustabout and short-order cook." Dick Meryman and Pat Moynihan had had their adventure. But Moynihan remembers one incident that seems to symbolize the basic decency of ordinary Americans.[36]

He and Dick Meryman decided to take a boxcar back east. They slipped into the rail yard at midnight, found an open car and disappeared inside. Thirty minutes later there was a sound outside, the crunch-crunch of boots on cinders. A flashlight shone on them as they cowered at the back of the car. "Where are you two headed?" "To Chi-Chicago, sir!" "Well, you can stay here if you want, but this car isn't gonna move for two weeks. Come on, I'll show you where to get on the next train."[37]

In Chicago, they separated. Meryman went east, and he understood that Moynihan went west to look for his father. But he can't be sure: "He sort of mumbled." That summer the future ambassador failed his Foreign Service exam. In the fall of 1949, he started work on his doctorate, and to help support himself he got his first teaching job. In the spring of 1950, he was back running Moynihan's Bar again, but the Hell's Kitchen period was coming to an end. That summer Margaret Moynihan sold the bar. On May 27, Pat received a letter confirming that he had been given a grant from the U.S. government under the Fulbright program to study "trade unionism" at the London School of Economics.[38] Pat spent the 1950 summer session at Harvard, and on September 9 he left New York for Britain. He landed at Southampton on September 16, 1950, and registered with the Metropolitan Police aliens registration office on September 29, just within the statutory two-week period. His Fulbright grant was supposed to last nine months, but he stayed for three years.

The London experience, as both Pat and Liz Moynihan agree, was "crucial."[39] It was not, however, a high-pressure commitment to rigorous academic work. Pat signed on at the London School of Economics as a "research fee student." Dr. Ann Bohm,[40] who ran the graduate school and knew Moynihan well, says, "He didn't have to take, and in fact didn't take, any exams." Most American students in those days worked for an American degree. Ironically for one who grew into such a phenomenally hard worker, Pat worried in his journal about the difficulty he experienced in getting down to work.[41] He also spent quite a lot of time as a Boswellian "man of pleasure." The journal is headed: "An Intellectual History of Our Times: Being a Descriptive Journal of adventures & meditations having occurred to the author during a Grand Tour of Great Britain, Ireland & the Continent of Europe."

Although the journal is dated "AD 1950–51," it actually covers most of Moynihan's three years in Europe. It is fairly full of accounts of love affairs, some longer and more serious, some exceedingly brief. It also contains long "meditations" on the progress of Moynihan's psychoanalysis. As early as December 1950, the journal records that Moynihan was seeing an analyst identified as PDM, Patrick de Maré. Among Moynihan's troubles were his difficulties in settling down to work, his feelings about his father, the Medford episode, and other postadolescent worries. The analyst appears to have been a somewhat conventional Freudian,[42] and while from time to time the patient noted in his journal that the analysis was helping, particularly in relation to his feelings toward his father, which became warm and forgiving, he seems to have remained a skeptic about both his own analysis and psychoanalysis as a whole. It should be said that psychoanalysis, and especially the rather orthodox Freudian analysis favored at the time by Dr. de Maré, were far more usual in the early 1950s than would be the case among students today. Moynihan's sessions should certainly not be taken as evidence of any very profound psychological trouble.

In London, for the first time in his life, Pat was fairly affluent, both by the standards of American students like those at Tufts, and even more so by comparison with his fellow students at the LSE. Besides his Fulbright scholarship, which paid his fees and gave him a monthly stipend, he had the GI Bill, which paid him $225 a month.[43] "Fulbrights were well off," says Dr. Bohm. "Most of them acquired a library in London."[44] (Later he found relatively well paid work as an administrator for the U.S. Third Air Force headquarters at Ruislip, in suburban London.)[45] He now could make the most of a city where a good many exciting things were happening. He could, and did, afford to go to concerts, to the theater, even to the opera. Sander Vanocur remembers going with Moynihan to see Michael Redgrave as Hotspur in *Henry IV, Part I* at the Old Vic, where you could get a stall seat for a few shillings. They also went to *Ring Round the Moon* by Jean Anouilh and starring the great Paul Scofield and the young Claire Bloom, and to see Joan Littlewood's experimental theater at the other Stratford, in the heart of the working-class East End. Moynihan also went to concerts at the elegant Wigmore Hall in the West End, and he attended the opening of the Festival of Britain on the South Bank in 1951.

He was attached, if by his own choice a little loosely, to a world-class academic institution at a very interesting point in its history. No wonder that the three years he spent in London were a time of budding intellectual, emotional and personal development. Dr. Bohm remembers that his life was "very much outside the school."[46] She also remembers that "he introduced me to some nice pubs," including the Windsor Castle, with a beer garden in back, on Campden Hill in Kensington. Moynihan's supervisor was William Pickles, an expert on French politics and well-known radio broadcaster. They got on "extremely well." It wasn't a "staff-student relationship," says Dr. Bohm, and Moynihan worked in fits and starts at a Tufts doctoral dissertation on the International Labor Organization in Geneva.

The LSE has been misunderstood and misrepresented, not least by Moynihan himself in a famous essay ("The United States in Opposition"), in which he portrayed it as filling the Third World with Fabian socialists. It is perfectly true that the school had been founded by Fabians like Beatrice and Sidney Webb and Graham Wallas. (They called themselves Fabians, after the Roman general Quintus Fabius Maximus Verrucosus, known as the Cunctator, "Delayer" in Latin, so called because he avoided battle with Hannibal. They took this name in order to emphasize the difference between themselves and revolutionary socialists.) It is also true that the most famous single figure at the LSE between the wars was probably Harold Laski, renowned for his published correspondence with his friend U.S. Supreme Court Justice Oliver Wendell Holmes. Laski was a socialist, and a powerful influence behind the scenes in the Labour government, which took power in Britain in 1945.

An equally influential figure, however, was William Beveridge, one of the intellectual founders of the welfare state, but Beveridge was a liberal, in the British sense of the word, meaning an advocate of moderate capitalism, and certainly no socialist. The first director, W.A.S. Hewins, was later a Conservative member of Parliament.[47] The school was dedicated to innovation and committed to "new" disciplines like economics, politics, sociology and "social administration." It was, quite intentionally, sharply contrasted with the academically conservative ancient universities Oxford and Cambridge, though to be fair Cambridge in the 1950s was a dynamic center for such key "modern" disciplines as economics and nuclear physics. But the LSE was never anything like an academy of the Left. Moynihan's friend, the brilliant Canadian political scientist Bob McKenzie, took a straw poll of the faculty and found that more than half of them said they voted Conservative.[48]

By the time Moynihan arrived, the intellectual energy had in any case already moved to the Right. Harold Laski died in March 1950, a few weeks before Pat Moynihan enrolled. Laski's death was "a watershed,"[49] says Ralf Dahrendorf, the German-born sociologist who, after a dazzling career in German and European politics, was himself to be the director of the LSE in the 1980s and then its historian. As head of the Politics Department, Laski was succeeded by the conservative Michael Oakeshott, who courageously devoted his inaugural lecture, in March 1951, to a skeptical analysis of politics which would have horrified his predecessor. By 1950, says Dahrendorf, "the School was beginning to find a new normality." It was, given the school's great tolerance of differing opinions, on the whole a conservative normality. The most influential single figure was the passionate free-market advocate, the economist Lionel Robbins. It was Robbins who nineteen years before had recruited Friedrich von Hayek from Austria, and it was only in 1950 that Hayek departed for Chicago.[50] In philosophy, the star was Karl Popper, author of *The Open Society and Its Enemies,* and a scourge of the totalitarianism of both Left and Right. Other stars, in a college that had at the time a faculty of only 154 for roughly 3,600 students, were the three future Nobel Prize winners, George Stigler, another conservative, who also went to Chicago; the West Indian economist Arthur Lewis; and James Meade.

Legend has it that the school was packed with Indians. In fact, in a given year in the mid-1950s, there were something like 120 Indians, 150 Africans and 200 students from North America. Moynihan did, however, meet a lot of Indians. He and his friend Vanocur decided that the food in the LSE canteen was inedible, so they took to migrating across the Aldwych to the Indian restaurant in India House, the diplomatic mission of the newly independent republic of India. There they found themselves in constant argument with Indian students, many of them acolytes of Krishna Menon, the left-wing and very anti-American Indian foreign minister. Before independence, Menon had been elected as a Labour councilor in one of the London boroughs.[51] (Moynihan likes the story that when some particularly unpleasant "non-aligned" delegate was hectoring the United Nations, someone said, "it made one nostalgic for the days of Krishna Menon!")[52] The first thing Moynihan ever wrote that saw print was a long letter to the *New Statesman,* a left-wing weekly with a high literary reputation at the time, rebutting an article by a well-known British socialist intellectual, G.D.H. Cole, who blamed the Korean War on "American imperialism." Like many a sensitive young man before and later, Pat found his patriotism strengthened by the experience of living abroad and hearing people say unkind things about his country.

Pat loved London and got on very well with ordinary Londoners. "The British were singularly welcoming to Yanks in those days," he remembers. "Needs to be recorded. Give you endless cups of tea in ministries, tours of housing projects, invitations to lectures, trade union meetings, council meetings."[53] Pat was immediately drawn to the world of the Labour party; but significantly not to the world of the sophisticated Marxist intellectuals around Aneurin Bevan, by whom he "wasn't much impressed," or to Tony Crosland and his social democratic friends, who were trying to move Labour to the right, but to the world of working-class rank-and-file members.

Early in his stay in London, at a Labour political meeting, he met Mrs. Gollogly, who represented Greenwich borough on the London County Council, the city's elected government. Her husband, Jock, who was a longshoreman and also chairman of the local Labour party, became a sort of father figure. And Mary, their beautiful and cultivated daughter, became the principal of Pat's numerous girlfriends; they went for long walks, she cooked him delicious omelettes and took him to hear the Boyd Neel Orchestra play Mozart at the Wigmore Hall.[54]

Pat loved the Golloglys' local pub, the Bunker, with Bill the bartender, who had the hugest hands ever. Nothing like it in America, he said; he and his new friends would get tight on Guinness while Jock nursed two whiskeys. These were manual workers with lively minds. One night at the Bunker, one of the locals read them a poem by Alfred Austin about the Jameson Raid in South Africa in 1895, and there was a bus conductor who had theories about Sir Christopher Wren's plans for rebuilding London after the Great Fire of 1666. He became aware, too, that he was coming to be accepted as a recognized suitor for Mary, and agonized in his journal about whether this was the woman with whom he wanted to share the whole of his life.

Pat still speaks affectionately of "those wonderful Labour party folk in London who aspired to be nothing more than what they were." But this was a young man who was already thinking and planning far ahead. He intended to "take a chance and finish this thesis." He wrote: "I want to advance socially because only in so doing will I have chance to do the work I want to do and that is important. In a sense I want to improve personally because only then will I really feel up to picking myself a wife — today I'm still out for delicious sex or a mother . . . A wife & a job — simple enough."[55]

Meanwhile, he was happy to get involved in Labour party activities. On November 23, 1950, he attended a meeting of the River South ward of the Woolwich Labour party. It is not far-fetched to see the Golloglys as having had a lasting influence on Moynihan's politics. Jock Gollogly was a Catholic Ulsterman who had come down to London by way of Glasgow.[56] He was a staunch Labour man, steeped in the culture of trade unionism, as much — Moynihan remembers — about "good fellowship" as it was about politics.

One attitude that Moynihan had long held was confirmed and strengthened by the Golloglys: anti-Communism. Irish Catholic America, and Catholic America as a whole for that matter, never had any doubts about that in the 1930s or in the 1950s. Labour party members, too, had come across the Communists in their unions, and they didn't like what they saw. Moynihan quotes the apocryphal story about British Foreign Secretary Ernest Bevin, an illegitimate child brought up as a teamster on the Bristol docks. Before he went into politics he was a tough union negotiator. On his return from the Potsdam conference with Stalin in 1945, Bevin was asked what the Soviets were like. "Why," he said, "they're just like the Communists!" That was Jock Gollogly's attitude, too. "They were distant Catholics," Moynihan says, "but fierce anti-Communists."[57] This birthright anti-Communism was confirmed, too, by Moynihan's travels from London.

As early as March and April 1951, he was exploring France and Spain. In June, he was off to Ireland with his friend John Barry; they visited Dublin, saw Headford Junction and went as far as Valentia Island, in the far southwest tip of Ireland, before returning to London.[58] That winter Moynihan and also his friends John Cole Cool and Sander Vanocur were called up for a secret mission to Bremerhaven, the naval base on the North Sea coast of Germany. (It seems that the United States was planning to set up a U.S. Navy headquarters there, but the plan came to nothing, probably because Winston Churchill, then in his last term as British prime minister, refused to have an American admiral commanding the Royal Navy's home fleet.)[59] The

West German economic miracle was just beginning, but the young Americans were still impressed by the devastation left by the British and American bombing of seven years earlier. "There was utter desolation," Cool remembers. "People were living in pieces of canvas strung over the rubble."[60]

The young reserve officers mustered at the American embassy in Grosvenor Square, and by late afternoon they were leaning back against the cushions as their train crossed Holland. Moynihan had brought along a copy of Hannah Arendt's recently published book, *The Origins of Totalitarianism*. Settling down, he read the first paragraph: "Two world wars in one generation, separated by an uninterrupted chain of local wars and revolutions, followed by no peace for the victor, have ended in the anticipation of a third World War between the two remaining world powers. This moment of anticipation is like the calm that settles after all hopes have died."[61]

He read it again, aloud, to his companions. There were six of them in the carriage, two of them veterans of the carrier wars in the Pacific. None of them demurred. Two years later, on his way back to the United States, Moynihan was in Germany again and visited Berlin. He drove through the Brandenburg Gate, which separated the democratic West from the Communist East, with Paul Niven, a close friend in London who later became well known as an NBC network television correspondent, and a British journalist. As they drove along the Stalinallee, the main drag of East Berlin, the Englishman said, "There's nothing here but the handwriting on the wall."[62] Moynihan, elevated to lieutenant in the U.S. Navy after the Bremerhaven trip, belonged to the generation who took the Cold War seriously because they would have been the ones to fight it if it ever turned into a hot war.

Decades later Moynihan summed up the political influence of the LSE years. "I did know Karl Popper, went to his lectures, having read *The Open Society and Its Enemies* while at Fletcher. But nothing and no one at LSE ever disposed me to be anything but a New York Democrat who had some friends who worked on the docks and drank beer after work."[63]

While the Golloglys became almost family to Pat, to an extent that caused him some troubled questioning in his journal, the core of Moynihan's group of friends in London was made up of fellow Americans. Some of them he met on the trip over, like John Cole Cool and

John Barry. (He didn't meet John Tower, Paul Volcker or Canadian Prime Minister Pierre Trudeau, all of whom were at LSE at the time.) They had a fairly riotous time. Pat lived in three flats in succession, one in Queen's Gardens, one in Edwardes Square and one in Emperor's Gate, all in fashionable Kensington, and all very smart addresses, then and now.[64] He shared the third with two Englishmen who have remained lifelong friends, the London lawyer Dante Campailla, and Frank Fenton, a brilliant classical scholar who became an industrialist.[65] Through them, he met the distinguished Cambridge historian of eighteenth-century England, J. H. Plumb, another friend for life. It so happened that Campailla and Fenton were looking for a flatmate when Moynihan had left another place.

The three of them agreed to share living quarters. The Emperor's Gate flat had a dining room, a kitchen, two front rooms and a room at the back for Moynihan, dark and hideously untidy. The rental was $40 a week. Food was still rationed in London then, but Pat had access to the United States Air Force post exchange store at Ruislip, which enabled him to bring home, among other things, a case of Schenley's gin every month. They drank it with orange juice, and the joke was that if you didn't finish a bottle, it would go bad. There was a lot of drinking and partying, but also concerts, theater, lectures and other culturally improving activities: Pat used to pin his theater tickets to the lampshade. He visited the Oxford University Union debating society, and had a holiday in Stratford and Warwick.[66] There were also parties, pub crawls, light-hearted expeditions and serial love affairs, all washed down with companionable drafts of beer, gin and whiskey.

One of Pat's favorite expeditions was to the House of Commons. He used to go there with Sander Vanocur and Paul Niven to listen to old lions like Winston Churchill and young tigers like Enoch Powell.[67] The story that he affected a monocle in London is pure invention. But Dante Campailla does remember him sporting a brown derby, not quite the uniform of the City of London gent, who would have felt undressed in those days without a black bowler hat (the helmet), a copy of the London *Times* (the shield), and a rolled umbrella (the sword) that made up the full panoply of the knight of commerce. But Moynihan wore a derby just the same. And it is true that, as another friend who knew him in London recalls, if he was at home with Labour party activists on the docks, he was also vastly impressed by the manners and mannerisms of the parliamentarians.[68] From them he took some of the lingering mannerisms of Edwardian England that have left traces in his manner and oratorical style.[69]

What else did these three years in London do for, and to, Moynihan? It was a time for exploring and meeting new ideas, new ways of doing things, and new friends. It was also a crucial opportunity to explore himself, both through the formal but rather crude mechanisms of psychoanalysis and in a more lasting way through reading, introspection (some of it recorded in his journal) and endless conversation with friends and lovers. There were more specific acquisitions in London, too. At the LSE, he picked up some ideas: one of them, says his friend John Cole Cool, who was working on a doctorate in anthropology, was an interest in ethnicity. Another was an interest in demography and a third, a lifelong interest in architecture. Yet another was a sense of history, and in particular a respect for the great Victorians, among them Disraeli, the champion of "Tory men and Whig measures," as he was to tell Richard Nixon. Through the Golloglys, but also through contact with a Labour party struggling to hold on to the dramatic gains of its six years in power after 1945, Moynihan watched the travails of a certain kind of democratic Left. His rejection of Communism was reinforced; so was his devotion to a certain kind of intelligent liberalism.

He had planned to stay for nine months. He stayed for almost three years. But it was time to go home. Early in February, he visited Rome. In mid-August, he was in Berlin. On August 24, he arrived in Italy by train from Yugoslavia. He left Genoa by sea on September 4 on a slow boat. On September 14, he went ashore for a day in Canada, and a couple of days later he was back in New York.

3

Chance Encounters, Random Walks

HARRIMAN, MARRIAGE AND
J. EDGAR HOOVER

> Every man is the maker of his own fortune.
> — Sir Richard Steele, *The Tatler*, No. 52

> Coincidences are a spiritual sort of puns.
> — G. K. Chesterton

ALEXANDER THE GREAT believed in his own luck, and so did Napoleon. Pat Moynihan, more modestly, believes something subtly different: that "almost everything that has happened to me has taken place by chance." It has been like that, he says. "Chance encounters, random walks." That, he muses, "can be the mark of someone whose certainties got knocked about early on."[1]

Before he even set foot back home in New York, he had one enormous lucky break, one that led forward in his life so far that in a sense he is still benefiting from it, almost fifty years later. In the second-class lounge on the *Andrea Doria,* he was typing away at his LSE thesis when a New York lawyer-politician called Paul Reilly introduced himself. They talked and got on well enough that Reilly asked Moynihan what he planned to do. Moynihan said he had no idea. So Reilly offered to introduce him to Adrian Burke, who was running Robert Wagner's campaign for mayor.[2]

Within days of landing in New York, Moynihan was working for Jonathan Bingham on the Wagner campaign. Jack Bingham, as he was known, came from a patrician family. He was educated at Groton and Yale. His father, Hiram R. Bingham, had been a Republican member of the United States Senate and governor of Connecticut.

Bingham went on to sit in the U.S. House of Representatives himself. Liz Moynihan says, "We were blessed in having Jack Bingham as a friend,"[3] and in fact Bingham and his wife, June, played an important part in getting the Moynihans started on the political ladder.

Pat Moynihan's luck had held. He had landed right in the middle of New York Democratic politics at an unusually volatile moment even in that state's habitually turbulent machinations. His political thinking was to be stamped for life by the conflicts he observed within the Democratic party between 1955 and 1958. The balance between the overwhelmingly Protestant Republican vote upstate and the largely Catholic and Jewish Democratic turnout in the city was traditionally close; yet in 1953 the Republicans had dominated state politics for more than twenty years. New York City's great mayor from 1933 to 1945, Fiorello La Guardia, though a half-Jewish and half-Italian Episcopalian and liberal verging on socialist, was in fact a Republican; and Thomas Dewey, Republican candidate for president in 1944 and 1948, had been governor since 1943.

After working as a volunteer on the successful Wagner campaign, Moynihan needed a job. He tried for work with a number of advertising agencies, without success. (It is intriguing to think of his prose style applied to advertising copy.) Instead, on the strength of his two brief visits to Berlin, he got a job with a volunteer agency, the International Rescue Committee, whose purpose was to help refugees. Even a minimal experience of Berlin was relevant because the IRC was helping refugees from the East, where protests surged against the Communist regime, to move to the West. The job was no great shakes. Moynihan spent most of his time writing press releases. But it paid $8,000 a year, enough then for him to rent a large room in a brownstone on 14th Street. It was soon as messy as the room in Emperor's Gate. He spent agreeable evenings listening to jazz in Greenwich Village, or just drinking beer in the White Horse Tavern or McSorley's saloon. This classic establishment had been recorded by painters like John Sloan and celebrated in the loving, richly varnished prose of Joseph Mitchell's *New Yorker* pieces. It was known for its Irish eccentrics, its argumentative old-timers and its "thick, musty smell" of pine sawdust, tap drippings and the cheese and onion sandwiches Moynihan devoured there between beers with Sandy Vanocur and other companions.

Politics, if less soothing than McSorley's, were more exciting than the IRC. Moynihan joined the Tilden Democratic Club, based in the

Gramercy Park area. Again, as he had done at the LSE, he had arrived in an interesting place at a time of change and opportunity. Democratic politics in New York City in the 1950s were obsessed with the conflict between what Moynihan himself in a 1961 article called "bosses" and "reformers."[4] The "bosses," and Moynihan used quotation marks to show that he did not share the general contempt in which they were held by the literati, were almost invariably Catholics and mostly Irish. By the 1950s, the leaders were mostly middle-class lawyers, but the rank and file they led were still working-class, and they adopted the style of the respectable, upwardly mobile, sober-suited and — contrary to mythology — abstemious. "There is no greater nonsense," Moynihan has written, "than the stereotype of the Irish politician as a beer-guzzling back-slapper."[5]

The reformers were either upper-middle-class or even upper-class Anglo-Saxon Protestants, or — more typically — Jews. To a degree that was then unusual in politics, they were women. Their leaders were Eleanor Roosevelt; her son, Franklin D. Roosevelt, Jr.; and Thomas K. Finletter, a lawyer with the prestigious Cravath firm who had been secretary of the air force in the Truman administration and who aspired to return to Washington as a senator. The Democratic clubs had a long history. But it was only with the defeat of the Truman administration by President Eisenhower in 1952 that idealistic, highly educated New Yorkers transferred their attention en masse from the national to the New York political scene, and proceeded to take over the clubs.

The Democratic clubs were liberal. Their *raison d'être* was to keep the ideals of the New Deal alive. Very different was the political tradition of the regular Democrats. The great schism in New York Democratic politics dated back to the party's decision to turn its back on Al Smith, an Irish Catholic "from the sidewalks of New York," and nominate Franklin Delano Roosevelt, scion of Dutch merchants and patroons, educated at Groton and Harvard. They had followed Jim Farley when he had broken with Roosevelt in 1940 over the approaching war and domestic politics. The name of Roosevelt held little magic for them, and the personality and policies of Eleanor Roosevelt none at all.

Although the young Pat Moynihan was always in policy terms a liberal, in many other respects he did not share the reformers' visceral suspicion of the bosses. The liberals spoke of Tammany with revulsion, as of an evil conspiracy. Moynihan knew the West Side, where the writ of the McMani ran. Their real name was the McManuses, but in a culture where people still had a smattering of church Latin they were always called the McMani, and they ran the neighborhood from its "clubhouse" on 44th Street for four generations, since 1890. They lost about seven city blocks when the Lincoln Tunnel was built in the 1930s. But still, when Margaret Moynihan was running her saloon, if you got into any difficulty with the city or anyone else, you still talked to the McMani.

With his background, Moynihan was aware that since the days of Charles Francis Murphy (who drank in McSorley's in his time) and under his protégés, Al Smith and Robert Wagner, Sr., the New York Democratic machine had supported the most advanced labor, health and safety measures in the world. Even in 1953, Moynihan could see that the Democratic party regulars were led by a man, Carmine De-Sapio, who was not only the most accomplished politician in the state, but also deeply committed to a liberal agenda — though not to one that would upset the essentially conservative Catholic working class he represented. The party was capable of producing candidates for high office of the ability and unquestioned probity of Frank Hogan, the Manhattan district attorney of whom Moynihan still speaks with deep respect, more than forty years later.

Moynihan's financial adviser John Westergaard remembers how strongly his friend supported Hogan back in 1958. "The club was about to nominate Harriman. Then there was a question: do you nominate Frank Hogan or Tom Finletter for the Senate. Hogan got tarred with being the machine candidate. The club wanted to go dedicated to Finletter. The leader asked [Moynihan] to come down. I was chosen to speak up for Finletter. I gave a rousing speech. I won the day. But ever since I figured I better not take Moynihan on. I better join him instead."[6]

Moynihan could see, too, that behind the rivalry between Irish Catholic regulars and Jewish or Wasp reformers lay the division that, in 1950s America, dared not speak its name: class. However ambiguous, in class terms, Moynihan's own background might be, as a naval officer and the grandson of a lawyer and a business executive who had gone to school in Harlem and lived in Hell's Kitchen, Moynihan understood class and what the sociologist Richard Sennett has called its "hidden injuries."[7] His time in London and his friendship with the Golloglys had cemented the understanding he had from his New York childhood that there was such a thing as a working-class culture that was in no way subversive, but on the contrary deeply conservative. Much as he might aspire to succeed in life, and so to rise through unspoken class barriers, he identified emotionally, not with the middle-class liberals, but with the more conservative working class.

There was, he adds, a more ideological dimension. By 1953 and 1954, he says, when he was getting into New York politics, the schism between the traditional working-class Catholic Democrats and the new Left liberals was becoming plain for all to see. He had been signed on by Jack Bingham to write position papers on the general theme that Catholic social doctrine was not in conflict with liberal ideas, but was on the contrary solidly liberal: why, in short, "Al Smith would have voted for Adlai." It would have been difficult to persuade the members of the Lexington Democratic Club on the Upper East Side of this proposition.[8]

After Wagner won, Bingham came out for Franklin D. Roosevelt, Jr., for governor of New York, and so did his position-paper writer Moynihan. The relationship between Harriman and FDR Jr. was delicate; they were fellow liberals, but also rivals. Harriman had already run for president in 1952, "holding aloft," as the political columnist Murray Kempton put it, "the lamp of the New Deal," and at the convention in Chicago it was FDR Jr. who proposed him as a "great troubleshooter in a troubled world." Defeated, Harriman decided he wanted to run for governor of New York.

FDR Jr. did not give up without a bloody floor fight in the nominating convention that left a good deal of rancor. It was former Senator Herbert Lehman who came up with the solution. He called from Sun Valley, where he was skiing, to suggest that FDR Jr. should be offered the attorney general slot on a Harriman ticket. When Roosevelt accordingly duly withdrew, Bingham went to work for Harriman as his research director (his title was secretary) and asked Moynihan to come to Albany with him. Moynihan went to his bosses at the IRC, Leo Cherne and Dick Saltzman, and asked them for a leave of absence. They were not surprised. "The next thing," Moynihan puts it, "I am carrying the briefcase, literally, of one of the central world figures of the midtwentieth century"[9] and writing Harriman's speeches. On the last day of 1954 he was driven up the Hudson by his sister, Ellen, and her husband to start a new set of random walks.[10]

Much later, Moynihan was to write an unpublished history of the Harriman administration in New York State.[11] It was, in more than one way, an anticipation of the Kennedy administration in Washington. For liberals, in 1955, there was no other game in town. Washington was firmly in the grasp of the Eisenhower Republicans, men who had come from the corporate world, who believed that what was good for General Motors was good for America. Harriman, like Kennedy, came from a more patrician tradition. He promised a "bold, adventurous administration," and bold, adventurous spirits, who believed that government could and should tackle what they saw as the residual problems of social injustice and inequality, rallied to his flag. In office, Harriman disappointed many of his supporters. Horrified to find that New York State had been left by Governor Dewey to all intents and purposes broke, Harriman followed his instinct as a tightfisted multimillionaire, rather than his political ideals, and took disappointingly few initiatives in comparison with his rhetorical promises. But he did attract to Albany, which his wife, Marie, only half-jokingly referred to as "Albania," a gathering of talented and idealistic people who foreshadowed the crowd that assembled six years later on the New Frontier.

His budget director, Paul Appleby, had worked in Washington for FDR and for Harry Truman. Philip Kaiser, a labor expert who later served as an ambassador under Kennedy and Johnson, was in theory responsible for the problems of the aging; in practice he was a link with the labor unions.[12] James L. Sundquist, later well known as a political scientist, looked after the governor's national ambitions, and Isador Lubin worked at what was called an "attack on poverty." The redoubtable Dr. Persia Campbell looked after consumer interests and did not take no for an answer. Matt McCloskey, who later became one of the Moynihans' closest friends and "Uncle Matt" to the Moynihan children, pioneered the study of policy in the field of juvenile delinquency. But right at the heart of the Harriman administration was its executive secretary, Jonathan Bingham. His assistant was Daniel P. Moynihan, and his secretary was Elizabeth Brennan.

In 1954, Elizabeth Brennan had been in New York for a couple of years. She was working for a small outfit there called the Health Information Foundation.[13] In those days, young women from middle-class families in straitened circumstances didn't often go to college, and it was hard to find jobs that were not secretarial, except in teaching or nursing. On the seventh day she was there, she met a painter called Jerry Weinstein. When he learned she was only twenty, he said, "Your mother should never have let you out alone." She was a beautiful young woman, on the run from a miserably unhappy adolescence. Her father left home when she was three, then reappeared when she was five. The relationship between her mother, Thérèse, and the only daughter was sometimes stifling, and Liz had a fierce desire to see what more life had to offer. The family was Irish, respectable and solidly middle-class, and had been in the United States for many generations, unlike the Moynihans. Liz and Pat had, they later discovered, other things in common, though. Both of their fathers left home. Both married again in church and had second families. One of his half brothers was a priest, and one of her half sisters was a nun.

Liz loved New York. So it was a blow when she learned that the foundation was due to move to Chicago. She looked for a job with a public relations agency, then discovered that its main client was the Republican National Committee. There were things nice Irish Catholic girls from Massachusetts didn't do in those days, and one of them was working for the Republicans. It was Jerry Weinstein who came to her rescue. He had a friend, Lib Filman, who was running Volunteers for Harriman. Thomas K. Finletter was chairman of the citizens' committee. He wanted a volunteer who would go to all of his meetings and keep a record of everything that was said. She became friends with Finletter and loved the job. It was "wonderful, incomparable." She met Eleanor Roosevelt, Carmine DeSapio, even Harry Truman. Then Harriman was elected governor. Liz Brennan did not want to go to Albany. But she was hired by Harriman, "the gov" himself, to answer his personal correspondence. "So here I was," she reminisced forty-five years later, still a little in awe of how swiftly her life had been transformed, "answering Winston Churchill and all these people. I can still do Harriman's signature."

One day Jerry Weinstein came in and took Liz down to introduce her to a tall young man in Jack Bingham's office. Shortly after that they were both in Albany (though Liz was careful not to give up her apartment in New York). Pat's job was to do whatever he was told to do, whether it was talking to an important visitor who had to be kept waiting, or writing mood speeches for the governor, or, increasingly, working with the groups who were hammering out social reform policies, not all of which Harriman was willing or able to fund.

They saw each other daily, but they hadn't had anything that could be called a date until Liz went up to Massachusetts to ski with a fellow she had been seeing. She broke her leg on the slopes and came back one Sunday night with a plaster cast. Her apartment was on the second floor, without an elevator, so the governor's secretary, Bernice McCrae, let her use her own room at the Ten Eyck Hotel. That night there was a reception in the hotel. Pat was one of the guests, and shot upstairs for a few minutes to say hello to Liz. He did not waste time. He announced that he was going to marry her. Some of her friends advised her against it, but she knew her own mind. The great attraction about Pat, she has said, was that he was the funniest man she knew — that, and the fact that he was unmistakably going places. Both of them were ambitious, determined to seize opportunities they could never have dreamed of having even a short time before. And they were both irredeemably hooked on politics. They were married in church in Cohasset, Massachusetts, Liz's mother's hometown, in May 1955. He was twenty-eight, she was twenty-four. This decision was not put down to chance, then or later. Pat had found the woman he had sketched out for himself in his London journal, the woman who was going to walk by his side, and he would find out how far they could go together.

For a while the Moynihans lived in Liz's apartment on Washington Avenue in Albany (Liz's former roommate moved into Pat's old apartment). Then they bought a house thirty miles out of town at a place called Coeyman's Hollow. They found it through an ad in the *Saturday Review,* which said, "partially furnished house by noted architect," though it should have read "partially finished." Liz remembers it as "a fantastic house." It was the last house in the county on a dirt road that rose a thousand feet in the first mile from the paved road. "Today," she says, "I wouldn't dream of living in such an isolated place with small children, but then I didn't know better, and it was OK." In fact they loved the place, and thought they would keep it as a second home if — as they expected at the time — they went to live in New York City. Liz stopped working full-time. Her first child, Tim, was born in 1956, and her daughter, Maura, in 1958. John was born in 1960.

At first, Moynihan's reputation in the Harriman administration, to those who knew him casually, seems to have been that of an entertainer, almost a buffoon. He was appreciated as a boon companion at Yezzi's or in the bar of the Ten Eyck, a raconteur with a vast stock of historical anecdote and local knowledge, a man who could mix a punch, tell a tale, escort a visitor around the Capitol or expound the intricacies of state politics, but also a man who was a little hard to place, a New York Irishman in an LSE blazer, a pol and a political scientist all in one, who left some of those who did not see his work directly a little puzzled and suspicious. To the intellectuals, even then, he could look like a pol; to the pols, an intellectual.

Jack Bingham, however, who saw the drafts Moynihan wrote of speeches and legislative documents for the governor, recognized that this was a political animal of no ordinary quality. In 1956, he put Moynihan in charge of reports, with a salary increased to $10,500. It was a job where a combination of political and analytical skills was exactly what was needed. Moynihan was expected to keep track of what all departments of the state government were doing, and he set up a sort of situation room and an elaborate reporting system. At the same time, his job was political in the down-to-earth sense of the word; Pat let the media know about the good things the Harriman administration was doing for the people of New York. In 1958, Jack Bingham took a leave of absence to run for the state senate from the Bronx. Moynihan took over as acting secretary. Now he was one of the most important officials in an administration responsible for a population the size of Holland or Australia. But not, unfortunately, for long.

Averell Harriman was a dashing and brilliant figure, a polo player and lover.[14] He had handled delicate business negotiations in the prewar Soviet Union, conducted the affairs of a big investment bank, represented President Roosevelt as his personal emissary to Winston Churchill and then as ambassador to Stalin in the darkest days of World War II. He had sat with the three titans, Roosevelt, Stalin and Churchill, in the Livadiya Palace at Yalta in the hour of victory. In 1952, he had come within a respectable distance of winning the Democratic presidential nomination. Late in life, he married his former mistress, the ubiquitous Pamela Digby Churchill Hayward, who became the most influential Democratic political hostess of her time. Harriman had always enjoyed the best of everything: jobs, polo ponies and wives. He was, in short, a great American statesman. But he was also an unusually maladroit politician, and in 1957 and 1958 he blundered from one crass political mistake to the next.

Harriman mishandled the scandals surrounding the parole of Joseph "Socks" Lanza, a hoodlum once known as "the Czar of the

Fulton Fish Market,"[15] and the mysterious affair of the organized-crime summit at Apalachin.[16] Worst of all, out of a mixture of complacency and misplaced upper-class solidarity, he promoted Nelson Rockefeller by putting him at the head of a constitutional convention. Rockefeller handled the assignment astutely, leaving the constitutional amendment process in ruins, and himself as the inevitable Republican candidate for governor.

Harriman was nevertheless sure to be chosen as the Democrats' next candidate for governor. The question was: Who would run for the Senate? But on that question the party fell apart disastrously. The liberals' candidate was Liz's former boss, Thomas K. Finletter. Carmine DeSapio was for Frank Hogan. Robert Wagner, mayor of New York, would have been a perfect compromise candidate. But then Harriman committed the gross blunder of announcing to Warren Weaver, the *New York Times* correspondent in Albany, on a plane trip,[17] that his first choice for the contentious nomination was Finletter, his second choice one Thomas Murray, known only as a former member of the Atomic Energy Commission. The night before the Buffalo Democratic convention that was to approve the party's slate, the bosses gathered for a tense meeting that went on until 4:00 in the morning.[18] Wagner refused to run, saying he had promised New Yorkers that he would finish his term as their mayor. DeSapio continued to back Hogan. Harriman could not switch to Hogan without looking like Tammany's man. As the salty Marie Harriman put it affectionately but mercilessly in her socialite growl, "They gave ole Ave a real ole Philadelphia rat fucking."[19]

Rockefeller won easily. Hogan was beaten by Kenneth Keating. It was the beginning of the end for DeSapio, who went to jail a decade later.[20] Moynihan had watched the political disintegration of the Harriman administration from the inside. He did not blame Harriman so much as he blamed the liberals. Yes, he admitted in 1998, "I hate the radical/liberal contempt which was so arrogant."[21] The Buffalo convention was formative. If one of the enduring paradoxes about Moynihan is that he shares many of the liberals' goals, but is uncomfortable in the company of the people who promote them, some of the reason lies in those months and years when he watched the New York "reformers" unable to forge any sort of lasting coalition with the party regulars who shared their objectives, because they despised them, and on class grounds, as Moynihan saw it and still sees it.

So the acting secretary found himself — with a wife and two children and without Harriman's great wealth — out of a job. Or rather he did have a strange sort of consolation prize. Harriman was looking for someone to write the history of his administration.[22] His papers were to be consigned to the Maxwell School of Citizenship and Public Affairs at Syracuse University. The chosen author would be paid a salary by Harriman himself. In January 1959, Harriman met with Moynihan and Harlan Cleveland, dean of the Maxwell School, and agreed that Moynihan, as the head of a New York state government research project, should write the book.

Liz was snowed in for six weeks after Pat started work at Syracuse.[23] They decided to sell the house at Coeyman's Hollow, but they had to wait until the spring before potential buyers could actually get up the road to view it. In Syracuse they rented from the university a big, comfortable house that was falling apart. In fact it was bulldozed three days after they left. The two years the Moynihans spent there were happy years personally, though they were frustrating in some ways for Pat. He worked away at the history of the Harriman administration, and in fact finished a typescript almost five hundred pages long, now in the Library of Congress, though it was never published.[24] Moynihan, who never quite forgave Harriman's second wife, Pamela, for supporting Bella Abzug against him in the New York primary in 1976, now says that Harriman refused to publish his book because it wasn't flattering enough.[25] But it was quite flattering, he concedes. In fact, Moynihan wrote that Harriman "combined the energy, initiative and rapacity of the robber baron with the strength of tradition and poise of responsibility which in other times and lands we are told adorned the ancient nobility."[26] But "nothing could have been flattering enough for Harriman."[27]

Those two years, however, were not wasted. For one thing, Moynihan used them, with the encouragement of Harlan Cleveland, to finish his doctoral thesis for the Fletcher School, on the International Labor Organization. He had almost wholly lost interest in it. Indeed, when after their wedding he moved into Liz's apartment, he left the typescript in the hall to be thrown away until a neighbor persuaded him to save it. In order to qualify for his doctorate, he had not only to finish his dissertation, but also to reach a reasonable standard in French and Spanish, something he found hard, even with help from Liz.[28] But a doctorate was the professional qualification for a trade. With his doctorate, Moynihan became a card-carrying member of the academic trade union, a position that gave him economic security, professional acceptance and psychological assurance.

At the same time, however, in these same years he won his spurs in another profession, the one, perhaps — if indeed it is a profession at all — for which he was most richly gifted: journalism. The connection took place because of Moynihan's interest in what was to be one of his lifelong preoccupations: roads and traffic safety.

One of the very able people who had been attracted to Albany to work for the Harriman administration was Dr. William Haddon, Jr. A graduate of MIT and the Harvard Medical School, where he earned a master's degree in public health as well as his M.D.,[29] Haddon brought together three ideas that revolutionized thinking about traffic safety. First, he was impressed by the work of Hugh DeHaven on protecting accident victims. DeHaven, who was for decades head of the automotive crash inquiry research project at Cornell University, had been the only survivor of a midair collision of two biplanes in 1917. During World War II, DeHaven developed cockpits that could survive high-speed impact and provide a safe environment for pilots. He invented lap straps and shoulder belts. In the same vein, Haddon stressed that "if a car hits a tree, nobody gets hurt until the person in the car hits the inside of the car. . . . A second collision. Therefore, think seat belt. Think padded dashboard. Think air bag. Think divided highway. . . ."[30]

Haddon's second idea was that traffic accidents are a public health problem like any other, and can be studied, like cancer or tuberculosis, by epidemiological methods. And his third contribution was to publicize the idea, already put forward by others but always firmly sat on by the automobile industry, that traffic accidents were not only caused, as the industry had always insisted, by driver fault, but also by car failure. In the 1950s, Detroit was happy to take part in bodies concerned with traffic safety, but usually recommended more driver instruction in high school or stricter highway policing, not government regulation of the design and manufacturing process.

Urged to do so by Jack Bingham, who was alive to the possibilities of the subject, Moynihan worked closely with Haddon in Albany on traffic safety and, after he got to Syracuse, he wrote his first important magazine piece. It was sent to *The Reporter*, a magazine started and published by the Italian antifascist journalist Max Ascoli. Moynihan's original connection was through the magazine's managing editor, Robert Bingham. But the *Reporter* connection was to be a lasting and significant one. For under Ascoli the editor was Irving Kristol, who would become a close friend and in some degree a patron of Moynihan for many years. The Washington editor was Douglass Cater, who later went on to work for President Johnson in the White House and to work closely with Moynihan on civil rights issues. And Meg Greenfield, who joined *The Reporter* as a researcher but was writing for the magazine by 1961, later went to work for the *Washington Post* and eventually became its editorial page editor; she remained one of Moynihan's closest journalist friends.[31]

Moynihan's article was called "Epidemic on the Roads," reflecting one of the key ideas he had picked up from Haddon.[32] It began by pouring scorn on the activities of the National Safety Council, an industry-supported body. A few months after the council published what it claimed was the "official" figure of 1,400,000 deaths and injuries due to motor vehicle accidents, the U.S. Public Health Service revealed that the true figure was nearer to 5,000,000. Campaigns against speeding produced little diminution in the accident statistics, and a high proportion of accidents took place when vehicles were traveling at well below the speed limit.

Moynihan drew on his own experience in Albany when he described a typical bureau of motor vehicles run by an assortment of "genial 'pols' with utterly no training or interest in traffic safety except as it provides an opportunity to do small favors," such as passing out low-number license plates.[33] Moynihan himself, in Albany, hit upon an ingenious way of doing favors when he increased the number of digits in so-called "vanity plates" from two to three, thus increasing from 676 to 17,576 the number of vanity-plate numbers available for the state to use for patronage.[34]

"Into this troubled scene of ignorance and misinformation," Moynihan wrote, there stepped a new protagonist, a figure of scientific enlightenment in the shape of the epidemiologist. To those trained in that discipline, it seemed more sensible, instead of trying to influence the behavior of some eighty million drivers in the United States, to concentrate on something "subject to control by perhaps a dozen persons," namely the faulty, or worse, design of the package that surrounds the driver or passenger in an automobile. This idea had begun to spread in the middle 1950s. As early as 1956, Harold A. Katz wrote an article in the *Harvard Law Review* arguing that automobile manufacturers might be held liable for injuries sustained as a result of negligent design.[35] In February of that same year, the Committee on

Trauma of the American College of Surgeons sent a resolution to the manufacturers stressing occupant safety in automobile design.[36] But in 1956, when Ford did redesign its cars, it took a beating in the marketplace as other manufacturers concentrated their advertising on speed and performance. Interestingly, in the light of the way discussion of public policy has proceeded in many different fields since 1959, Moynihan ended his first important article by calling for government regulation. "The Federal government," he concluded, "will have to do the job." The article was hard-hitting but civil in tone.

A few years later in a paper first read at a seminar at Wesleyan University in March 1966 and later published in *The Public Interest,* Moynihan was less circumspect. The automobile industry, he said then, was the most profitable enterprise in the world, and "these profits are drenched in blood."[37] In 1960, he went on, Dr. William Haddon, Jr., and he had made "tentative calculations that something like one-third of the automobiles manufactured in Detroit actually end up with blood on them."

If Moynihan was a pioneer in bringing the new thinking about traffic safety to the general public, though, he was not the first. Nineteen days earlier, an article on the same subject appeared in *The Nation.* It was contributed by a thin, intense Lebanese American, a graduate of Princeton and the Harvard Law School currently serving as an enlisted man in the U.S. Army at Fort Dix. His name was Ralph Nader, and one of his friends at Harvard, Frederick H. Condon, had been confined to a wheelchair by a road accident.[38]

Moynihan's interest in traffic safety, and in particular in Haddon's epidemiological approach and his emphasis on automobile design as opposed to driver fault, lasted long after he left Albany. When he went to work for Arthur Goldberg in the U.S. Department of Labor in Washington, he found himself representing Goldberg on the President's Committee for Traffic Safety. Moynihan took the view that the executive director of the committee was a General Motors company man and that no one was taking an overall look at the issues.

In 1964, therefore, he hired Ralph Nader as a consultant to his planning staff on highway safety at $50 a day. For the previous five years, Nader had been floundering. He opened a law office in Hartford, taught law, wrote freelance articles, and visited Scandinavia, Latin America and the Soviet Union. Moynihan had not forgotten him, however, and found a use for his obsessional digging and his unappeasably suspicious mind. Working at night, in a "sea of books and papers," Nader was convinced that his phone was being tapped. In the spring of 1965, he finished a report "on the Context, Condition and Recommended Direction of Federal Activity in Highway Safety." It ran to 234 double-spaced pages of text and 99 pages of notes.

Moynihan wanted the government to act on road safety. He wanted legislation that would pinpoint faulty design and manufacture as the main cause of accidents, and he lobbied for it within the government. It was Nader, however, who created the climate of opinion in which public thinking about traffic safety was transformed and legislation became possible. But it was not his report that did it. First Nader lost his research notes in a taxi; then his report itself seems to have disappeared. In September 1964, Richard Grossman, of Grossman Publishers, bought Nader lunch and commissioned a book on traffic safety. In November 1965, it was published as *Unsafe at Any Speed*. The book was devastating enough, with its hair-raising allegations about how GM's Corvair would suddenly flip and turn turtle, killing or maiming even careful drivers. But what really converted public opinion to Nader's jaundiced view of the automobile industry were GM's heavy-handed attempts to discredit him. Even before publication of *Unsafe*, GM had hired a private detective agency, Vincent Gillen Associates. A month later agents were checking Nader's "politics, his marital status, his friends, his women, his boys and so forth, drinking, dope, jobs." In March 1966, James Ridgeway did a piece in *The New Republic* on GM's undercover intimidation, and Morton Mintz did another in the *Washington Post*. On March 22, the president of GM, James Roche, testifying to Senator Abraham Ribicoff's subcommittee, apologized to Nader.

By 1966, the reputation of the American automobile industry had been destroyed for a generation. In 1964, Moynihan has suggested, the Johnson administration had been dependent on political contributions from the automobile industry; by 1965 that had changed. On September 9, 1966, President Johnson signed the Traffic and Motor Vehicle Safety Act. Moynihan had signed a contract for another book about traffic safety, but he never wrote it. There has been a certain competition between Moynihan's friends and Nader's over who deserves the most credit for the shift in public opinion and for the ensuing legislation. It is clear that both men are responsible. They produced articles, drawn on very different exposure to the problem, at about the same time. Moynihan then plucked Nader from obscurity, and Nader, helped by the folly of General Motors, knew how to seize his opportunity. He played an important part in changing both public and government attitudes to an issue that affected millions of American lives. Nader's work showed how academic research, skillfully transformed into campaigning journalism, could transform public attitudes and prod the government into action, even in the face of ruthless opposition by one of the most powerful interest groups in the country. The traffic safety issue created Ralph Nader as an eternal gadfly, demanding more honest and more truthful behavior from the great forces in American life. Less obtrusively, Pat Moynihan, too, learned from the experience. It was, in any case, among other things the first example of his gifts as a journalist.

Irving Kristol, one of the shrewdest editors of his generation, had spotted those gifts too, and used him steadily as a contributor to *The Reporter*. Moynihan was, the sociologist Nathan Glazer remembers, "taken up" by Kristol. He was introduced by Robert Bingham to Kristol, who had recently returned from editing *Encounter* in London for the Congress for Cultural Freedom, funded, as later came out, by the Central Intelligence Agency. "Pat had enough wonderful ideas for articles to fill up his own magazine," says Kristol. "We finally agreed that he would write a four-thousand-word piece on automobile safety . . . I had high hopes, but they fell far short of reality when, a little more than a week later, I received a ten-thousand-word article that was an editor's dream."[39] For Kristol, Moynihan wrote a series of long pieces in which he developed what became a characteristic style, based on solid research, illuminated by flashes of wit and often sarcasm, yet always seeking to persuade, not to bludgeon. On June 11, 1959, he wrote in this manner about the unseemly panic over *Sputnik* and how it had led to the National Defense Education Act of the previous year, which Moynihan characterized as kicking the educator "into the trough of Federal aid." Then on April 14, 1960, came "New Roads and Urban Chaos," exploring a theme Moynihan would continue to be interested in as chairman of the Environment and Public Works Committee of the U.S. Senate. Once again Moynihan deployed a good journalist's eye for telling detail. Three supernumerary interchanges in remotest Nevada, he discovered in a General Accounting Office report, would serve only "some old mines, a power line, four or five small ranches, and a house of ill repute." But the sprightly manner concealed massive research and an unerring grasp of the strategic point. As ever, there was an unresting skepticism of the claims of interested parties in and out of government, and an enduring concern for the American city and its people. Rhapsodies about the highway and the freedoms it conferred, he observed, "startled many of those who have been concerned with the future of the American city," and he added a comment that was well in advance of its time in 1960: "To undertake a vast program of highway construction with no thought for other forms of transportation seemed lunatic."

Kristol was drawing these long, authoritative articles out of the knowledge Moynihan had acquired in Albany and through his access to information about government in the Harriman papers. Moynihan was staking out areas of what would be lifelong interests. The last of these, which appeared in *The Reporter* after its author had moved on to another sphere of life, was called "The Private Government of Crime." It arose out of Moynihan's exposure in Albany to organized crime, and was to have unanticipated consequences.

Averell Harriman had used the issue, in the specialized shape of corruption at harness-racing tracks, in his campaign to capture the New York governorship from Thomas Dewey, and then promptly dropped the issue until there was a stir about an attempt to fix a parole-violation charge for Socks Lanza, the fish market czar. It was an old tradition. Dewey in his day had won the governorship by boasting of his prowess as a "crime buster," then conveniently shut up about crime for a decade. It became more difficult for Harriman to ignore organized crime after Albert Anastasia, a Mafia killer, was murdered in a New York barbershop and the McClellan Committee (with the young Robert Kennedy as its counsel) held hearings on the links between the Teamsters union and the crime syndicates. Then, on one night in the late fall of 1957, the suspicions of the solitary New York state trooper who maintained law and order in the hamlet of Apalachin, Sergeant Edgar Croswell, were aroused by the appearance of dozens of men with Italian names in fancy suits and large limousines. Like a child blundering onto a wasp's nest, he had stumbled on a Mafia summit, a sort of Versailles of crime. Some sixty-five Mafiosi from as far away as Puerto Rico and California, including the heads of three of the major crime families, had converged on Apalachin; but if some of their expensive clothes got snagged as they ran for cover into the woods, the police had no grounds for holding them.[40]

Overnight, organized crime became the hottest issue of the day. Nelson Rockefeller, in his turn, seized on it to defeat Harriman, as

Harriman had used it to overthrow Dewey. Moynihan used it to try to get himself a job in Washington. Instead, as we shall see, it almost prevented him from appearing at all on the New Frontier.

In the meantime, Irving Kristol had helped Moynihan find an opportunity that was to have an even more lasting effect on his career. One of Kristol's friends, going back to City College in the 1930s, was Nathan Glazer, who had been pondering ethnicity in America since he majored in sociology at City College, from 1940 to 1944.[41] He was associated with the *Contemporary Jewish Record*, which became *Commentary* magazine in 1945. Glazer was drawn to the issue of ethnicity by his interest in two groups, Jews and Negroes. His first major article about ethnicity in America was "America's Ethnic Pattern: 'Melting Pot' or 'Nation of Nations'?," which appeared in *Commentary* as long ago as 1953. The following year it appeared in a scholarly version.[42] Glazer's friend Daniel Bell suggested that studies of the main ethnic groups in New York could be used as the basis for a series of articles in the *New York Post*, whose editor, James Wechsler, was a friend of Bell's. Glazer's original plan was to get a New Yorker of Italian stock to write about the Italians of New York, a black writer to write about the blacks, a Puerto Rican to write about the Puerto Ricans, an Irishman on the Irish, and a Jew, himself, on the Jews. The central idea was that most discussions of minorities and ethnic groups had focused hitherto on the immigrant generation and on discrimination. Glazer wanted to emphasize the emergence of second generations and the distinctive characters of each group, as opposed to their supposed submergence in the American type.

The project was to be funded by a grant of $50,000 from the New York Post Foundation, controlled by the paper's publisher, Dorothy Schiff. There were difficulties about administering the grant, however. The Joint Center for Urban Studies of Harvard and MIT was then being established, headed by another friend of Glazer's, Martin Meyerson, and it seemed a good idea to have the center manage the project.

As a publishing venture, *Beyond the Melting Pot* was not altogether a triumph. Literary collaboration is rarely entirely free from tension, and although the Glazers and Moynihans, close neighbors for years in Cambridge, Massachusetts, have remained friends, the relationship was not wholly an exception.

When Glazer submitted the first three treatments (Negroes,

Puerto Ricans and Italians), the *Post* decided it didn't like them, and cut off the grant after paying only about $15,000. Glazer still went on to write about Jews as well, along with most of the introduction. Moynihan wrote the essay about Irish New York and most of the concluding chapter, "Beyond the Melting Pot."

Glazer's plan for the book called for studies looking at ethnic groups in the light of up-to-date social science. That meant, first, that they should not be seen just as immigrant groups, destined to disappear through assimilation. Glazer's interest in Zionism and the Jewish experience was obviously relevant to this conception of how other ethnic groups had evolved. Second, he wanted to emphasize the way ethnic groups continued to keep a distinctive culture, in the anthropological sense, as defined by different patterns of family life, child-rearing and so on. This "personality and culture" approach had been reinforced by Glazer's collaboration with David Riesman on the project that became another bestseller of the day, *The Lonely Crowd*. As a result, Glazer kept pressing anthropological studies like Conrad Arensberg's *The Irish Countryman* on his collaborator. Moynihan, Glazer suspects, "didn't cotton to this aspect of ethnic studies."[43] The different approaches show through in a letter Moynihan wrote to Glazer in March 1962, enclosing "the Introduction and Conclusion as they emerge from our collaboration." He goes on, "You will find that almost all of your introductory material is here, although less of the conclusions. The feeling in Cambridge appeared quite firm to the effect that the sociological discussion in our conclusion was really out of place. I think I might agree, although I was much interested in what you had to say. It seems to me that we would not be entirely wise to identify what we have done as Sociology . . . For one thing, I am not a sociologist."[44]

The book was finally published by the MIT Press. At one time, Glazer wanted it published by a trade publisher, but Martin Meyerson was unwilling to exclude it from the general arrangement he had with the university press for all the Joint Center's books. In 1964, Glazer was writing long letters to Moynihan explaining the complexities of royalties, and so on.[45] Neither author made serious money out of the venture.[46]

The book was, however, highly influential, both in spreading the idea of ethnicity as a subject worthy of study, and also in its decisive effect on Moynihan's career. Its conclusion that, as the authors put it, "the melting pot doesn't melt," that "the principal ethnic groups of

New York City will be seen maintaining a distinct identity, albeit a changing one, from one generation to the next," came at just the right moment to explode the Fourth of July pieties of most previous writing about the immigrant experience. Its observations were sharp and credible.

It was also a courageous book. The apology that the authors included in their preface might have been written in foreknowledge of the reception of the Moynihan Report: "Understandably enough, the unevenness of achievement . . . is the source of resentment and even bitterness by many individual members of the different groups. It may be that our discussion will also be resented . . . We would therefore, in advance, ask a measure of forgiveness for taking up a subject which needs to be discussed, but which cannot be aired without giving pain to some."[47]

Moynihan's short history of the Irish in New York revealed how much he had read and how much he had assimilated of the Irish Catholic experience. It takes its place with his articles " 'Bosses' and 'Reformers' " and "When the Irish Ran New York" (based on the section in *Beyond the Melting Pot*) as his contribution to the tribal history. But it was the last chapter, largely his, though incorporating some ideas that Glazer had been exploring for more than a decade, that spelled out the book's essential message. The title referred back to the 1908 hit play *The Melting Pot,* written by an English Zionist, Israel Zangwill. Its hero exults that "America is God's Crucible, the great Melting Pot where all the races of Europe are melting and reforming." Not so, said Glazer and Moynihan. "The experience of Zangwill's hero and heroine was not general. The point about the melting pot is that it did not happen."

In 1960, while marooned in comparative isolation from the political process at Syracuse, Moynihan took a limited part in John F. Kennedy's presidential campaign. He had remained the secretary of the New York State Democratic party's Public Affairs Committee, and had already had some contact with some of Kennedy's people, including his key aide, Kenneth O'Donnell. Moynihan was selected as an alternate delegate to the Democratic Convention in Los Angeles, and wrote a brief speech that Governor Harriman used to second Kennedy's nomination. The wild demonstrations on the part of the Stevenson delegates, and their reluctance to accept Kennedy as the candidate, reinforced Moynihan's reservations, verging on hostility, toward the reform wing of the party. His only contact with the candidate, on the other hand, was brief and irritating. Moynihan was talking to Governor Harriman in a hotel lobby when Kennedy came up. Harriman introduced the two, mentioning that Moynihan taught at Syracuse. Kennedy said he had an honorary degree from Syracuse and left without further conversation. His manner appears to have rankled with Moynihan, but in no way diminished Moynihan's admiration for the first Catholic candidate for the presidency since Al Smith.

Back in Syracuse, Pat's ability to campaign for Kennedy was limited. He made a number of speeches for him. A reporter's notebook preserved in his papers and full of his scribbles from the 1960 election suggests a considerable degree of involvement, however.[48] On election day, he served as a poll watcher, and is said to have made a dramatic appearance, clad in a trenchcoat and tweed hat, demanding that a certain room be unlocked, as Republican chicanery was taking place inside. Unfortunately, once the key had been found, the room proved to be empty.[49] Liz Moynihan, on the other hand, took an active and highly effective part in Kennedy's election. She discovered a lifelong passion for campaigning and a formidable talent for it.

With Kennedy on his way to Washington, ambitious young politicos and academics, birthright Democrats excited by the prospect of a youthful president, liberal on domestic issues but reliably anti-Communist, replacing Eisenhower and his tired legionaries, were desperate to get a job in his administration, and the Moynihans were no exception. Liz was as keen to leave Syracuse as Pat.

There were difficulties, however. There was the matter of the book about the Harriman administration, which was not finished by election day. There was the matter of finding a job. Moynihan first tried to land a job in the Justice Department under Robert Kennedy, stressing his organized crime experience in Albany. That didn't come off, in part because Averell Harriman told Kenneth O'Donnell that Moynihan wanted to stay in Syracuse until he had finished the book. He also tried for jobs in Health, Education and Welfare, and for a job in the Commerce Department, as deputy undersecretary for transportation, and apparently also in the Bureau of the Budget.[50]

Help came from an unexpected direction. Sandy Vanocur was at NBC and doing everything he could to find a job in Washington for his friend.[51] "Nothing worked," he says. Then Arthur Goldberg, newly appointed secretary of labor, who was recruiting staff for his department, asked Vanocur if he knew any bright young economists. It was perhaps stretching a point to call Moynihan an economist, but he was a social scientist. (He had just received his doctorate from Tufts.) And he had studied at the London School of Economics, though not, as it happened, economics. Vanocur introduced Moynihan to Goldberg's assistant secretary, Willard Wirtz, who wanted to take him.

In the spring of 1961, after he knew he had landed his job at the Department of Labor, Moynihan telephoned Stephen Bailey, the new head of the Maxwell School at Syracuse, and told him he would be going to Washington. He promised to finish the Harriman biography after he got there. Bailey asked Moynihan to show the manuscript, not quite finished as it was, to Harriman, to the university's chancellor, Clark Ahlberg, and to Paul Appleby, the former dean of the Maxwell School who had worked as budget director for Harriman in Albany. Both Ahlberg and Appleby thought the manuscript was too critical. Specifically, they were unhappy with Moynihan's account of the Apalachin episode and Harriman's handling of the organized crime issue generally. Bailey flew to Washington and took Moynihan to lunch at the Cosmos Club to explain that he had decided not to publish, and why. Moynihan said little at the lunch, but afterward wrote Bailey a letter suggesting that Harriman had pressured him into refusing to publish. It was, he argued, an issue of academic freedom. But in the end he decided not to press his point. Washington summoned, and Syracuse could not hold him.[52] On July 5, 1961, he was able to write to his pal in the White House Richard K. Donahue from his desk at the Labor Department:

> Dear Dick:
> Reporting aboard, Sir.
> Best,
> Pat M

This had been no random walk, but a determined scramble to ascend from the provincial world of Syracuse to the center of things.

At the last moment, there was another problem. Moynihan called Vanocur at one in the morning and said, "It's being held up by J. Edgar Hoover."[53] It was true. The FBI director had not been pleased by what he had heard of Moynihan, especially by some remarks in Moynihan's *Reporter* article "The Private Government of

Crime," which had just appeared. In it, Moynihan had been severe on Hoover and the Bureau. Worse, he had mocked. Worse still, he had made fun of Hoover's proudest instrument of self-glorification, the FBI's Black Museum and guided tour. He argued that "for thirty-seven years" Hoover "has sought to avoid any assignment that would involve the FBI directly" with fighting organized crime.[54] The article may have been written in the first place to help Moynihan's credentials in Robert Kennedy's Justice Department. It almost blocked his appointment to the Department of Labor. According to Vanocur, Hoover also brought up Moynihan's brief incarceration after the incident in Medford in 1948.[55] Indeed, many years later, Moynihan revealed that a few weeks after the article was published, and after he had started work at Labor, J. Edgar Hoover ordered what Moynihan described as a "raid" on the Department of Labor.

"They hit the Secretary's floor in unison, went door to door, told everyone save the hapless author but including the Secretary himself, that a dangerous person had infiltrated their ranks with the clear implication that he should go." Goldberg stood by him. On August 2, C. D. "Deke" DeLoach, J. Edgar Hoover's right-hand man, informed him that "it would appear to be impossible to deal with Moynihan on a liaison basis in view of his obvious biased opinion regarding the FBI." Goldberg called Moynihan in, and said, "Pat, you have a problem. Go and explain your point of view to the Director." He didn't get to see Hoover, but the next day he went to see DeLoach, who "made it plain he could barely stand the sight of him." DeLoach sent a three-page, single-spaced memo of the conversation to Hoover. It ended as follows:

> Moynihan is an egghead that talks in circles and constantly contradicts himself. He shifts about constantly in his chair and will not look you in the eye. He would be the first so-called "liberal" that would scream if the FBI overstepped its jurisdiction. He is obviously a phony intellectual that one minute will back down and the next minute strike while our back is turned. I think we made numerous points in our interview with him, however this man is so much up on "cloud nine" it is doubtful that his ego will allow logical interpretation of remarks made to other people.

The Director noted in his own hand: "I am not going to see this skunk."[56]

There was also a case of mistaken identity, perhaps accidental, perhaps not, to be overcome. The Bureau had reported to Dick Donahue in the White House that Moynihan had been picked up on a drunk-driving charge. Moynihan responded in writing to Donahue's inquiry, "The only motor vehicle operator's license I have ever held was issued in New York State in 1955. I still hold it. At no time before or since have I ever, here or abroad, been charged with or convicted of any offense relating to driving under the influence of alcohol."[57] Donahue wrote back, "The record is entirely clear. The information furnished to us on security clearance was inaccurate — there was another similarly named individual."[58]

In the end, Hoover was persuaded, if not to forgive, to calm down. He had demonstrated yet again that he was a dangerous enemy to cross. Arthur Goldberg had shown that he was not to be intimidated. (Moynihan thinks he was the only cabinet officer in the Kennedy administration who would have resisted a full-court press by the FBI of this kind.[59])

The row with Hoover paid an unexpected dividend for Moynihan. Some time in 1962 he was invited to give a talk on crime at the Joint Center for Urban Studies in Cambridge, Massachusetts. At the end of the lecture a Harvard junior faculty member came up and introduced himself. His name was James Q. Wilson, and he had been a pupil of the well-known urban scholar Edward C. Banfield, whose catalog of the woes of urban life, *The Unheavenly City,* was to have a great impact when it was published in 1970. Wilson thought it was an astonishing thing. "I was quite impressed that a fellow would talk critically about the FBI in public, as I thought they deserved to be spoken of, for their neglect of, or denial of the existence of organized crime."[60] Those were the days when J. Edgar Hoover was extremely powerful; he had after all intimidated President Kennedy and would intimidate President Johnson into retaining him as FBI director. Jim Wilson admired Moynihan's guts, and he told him so. They were to become the closest of friends, and each was to influence the other more than a little.

Moynihan had made it into the Kennedy administration, and in spite of his passage with Hoover, he had not, thanks to Arthur Goldberg, been immediately hurled into outer darkness. Now it was time for him to show, to paraphrase John F. Kennedy's inaugural, what he could do for his country, and to discover what his country would do for, and to, him.

4

On the New Frontier

1961–1965

> Our revels now are ended.
>
> — William Shakespeare, *The Tempest*, quoted by
> Daniel P. Moynihan in a radio interview after
> President Kennedy's assassination

THE FRONTIER in American history was not just a line marching inexorably west between the settled and the unknown, the desert and the sown. It was also a social organism, drawing to it all manner of men and women: cattlemen and sodbusters, trappers and miners, lawmen and outlaws, preachers and prostitutes, church builders and hell-raisers.

So it was with John Kennedy's New Frontier. It was, of course, a metaphorical frontier. Although Kennedy flirted for a while with the idea that space itself would be the New Frontier,[1] really the phrase was not much more than a political slogan, like Franklin Roosevelt's New Deal or Harry Truman's Fair Deal. Still, the prospect of a new, young Democratic president, open to new ideas, yet full of "vigor" — one of Kennedy's favorite words — did attract to Washington in the winter of 1960 and 1961 a varied population of political and intellectual adventurers. They came from New York and San Francisco law firms, from state and city politics across the nation, from the growing world of foundations and pressure groups, and of course from the great graduate schools, swollen by the postwar demand for academic manpower. It was the natural thing for a birthright Democrat, from New York City by way of Albany and a graduate school of public administration, to join this energetic and high-minded throng.

The prevalent image of the New Frontier, carefully cultivated by Kennedy's boosters in and out of the administration, was one of youth replacing tired middle age. Young, athletic millionaires in blue suits who played tennis were taking over from portly millionaires in brown, who played golf. The mood was strangely blended from ambition and idealism, aggressive social climbing and a sense of youthful adventure.

For all the emphasis on youth, the best address for New Frontiersmen was the very oldest part of town. Georgetown[2] was the first choice for those who could afford it. Rediscovered in the New Deal years, in the 1960s it was a quiet, elegant settlement of brick or stuccoed houses, surrounded by tiny gardens with box hedges, magnolia trees and ivy ground cover, and redolent of the unmistakable scent of money, earned or more often inherited. That was where the Chester Bowleses lived, and the Joseph Krafts, and the Joseph Alsops, and the Yale men from the CIA, and the Philip Grahams, who owned the *Washington Post* and the Averell Harrimans, who installed their Picassos, Matisses and a Van Gogh called *White Roses* in a large red brick mansion on N Street. The Kennedys themselves lived on N Street, the other side of Wisconsin Avenue, until they moved into the White House. With such affluent citizens besieging the Georgetown real estate offices, plain folk had to look elsewhere for a place to live.

Some New Frontiersmen, including the president's brother Bobby, moved out to the Virginia suburbs. But if you couldn't live in Georgetown, the second best address on the New Frontier was Cleveland Park. This was a late-nineteenth-century suburb, originally settled by prosperous families who had their main residence in the city; in the days before automobiles and air conditioning, the families and their servants would decamp a couple of miles up Connecticut Avenue to a leafy neighborhood where the air was fresher, the temperature, in Washington's steamy summers, a degree or so more bearable. In the 1960s, the Nicholas Katzenbachs lived there on Highland Place; he was a Wall Street lawyer who was Robert Kennedy's deputy at the Justice Department. So did the McGeorge Bundys: he was President Kennedy's national security adviser. Tregaron, one of the few big estates left in Cleveland Park by the 1960s, a steep place, densely wooded, had belonged to Marjorie Merriweather Post, of the Post Toasties family, and her husband, Joseph E. Davies, who was sent by Franklin Roosevelt as America's first ambassador to Moscow after the United States recognized the Soviet Union in 1933. By the 1960s Tregaron was the Nationalist Chinese embassy, but the ornate wooden Russian dacha, which the Davieses packed up and brought back from Moscow, the way someone else might have brought back *matryoshka* dolls, was still standing on the grounds, along with the stables.

When the Moynihans first came down to Washington in the early summer of 1961, they lived in a rented house at 3016 Cortland Place. It was a real wife-killer, Liz remembers, with the laundry in the basement and the kids on the third floor.[3] But it was across from the Klingle Road entrance to Tregaron. It wasn't long before Liz had found what is still called the Farm House, a white clapboard structure, once part of the estate's stable block. The estate was managed by a bank, and Liz was able to rent the Farm House, with $2,500 allowed off the rent by the bank for putting it in order. It had ten rooms and four bathrooms. Always clever at finding and fixing houses, Liz took down a wall, put in a rolled steel beam and took out the sinks that remained in every room. It was a nice place when she had finished, she remembers, "And there were we, the poorest folks in the Kennedy administration, with all those gorgeous acres in the middle of town." Tim went to Sidwell Friends School, then still on Wisconsin Avenue in the neighborhood. But when the lower school moved out to Bethesda, Liz put Tim in John Eaton, the public school less than a block away, where Maura was already a student. The "enrichment" was done by parents; Liz ran an art room two mornings a week. She also found the energy to run a play school at Tregaron, the "Shed School," for John and four other little boys. Each day a different mother stayed, but Liz did the juice and the crayons.

She also gave wonderful dinners in the Tregaron house. Pat invited fellow New Frontiersmen, journalists and writers, architects like Charles Bassett from San Francisco or the priest Andrew Greeley, also a social scientist and future mystery writer. Liz's cooking was excellent, and Pat's wine copious. There was a nucleus of friends from Albany, from Syracuse and from the media, including Vanocur, Howard K. and Bennie Smith and Paul Niven, Mary McGrory and Meg Greenfield, and colleagues from the department and gradually from a wider swath of the administration.

The Tregaron years were a time of happiness and personal expansion for both Pat and Liz in many ways. Liz took up sculpture and discovered a real talent for it. Some time after he got to Washington, Pat had lunch with Richard Meryman and confided that for the first time in his life, with his assistant secretary's salary, he felt financially secure. In 1964, Congress gave federal employees a substantial pay boost. Overall it averaged 33 percent. Top civil servants (GS18) got a 23 percent rise to $24,500, assistant secretaries about the same. Even before the pay rise, Pat began to feel able to indulge his taste for good clothes and antique furniture. In September 1963, he wrote to Mr. Taylor of Taylor & Solash, of Great Marlborough Street in the West End of London, saying "the plaid suit has been a source of constant joy," and a week later he got a reply enclosing swathes of blue cloth and quoting £37 (about $100 at the time).

The Tregaron Farm House was rented. But now the Moynihans wanted a home of their own. Their weekend entertainment started on Saturday evening with the spreading of topographical maps on the table, maps that showed every building that existed before 1900, and tracking down the places offered in the letters that came in answer to their ads for country properties. Then on Sundays they would pack the kids in the car and hunt for a home. They didn't find what they were looking for until after the Kennedy assassination. It was on the bend of a country road at Pindars Corners, in West Davenport, close to Oneonta, New York, about eighty miles west of Albany in Delaware County.[4] It was a pre-Revolutionary house, L-shaped, in white clapboard with a handsome pediment, set on a plinth of massive field-stone. The sale took some time. As early as February 25, 1964, Pat was writing to Dean James A. Frost of State Teachers College at Oneonta, praising his *Short History of New York,* and saying, "It so happens that I am just in the process of buying an old farm up Charlotte Creek." In January 1965, the deal had still not gone through.[5] Liz finally bought the property, with about two hundred acres, for $10,000. While the owner was deliberating with the agent about whether to sell, Liz marched in and slapped down a check for $1,000. In upstate New York, in 1964, that was enough to make up his mind.[6] The house with its stable and big red barn, its pond, stream and surrounding wooded hills, where no trace of human habitation can be seen, has been a refuge and a sanctuary ever since.

Although Pat was a popular and increasingly respected member of the Kennedy administration, the Moynihans were not personally intimate with the Kennedys. "Pat was never that close to the Kennedys," says Stephen Hess, who knew him well at the time and later.[7] On October 13, 1964, Moynihan, who was speaking at a National Catholic Social Action Conference at Boston College, visited Edward M. Kennedy in New England Baptist Hospital, where he was recovering from a plane crash. This visit is the closest to social contact with any member of the family revealed in Moynihan's voluminous personal and official correspondence, though in the fall of 1964 Moynihan did speak for Robert Kennedy during his senatorial campaign in New York. Moynihan knew many of "the Kennedy people." He had met the president and the attorney general on a handful of occasions. He admired them, even idolized them. Many young Catholics and especially Irish Catholics identified with the first Catholic to be elected president. But he didn't know them very well.

He did, however, during the Kennedy years, compile an immense acquaintance among the politicians, officials, intellectuals and assorted celebrities, major and minor, who orbited around the dazzling blaze of the president and his brother. Already, he was compiling one of the most remarkable Rolodexes in America. His correspondents in his years at the Department of Labor included Dean Acheson; his former boss Averell Harriman; the great British expert on American politics, D. W. Brogan; the poverty expert Michael Harrington; and Richard Neustadt, the author of a remarkable book about the presidency. There were letters from Bayard Rustin, one of Martin Luther King's most trusted advisers; from the young historian Simon Schama, then an undergraduate studying with Moynihan's old friend J. H. Plumb at Cambridge University; and exchanges of correspondence with Hunter S. Thompson, the self-styled "gonzo journalist" from Colorado; with Harry Van Arsdale, the New York union leader; the documentary maker Ted Yates of NBC; and Theodore White, author of a famous series of books about presidential elections. And this list is the merest sampling. It is clear that it reflected Moynihan's immense range of interests and his intellectual curiosity. It was also the contacts book of a man with more than ordinary political ambitions.

Sometimes his desire to make friends took him close to, occasionally over, the line between politeness and flattery. "I think I shall remember the year for two things," he wrote to the writer Barbara Deming in mid-1963 after the murder of the Mississippi civil rights leader Medgar Evers, "the words 'Mrs. Evers spoke over her husband's body,' and your article in The Nation."[8] He wrote to congratulate Luther Hodges, retiring secretary of commerce, on his "wise, humane and immensely effective leadership," ignoring the protocol that might have told him that his letter was a little out of the ordinary for a subordinate official in another department. More egregiously, he wrote to J. Edward Day, on his retirement, "You have been the greatest Post Master in our history. It has been a grand thing just to be in the same city with you." At one point he tried to persuade Stewart Udall, secretary of the interior, to tramp around Tregaron because it would make an ideal residence for a vice president. And in July 1963, in what looks in retrospect like an attempt to join the inner circle around the president, he wrote to Kennedy's personal physician, Dr. Janet Travell, complaining of a ruptured lumbar disc, and asking for an appointment to see her at the Bethesda Naval Medical Center. "This Spring," he wrote, "I managed to fall off a dais (making room for the President!) and it has since got somewhat worse." In fact, Moynihan had suffered from back problems since his fall in Narragansett Bay in 1946. His correspondence reveals a restless intellectual who was also a hungry politician, avid for friends and contacts.

Over the preceding two or three years, Moynihan had come to be recognized by the Church as a promising Catholic intellectual. Monsignor George Higgins of the National Catholic Welfare Conference was writing to Moynihan fairly frequently as early as the beginning of 1963. In May that year, there was a mildly comic correspondence with a Father Thurston N. Davis about the government's failure to promote a certain Miss Finnerly in the Social Security Administration. Father Davis had got hold of the wrong end of the stick, but he clearly saw Moynihan as a Catholic official who could be enlisted to lobby for a Catholic woman who had been passed over. Moynihan made inquiries, found that the Jesuit was misinformed and gently put him off. He displayed even more tact when invited by Father Malcolm Kennedy of Opus Dei to a mass and spiritual conference at the secretive order's headquarters near the White House. Moynihan apologized for having mislaid the letter "in a drawer" and said he would be honored to attend. "On the other hand," he added, "it is difficult in the middle of the day and I am often away from Washington."

On May 19, 1965, even the London Catholic weekly *The Tablet* reported that the Church had discovered Moynihan.[9] The impression is that in those years before his name became controversial, the Church made more calls than later on Moynihan's time, to write for Catholic magazines, to speak at Catholic gatherings, attend retreats and make what for a middle-level bureaucrat with a family to support were rather generous donations to various Catholic charities.

The story is that on the drive to his inaugural on January 20, 1961, President Kennedy noticed how tacky Pennsylvania Avenue had become. The ceremonial way, linking the White House and the

Capitol, the executive and the legislative poles of constitutional government, was lined on one side with the monumental buildings
of the Federal Triangle, most of them in the Beaux Arts manner.
But the other side of the great street was lined with ancient brick
buildings with cracking paint and rotting woodwork, crummy old
souvenir stores or boarding houses that had rented rooms to impe-
cunious Southern congressmen and their corn whiskey since Lincoln's day. Between the Treasury and the Capitol, Moynihan later
maintained with some hyperbole, the only light to be seen came
from Apex Liquor, at Sixth and Pennsylvania. Kennedy, in an official account, remarked on this urban decay at the heart of the nation's capital to Arthur Goldberg, and it was Goldberg who assigned
Moynihan, as his young head of research, to look into what could
be done.

Moynihan is so loyal to the memory of John F. Kennedy that he
still insists it was Kennedy's idea to fix up Pennsylvania Avenue. In
fact it was his own. When you are only an assistant to the secretary of
labor, you have to pretend that your ideas are someone else's. But,
says Robert Peck, now the commissioner of the Public Buildings Service at the General Services Administration, the idea was Moynihan's. "He turned a cabinet meeting which was mainly bitching
about parking in federal buildings — all right, it was supposed to be
about office space, but it was also about parking, it always is — and he
turns that into 'Guiding Principles for Federal Architecture!' "[10]

So Moynihan seized his opportunity. He was assigned to write the
report of what was called an Ad Hoc Committee on Federal Office
Space, released on June 1, 1962. Moynihan claims credit for the three
pages tacked on to the end of that report on the "Redevelopment of
Pennsylvania Avenue." He also wrote the previous page, to which
Peck referred, "Guiding Principles for Federal Architecture." There
is a tone to this short paper that had not been heard in Washington
for many years: a tone of pride in the achievements and the task of
the American federal government. The government's architectural
policy, Moynihan pronounced, should "reflect the dignity, enterprise, vigor and stability of the American National Government." Its
buildings should embody the finest contemporary American architecture. Where possible they should incorporate fine art, with an emphasis on the work of living American artists. They should be constructed of materials and by methods of proven dependability and
"the development of an official style must be avoided." This was a

bold and farseeing paper to come from a young middle-rank official, but there was more. It should be our object, Moynihan wrote, to meet the test of Pericles' address to the Athenians, which the president commended to the Massachusetts legislature in his address of January 9, 1961: "We do not imitate — for we are a model to others." In that sentence, for better or worse, the government sent the Beaux Arts style back where it came from.

The paper went on to trace the history of the architecture of the nation's capital since the original plans of Major Charles Pierre L'Enfant, of which Pennsylvania Avenue was to have been the "grand axis." It "should be *the* great thoroughfare of the City of Washington," Moynihan wrote. "Instead it remains a vast, unformed, cluttered expanse at the heart of the Nation's Capital," and the main court of the Federal Triangle "was left to become a parking lot of surpassing ugliness."[11] Large parts of the north side were decayed beyond restoration, and many buildings would have to be torn down and replaced whatever happened. "This," Moynihan pointed out, "is an opportunity not to be missed. It will not come again for a half century or more." But he also made an important point that anticipated changes in public taste then still in the future. The Capitol should not be left in isolation, the young Labor Department official warned, as it would be if the north side of the avenue, like the south side, were to be lined with public buildings. "Pennsylvania Avenue should be lively, friendly and inviting, as well as dignified and impressive," he wrote. It should be a street on which it would be pleasant to walk as well as possible to drive. "Benches, arcades, sculpture, planting and fountains should be encouraged." And they have been. One idea that occurred to the enthusiastic planners was not pursued. At the very first meeting of the President's Council, William Walton and Moynihan wondered whether an old-time bawdy house might add to the friendly qualities of the boulevard. Moynihan later joked, "Walton promptly sketched a portrait of 'Miss Pennsylvania Avenue of 1965,' complete with the oversized handbag and sturdy high heels of that ancient calling."[12]

The Periclean ideal attracted President Kennedy. A President's Commission on Pennsylvania Avenue was set up. It was headed by Nathaniel Owings, head of the most successful commercial firm of architects of the day, Skidmore, Owings and Merrill of San Francisco. By mid-1963, Owings had drafted, and the council had approved, a plan. One of Kennedy's last instructions before leaving for Dallas was to arrange a coffee hour to show this document to congressional leaders.[13]

The Pennsylvania Avenue project did not die with him. When Jacqueline Kennedy left the White House, Lyndon Johnson asked her, as she wrote later in a letter to Moynihan, what he could do for her. "Finish Pennsylvania Avenue," she said. "It was something Jack cared deeply about."[14] By October 1964, Moynihan could report to President Kennedy's close aide and biographer Theodore Sorensen that President Johnson had accepted in principle the proposals of the President's Commission on Pennsylvania Avenue, and by May 21, 1965, the President's Temporary Commission on Pennsylvania Avenue met for the first time.

In July 1963, as he recalled later, the Labor Department "had done all the policy planning needed for the moment."[15] There was little for a newly appointed assistant secretary to do except read the morning papers. The problem, as the economy recovered and concern with unemployment faded, and as Congress stubbornly refused to pass President Kennedy's domestic program, was not to think of new things to do, so much as to look for new arguments to advance the department's existing agenda. One morning, Moynihan's daily reading of the *Washington Post* suggested an intriguing idea. General Lewis B. Hershey, director of the Selective Service System, better known as the draft, had reported yet again that roughly half of the young men called for examination had failed the physical or mental tests or both.

Moynihan was perfectly aware of the politics of that fact. This was the heyday of Cold War liberalism, the combination, that is, of a commitment to anti-Communist vigilance and strong national defense, with a zeal for using the action of government to "improve" society. A national highway system had been passed under the Eisenhower administration on the grounds that it would enable troops to be moved more quickly from one part of the country to another. Universities had benefited from the National Defense Education Act to strengthen departments — such as art history or classics — not obviously related in any close way to military preparedness. In Albany, and at Syracuse, Moynihan had observed how the sacred plea of national security could be used to persuade politicians to support causes they might not otherwise care two pins about.

In no time, he had persuaded Willard Wirtz, who succeeded

Arthur Goldberg as secretary of labor on Goldberg's appointment to the Supreme Court,[16] to make him secretary of a presidential task force. For ninety days, Moynihan and his colleagues scarcely left their offices in the Department of Labor, and by New Year's Day 1964 the report was finished.[17] Its conclusions were startling. "One-third of all young men in the nation turning 18 would be found unqualified if they were to be examined for induction into the armed services. Of these, about one-half would be rejected for medical reasons. The remainder would fail through inability to qualify on the mental test."

Such a conclusion, in an important, presumably dispassionate government report, would be disturbing today. In 1964, when the report was released, it had a special edge. Most Americans saw themselves as engaged in what President Kennedy, in his inaugural address, had called "the long twilight struggle" of the Cold War. To a generation that had lived through military triumph in World War II and now saw itself challenged in a way that could easily lead to war again, the idea that a third of the country's young men were unfit for military service was shocking.

Two more conclusions in the report touched sensitive nerves. The mild recession of the late Eisenhower years had set off widespread anxiety about the possibility of a return of unemployment, virtually vanished during the war and after it. In particular, there was widespread concern that what was called at the time "automation" would cause an increase in unemployment. The young men unqualified for military service, and especially those unqualified by mental and educational shortcomings, the report said, "face a lifetime of recurrent unemployment unless their skills are sufficiently upgraded."

So far, there was nothing especially startling in the facts recited in "One Third of a Nation." Upon receiving the report, however, President Johnson ordered that, starting in July 1964, *all* eighteen-year-olds should be tested regardless of their draft eligibility. In this way the administration hoped to find out as soon as possible how many young men would be coming into the workforce without the equipment to make a living. Early in May 1965 the results were in. They showed that 26 percent of all eighteen-year-old males had failed the "mental" test, the equivalent of a seventh-grade education. In the District of Columbia, however, the failure rate was 53 percent, and as Moynihan commented at the time, it was a safe assumption that the great majority of those taking the test in the District were black. The failure rate for blacks in the previous year, nationally, had in any case been 56 percent.[18]

Up until the publication of "One Third of a Nation," Pat Moynihan was just one of the bright young men brought to work in Washington by the New Frontier. His work at Labor had been noticed by Kennedy's connoisseurs of the new Stakhanovite bureaucracy. "One Third of a Nation," for example, thirty-four double-column pages, crammed with tables and statistics, with as many pages of appendices, was researched and written in some three months before being given to the president on January 1, 1964.

By then the administration, first under Kennedy and then under Johnson, had become committed to what became known as the War on Poverty. Moynihan was deeply involved in the planning of this ambitious enterprise. Specifically, he became embroiled in a bitter argument between those who wanted poverty to be attacked by a "community" strategy and those more pragmatic thinkers, like Moynihan himself, who thought that what the poor needed most was not community action, but jobs and money.

Early in 1963, President Kennedy's restless eye fell on an "essay review" by Dwight Macdonald in *The New Yorker*.[19] It was a summary of a recently published book by the socialist intellectual Michael Harrington called *The Other America*.[20] Its thesis, an unfamiliar and shocking one at the time, was that in affluent America there were nevertheless tens of millions of people who were poor.[21] By this time Kennedy was looking around for new worlds to conquer, but he was also aware that poverty was an issue on which some Republicans were thinking of attacking him politically. So he summoned the chairman of his Council of Economic Advisers, the Minnesota liberal Walter Heller, and asked him to look into the matter of poverty. Heller assigned an economist called Robert Lampman, from the University of Wisconsin, to prepare a paper, which was ready by May 1963.[22] Harrington's thesis was correct, Lampman reported. And — contrary to what was generally supposed — the number of poor people was not shrinking but growing. By the fall of 1963, the Council of Economic Advisers was able to circulate a staff memo proposing "a Concerted Assault on Poverty." It spoke of the "poverty cycle," the trap whereby people slipped into poverty and found themselves deprived of the opportunity and ultimately the motivation to escape.

At this point the idea of the government attacking the problem of poverty became mixed up, in the way that such things happen in large bureaucracies, with a different set of concerns and with proposed solutions originally devised in a quite different context. As far back as 1957, the Henry Street Settlement, established to combat the grinding poverty of the Lower East Side in the late nineteenth century, had set up what it called Mobilization for Youth to deal with what was perceived as the new problem of juvenile delinquency. Meanwhile, the nation's largest charity, the Ford Foundation, had become interested in "community development." The idea of combating juvenile delinquency with community action to provide greater opportunity was in the air. In October 1960, the sociologist Lloyd E. Ohlin produced a paper for a Ford Foundation conference on this concept, and in the same year Ohlin and another social scientist, Richard A. Cloward, published a study of delinquent teenage gangs in New York called *Delinquency and Opportunity*.[23] The Children's Bureau, too, in that same year, published a report on juvenile delinquency.[24] And in December 1961, Mobilization for Youth published a 617-page proposal for preventing delinquency by expanding opportunity.[25]

Early in the Kennedy administration, the president asked his brother Robert's close friend, the former college ice-hockey star David Hackett, to look into the problem of juvenile delinquency. In May 1961, Hackett was put in charge of a presidential committee on juvenile delinquency. Hackett's thinking was strongly influenced by New York social scientists like Ohlin, Cloward and Albert K. Cohen, author of the study *Delinquent Boys*,[26] and by the Ford Foundation officials who had come under their influence.

So when, on October 30, 1963, Walter Heller asked for ideas about assaulting poverty, most of the government could not come up with much in the way of answers. But Hackett and his men were ready. When the Bureau of the Budget asked them to submit proposals, they requested $500 million to be spent on "community action." In early November, Hackett sent a memo to his friend Robert Kennedy, arguing that opportunity, or the lack of it, was the key to eradicating poverty, that community action would be the method, and that the specific tool would be the formation of a "domestic peace corps," to bring home some of the glamor won by the Kennedy administration's single most successful initiative, the Peace Corps that had sent idealistic Americans to work in poor countries, improving the image of the United States abroad.

———

On the morning of November 22, 1963, Assistant Secretary Moynihan had been testifying on Capitol Hill. It was an interim report on the disappointing statistics about how young black men performed in the tests for selective service. There were TV crews waiting in his office to interview him about his testimony. But he was deep in a meeting with the president's friend William Walton and the Washington lawyer Charles Horsky about Pennsylvania Avenue when the White House called. Moynihan went right out, and said, to the cameras, the sentence that would help to make him famous. "I guess there's no point in being Irish," he said, "if you don't know that the world will break your heart one day."[27] Mary McGrory, then with the *Washington Star,* called up. "We'll never laugh again," she said. "No, Mary," he said. "We'll laugh again, but we'll never be young again."[28]

Moynihan went over to the White House with Walton, and he was there when the news came through that the president was dead.[29] He and a dozen others, he has recalled, were in the southwest-corner office of a White House aide called Ralph Dungan. Hubert Humphrey, who was present, threw his arms wide, embraced Dungan and said, "What have they done to us?"[30] "They," Moynihan has subsequently explained, meant "the Texans": not, he implies, the Texans around the new president, but "the reactionaries."[31] And it is true that the first response of many in Washington that day was to assume that Kennedy had been assassinated by the far Right, even though the assassin, Lee Harvey Oswald, had far more obvious connections with the far Left.

Moynihan went on to describe how no one did anything, except McGeorge Bundy, Kennedy's national security adviser, who went to a telephone in the next room and called Robert McNamara, the secretary of defense. Moynihan "drifted off" with William Walton. He has described, too, the shock with which they both saw the flag on the White House come down to half-staff.

According to his account, highly emotional and written four years or so later, Moynihan went back to his office at the Department of Labor, then returned to the White House to "take one last look at the Oval Room, which I did not expect to see again." He wrote, "I had hardly been a regular visitor, but even so I had been there, with him in the rocking chair, and had once, even, corrected his arithmetic; and now this was all finished."[32]

They were, he recalled, fixing the rug, so that the furniture was piled out in the corridor. He left, picked up a photograph of Kennedy from the desk of his secretary,[33] and was about to leave when "on sudden impulse, I saluted, turned, Officer of the Day style, and marched off. A guard asked for my Secret Service pass, and I asked, 'What difference does it make?' "

Then another side of his personality asserted itself: that recurrent, pessimistic sense of the dangers of life. At midnight, he was at Andrews Air Force Base to meet the plane that had brought most of the cabinet back; it had been halfway to Japan. There began, he says, "a decisive experience." He tried, in vain, to impress on the hierarchy of officials that it was essential to secure Oswald. He might be an agent of Texas reactionaries, or of world revolution. In either case, Moynihan saw it as vital that Oswald live, and that his case be "remorselessly investigated," not because — as bewildered officials supposed — he thought there had been a conspiracy, but because he feared that people would believe there had been, unless the suspicion was promptly and effectively scotched. After Oswald was shot, Moynihan found only one official who shared his sense of urgency about that, John Macy, chairman of the Civil Service Commission. Together, they went the rounds of shell-shocked official Washington. Moynihan carried with him a recently reprinted Protestant tract,[34] which claimed to have proof that John Wilkes Booth "was nothing but the tool of the Jesuits. It was Rome who directed his arm, after corrupting his heart and damning his soul." It is not perhaps surprising that he found few who understood his point, for it was a subtle one, and Washington had more urgent tasks: to mourn a president, to reassure the American people and the world and to try to come to terms with a new president. Yet Moynihan's perception was correct: only relentless exposure of the truth could have dispelled the miasma of paranoid myth that still hangs over the assassination.

"Let us continue," said Lyndon Johnson in his very first televised address to the nation as president. It was plain that he intended to differentiate himself from Kennedy not by changing political direction, but by showing how much more effective he could be in carrying out the policies that Kennedy had already outlined. One of these was what Kennedy had called an "assault," and Johnson now declared was to be a "war," on poverty. On January 8, in his State of the Union speech, the president committed himself to sending a poverty program to Congress. By January 21, Lee White, his assistant special counsel, sent to the Labor Department as well as to the other domestic cabinet departments "draft specifications" for a poverty bill.

The brightest and best in the Kennedy-Johnson administration (for that is what it still was) threw themselves into one of those headlong, workaholic fits of bureaucratic enthusiasm that were that administration's characteristic way of approaching difficult problems. Assistant Secretary Moynihan found himself right in the middle of the effort to draft legislation. He was naturally assigned those measures that were the province of the Labor Department, including "Draft rejectees. Simple jobs for old people. Dependent mothers (and note day care item . . .) Other projects worth considering," to quote from a memorandum prepared for a meeting on February 5 by the former Harvard University law professor and Pentagon official Adam Yarmolinsky.[35]

Even before that early date, the team assigned to make war on poverty was sharply divided, so much so that in February 1964 Johnson appointed President Kennedy's brother-in-law, Sargent Shriver, "to impose order."[36] The division directly opposed Moynihan and his boss, Willard Wirtz, the secretary of labor, and some other officials, and supported another group of officials influenced by the social work tradition, rooted in the Columbia University School of Social Work, which had also colonized the powerful Ford Foundation. The argument was to have a lasting influence on Moynihan's thinking. Ford Foundation officials like Paul Ylvisaker, themselves influenced by the social scientists, had succeeded in persuading David Hackett that the answer to the problem of juvenile delinquency was to provide potential delinquents with greater opportunities through "community action." To this they attributed almost magical powers. It was, Moynihan wrote much later, nothing less than the "direct transmission of social science into governmental policy."[37] Moynihan, like Wirtz and, for example, the authors Michael Harrington and Paul Jacobs, both of whom had been hired by the government as consultants, kept repeating that what the poor needed was money; and that the best way of giving them money was to give them work, that is, to reduce unemployment.

On February 25, Moynihan broke bureaucratic cover with a strong speech in which he warned that welfare was "rotting the poor." This assertion provoked an angry response from the welfare lobbyist Elizabeth Wickenden. Secretary Wirtz, though in general, like Moynihan, favoring jobs as opposed to community action, thought his assistant secretary had gone too far. An exchange of memoranda followed, in which Moynihan pointed out that a conservative Republican, Thomas Curtis of Nevada, was sufficiently impressed by Moynihan's speech to have read it into the *Congressional Record*. Those, like Wirtz and Moynihan, who favored an emphasis on job creation, as opposed to welfare, were prepared to use conservative opposition to welfare to help them win their argument inside the administration.

Working at remarkable speed, the administration sent detailed proposals for legislation to Capitol Hill on March 16, 1964. The poverty bill passed the Senate on July 23, passed the House with some amendment and was signed into law by the president on August 20, 1964.

The Economic Opportunity Act of 1964 embodied compromises between two rival social philosophies.[38] One, to which Moynihan subscribed, remained firmly within the American tradition of self-help. This tradition recognized that there would be people who, from time to time, because of their individual problems or because of unemployment, would need public help. It rejected the rival, more social democratic tradition, which was willing to contemplate measures of economic redistribution to achieve greater equality and in some circumstances, at least, to offer "income as a right." This argument had been fought out since the later days of the New Deal. In one corner stood the more radical National Resources Planning Board, which, many scholars believe, might have led to a "full employment welfare state."[39] In the other was the more cautious Social Security Administration. Although in his last, 1944, reelection campaign, President Roosevelt sometimes spoke as if he favored a second, economic Bill of Rights, guaranteeing every citizen a more than minimum level of economic prosperity as well as education and health care, by the time John Kennedy was elected in 1960 the champions of a full welfare state had lost the argument. By the 1960s, American liberals did not contemplate replacing capitalism with a welfare state. They agreed with J. K. Galbraith that "American capitalism works, and in the years since World War II, quite brilliantly."[40] But they did want the government to intervene to mitigate the sometimes harsh consequences of capitalism. They believed devoutly that economic growth was the great engine that would release resources for distribution, and so obviate the need for redistribution, giving to all, and taking away from none. And — not surprisingly, in view of how heavily postwar liberalism was intertwined with and dependent on the labor movement — they believed that government should do all it could to promote full employment.

The Johnson administration's commitment to a war on poverty, revealingly called a campaign for economic opportunity, was well within this more cautious, less radical liberal tradition. "The Economic Opportunity Act," one recent scholar has written, "helped to place the new President's vision of a Great Society firmly within America's core individualist tradition."[41] Great Society liberalism, as President Johnson and his aides, including at this time Daniel Patrick Moynihan, saw it, was not an insurgency against the American way.

But there was such an insurgency, and it came from the social work tradition and the prophets of community action. It may be historically ironic, but it came as no surprise to Moynihan, with his suspicions of the economic elite's social policy, that it was the Ford Foundation, one of the biggest charitable enterprises in the country, funded by the wealth of one of the most ruthlessly antilabor corporations of the 1930s, that encouraged and financed this rebellion against the American way and the established lines of political authority.

It did not take long for those established authorities to make plain their outrage that the federal government — as they saw it — was giving money to unelected radical activists to compete with and subvert the Democratic party of which the president was supposed to be the head. Mayors, in particular, were furious. In the summer of 1965, Mayor Daley of Chicago made his indignation plain. He was not alone. Elected Democratic officials had no intention of letting "maximum feasible participation" by the poor in the antipoverty campaign mean handing over control of the money, the programs and the gratitude they might engender to "community" activists, all too often aggressive black radicals.

This, too, Moynihan saw differently from most liberals. New York politics had made him suspicious of radical middle-class intellectuals. London had given him a respect for regular working-class social democrats. His whole experience made him see community action as an absurd and dangerous deviation. He was not surprised, and was perhaps not wholly displeased, therefore, when on August 16, 1964, the *New York Daily News,* "the hands-down favorite reading-matter of the poor people of New York City," a conservative tabloid read by the working class, reported that Mobilization for Youth was "infested with subversives."[42] Among many wild charges, the *News* alleged that MFY equipment had been used to print posters that inspired black rioters: WANTED FOR MURDER, GILLIGAN THE COP. (Gilligan was believed to have killed a young black man.) In the summer of 1964, unrest became rioting in several U.S. cities. It would be the start of a series of violent summers. The idea was firmly implanted in the minds of millions of working-class white citizens in the industrial East and Middle West, not to mention the South, that radical community action to abolish poverty was in some part to blame for the growing urban tension.

The experience of the war on poverty had a lasting influence on Moynihan's thought. But before he could turn it into policy, his attention was diverted by an even larger problem, and one laden with infinitely sharper political dangers.

Over the Christmas holidays of 1964, Moynihan called two staffers, Paul Barton and Ellen Broderick, to his corner office and asked them to start research into the relationship between black unemployment and the collapsing black family. At his urging, they ranged much more widely in their search for data than civil service inquiries usually do. Paul Barton trained in social science at the Woodrow Wilson School of Public and International Affairs in Princeton in the 1950s. As a civil servant who began his career at the Bureau of the Budget, Barton remembers that his job at the Department of Labor, which he started in 1963, entailed reading widely in the literature of slavery.

Moynihan was already aware that scholars were taking a new look at the literature of American slavery, and in particular at the evidence for the damage it did to the psyche of slaves and to the black family. In 1946, Frank Tannenbaum wrote his *Slave and Citizen: The Negro in the Americas*,[43] in which he compared slavery in the Hispanic and Portuguese colonies and in the British and American ones, and asked why the British and American versions of slavery were so much harsher. In 1959, Stanley Elkins's study, *Slavery*,[44] confirmed the severity of North American slavery and showed that slaves in Brazil were protected by the Crown and encouraged by the Church to think of themselves as having a religious life, and to raise a family, both consolations denied by law to slaves in America. As early as 1939 the great black sociologist at the University of Chicago, E. Franklin Frazier, pointed out the consequences of the denial of family life in American slavery, and so first drew attention to what a later black scholar, Kenneth B. Clark, called the "pathology" of the black family. Moynihan was aware of this work. His coauthor Nathan Glazer presented him with a copy of Elkins's book, to whose second edition Glazer had written the introduction. Moynihan borrowed Clark's word *pathology*, writing in his Report of the "tangle of pathology" in the black ghettos. In view of the later attacks on him, it is interesting that the two writers, Frazier and Clark, on whom Moynihan chiefly drew for his interpretation of the Negro family, were both African Americans.

There has been speculation[45] that Moynihan was motivated in writing what was later known as the "Moynihan Report" by the need to pull off a spectacular bureaucratic-cum-intellectual triumph, either because he already sensed that, as a perceived associate of Robert Kennedy, he was in danger of incurring President Johnson's hostility, or because he was already planning to run for office. It is hard to be so specific. It was all too apparent to anyone, certainly to anyone who had served in the Kennedy and Johnson administrations, that the nation was approaching a new and frightening crisis over race. It was after all Moynihan's job to present and analyze data bearing on jobs and unemployment. No doubt as an ambitious public servant he was aware that anyone who could contribute to the understanding, let alone the alleviation, of racial inequality would acquire merit in the Johnson administration. No doubt, too, Moynihan had already thought of running for public office. But there is no evidence that he had any plans to do so until the opportunity presented itself at midsummer.

The work went fast. Barton and Broderick passed along the ammunition, and Moynihan transformed it into urgent prose. The argument was certainly his. The nub of it is contained in an outline, a dozen pages long, and annotated by Moynihan.[46] He began, "The major political, administrative and legal events of the Negro American revolution are now behind us." Now came a "period of maximum danger and opportunity." The contrast between expectation and reality for black people was widening, and the focus was shifting from Southern blacks to the Northern working class, and to those who could not find work — from "Tuskegee," Moynihan put it, "to Harlem."

"What are we trying to change?" he asked, and then answered his own question. He was looking for "changes that break the cycle." He defined his thesis forcefully. "The principal effect of exploitation, discrimination, poverty and unemployment on the Negro community has been profound weakening of Negro family structure." He traced the roots of "the present problem" to the legacy of slavery, to Reconstruction and to the Jim Crow laws that reimposed something not so very different from slavery on the freedmen, to unemployment and urbanization. He cited E. Franklin Frazier's ominous warning that in "the travail of civilization" the family that had evolved in the isolated world of the African Americans must become more disorganized.

Then in his outline Moynihan announced what was to be one of his recurring themes, one no doubt rooted in his own painful personal experiences as the child of a broken family himself, as well as in his London experience of psychoanalysis, his Catholic upbringing and his reading in social science. He stressed the paramount importance of the family. It was "the key institution for socialization." It lay "at the core of psychoanalytic theory." When the family breaks down, he said, as it does in slavery, and in times of extreme social unrest and abrupt economic change, "the delicate line of fatherhood transition is broken."

The Negro family, he argued in his outline, was disintegrating. "Where marriage exists, it is not producing families," and where marriage does not exist, children are produced without families. Where in 1962 only 3 percent of white births were illegitimate, 23 percent of nonwhite children were born outside of marriage. The figures were getting worse, and "at the leading edge," in parts of Harlem and the District of Columbia, they were already much worse; in both places the illegitimacy rate had passed 40 percent.

The consequence was a sharp increase in the proportion of African American families headed by females, and in the number of children without two parents. These trends were producing a boom in the demand for the welfare program called Aid to Families with Dependent Children. Not only that: it was transforming the whole nature of that program. AFDC had evolved from Mother's Aid laws designed to help working-class women whose husbands were dead or who were unable to work to bring up their children. But now AFDC was becoming increasingly a program for black mothers and their children, many of whom had never had fathers at home. Almost half of the children whose mothers were receiving AFDC, Moynihan said in his outline, 69 percent in New York, and 94 percent in the District of Columbia, were nonwhite.

By late February, Moynihan and his team had made a discovery that was to have far-reaching effects, both for him and for the whole frame through which Americans would come to see their society. He has described this discovery himself many times, in language that varies from the scholarly to the sensational. "The numbers went blooey on me," he told writer Nicholas Lemann.[47] He told me that what his friend James Q. Wilson later called "Moynihan's scissors" showed up the moment Paul Barton ran the two graphs for him on one chart. In the past, the two lines, one representing the unemployment numbers for black men, the other showing the take-up of AFDC, had run closely parallel. That was logical, because when a black father lost his job, there was a strong likelihood that he would quit his home, leaving his children to be brought up without a father, and that their mother would then claim AFDC.

> It may be noted, for example, that for most of the post-war period male Negro unemployment and the number of new AFDC cases rose and fell together as if connected by a chain from 1948 to 1962. The correlation between the two series of data was an astonishing .91 . . . In 1960, however, for the first time, unemployment declined, but the number of new AFDC cases rose. In 1963 this happened a second time. In 1964 a third. The possible implications of these and other data are serious enough that they, too, should be understood before program proposals are made.[48]

A graph showing "cases opened under AFDC compared with unemployment rate for non-white males" shows that the crossover occurred in 1963. After that, the unemployment rate for black men fell steeply, while the AFDC caseload shot up, from about 400,000 in 1963 to more than 700,000 in 1968.

In a paper published in 1967,[49] Moynihan made another point in academic language. He showed that the "scissors" could be seen at work in other statistical relationships; for the period from 1953 to 1964 there was, for example, a high correlation between the unemployment rate for black men and the number of nonwhite women separated from their husbands; but there, too, when the unemployment rate went down, the separation rate went up. A second set of numbers confirmed the intuition he had had in 1965. "With the onset of the 1960s," he concluded, "the strong presumed influence of employment on family structures appears to give out, so that the separation rate begins to rise even when the unemployment rate is falling."

Moynihan instantly saw what the sudden crossing of the two lines meant, and understood that its implications were anything but dull. They would be worked out in frustrated and wasted lives, and in crime and other forms of hostility between black and white

Americans. For some reason, he grasped, the normal processes of economic opportunity, which had floated off one immigrant group after another on the rising tides of economic expansion as successive recessions ended, were no longer doing that healing job for blacks. "If this continued," he reported his own mental processes in a 1973 book, "if microeconomic forces had lost their apparent influence on social structure — there would form an urban underclass which, because of its racial identification, would lead to a new and wholly unexpected range of social conflict."

One other point is worth making.[50] What was most distinctive about the Moynihan Report was not so much Moynihan's analysis of the consequences of the damage done to the black family by slavery; this had been noted by many scholars before him. What was truly original, and remarkably courageous, is that Moynihan was willing to come out for affirmative action. There is a special irony about this: so far from wanting to "blame the victim," as his liberal critics later accused him of doing, he was prepared to go beyond New Deal tradition to the extent of actively intervening to compensate for the previous neglect of black people. As a political animal with exceptionally sensitive antennae, to be sure, he understood that affirmative action would have to be achieved to some extent by stealth. Social programs should be pursued that would disproportionately help black people. But they must at all costs not be presented as programs to help black people as a race. This, incidentally, is consistent with the rationale behind his later, notorious, "benign neglect" memo. But the Report remains, what Moynihan called it, a "case for national action," and that included what came to be called "affirmative action."

In the spring of 1965, even before the Report was finished, Moynihan's curiosity took him to the South, which he didn't know well. On February 15, he wrote to a new friend, Father Theodore Hesburgh, president of Notre Dame University (which Moynihan's father had attended), mentioning a trip he had made to Mississippi. While there, he visited Oxford, site of a savage riot three years earlier and home of the novelist William Faulkner, who had died shortly after the riot. Moynihan sought out Faulkner's housekeeper and was thrilled when she told him something about the great writer's strange working routine. Mr. Faulkner drank an awful lot, she said, but he couldn't get to sleep. So after an evening's whiskey he would get out his horse and ride off into the woods behind the house. She would stay awake until she heard him come home, because she was afraid he would stumble or be knocked off his horse by a branch. Then, for an hour or more she could see him sitting motionless on his horse in the moonlight in the field behind the house, until he came in, stabled the horse and went to his study to write furiously for an hour, and only then collapse exhausted into bed. Moynihan understood that Faulkner used to drink to suppress inhibitions about writing, rode to clear his head, sat on his horse to compose a paragraph or a page and then wrote furiously to catch his thoughts before he slept.

After his return, the threads of Moynihan's public life were being twisted together at extraordinary speed. Quite a few of them connected him to a new close friend, Harry C. McPherson, Jr., one of Lyndon Johnson's aides who was made assistant secretary of state for educational and cultural affairs, then secretary of the army, before being called into the White House as special counsel. A Texan graduate of the University of the South at Sewanee, Tennessee, with an interest in classical music and literature, he met Moynihan in 1964. Moynihan, McPherson has said, is "one of the most exciting men in the world, full of more intellectual spin-off than most men acquire in several lifetimes."[51] The two men were equally concerned by what was happening to the civil rights movement. That spring, McPherson, on loan from the State Department to the White House, was in the hospital having surgery on a hernia. At 5:00 one boiling afternoon, Moynihan arrived with a full bottle of Johnnie Walker Black and the Moynihan Report. "It's going to be dynamite, I think," Moynihan said. The two friends drank Scotch together for four hours and began to yell and scream at each other. McPherson's concern was that the Report would make perfect ammunition for Southern opponents of the administration's liberal policies. But the trouble, when it came, did not come from that direction at all.

McPherson might have worried about what the Southerners would say, but he helped to persuade colleagues in the White House, including Bill Moyers and Douglass Cater, to take on board Moynihan's "Case for National Action." And President Johnson accepted as his own the main lines of the Report's strategy. He decided to take the opportunity of a major speech to argue that nothing would do short of a major effort to help black Americans achieve equality by compensating for the historic injustices of slavery and segregation. He

and his staff seized on an invitation to speak at the upcoming commencement of Howard University in Washington, perhaps the nation's leading black college, as the place to make such a commitment.

There is some dispute about Moynihan's precise part in the drafting of the Howard speech. The final draft, it is agreed, came from the
typewriter of Richard Goodwin, a saturnine holdover from the
Kennedy circle who was generally admired for his skill as a speechwriter. A file in the LBJ Library in Austin, Texas, contains several versions of the speech, including the TelePrompTer roll from which the
president actually read. In that file there is a draft, annotated by Johnson's favorite speechwriter, Horace Busby, who found little fault
with it except that it was too long, and headed simply, "Howard
speech, First Draft, RNGoodwin." The same file, however, contains
a copy of the Moynihan Report, and a somewhat innocent note by a
relatively junior White House staffer, Dorothy Territo, which read
"Lee White [Associate General Counsel] said this report was used for
the Howard University speech. It is therefore made a part of this
speech archive."[52] Harry McPherson remembers sitting with Goodwin in a Greek American café across from the executive office building on Seventeenth Street, expounding Moynihan's argument to
Goodwin over many cups of indifferent coffee. Moynihan remembers
working into the small hours of June 4, the day set for the speech, on
drafts for Goodwin to fit into the president's speaking text. Early that
same morning, he took himself out of Washington on an errand that
was to be both incongruous and fateful for him.

The president's speech did not mention the Moynihan Report, and
it is possible that he read neither the Report itself nor the covering
memo, written by Moynihan, with which his boss, Secretary of Labor
Willard Wirtz, forwarded it to the president's key aide, Bill Moyers.
That is not as significant as it sounds, however. Presidents do not
have time to read all the documents, not even all the important documents, generated by their staff and by the bureaucracy of the "permanent government." That is why they are surrounded by assistants.
And the ideas argued in the Moynihan Report were well understood
by a whole tier of very able assistants in the White House: by Moyers,
McPherson, Cater and Goodwin, among others. The Howard University speech was written, at the president's desire, by Goodwin,
with the help of Moynihan's Report, whose ideas it unmistakably
expressed.

The speech developed, with considerable eloquence, the theme that while African Americans — with help from white people, not least from Lyndon Johnson — had made great strides toward freedom, nevertheless "freedom is not enough." The key passage of the entire speech began with that phrase. It went on:

> You do not wipe away the scars of centuries by saying: Now you are free to go where you want . . . You do not take a person who, for years, has been hobbled by chains and then say, you are free to compete with all the others . . . It is not enough just to open the gates of opportunity. All our citizens must have the ability to walk through those gates. This is the next and more profound stage of the battle for civil rights. We seek not just freedom but opportunity — not just legal equity but human ability — not just equality as a right and a theory but equality as a fact and as a result. . . .
> To this end equal opportunity is essential, but not enough.[53]

The "harsh fact," the president went on, was that too many black Americans were losing ground. No one knew quite why this was. The causes were complex. But "we do know the two broad basic reasons." One was that "Negroes are trapped — as too many whites are trapped" in poverty. The second reason, however, was that "Negro poverty is not white poverty." For blacks, there was the "devastating heritage of long years of slavery, and a century of oppression, hatred and injustice."

It was "the glorious opportunity of this generation," Johnson said, "to end the one huge wrong of the American nation." The president promised to convene a White House conference of scholars, experts and black leaders "to fulfill these rights." And he pledged that it would be "the chief goal" of his administration to "dissolve, as best we can, the antique enmities of the heart," which had denied justice and equality to black Americans.

The speech was the high-water mark, not only of the Johnson administration's commitment to active efforts in the cause of greater equality for African Americans, but also — as it turned out — of the whole liberal enterprise. A central theme of liberalism since the New Deal, after all, had been to use the power and resources of government, and especially of the federal government, to promote greater equality.

Not everyone within the administration, to be sure, conceded Moynihan's major role in the speech. His immediate boss, Willard Wirtz, who had forwarded the Report to the president, is skeptical about his former colleague's influence. Speaking in 1998 with great care, he said in an interview that reports of Moynihan's significance in the Johnson administration were exaggerated. "I have heard a number of times of [Moynihan's] large-scale participation in the Howard speech. I didn't know it at the time, and I have doubts."[54] On the other hand, it is not clear that Wirtz would necessarily have been privy to the preparation of even a major policy speech: The testimony of Harry McPherson, among others, tends to confirm Moynihan's own estimate of his own role.

If so, it was an extraordinary triumph for a middle-level federal official. Many labored for years in the vineyard and were grateful if a phrase, the shadow of an idea, appeared in a presidential message or speech once in a decade. Here were Moynihan's ideas, ideas clearly identified with him within the government, being given a detailed endorsement by the president on a solemn occasion. But the Report would come to be the cause of bitter recrimination. The triumph would turn to dust in Moynihan's mouth.

5

The Dark Hour

THE ELECTION AND THE REPORT, 1965–1966

En una noche oscura (In a dark night)
— St. John of the Cross, *Poems*

A N HOUR before the president began to read his speech at Howard University, Moynihan was airborne, bound for Yugoslavia. At one level, the trip was to be something of a holiday. Pat and Liz Moynihan, as befitted parents with three children, flew separately to London, where they had dinner with Pat's old flatmate, the lawyer Dante Campailla, and saw other friends.[1] Then they flew together for a few days in Rome, where Liz was to stay, seeing more friends and visiting museums. Pat flew on to Zagreb on June 7 and then on to Ljubljana (now the capital of the independent republic of Slovenia, but then in Yugoslavia). They returned to Washington on June 24. There was a Catholic flavor to the trip, too. Moynihan had arranged for an introduction from Monsignor Higgins to the Vatican, where he met with an Italian American monsignor called Luigi Ligutto. From Rome he wrote back to Willard Wirtz that "Liz and I will say a little Roman prayer" in St. Peter's for Wirtz's father, who had just died.

Thanks to the monsignor's good offices, the Moynihans received an audience with Pope Paul VI. There is a photograph extant of Pat and Liz, in a veil, on their knees to receive the Holy Father's blessing.[2] Suddenly, consternation. Liz became aware that her husband, contrary to all protocol, was addressing the Pope. And what he was saying was even less to be expected. "Holy Father," Pat said, politely but distinctly, "we hope you will not forget our friends the Jews!"

The Pope became, as Liz put it later,[3] "very Italian." He kept saying over and over again, "But we love the Jews!" The entourage, however, was unmistakably flustered. The cardinals and bishops were startled. When the Moynihans finally rose from their knees and left the pontifical presence, the bishop from Chicago who had accompanied them expressed the general feeling of the American pilgrims succinctly. "We need a drink," he said. Pat said simply, "If they're going to behave like a medieval court, they must expect us to take an opportunity to petition him."

Moynihan's breach of etiquette was not, however, a random act. It arose out of a current controversy about whether the Church would drop its insistence on the collective guilt of the Jewish people for the crucifixion of Christ. Pope Paul had recently made a sermon in which he declined to eliminate mention of Jewish guilt, and it was in reference to this that Moynihan seized his opportunity at the Vatican.[4]

Before long Moynihan had another opportunity to address a subject of great concern to American Jews: the status of Jews in the Soviet Union. This came about at a United Nations seminar in the former Yugoslavia.

Moynihan was beginning to develop international interests and the beginnings of an international reputation. In the spring of 1965, he was asked by Harlan Cleveland, his former dean at the Maxwell School of Citizenship and Public Affairs at Syracuse, who had become assistant secretary of state for international organizations, to represent the United States at a UNESCO conference on the multi-ethnic society. It was to be held at Ljubljana. The idea had emerged from conversations with friends, especially McPherson. Moynihan sent McPherson a memo promoting "an idea I have had for some time, namely that the U.S. should put the question of ethnic conflicts on the world agenda." At Cleveland's suggestion, he circulated copies of *Beyond the Melting Pot* to all delegates. "Ljubljana is lovely, and incredibly prosperous," he wrote home to a secretary from the conference, though the meeting was "incredibly disorganized and wasteful of time and energy, but it is, I think, worth it to me." To the worldly and sardonic Dick Goodwin, he cabled a summary of the conference, saying, "I have seen the Austro-Hungarian empire, and it works."[5]

Moynihan was able to take advantage of the meeting to score a point on the Soviet attitude to ethnic issues. Specifically, he anticipated by ten years his later dramatic championing of the Jewish people as U.S. ambassador to the United Nations. Most surprising of all, he was actually able to embarrass the Soviet delegation into reversing its traditional aversion to allowing minority groups and their members — and especially Soviet Jews — to make contact with both national organizations abroad and international organizations, and with individuals in other countries. It was to be a long time before the Soviet authorities began to act on that principle, and even then they acted only sporadically and with bad grace. But Moynihan did succeed in pushing them into accepting the principle, and that was not nothing.

The Soviet delegation to the meetings in Ljubljana's Pionirski Dom (headquarters of the local young communist Pioneers) consisted of safe, ethnically diverse party hacks. There was a "head of delegation from Tajikistan . . . a woman deputy, also of Asian stock, a Ukrainian and a Jew, but also, of course, a young man from Moscow who was in fact in charge."[6] The Soviet intention was to use this conference, as the Soviet Union in those days and for long years afterward habitually used all international gatherings, to denounce colonialism and the West. But on this occasion the gathering refused to be used in this way. The Israeli delegate asked the Soviet representative how it was possible to justify the fact that some three million Soviet Jews were not allowed to associate either with one another or with Jews abroad. The Indian delegate pointed out that laws protecting the rights of minorities, such as were supposed to exist in the Soviet Union, were meaningless without an independent judiciary.

Moynihan was asked to lead a discussion on the right of association. The crucial issue, he argued, was whether the right of association, which most governments acknowledged in theory but denied in practice at one time or another, extended across national borders. He was furiously denounced by the head of the Russian delegation, who tried to argue that individuals had no rights in international law, but that contention was swept away. The turning point came when a Yugoslav delegate, a Slovene scholar with a distinguished record in the wartime resistance against the Nazis, raised his hand and said he accepted all of Mr. Moynihan's points.

The young man from the Soviet foreign ministry then approached a senior American foreign service officer accompanying Moynihan and asked smoothly why there should be any differences between the Soviet Union and the United States. In the end, after a four-day wait, presumably while an agreed text was checked with Moscow, the Soviet delegation accepted the right of organizations and individuals to associate across national boundaries.

Moynihan's own conclusion, reached in a somewhat triumphalist account of the conference,[7] was certainly prophetic. The Soviet leadership, he said, was too conscious of world opinion to have a major row on the issue. They were well aware that the individuals in the Soviet Union most interested in associating with coreligionists elsewhere were Soviet Jews, and that this was a political question. It could affect Jewish relations with, and Jewish migration to, Israel, and therefore the balance of power in the Middle East. Moynihan already understood, too, the strategic advantage to the United States in clearly posing its own democratic principles as a banner to which in the end others would repair. "The oppression of people anywhere," he concluded, "is the concern of democratic nations everywhere." Such concern on the part of the American people and government "has been an abiding force for liberty and freedom from oppression throughout the world. It should continue so."

The conference began on June 8 and was scheduled to end on June 20. On June 18, Pat Moynihan was woken by a call from a *New York Times* correspondent in Belgrade, who asked him for his reaction to a report of his possible nomination as a candidate for mayor of New York.

Mayor Moynihan! Here was the first gust, loud and unmistakable, of the storm that, before it blew itself out, would have carried him far from the smooth course of the rising young federal official. Moynihan was taken aback. But he had also no doubt been preparing subconsciously for questions like this for a long time.

"Mr. Moynihan paused for 10 seconds," the *Times* reported, "caught his breath and asked 'What?' "[8]

He then responded with considerable political sophistication. He said, in fact, just the right things. The subject of his running for mayor had been put to him by "some respectable political people" in New York over the past six months, he said, but he had not considered it seriously. "I wish Mayor Wagner was running again," he went on. "No one appreciates how good a mayor he was." He hesitated to commit himself to running for mayor, but he did say "I am a New York Democrat. I live in New York" — he could indeed be said to live in New York State, though not in New York City, whose mayoralty was at issue —"I love New York and I believe in party regularity. If anyone thinks I would make a candidate, let him say so." It was far from what is known in the trade as a Sherman declaration.[9] Indeed it was a rather subtle appeal for support. And for good measure he included a broad swipe at John Vliet Lindsay, the Republican candidate. Asked whether he would enjoy running against Mr. Lindsay, the *Times* reported, Moynihan raised his voice and said, "Good God, yes! Any decent man would oppose a candidate who knows little and cares less about New York."

By the spring of 1965, a new factor had entered the equation. It had potentially both positive and negative force. Robert Kennedy had moved to New York. The man whom Moynihan regarded, if anyone, as his political chieftain, announced on August 25, 1964, that he was running for the Senate from New York, after Lyndon Johnson, with some agonizing delay, had removed him from the list of possible vice-presidential running mates. Both Johnson and Kennedy won by landslides that fall. A great quarrel had been postponed.

It is not known what private soundings Moynihan may have received on the matter of his running for mayor. From time to time friends and political admirers did suggest that he should run for one office or another. Thus on March 4, 1964, for example, his former boss at the International Rescue Committee, Richard R. Salzmann, wrote:

Dear Pat,
     Have you thought of trying to take on Senator Keating this year? . . . I believe you could beat him this year.

To which Moynihan responded in jocular vein:

Dear Dick,
     I should be delighted to run if you would agree to be the finance chairman. Alternately, I should be delighted if you would run and I would be finance chairman.[10]

As 1965 wore on, Moynihan was in an exquisitely difficult political bind. He was instinctively on the side of the Kennedys. He would have liked to be a member of the Kennedy inner circle, but he was not. And he *was* making a career, might even, if things carried on satisfactorily from the Howard speech, make himself a brilliant career, in the Johnson administration. Only if and when it became plain that these hopes from Johnson would not be realized would it make sense, politically, to break with him. And Moynihan can have been under no illusions: too close a political friendship with Robert Kennedy would indeed mean a breach with Johnson.

The most obvious feature of the political landscape in the Democratic party in 1965 was the bitter suspicion and rivalry between Robert Kennedy and Lyndon Johnson. The causes hardly matter. Texas and Boston, youth and age, Catholic and Protestant, didn't mix. Johnson saw himself as having fought his way up from hardscrabble poverty and saw Kennedy as a spoiled brat whose daddy had given him a $10 million trust fund. But he was also proud to be the descendant of sheriffs and state legislators,[11] and he despised Kennedy as an upstart who had been no more than a junior staffer, and for Joe McCarthy's notorious committee at that, when Johnson was already the feared leader of the Senate whales.

Although Johnson contrived to be civil to Kennedy, he never tired of telling his staff of his contempt and suspicion of him. The dislike was fully reciprocal. Bad blood had been curdled by many an incident. It dated back at least to Kennedy's role in trying to deny Johnson the vice presidency in 1960. It was made rancorous by misunderstandings in the immediate sequel to President Kennedy's assassination and in the version Kennedy and his friends were — rightly or wrongly — suspected of feeding to William Manchester when he was preparing his account of the assassination, *The Death of a President*.[12] Lyndon Johnson and Robert Kennedy, one student of their relationship concluded, "loathed each other."[13] "This man," said Kennedy of Johnson, "is mean, bitter, vicious — an animal in many ways." Said Johnson of Kennedy, "A grandstanding little runt."

So in the fall of 1964, Robert Kennedy moved into an apartment in UN Plaza on East 49th Street, and Pat Moynihan went up to New York from time to time to campaign for him. It didn't amount to much; mostly a little speechwriting. But it marked Moynihan out, in the feverishly suspicious eyes of Lyndon Johnson, as a Kennedy man. Reports reached the White House, too, that conversation around the dinner table at the Moynihan home in the Tregaron farmhouse, if not as savagely contemptuous as the table talk at Robert Kennedy's Virginia home, Hickory Hill, permitted a fair amount of Johnson mocking.[14] Willard Wirtz, for instance, offered accounts of such criticism to his inner circle.[15]

Moynihan's name found its way into print as a possible candidate for mayor of New York as a result of a tip from Tom Wicker, then the bureau chief of the *New York Times* in Washington, to another *Times* correspondent, Warren Weaver, Jr., who covered New York State politics. Unfortunately Wicker does not remember where he got the tip.[16]

What Moynihan believes is this: While he was in Ljubljana, there was a dinner at the Harrimans' home in Georgetown. Bobby and Ethel Kennedy were present, and so he thinks was Arthur Schlesinger, a trusted counselor of the family.[17] Kennedy was looking for a strong ticket in New York, and in particular for a candidate who could beat John Lindsay. He also wanted a mayor he could work with. Although later Governor Harriman came to have reservations about his former protégé,[18] at the time the Harrimans would have been happy to advance the career of a former staffer. It was known that Moynihan had played an important part in the Howard speech, of which the company would have approved. Moynihan was known as a thoughtful, moderately liberal Democrat. He was assumed to be a native New Yorker, and a man at ease with New York politics and New York politicians. Someone said what the ticket needed was someone like Moynihan as candidate for mayor. Why not Moynihan himself? said someone else. And someone rang Warren Weaver, Jr., a *New York Times* reporter. Tom Wicker's recollection is slightly different. What is certain is that Wicker picked up some "Moynihan for mayor" talk in or around the White House, and passed it on to Weaver, who floated the trial balloon, with fateful consequences for Moynihan's career. Moynihan's hat was in the ring.

The early press comment was highly positive. It reflected both Moynihan's talent for self-promotion, and the journalists' recognition, even at this early stage of his career, that his personality and intellect were both out of the ordinary. On June 20, Moynihan's friend Mary McGrory wrote in her column in the *Washington Star*, "Faced with an embarrassment of candidates in New York City, the Administration has suddenly come upon a dazzling prospect on its own doorstep." Moynihan's file was passed around the White House, she reported, "with rising joy."[19] But there her loyalty to her friend had outrun her judgment of the situation.

Both the *New York Times* and the *Washington Post* wrote favorably about Moynihan's prospects. On Tuesday, June 22, Julius Duscha reported in the *Post* that New York Democrats "would like the President to make two telephone calls that they think would open the way to a harmonious settlement of the fight for the Democratic nomination."[20] The two calls would be to Paul Screvane and Franklin Roosevelt, Jr., and "the purpose of both calls would be to let the candidates know that the President believes they should withdraw in the interests of Party harmony." The president never made those calls.

The problem was that there were six candidates in the race to replace Mayor Robert F. Wagner. Some had announced, others were just assumed to be interested: Paul R. Screvane, present of the city council and former sanitation commissioner, was widely seen as Wagner's heir designate. But also considering a run were Franklin D. Roosevelt, Jr., heir to an even more august tradition; liberal Congressman William F. Ryan; City Councilman Paul O'Dwyer, another liberal; the city's comptroller, Abraham D. Beame; and the U.S. district attorney in Queens, Frank D. O'Connor. Screvane and Ryan reacted to reports of a possible Moynihan candidacy by welcoming him in the traditional manner, that is, tongue in cheek. He would be joining a happy throng, said Screvane; the more, the merrier, said Ryan.

Willard Wirtz says he would not have objected to Moynihan's running for office in New York.[21] But besides being preoccupied with his own father's death and with the death of his own former boss, Adlai Stevenson, who had a heart attack on a London street on July 14, Wirtz was unenthusiastic. Instead, Moynihan enlisted the help of a far more influential figure, *his* former boss Arthur Goldberg.

Three legal-size sheets of paper, covered with scribbles in Moynihan's handwriting and with doodles, survive in the Library of Congress.[22] Together they make it plain that, however briefly, he did take seriously the idea of mounting a campaign for mayor of New York. They probably date from Moynihan's days in Rome shortly before his departure for Ljubljana, though on one of them Moynihan scrawled "in Rome on way home." One scribble says "seeing the Pope tomorrow"; another notes the flight number of a Pan American flight to Friendship Airport, between Baltimore and Washington. On a second sheet, he wrote, "Goldberg called," and noted what the Supreme Court justice, shortly about to become Johnson's ambassador at the United Nations, had said:

1. Spoke to LBJ said Pat was fine fellow. Very noncommittal. Same comment to Kraft.

2. Dubinsky [David Dubinsky, powerful head of the International Ladies Garment Workers Union] heading towards Lindsay. Trade union not keen. Rose [Alex Rose, head of the New Liberal Party] was in favor.

3. Not say word to the press about seeing the President.

The next four jottings presumably also refer to Goldberg's advice. They read "Go through Moyers," "Call Moyers earlier," "Irving Kristol" and "see Arthur" [Goldberg].

The third sheet is covered with notes about who should call whom, such as "McPherson — Kraft" and "Moyers — Mary [McGrory]." It also says "Lunch with Schiff. Blair Clark would lay it on." Mrs. Dorothy Schiff was the publisher of the *New York Post,* and Blair Clark was her close friend. "Should talk to the Liberals." And, most interestingly of all, "Talked to Bob Kennedy — delighted." Taken together these notes make it plain that Moynihan made a serious attempt to drum up support for his campaign for mayor.

It was not, however, successful. Instead, Moynihan had to settle for a place on Paul Screvane's ticket. He accepted on Thursday, July 8.[23] Liz Moynihan's reaction was simply "Why not?" Pat went up to New York on Sunday morning. Liz and the children had to be in New York for the press conference on Monday morning. They emptied the fridge, washed some clothes, packed up the dog, Mr. Dooley, and drove to the city.[24] They stayed with their friends the McCloskeys[25] at 135 East 35th Street; they voted from there in the fall. The children were taught to chant the address, ready for the press conference, so as to be ready with a New York address when asked where they lived, and Maura in particular chanted faithfully. The truth was that their real address was 3100 Macomb Street, NW, Washington, D.C., but the rules of the game demanded that they be instant New Yorkers.

It is plain that it was Lyndon Johnson who decided that Pat Moynihan should not run for mayor of New York, equally plain that Johnson's reason lay in personal hostility. He had certainly heard reports of the sometimes bitter anti-Johnson mockery at the Moynihans' dinners,[26] and they would have lost nothing in the telling. Harry McPherson, with some courage, risked his own standing with the president to defend Moynihan. On June 24, when Moynihan was on his way back from Rome, McPherson sent a memo to Johnson headed "Thoughts on Bobby Kennedy and loyalty." It was in part an analysis of how Robert Kennedy could be expected to behave. But it also said:

"There are many able men in government now who came because of the change Kennedy represented . . . we cannot afford to lose them. Neither, in my opinion, can we afford to give them a polygraph loyalty test . . . In the long run there is an even greater danger in applying a test requiring fealty to you alone . . . If the word gets around that one has to put on horse-blinders to work for you, you will probably come out with a bunch of clipped yes-men who are frightened of their own shadows and terrified of yours.[27]

It was a brave try.

It is customary for presidents to write a note of thanks to all senior presidential appointees. On July 18, 1965, Moynihan wrote to the president, tendering his resignation as assistant secretary of labor in order to run for president of the City Council of New York. The president did not reply. Instead, on August 6 he scrawled simply, "Accepted LBJ."[28] McPherson made several attempts to get the president at least to write a note of thanks for Moynihan's services, but Johnson would not do it. McPherson enlisted the help of Bill Moyers, who was, if anything, even closer to the president, but again Johnson would have none of it. On September 29, McPherson wrote once again, asking him to sign a draft letter of thanks to Moynihan, and the president scrawled on it in pencil: "Here [sic] this (1) I didn't like to start writing to Asst Secretaries;[29] (2) or to people who tried to involve me in NY election or to any person who calls for it — but as usual I yield to your judgment. L."[30]

Moynihan, it is clear, was in the president's bad books. The "feud that defined a decade"[31] was too bitter. Lyndon Johnson's suspicion of men with Moynihan's background was too deep; Austin was still a long way from Boston.[32]

Years later, in March 1971, when the tables were turned, and Johnson was a defeated ex-president and Moynihan a powerful aide to his successor, the latter wrote the former a long letter that seemed almost apologetic.[33] He began by making an excuse for writing to his former boss. Then he said he was sorry that his name had "somehow got into the papers" in connection with the Howard University speech, "But I should tell you that I left for a UN conference in Yugoslavia three hours before you gave it. Someone told someone, but it wasn't me. I was over the Atlantic." He went on — without mentioning the question of his running for mayor — that he was asked by Bob Wagner to run with Paul Screvane on a kind of center Democrat slate. And that he used every contact he had in the White House to get your guidance as to what to do, but to no avail. Finally McPherson told me that I would simply have to make up my own mind. Remembering your story about the story of the congressman who had said of some great statesman that he wished he had "just once run for sheriff," I went up and ran. Lost and went to Harvard, which is not bad for a CCNY man, but which perhaps associated me in your mind with other things.

Johnson did not deign to reply, but even that was not the end of Moynihan's efforts. In March 1972, when Johnson was already growing his hair long, drinking and smoking heavily, and acting as if he were indifferent to his own approaching death, Moynihan wrote again, thanking him for an invitation to a symposium at the LBJ Library in Austin. "To be frank," he wrote, "I was surprised not to have been asked to the opening of the library." Moynihan then asked Johnson to autograph a text of the Howard speech, "not only a great event in your life, but one in mine as well." He had left for a UN conference in Yugoslavia "just an hour before you were scheduled to speak," he repeated. He was away for three weeks "and returned to a rather different Washington." Somehow, he said, word had got to the press that he had helped to draft the speech. "As I can best reconstruct, the leak came from the White House and was meant to be a friendly act. But you were distressed, as you had every right to be. At this time the question arose of my succeeding Harry McPherson as assistant secretary of state for cultural affairs. You turned down the proposal in terms that made me feel that I had best leave Washington, which I did a few weeks after returning."[34]

There is an obvious element of special pleading in this letter. Whether or not the question of his becoming assistant secretary of state ever proceeded beyond conversation, Moynihan did not leave Washington because of sensitivity about the terms in which the idea was turned down by the president: he left to run for office in New York. Having failed to find support for his candidature for mayor, he accepted a lesser place on the ticket. That he had annoyed Johnson is plain enough. What is interesting is how hard he tried to get Johnson's absolution. In so doing he revealed a remarkable ability to reinterpret history to fit in with the way he wanted to remember it.

———

It is after all not so surprising that Johnson did not help Moynihan to become mayor of New York, or even president of the city council. What is less obvious is why Kennedy, too, backed off from helping him, especially if, as Moynihan believed when he scribbled that note about his prospects, Kennedy was truly "delighted" to have him run for mayor. The explanation lies, probably, not in Moynihan's relations with Kennedy, which were not particularly important to the New York senator, however important they may have been to Moynihan, but in the feud between Kennedy and Mayor Wagner. At a deeper level, it lies in Kennedy's strategy (one entirely congruous with his family's whole political tradition) of trying to achieve reformist goals through alliances with conservative political forces.

After Kennedy's election to the Senate in the fall of 1964, the Democrats found themselves in a stronger position in New York State than they had been since the 1930s, and — perhaps partly as a consequence — bitterly divided. Kennedy immediately challenged Wagner's power and that of the party leadership in Albany. Over the winter of 1964 to 1965 a battle royal raged. The dispute was seen not as pro- or anti-Kennedy so much as pro- and anti-Wagner. The mayor, son of a much-admired United States senator who had the good fortune to be half-Irish and half-German, was not a reformer, but not part of the organization either. Rather, as one observer put it, he presided over a world where "coteries and interlocking alliances of politicians, political lawyers, contractors, franchised businessmen, public relations men and fixers and hangers-on of various kinds" struggled for and over money in multifarious forms.[35]

On June 10, 1965, Wagner abruptly resigned, setting off the conflict Pat Moynihan was briefly invited to join. The Democrats split four ways. Wagner loyalists rallied to Paul Screvane. The organization regulars from the Brooklyn and Bronx machines went for Abe Beame. Reformers and radical liberals were split between William Ryan and Paul O'Dwyer. Kennedy first tried to persuade Frank Hogan, the much-admired Manhattan district attorney, to run for mayor. Then he switched his support to Theodore W. Kheel, a well-known labor negotiator. However much some of his aides and friends might have been attracted to the idea of running Moynihan for mayor, and whether or not Kennedy himself ever seriously thought about that idea, when it came to the point, Kennedy was not there.

And so Moynihan agreed to run for president of the city council, on the Screvane ticket, with Orin Lehman, a relative of former U.S. Senator Herbert Lehman, as candidate for comptroller. The slate was announced on July 19, and the same day Paul Screvane's ticket, with Moynihan on it, won the endorsement of the New York County Democratic organization, though only by a narrow margin that underlined deep divisions among the Democrats. Ominously, most of the Harlem leaders, taking their cue from Congressman Adam Clayton Powell, who stalked out of the meeting after only twelve minutes, abstained. Moynihan made a brief but emotional speech on his invitation to run on the Screvane ticket in which he looked forward to what was to be another of his constant themes, saying he had "come back to New York out of the further conviction that our nation is at last about to come to grips with the problems of the American city." There was little or no reference to the Moynihan Report in the campaign, but there were other echoes of Moynihan's involvement in what were already the unraveling politics of the Great Society. Congressman William F. Ryan, the most liberal of the candidates for mayor, attacked Moynihan for "whitewashing" an attack by Screvane on Mobilization for Youth. And an Italian American chose to denounce the two-year-old *Beyond the Melting Pot* as "a mass of twisted facts, contorted conclusions and hearsay statements."[36] Moynihan shot back that "if there is anything that sins against the spirit of the people of New York, it is the effort to exploit and worsen the relations between ethnic and religious groups for gritty political purpose."[37]

He devoted his sole major policy speech of the campaign, at the Overseas Press Club, to what should become of a federal surplus of $40 billion — the result of a booming economy. This surplus must not be hoarded, he said. There were only three ways in which it could be spent: by reducing the national debt, by cutting taxes, or by increasing government spending, and he came out strongly for the latter. Neither New York City nor the state could find more money. The country's "major domestic challenge" was to revitalize its cities. The money would be available in the federal surplus, and he called strongly for it to be spent.

Moynihan was finding his political style. Although several candidates did traditional handshaking election tours, this campaign was one of the first fought mainly in the media. The future professor and senator and former longshoreman adopted a style that was a mixture of the proletarian and the professorial. The trouble was not that people didn't like him; they did. They didn't always know what the hell he was talking about. But he was a surprisingly effective campaigner. The Screvane ticket suffered because Ryan was siphoning off liberal votes. An Oliver Quayle survey a week before polling day found that Frank O'Connor, his opposite number on the Beame ticket, was still ahead by about 27 to 23 percent, but that Moynihan had more than doubled his support in two weeks to pull "within striking distance."[38] There was trouble in Queens, where a number of district workers said they would split their ticket and back O'Connor, the local man. Mayor Wagner, who had endorsed the whole Screvane ticket, made some phone calls to get them back, and told reporters that Moynihan would win. But he didn't. In the primary on September 14, Beame beat Screvane by 336,000 votes to 271,000. Moynihan lost slightly more heavily to Frank O'Connor by 262,000 to 350,000.[39]

Pat Moynihan was desperately disappointed in the result. A photograph shows his face drawn, and the *Times* reported that he left his headquarters in tears.[40] On election night, there was a contretemps of some kind. Robert Kennedy took no position on the candidates as he toured their headquarters, accompanied by his usual entourage of sharp young aides in sharp suits, well-dressed women with sunglasses pushed up on the top of their heads and several camera crews from local TV stations. The Moynihans, Liz especially, were not pleased. At the time, there were awed accounts of how Liz had slapped Bobby's face.[41] She has no such recollection.[42] Her husband recalls that what happened was that Kennedy "made to kiss Liz, but she reeled away."[43] The senator must have been startled. Few women refused such a tribute from a Kennedy in those days.

Both Liz and Pat had reason to be disappointed with Robert Kennedy. Moynihan had after all admired John Kennedy and mourned him more eloquently than most. He had worked closely with Kennedy's aides and with his brother-in-law Sargent Shriver in the War on Poverty. He had campaigned for Robert, and visited his brother Ted when the latter was injured in a plane crash. And yet Kennedy was not only unwilling to back Pat for mayor, he was not even willing to come out and back him for a lower office. During the campaign, Moynihan told an interviewer on WNBC-TV that while he was not in city politics on Senator Kennedy's orders, he had taken the senator's advice.[44] Of course, the Moynihans understood that Kennedy did not want to offend the machine politicians, like Charlie Buckley in the Bronx and Stanley Steingut in Brooklyn. Moynihan was quite capable of understanding that, as Kennedy put himself, with a cynicism worthy of his father, "Whichever ticket wins, I'll have a man in City Hall to look after my interests. If it's Beame, Steingut and Buckley; if Screvane, Moynihan." But to understand the calculus behind rejection does not make it any easier to bear. To those who saw themselves as devoted followers of the Kennedys, inspired by their ideals, it must have felt a little like treason.

Between them, Robert Kennedy and Robert Wagner had left the New York Democratic party in a shambles. In the fall, Kennedy eventually bestirred himself to vote for Abe Beame, but it was too late. In spite of a three-to-one advantage in registrations, the Democrats managed to lose control of the city for the first time in twenty years. By his failure to come out for Moynihan for mayor, and for the Screvane ticket as a default, Kennedy made it impossible to build a New Frontier Democratic party, centrist but progressive, in New York. The only consolation, and it was a cynical one, was that the task of facing the multiple crises — racial, social, fiscal, economic and criminal — about to fall on the great city would now be in the hands of a Republican, John V. Lindsay.

Moynihan's own reaction to the New York election was summed up in a wry note to a friend, Robert Dowling. "I am reminded," he wrote, smiling, you might say through the tears, "of Oscar Wilde's observation that Niagara Falls would be more impressive if it flowed the other way."[45]

For Moynihan, the second half of 1965 had started disastrously. In three short months, he had lost a key position, influential and admired, in the executive branch of the national government. He had lost what for a brief moment looked like an enticing opportunity in elective politics in New York. He was out of a job. And there was worse to come.

The Moynihan Report had been "published" within the government on March 25 but not made public.

On August 18, the syndicated columnists Rowland Evans and Robert D. Novak headlined their nationally syndicated *Wall Street Journal* column "The Moynihan Report." Moynihan has commented recently that "Rowly and Bob got it."[46] But in fact their coverage was an extraordinary mixture of accurate reporting and tendentious misinterpretation.

In a "78-page report largely based on unexciting census evidence," Evans and Novak reported, Moynihan showed "that broken homes, illegitimacy and female-oriented families were central to big-city Negro problems."[47] They explained, to be sure, accurately, that the ideas in the Report had influenced President Johnson's Howard University speech. They reported that there was intense debate within the White House and the administration generally about the role of the family in black poverty, and they were aware of the concern that the Report might lead to discussion of preferential treatment for black people. But where Evans and Novak were wrong, and where, just because their column was so influential, it was so disastrous for Moynihan, was that it gave the impression that the Report's main thrust was that the troubles of black people in the cities were the consequence of the breakdown of the Negro family. They did not mention Moynihan's other, crucial contention: that whatever might have been the long-term historical consequences of slavery and discrimination, it was poverty and unemployment that were the immediate causes of the breakdown in black family life, and not the other way around.

Evans and Novak left out the absolutely vital point that Moynihan saw unemployment as the *direct* cause of the breakdown in the African American family. Moynihan specifically mentioned "the impact of unemployment on the Negro family" as "the least understood of all the developments that have contributed to the present crisis."[48] But then he cited the work of a sociologist, Edward Wight Bakke,[49] who had studied the effect of unemployment on family structure. After the male worker had lost his job, exhausted sources of credit and seen his wife go out to work, the unemployed man found his life dominated by two women, the housewife and the caseworker. At this point, Moynihan's own experience of the dynamics of family breakdown gave him an insight into what was going on. The father was no longer the provider, he said, and the elder children became resentful. The father lost his authority and eventually was likely to lose his home. The Report was quite clear. Slavery and the black experience in America since slavery may predispose the black family to unemployment and poverty. But it is unemployment that is the cause of the family breakdown.

There is, to be sure, an apparent paradox. Moynihan maintained that families continued to disintegrate even after the rate of unemployment began to go down. But that does not mean that there was no connection between unemployment and family breakdown.

With the publication of that column, Daniel Patrick Moynihan became a celebrity. But his new, unwelcome fame was based on interpretations of his Report which had more to do with the search for policy than with what the Report had actually said. Misunderstandings multiplied. The major leaders of the civil rights movement, including Martin Luther King, Roy Wilkins of the NAACP and the veteran labor leader A. Philip Randolph, met with the president to discuss what should be done, and in particular to plan the promised conference "To Fulfill These Rights." They were unhappy about the Report, partly because they were afraid it might be taken as confirming hostile views of black "worthlessness," partly because they were defensive about female-headed families, from which a number of them (ironically, like Moynihan himself) came.[50]

Two days after the first leaks from the Moynihan Report appeared in *Newsweek*,[51] a traffic officer arrested a young black man in Los Angeles. A crowd gathered and began to attack white motorists. Thirty hours later, and two miles away, in Watts, in the south central section of the sprawling city, black people began firebombing white-owned property in the predominantly black neighborhood. Police, followed by National Guardsmen, moved in. By the time order had been restored, thirty-four people, all African Americans, had been killed, and the racial landscape in the United States had changed. There had been racially motivated rioting in many cities the previous summer. But up until the Watts riot, the worst since the Detroit riot of 1943, most white Americans preferred to focus on the progress that had been achieved. After Watts, attention shifted sharply to racial tension and the potential for violence in the cities of the North and West. In this new, apprehensive mood, the Report, then still known more in Evans and Novak's interpretation than in and of itself, was seen as the government's explanation for the riots. When Vice President Humphrey took some of the nationally known civil rights leaders on a boat trip on the Potomac in the presidential launch *Honey Fitz*, these dignified, moderate men "almost turned the boat over" in their indignation. The White House realized belatedly that it had a political nightmare on its hands.[52]

The immediate dilemma arose from the promised conference. It was plain that any such gathering would turn into a chainsaw massacre. Yet to cancel the conference would be even worse than to convene it. On October 4, the White House came up with a feeble compromise: a conference would be held, but it would not be *the* conference, only a planning conference. When this sheepish substitute did finally assemble, in mid-November 1965, Berl Bernhard, its executive director, tried to put the delegates in a better mood by joking that no such person as Daniel Patrick Moynihan existed — not such a good joke for the nonperson himself, who was present.[53]

The historic chiefs of the civil rights movement were unhappy enough about the Report. Their followers, who did not get invited to the White House or on boat trips for presidential schmoozing, were even more suspicious. One focus of furious opposition was the liberal Protestant milieu of New York. The Office of Church and Race of the Protestant Council, jointly with the Commission on Race and Religion of the National Council of Churches, convened a conference of their own, ahead of the White House's planning session. One leading figure was Dr. Robert Spike, executive director of the commission, founded during the Birmingham, Alabama, crisis of 1963. Moynihan regarded Spike as one of the chief organizers of the attack on his Report, as he wrote to Harry McPherson the following spring:

> When I read that Spike had been appointed to the Council to the White House Conference I assumed it reflected a conscious decision to repudiate the report and me, and I let it go at that: life is full of ups and downs. . . .
>
> Spike has been a *leader* of the effort to discredit me, which has been an organized effort. Hundreds on hundreds of the enclosed news release were sent out. For what it's worth, I feel that just below the surface has been an effort to discredit the President's initiative at Howard.[54]

Another leader of the Protestant churches' campaign against the Report was Dr. Benjamin F. Payton, a young black minister and sociologist. The meeting proposed that the Johnson administration commit an "Economic Development Budget for Equal Rights" in the then-gigantic sum of $32 billion.[55] More to the point, it demanded that the whole topic of "family stability" be struck from the agenda of the White House conference. To support this demand, Payton circulated several hundred copies of a bitter critique that demolished what Moynihan was reported in the press as saying, without seriously addressing what he was actually saying.

On the first day of the "planning conference" in November, Moynihan, who had not yet read Payton's paper, said nothing. After someone had shown it to him, he rose "on a point of personal privilege" and addressed Payton directly. He said he had difficulty in believing that Payton had actually read his report. He could not believe it could be taken as minimizing the importance of social and economic remedies for the crisis in the ghettos. "Do you see," he asked, "that the object of this report is not to say that jobs do not matter, but rather that jobs matter in the most fundamental way? . . . We can measure our success or failure as a society not in terms of income level, and not in the prettiness or attractiveness or peacefulness of our people, but in the health, and the living, loving reality of the family in our society."[56] Payton was not won over by this direct appeal. He continued to maintain, to Moynihan's face, that he was "outraged" by the Report. And on December 13, in the National Council's journal, *Christianity in Crisis*, he published a restatement of his views.

Meanwhile, other critiques of the Report were circulating. On October 15, the highly respected sociologist Herbert Gans published in the Catholic journal *Commonweal* a careful and not unsympathetic analysis.[57] He concluded that "in this desert of compassion, the Moynihan Report is a tiny oasis of hope, and if properly interpreted and implemented, a first guide to the achievement of equality in the years to come." The general tone of his account, however, was pessimistic. He feared that because the Report did not offer specific policy recommendations its conclusions could be "conveniently misinterpreted," which they certainly were. This was all the more likely, Gans said, because of the conflict between the two major themes of the Report: "that Negroes must be given real equality, and that because of the deterioration of the family they are presently incapable of achieving it." The "inherent sensationality of the data," he presciently warned, made it likely that "the handicaps of the Negro population" would receive more attention than Moynihan's appeal for an equality of outcomes.

Far more hostile and hurtful to Moynihan was the response of a Boston psychologist, William Ryan. Active in the Boston chapter of CORE (Congress of Racial Equality), Ryan taught at Harvard Medical School. As early as September, he started to write an attack on the Moynihan Report, which he had not read, but knew only through the *Newsweek* version. In October, he distributed fifty copies of this critique to friends and before long he had been asked for, and had sent out, another one hundred copies. On November 22, a version of his paper was published in the left-wing New York weekly *The Nation,* under the uncompromising title "Savage Discovery." It was also republished, significantly, in *The Crisis,* the journal of the NAACP. Ryan pummeled the Report's "serious shortcomings" with both fists: "Briefly, it draws dangerously inexact conclusions from weak and insufficient data; encourages (no doubt unintentionally) a new form of subtle racism that might be termed 'Savage Discovery,' and seduces the reader into believing that it is not racism and discrimination but the weaknesses and defects of the Negro himself that account for the present state of inequality between Negro and white."[58]

As if that was not enough, Ryan went on to call Moynihan's treatment of illegitimacy as "highly sophomoric" and "oversimplified," and the Report itself "heresy" and "sociological fakery."[59] Later he coined a refrain that expressed his indignant view of what Moynihan was doing: "blaming the victim."[60]

That was not the end of the attacks. "For a year," Moynihan wrote later, "I found myself the object of incredible accusations, some of them, from academia, going quite beyond the border of fair comment."[61] Just before the White House conference finally met in June 1966, for example, a publication of the Ferkauf Graduate School of Education at Yeshiva University devoted itself to the subject "The Moynihan Report and Its Critics: Which Side Are You On?" Moynihan responded, "The publication was not on my side, heaven knows, but, more importantly, it depicted 'my' side in terms near to absolute distortion." To omit from the bibliography all articles by black scholars such as C. Eric Lincoln, who agreed with him, was — Moynihan said angrily — "the scholarship of Che Guevara."[62]

The *annus terribilis* had almost run its course. Moynihan took these attacks extremely hard. It would be easy to say that he was oversensitive. But this was not an easy time in his life. He was in effect unemployed. Interviewed by the *New York Times* the day after his defeat in the primary, he said he didn't know what he would do. He was considering whether he might "try writing full-time," but he would have to hunt for a job, even though "tactful job offers were made before the polls opened Tuesday."[63] In fact, he did not need to worry about where his next salary was coming from. The day of the primary, he received an invitation to spend a year at the Center for Advanced Studies at Wesleyan.[64] But the longer-term future, for a man approaching forty with three small children, was less encouraging. He had resigned from the government to run for public office, had been disappointed of nomination for a greater office, then badly beaten in the primary for a lesser office. His former employer, the president of the United States, flatly refused to thank him for his efforts, and now he had to suffer being accused of the worst possible motives for efforts of which he had every reason to feel proud. It was no small thing, in that time and for a man with his commitments and ambitions, to be falsely accused of racism.

He experienced, he now remembers, something like what St. John of the Cross called "the dark night of the soul." Years later he was proud when a Catholic priest said that the experience would have broken "a lesser man"[65] and he says that he had been saved from a breakdown by two things: "a telephone call from Reinhold Niebuhr and a short story by Seán O'Faoláin."[66]

The call followed an article in *Christian Century*, on December 15, 1965. It was bad enough for Moynihan to be attacked by Benjamin Payton in *Christianity in Crisis;* to be patronized as he was by the writer of the *Christian Century* editorial was infuriating, and all the more so because Moynihan admired Reinhold Niebuhr, the magazine's founder, as an impressive moral force in liberal Protestantism. Niebuhr called to say that he had been invited to be honored at *Christian Century*'s anniversary, but he declined and called Moynihan to say why. "He thought," Moynihan says, "that what I had done was exemplarily Christian and possibly true and [that he] would have nothing to do with excommunication."[67] On February 26, he wrote to Mrs. Niebuhr, saying he was "appalled" to be the reason for her husband's not attending the celebration. "Please try to tell Dr. Niebuhr how much his action has meant to me," Moynihan wrote: "the whole affair has become a nightmare of misunderstanding, and misinterpretation, and misstatement."[68] Earlier, Moynihan wrote Niebuhr, "No one . . . has ever offered me more understanding . . . I am hurt right now, but I am not defeated."[69]

The morning of the New York primary, as Moynihan was contemplating the ruins of his career, he was approached by the novelist Paul Horgan, who was director of the Center of Advanced Studies at Wesleyan University, a small but comfortably funded institution with a beautiful campus in Connecticut. (The invitation, which Moynihan accepted, had been suggested by Douglass Cater, his former colleague on *The Reporter,* then working on civil rights in the Johnson White House.)

Another fellow at Wesleyan was the distinguished Irish writer Seán O'Faoláin. It has not been possible to identify the short story that Moynihan remembers, after all these years, as having restored to him a gleam of hope:[70]

> Seán has a story about a social worker who visits two ancient brothers in some godforsaken bog to see if they are alive and eligible. The oldest thinks he is there to deprive them of their dole. He leads [the social worker] to a place of no return and disappears. After things look grim — the man could die — the younger brother appears and brings him back to the road, as it were. As they part, the brother meekly asks if the social worker intends now to cut them off. No, he replies, I'm not that bad a man.

"Sean was writing about many things," Pat commented years later. "One was the situation I found myself in during that dark night."[71]

Helped by Liz's unfailing determination and support and by the affection of his friends, he was soon on the way back, though the experience of 1965 left lasting emotional scars. The effect on his political and intellectual orientation was like that of a force-nine gale on an explorer's ship in midocean. He was blown right off course. Characteristically, he himself wrote much later, that "correcting course in a storm is a way of staying the course."[72] As a consequence, he discovered coasts and made landfalls he would never have seen if he had not run into stormy weather. Eventually, he steered back to a course not so far from the one he had been on before. But, like Odysseus, he was doomed to wander for ten years and more before coming home.

6

The Era of Bad Manners

FROM HARVARD TO NIXON

An era of bad manners is certainly begun.

— Daniel Patrick Moynihan, "The President & the Negro:
The Moment Lost," *Commentary*, February 1967

U P UNTIL THE SUMMER of 1965, Moynihan had been a regular Democrat and — like most Northern Democrats in those days — an orthodox centrist liberal, if one who had more understanding of, and more sympathy with, the white working class than some liberal intellectuals did. As an officeholder under Governor Harriman in New York, and under Presidents Kennedy and Johnson in Washington, as a member of Americans for Democratic Action and a contributor to journals like *The Reporter*, as an important participant in the discussions over the War on Poverty, and as the author of an ambitious presidential initiative aimed at achieving equality of condition, not just of opportunity, for black Americans, his credentials as a liberal Democrat looked impeccable.

Gradually, however, he began to distance himself from some of his former liberal allies. He began to associate more with a group of them who were already critical of the New Deal tradition. One was his old friend Norman Podhoretz, the editor of *Commentary*, for which in late 1966 Moynihan distilled his interpretation of the controversy over the Report.[1] Until much later, Podhoretz stoutly claimed liberal credentials of his own. He has described in his own autobiographical writings how he moved from an orthodox liberal position to one unremittingly scathing about liberal dogmas and attitudes.[2] Still, in the late 1960s, a time when he was close to Moynihan and published a number of articles in which Moynihan expressed his changing views of the world, Podhoretz had not broken openly with the mainstream of liberal thought.

The same was true of the group of friends with whom Moynihan became closely associated in the years after the heckling of the Report: the editors of *The Public Interest*.[3] The twin driving spirits of the magazine were Irving Kristol and Daniel Bell, both of whom were to have great influence over Moynihan's career and ideas. It might be tempting to typecast Kristol as the man of business, raising the funding, making the decisions, and making the magazine happen, and Bell as the man of ideas. In reality the relationship was more complex. While Bell, who has remained a liberal, contributed greatly to the magazine's intellectual gravity and scope, he also brought in financial backers whom he had met as a *Fortune* journalist writing about Wall Street as well as his more habitual labor beat. These included men like Martin Segal and Harry Kahn. If it was Irving Kristol who ran the magazine (with the help of Vivian Gornick, later a distinguished feminist writer) out of his office at Basic Books, and Kristol who found the crucial angel, in Warren D. Manshel, whose financial backing made it possible to launch *The Public Interest* in the fall of 1965, it was also Kristol, whose adolescent socialism had long given way to conservative principles, who did more than any other single person to commit the magazine to its line of deep skepticism about the ability of government to solve social problems.

This line, however, took some time to emerge. Moynihan's contribution to the first issue, an article on "The Professionalization of Reform,"[4] related to it only peripherally, insofar as it called into question, rather gently, the claims of reformers to be activated by purely altruistic motives. It suggested that powerful professional and economic interests were now in play where schemes of social improvement were under discussion. Specifically, it made the point that the "war on poverty was not declared at the behest of the poor." Significantly, he mentioned the phrase that was to supply the title for his next book, the idea that under the Economic Opportunity Act community action programs should be carried out with the "maximum feasible participation" of the poor themselves. Then he added that "typically this measure was inserted in the legislation not because of any demand of the poor, but because the intellectual leaders of the social welfare profession had come to the conclusion that this was indispensable."[5] In this first article, Moynihan had not moved, and indeed he never has moved, to a position of opposition to the expenditure of public money to help the poor. What was beginning to emerge, rather, was a wary skepticism about the efficacy of such programs and about the ability of government to shape and aim them accurately.

It was Irving Kristol, who had met Moynihan when both were contributing to *The Reporter,* who got him involved in this new venture. Another of the editors was James Q. Wilson, whose introduction to *The Public Interest* was quite casual.[6] His friend and former supervisor Edward C. Banfield heard about the magazine and suggested to Wilson that he might want to write for it. Wilson phoned Kristol, saying he planned to be in New York soon, and Kristol, as was his custom with potential authors, invited him to lunch at a restaurant (now defunct) called the Italian Pavillion. More than thirty years later, every detail of the lunch remained clear in Wilson's recollection: the veal, the deference with which Kristol was treated by the waiters, and the invitation to write about political corruption in Massachusetts which Kristol published as "The Shame of the States." Thus simply was another new and talented contributor recruited. Kristol, Wilson comments, was "a terrific editor. He really knew how to give a magazine a point of view."

Moynihan's coauthor on *Beyond the Melting Pot,* Nathan Glazer, was also a contributor to *The Public Interest,* though at first he and Seymour Martin Lipset were not on the masthead as editors. Lipset and Glazer, as professors at Berkeley, the first great American graduate school to be hit by the tide of student radicalism, had already experienced something that Moynihan, in Washington, had so far been spared. Like many professors who had grown up as instinctive liberals, Glazer and Lipset were appalled by the intolerance and indiscipline and the sheer anti-intellectualism of many radical students, and in October 1971 Glazer wrote an influential article[7] in which he described how he had been changed by the intolerance of the radical movements of the late 1960s, by the "increasing vituperation, increasing disaffection with the country and its institutions." "How," he asked, "does a radical — a mild radical, it is true, but still someone who felt closer to radical than to liberal writers and politicians in the late 1950s — end up by early 1970 a conservative, a mild conservative, but still closer to those who now call themselves conservatives than to those who call themselves liberals?" Glazer went on to admit that he detested what student radicals were doing to the university and to the country.

The intellectuals who wrote for *The Public Interest* in its early issues were by no means all of one mind. Indeed, more than thirty years later it is a mistake to see them all as members of a neoconservative sect. If they shared, and to some extent still share, certain instincts and assumptions, there are few, if any, issues on which they all agreed. Even so, in the second half of the 1960s, as the country became engulfed in a political crisis and a sort of collective intellectual breakdown, Moynihan no longer needed to feel alone. Some of the most gifted of his friends shared his dark mood of resentment, misgiving and foreboding. They also shared some of his specific ideas about social science and public policy.

At one level, the cement that bound *The Public Interest* group together was a negative feeling, indeed a kind of double negative: anger at the destructive and unpatriotic tenor of much of the new radicalism thrown up by the peace movement, the civil rights movement and the campus upheavals. But there was always another key idea, which had to do with the claims of social science in relation to public policy. It was not a coincidence that virtually all of *The Public Interest* editors and the writers they published were social scientists trained in one discipline or another. They had all watched social science being used and, as most of them thought, misused, as a guide to public policy and government action. They shared a skepticism about the belief, which was a cornerstone of interventionist liberal thinking, that once social scientists identified a problem, it was the function of government to devise, fund and staff programs to deal with it, and the problem would duly disappear. Instead, says Seymour Martin Lipset, "What was special about *The Public Interest* was skepticism."[8] Its editors believed that most problems had multiple causes. Pat Moynihan has always said that the duty of a social scientist is to refine the hypothesis, not to prove a case. James Q. Wilson says the same thing in different words. "Pat has always thought, rightly in my view, that the task of policy-relevant social science was not to answer the question 'What should the government do?,' but to answer the question 'Now that the government is doing this, is it making any difference or not?' "[9]

I asked Professor Wilson how he explained the fact that, within weeks of helping to draft President Johnson's Howard speech, the high-water mark of liberal interventionism, Moynihan was joining with others in *The Public Interest* who were increasingly skeptical of the efficacy of government intervention in almost all circumstances.

"This goes to the core of Pat's being," Wilson answered:

> Pat has always been a Democrat. He always believes that the job of politics is to help those who can't help themselves. But he has a scholar's reluctance to accept the proposition that the government knows very much about how to help people who can't help themselves.
>
> When all that is required is to transfer money from person A to person B, as in the social security system, it works very well, and Pat has been a staunch defender of social security. But when it has to alter their character, when it has to alter whether men marry women with whom they begat a child, or when it has to reduce the crime rate, or has to deal with student radicalism, the fact of the matter is that government doesn't know much what to do.[10]

Throughout the crisis period from 1965 to 1968, in fact, as indeed through much of his career, Moynihan's experience rather accurately mirrored that of many other Americans. If he was in difficulty because he tried to rethink what it was that had denied equality to African Americans, others, too, found that exercise painful. If he was shaken by the schism in a predominantly liberal consensus, so were most of his generation; if he was shocked by the speed with which liberal optimism was being torn to shreds by the rising winds of foreign war and domestic discord, so too was almost everyone else. But, more than almost anyone, Moynihan epitomized the changes that were taking place in many Americans' assumptions. In the spring of 1965, he had taken the initiative to propose "the case for national action": nothing less than a campaign to make black Americans truly equal with whites. By the fall of that year, he was publicly associated with a group of writers whose work would challenge that philosophy at its roots. And by year's end, he was retreating from the scene for a while, to lick his private wounds and see what could be made of the rags into which in a few angry months the optimistic public philosophy of liberalism had been torn. If, by the end of 1965, Daniel Patrick Moynihan was distraught, so too was the better part of America.

Immediately after Pat's defeat in the New York primary, Liz drove the family up to Wesleyan. With two exhausted parents, three puzzled children and a hot family dog in the station wagon, she says,[11] they felt like Okies as their host, Paul Horgan, met them and led them to their new house on campus.[12] It was, Liz insists loyally, a great house, and they spent "one of the best years of our lives" there. It is true that they made great friends at Wesleyan: Paul Horgan himself, Seán O'Faoláin, the philosopher Michael Polanyi and his wife, Magda, among them. But for Pat, even while he was telling the undergraduate reporter from the *Wesleyan Argus* how "agreeable" and "stimulating" he found the largely automobile-free campus,[13] it was a time of emotional convalescence and intellectual readjustment. By March 1966, he had succeeded in organizing and fund-raising for a major conference on the problems of the "lower-class Negro family" to which he attracted political scientists and sociologists from the Ivy League as well as from predominantly black Southern schools like Fisk University. He told the Middletown newspaper that he planned to write a book of "unabashed prescription" about cities.[14] He didn't write that book. But he did write several important articles. One of them, appropriately enough, was a review for *Commonweal* of E. Franklin Frazier's study of *The Negro Family in the United States*, which had recently been republished, and had provided the foundations for the Moynihan Report.[15]

The most revealing of the articles in which he summed up his assessment of what had happened to the movement for black equality was not published until after Moynihan had left Wesleyan.[16] It is worth referring to at some length because it is not only the fullest and frankest response by Moynihan to the controversy stirred up by the Report, but it is a conspicuously shrewd analysis of an important moment in American history. And it is also a clear statement of beliefs that guided its author both long before and long after the public fuss over the Report and his own personal trauma had subsided.

The country, he began, had just passed through one of those comparatively rare periods, lasting roughly from the Kennedy assassination in November 1963 to the midterm elections of 1966, when it was exceptionally receptive to new ideas. There were two reasons. One was the assassination itself. The other was the defeat of Barry Goldwater in the 1964 presidential election and the immense Democratic majorities in the Congress. Together these events enabled Congress to "clean up the agenda" of the Roosevelt and Truman administrations.

Now, with the 1966 elections, the mood had changed again. The vote "was a bruising declaration that the electorate is fed up to the teeth with demonstrations and riots." For Negro Americans, the election might turn out to be a calamity. "For the second time in their history," he predicted, "the great task of liberation has been left only half accomplished." As during Reconstruction, Negroes had been given the forms of social equality, but the economic and political resources that are the bases of social equality had been withheld. "Negroes," he said, "did get a good deal out of this period. But not enough."

His view was that Johnson, in the Howard speech, had faced squarely "the most difficult problem of American life" (borrowing a phrase from the *Times*'s Tom Wicker), not the problem of enforcing legal equity for the Negro, but "rather the acceptance of the Negro as an equal human being rather than a 'separate but equal' human being—a man with a darker skin rather than a 'black man.'" Yet nothing had come of Johnson's initiative. Why not? One reason, Moynihan conceded, was Vietnam. The Howard speech was Johnson's last in peacetime. But another reason was that the development of a program to work toward black equality was "superseded by a preposterous and fruitless controversy" over the Moynihan Report, which, he claimed, "had been the original precipitant of the Howard speech."

Moynihan then launched into a careful but irritated account of the Report's reception. The welfare bureaucracy, as the sociologists Lee Rainwater and William L. Yancey wrote, found his "intransigent emphasis on color reactionary rather than radical." The word in the Department of Health, Education and Welfare was that he was "a subtle racist." The attacks by William Ryan, Dr. Robert Spike and Dr. Benjamin Payton were rebutted, as one would expect, with indignation and contempt. The most interesting part of the article, however, was Moynihan's account of the role played in the controversy over the African American family by "the liberal Left." He does not define this group. But he clearly associates it with those in the Protestant churches, in universities and elsewhere who had supported the civil rights movement, not, in general, with labor unions and their political supporters, or with the Democratic party as a whole. Here we can see the beginnings of a schism, conscious or not, and also Moynihan positioning himself on one side of that schism, and emphatically not that of the liberal Left.

He began, with a faint echo of Mark Antony's speech in *Julius Caesar*,[17] by paying tribute to the good intentions of his adversaries: Brutus was an honorable man. Moynihan wrote, "The nation needs the liberal Left. It has provided a secular conscience in a civilization where the immorality of large organizations has become . . . almost the central danger of the age . . . Had it not been for the liberal Left, it is unlikely that the civil rights movement would have had the extraordinary impact and success of the past decade."[18]

Having said that, Moynihan revealed his pent-up contempt for what he saw as the sheer naïveté, the indifferent self-indulgence, of middle-class liberals in one scathing passage after another. "Negroes want in. Read *Ebony*. Read Myrdal. Read the election returns from Lowndes county. The great, guilty, hateful secret is that Negroes are not swingers. They are Southern Protestants. They like jobs in the civil service. They support the war in Vietnam, approve the draft, back the president."[19]

The reaction of the liberal Left to discussion of the Negro family, he said, was, on the one hand, that no one was to talk about "their poor people" that way, and again that the dysfunction of the black family was not a problem at all, but a healthy adjustment to conditions imposed by a racist society. His critic William Ryan, he jeered, had introduced "a novel social indicator, the illegitimacy conception rate. . . . This rate reveals that white bourgeois females fornicate almost as much as, or even more than (although not of course so well as) Negro girls, and conceive almost as often. But thereafter they resort to (Park Avenue) abortionists. Thus the point becomes to establish *guilt* instead of to deal with a problem."

With all its virtues as a secular conscience, the liberal Left can be as rigid and destructive as any force in American life.[20]

At this point, it is plain, the once orthodox liberal had crossed the Rubicon, burned a bridge. There were, he concluded, two points of view. There was that taken by Martin Luther King, Jr., who described the life of poor black Americans as "social catastrophe" and in effect told the white world to "put up or shut up." And there was the position, taken by the novelist Ralph Ellison, among others, that there was no reason for blacks to conform to any standards but their own, and that children could just as well grow up in a Negro cultural pattern as in a white one.

Up to a point, Moynihan was prepared to go along. But "this country is not fair to Negroes and will exploit any weakness they display." And he ended with a prophecy that was at the same time the statement of a political philosophy that was realistic, if not pessimistic. "The time when white men, whatever their motives, could tell Negroes what was or was not good for them, is now definitely and decidedly over. An era of bad manners is certainly begun."

Quite early in his year at Wesleyan, Moynihan was already making plans for the time after this pleasant interlude ended. Moynihan's comforters might have included Seán O'Faoláin and Reinhold Niebuhr. His savior was to be James Q. Wilson, a junior faculty member at Harvard when he went to hear Moynihan speak on organized crime.[21] But by 1963 he had become the director of the Harvard-MIT Joint Center for Urban Studies. One of his first tasks in that job was to sort out some publishing problems associated with *Beyond the Melting Pot*. He visited Pat and Liz at Tregaron. "I was completely captivated," he admits. When Moynihan lost in the 1965 New York primary, "I began to wonder whether I could find a way to bring him to Harvard." In 1966, Wilson decided to step down as director of the Joint Center. "I recommended to the deans," he recalls, "that they appoint Pat to take my place, because I thought he brought intellect, experience with urban problems, familiarity with Washington. He had all the requirements. In fact he had more requirements than I had for the job."

The difficulty was in finding him a professorship. He had a Ph.D., to be sure. But it was essentially in international law or international relations. He had not published anything in academic journals, except an article that he and Wilson had written jointly for the *American Political Science Review*, his only peer-reviewed journal article to date. In fact, if his reputation was high, Moynihan's academic qualifications were not particularly impressive at that stage. His B.A. degree from Middlebury and some of the credits for his master's at Tufts were in naval science. He had no degree from the London School of Economics. "He couldn't calculate a chi square," said one of his closest friends.[22] He had not published the book for which he had been given his job at Syracuse. He had part of one brilliant book (*Beyond the Melting Pot*) to his credit, and a series of well-researched and persuasively argued articles in *The Reporter* and *Commentary* and elsewhere on a variety of topics, but on none of which he could be called an academic expert. So Harvard's reservations were understandable, and Harvard's willingness to give him a job creditable.

The academic discipline of urban studies, when founded by Martin Meyerson and Edward C. Banfield and a number of other thinkers in the 1950s, had been a gentle backwater. Scholars were working on the theory of planning, on urban renewal (which, in the joke of the time, "equals Negro removal"), on city politics. James Q. Wilson had written his doctoral dissertation on Negro politics, but in the textbook he published jointly with Banfield in 1963, *City Politics,* only one out of twenty-one chapters was about African Americans.[23] Now suddenly, after Watts, "urban studies" had become a euphemism for the hottest and fiercest political issue of the day, the problem of poor, angry black people in the inner cities. Harvard, always keen to offer expertise to politicians, desperately needed someone whose experience accredited him in a field where there were few generally accepted academic experts.

It was remarkably generous of Wilson to step down to make room for his friend. Wilson originally proposed that Moynihan should come to Cambridge as a lecturer.[24] Once one is a lecturer at Harvard, Wilson says, he can stay as long as he likes. Wilson thought that Moynihan was not going to remain an academic all his life, so tenure didn't matter. But it mattered to Moynihan. Wilson thinks this attitude is part of the legacy of his childhood. "Pat has always worried about where his next job is coming from. If you come from his background, broken family, living in the streets of New York, you can understand." So Wilson said, "If tenure matters to you, I will work it out." He was as good as his word. He approached Theodore Sizer, dean of the School of Education, and arranged for Moynihan to be given a professorship with tenure there, and he duly became director of the Joint Center.

The Center had been founded in 1959. Its first director was Martin Meyerson.[25] He attracted the interest of Paul Ylvisaker of the Ford Foundation, who had been deeply involved in the War on Poverty and had found small amounts of money to bring scholars from impoverished Southern Negro colleges to Moynihan's seminar at Wesleyan. Although the Center occupied modest premises in Cambridge, first above what is now Sage's Market on Church Street and then in the yellow frame building nearby that now houses the Harvard Institute of Sanskrit Studies, it was well financed. Ford alone gave it grants of about $1 million a year.[26]

So when Moynihan arrived he was able to make the Center something of an intellectual powerhouse and focus in a field that had suddenly acquired urgent importance. He gave a weekly lunch, with a reception beforehand, which was "a hot ticket," according to one regular attendee.[27] Everyone who was working in urban studies had to be there, and so did outstanding graduate students, including the educationist Mary Jo Bain, later an assistant secretary of Health, Education and Welfare in the Clinton administration, the sociologist David Cohen, the writer Edward J. Epstein and Chester E. "Checker" Finn, who was to work for Moynihan in India and later in the Senate.

The Moynihans soon settled into a very pleasant family life in Cambridge. Liz and Magda Polanyi discovered a large house belonging to the university on Francis Avenue, behind Memorial Hall, close to the Divinity School.[28] Nobody wanted it because it was too big and too gloomy. But the Moynihans loved it. "When it was painted it was cheerful," says Liz, "and kids always help to make a place so." The children had spent a year in the public schools in Middletown, but now Tim started fifth grade at Shady Hill, a local private school in Cambridge, while Maura and John went to the public school near Francis Avenue. Pat and Liz soon made plenty of friends, especially the Glazers, who lived around the corner, and Ken and Kitty Galbraith, who also lived on Francis Avenue. The Wilsons, the Glazers and the Moynihans had a movie club. A good deal of ingenuity went into finding appropriate movies; as a tease, Jim Wilson once spent a good deal of time trying, without success, to find Fred Astaire's *Top Hat*, which was the only movie shown on board the USS *Quirinus*, and which Pat had consequently seen several dozen times.[29]

Pat rapidly established himself as a star at Harvard, constantly in demand by the media. He became the darling of the networks and made a powerful television documentary about cities and their racial problems for NBC. He also produced essays on the distempers of the time — such as his speech to the Phi Beta Kappa fraternity at Harvard in the spring of 1967 — of surpassing elegance and wisdom. He did not, however, find the time for much deep scholarship, and there were those at Harvard who did not wholly accept him. For the time being, however, Moynihan made himself the focus of a great deal of attention by the faculty seminar he ran on the Coleman report on equality of educational opportunity.

The very first day he arrived at Harvard, in the spring of 1966, Moynihan met a group of colleagues in the Faculty Club.[30] One of them was Seymour Martin Lipset, who greeted him with, "Hello, Pat, guess what Coleman's found!" The Coleman report sprang from the provision of Section 402 of the great Civil Rights Act of 1964, that the commissioner of education should report to the president and the Congress on the lack of equal educational opportunities for individuals "by reason of race, color, religion or national origin."[31]

Professor James Coleman of Johns Hopkins University was one of a small committee of social scientists hired by the government to carry out this survey. Information was collected from and about some 570,000 children, 60,000 teachers and more than 4,000 schools. School facilities, teacher qualifications, resources and every other kind of input were inventoried and compared to outputs in terms of reading and other scores.

The purpose behind this massive exercise in quantitative social science, of course, was to demonstrate what the great majority of educationists then believed, that black and other minority children were educated in schools that had unequal facilities. Coleman himself told an interviewer while the survey was under way, "You know yourself the difference is going to be striking." What was striking, in the event, was how small the differences turned out to be.

The one characteristic that showed a consistent relationship to students' test performance was one to which most black children were denied access: classmates from affluent homes. When other things were equal, the data showed, factors such as the amount of money spent per pupil, the quality of physical plants and buildings, the number of books in the library or even differences in the curriculum made little difference to the children's performance.

The whole report shattered some of the deepest American assumptions, not only about education, but also about equality and about the relationship between equality of condition and equality of opportunity. Since discussion of the report focused on the lack of equality between groups, and particularly between blacks and whites, rather than on the differences among individuals, the report also raised sharp questions about race, and about the extent to which government could do anything to diminish racial inequality.

Since these were the very questions raised by the Moynihan Report, it was remarkably courageous of Pat Moynihan to hurl himself back into the fray. But that is exactly what he did. It was in a sense because of the accident of Jim Wilson finding him a tenured professorship in the Education School that he now focused on the educational aspect of racial inequality. But the Coleman report did go straight to the heart of the liberal assumptions about the relationship between public policy and social outcomes. And it did have relevance for the whole interaction of politics and social science.

Moynihan was not shy about taking the lead in examining the implications of Coleman. Together with a colleague from the Education School, Professor Thomas Pettigrew, he organized a faculty seminar.[32] He took the precaution of securing a modest budget from the Carnegie Corporation, some of which was spent on entertainment. "It was quite something, that seminar," one of its leading participants recalled later. "Pat always had the very best booze and the best cigars." He also understood how to generate intellectual enthusiasm and the sense that something of national importance was taking place every week at the Harvard Faculty Club. Harvard had seen nothing quite like it since the great days of Henry Kissinger's disarmament seminar, a dozen years earlier, at which the future strategic policies of the Kennedy administration were hammered out and the nucleus of the elite which was to implement them in government was brought together. Statisticians, economists, pediatricians, approached Moynihan in Harvard Yard and asked him if they could come along. Education had suddenly become fashionable. Jason Epstein from Random House and the *New York Review of Books* and Charles E. Silberman from *Fortune* came up from New York. Altogether, eighty people took part. Moynihan had shown Harvard what a draw he could be. He had also demonstrated that the focus of intellectual interest in the United States was shifting from international to domestic affairs.

Eventually, the seminar was to lead to more than one fierce row. One concerned the genetic basis of differential performance by black and white students. After all, if there was a difference between the outcomes of the two groups, and that difference could not be explained by wide differences in inputs, it was tempting to invoke genetically caused differences in ability. In 1969, Dr. Arthur Jensen of the University of California at Berkeley duly put forward the hypothesis that heredity might account for the differences between the IQs of individual blacks and whites and of whites and blacks as a group, a conclusion tentatively supported by a Harvard professor, Richard Herrnstein, two years later in the *The Atlantic Monthly,* who envisioned American society being sorted into "inherited castes." (Many years later Herrnstein coauthored, with Charles Murray, *The Bell Curve,* a book that caused a bitter controversy.)

The essays generated by the Moynihan seminar, which Random House published in 1972, showed a general agreement about the lessons of the Coleman report. But by the time they appeared, the social science community was bitterly divided both over what precisely the report meant, and over its implications for public policy. By 1969, as these academic rows were surfacing publicly, Moynihan was (for the time being) long gone from Harvard. But the debates over the Coleman report had nevertheless intensified his skepticism about traditional liberal policies and sharpened his criticisms of at least some of their defenders. "I think it had an enormous influence on his thinking," says James Q. Wilson. "It was a classic example of Pat paying attention to facts other people preferred to ignore. I think Pat felt that the Coleman report showed that simply spending money will not solve a problem that has a cultural root, and I think this view of his has remained essentially unchanged since then."[33]

Moynihan wrote, jointly with Frederick Mosteller, a Harvard social scientist, the introductory essay to the book of collected papers written for the seminar. However much Professor Mosteller contributed to earlier sections of the essay, there is little doubt that the concluding section expressed the way Moynihan's mind was moving at the time.

> It is simply extraordinary that so much has been done, and — again — scarcely to be remarked that it has not been done flawlessly . . . No small achievement! In truth, a splendid one. More the reason, as even more difficult goals are set for the future, to pause and take note of what has been accomplished. It truly is not sinful to take modest satisfaction in our progress.
>
> What is needed is innovation, experiment, effort, measurement, analysis. What may be hoped for is a process by which the great gaps separating the educational achievement of different ethnic/racial groups begin to narrow.[34]

The Moynihan Report, after all, had set out a case for national action. Now, in his response to the Coleman report, Moynihan was still ostensibly calling for national action. But in the same breath he called for "modest self-satisfaction," which sounds almost like national self-congratulation. He called not so much for vigorous government intervention, but for "measurement and analysis" alongside "innovation, experiment, effort." In an article in *The Public Interest* in 1972, he made even plainer how far he had become skeptical of the interventionist liberal tradition.[35] "The most striking aspect of educational expenditure," he wrote, "is how large it has become"; it had risen at almost 10 percent per annum, while the GNP had risen only by under 7 percent. "It is simply not clear that school expenditure is the heart of the problem." And he went further. Greater expenditure on education, he argued, might actually create greater inequality. How so? "Any increase in school expenditure," he wrote, "will in the first instance accrue to teachers, who receive about 68 percent of the operating expenditure of elementary and secondary schools. That these are estimable and deserving persons none should doubt, but neither should there be any illusion that they are deprived." Shortly after the education seminars, Moynihan crossed Harvard Yard and was heckled by a group of students about his involvement in the Nixon administration. He told them with some irritation that they were "defending a class interest." He meant that 70 percent of the money spent on education went to salaries. Because many Harvard students were likely to end up as teachers, they would naturally favor high social expenditure. The argument was perhaps overstretched. But at this stage of his life, Moynihan's impatience with liberal orthodoxies and his conviction that these were ultimately class-based were unmistakable. With teachers earning an average of $10,000, he argued in his 1972 article, and with many of them married women with well-paid husbands, "increasing educational expenditures will have the short-run effect of income inequality."

By the time those words were published, Moynihan had been through a whole cycle and was back again at Harvard. They probably misrepresent his state of mind in 1967 and 1968. For in 1967, he gave a lecture to the Harvard chapter of the Phi Beta Kappa fraternity, a lecture that expresses a surprising empathy and even sympathy with the student radicalism that so puzzled and infuriated friends like Nathan Glazer and Seymour Martin Lipset. The lecture, to which Moynihan gave the title "Nirvana Now" when it was published in essay form, is a classic illustration of how Moynihan at his best has always looked behind ideological name-calling to the realities of human feelings.[36] At the very time when he was coming to feel that the national disease might be hypochondria, and when he was most irritated by the negativism of the more radical liberals, he was still able to enter into the mind of the disenchanted and the dissenters and indeed to express their anger and disappointment more eloquently than most of them could express their own feelings.

In "the flamboyance of the hippies, the bitterness of the alienated college youth," he began by suggesting, in "the outrageousness of the New Left, . . . we may be witnessing the first heresies of liberalism."

Secular liberalism, he argued, had become the accepted creed of the ruling elites of the Western world, and the current wave of protest against this established church showed striking similarities with the great heresies of earlier ages. The New Left, for example, departing sharply from the materialism of earlier, working-class radicalism, was rebelling not only against materialism, but also against the rational commitment to logic and consistency "that can lead from game theory at the Rand Corporation to the use of napalm in Vietnam."

Who are these young people? he asked. They reminded him, he said, of the Christians newly arrived in second-century Rome, as they were represented by the aristocratic Epicurean Celsus: outrageous people, "bad citizens, refusing public employment and avoiding service in the army," boasting that "fathers and tutors . . . are mad or blind." For them, "the weavers and cobblers only are wise, they only have the secret of life!" To be a sinner, for them, was the only way to be saved.

He trawled through history, finding parallels between the unhappy rebels from American liberal secular society in the late 1960s and other heresies: the followers of the seventeenth-century Jewish cabalist Sabbatai Zevi with his doctrine of the holiness of sin, the Brethren of the Free Spirit in the medieval Low Countries or the Ranters of the English Revolution, with their cheerful chorus,

> About, about, ye Joviall rout,
> Dance antick like Hob-goblins;
> Drink and roar, and swear and whore,
> But yet no brawls or squoblings.

Implicitly, he compared to these heretics against past religious orthodoxy the young woman whom Hunter S. Thompson had interviewed in San Francisco's Haight-Ashbury. "I love the whole world," she told Thompson, "I am the divine mother, part of Buddha, part of God. Whatever turns me on is a sacrament: LSD, sex, my bells, my colors . . . that is the Holy Communion, you dig?" Perhaps not, the Catholic in Moynihan made him add. But he quoted G. K. Chesterton, another unorthodox Catholic controversialist: heresy is truth gone astray.

Not only did Moynihan, on the eve of yielding to his most conservative impulses, show a surprising sympathy for ranters and hippies. He might resent the unpatriotic character of the New Left; but that did not stop him drawing up a formidable bill of indictment against the ways in which liberal America had gone wrong. In three ways in particular, he told the Harvard students, many of them at that very moment trembling on the edge of dropping out, or at least of joining the New Left, America faced problems that arose from the tendencies of secular liberalism.

One was the desire to export the American system worldwide, "an effort doomed to fail." He quoted Michael Oakeshott, the LSE guru, that "to try to do something which is inherently impossible is always a corrupting enterprise." American democratic values were not yet secure at home. Secondly, "We have not been able to get rid of racism," he said, "or to secure an equal place for Negroes in our society." And, third, it was true that as the life of the educated elite in America became more rational, "the wellsprings of emotion do dry up." To the rational liberal, "the tribal attachments of blood and soil appear somehow unseemly and primitive"; that was why Americans had found it so hard to accept the persistence of ethnicity both at home and abroad.

So it was possible, he said, "not only to sympathize with the new protest, but to see much that is valid in it." At the same time, it was dangerous. To see history as evolving ever onward and upward from the peat bogs to the 1964 Democratic platform was too simple. Yet "things are better, and where they are best is in the liberal industrial democracies of the North Atlantic world." The rule of law, with its acknowledgment of the frailty of man and the persistence of sin and failure, was "not to be frittered away in deference to a mystique of youth." Yet "what we must do first of all is listen. Young people are trying to tell us something." We should neither brush aside the just criticisms of the new heretics, he was saying, nor out of panic surrender to their unworkable remedies.

This speech comes as close as Moynihan ever has to defining his political philosophy in a single discourse. It is a complex, subtle attempt at reconciling freedom and order, the public and the individual, pessimism and pride, in the effort to build an inhabitable society on foundations of truth. Many recurring themes of his thinking are touched on: among them trust in the central, Whig tradition of American faith in liberty and progress, tempered by a ruthless commitment to veracity and to self-examination. To this he added a sense, drawn no doubt from the eighteenth-century Irish politician Edmund Burke, of the place of the living in the historic procession between the dead and those to come. But perhaps most revealing is the rhetorical surprise with which he ended his speech: a fey anecdote that nevertheless reveals how deeply Moynihan has retained a Catholic sensibility among the underpinnings of his Whiggish humanism.

The fable concerns the building of the great Catholic Shrine of the Immaculate Conception in Washington, paid for with the pittances of "truck drivers, coal miners and cleaning women." It gains some of its effect from the contrast between the fairy-tale description, tongue in cheek, of what is, after all, not generally regarded as a masterpiece of architectural taste, and the sting in the sermon's tail. For Moynihan the American patriot, like Moynihan the American Catholic, acknowledges the beauty of the resplendent structure, but never forgets to ask in what spirit it has been built.

> Nothing was spared of precious metal and lustrous stone. Nothing was spared by way of design: elements of every architectural tradition in the world were skillfully incorporated in the soaring facade and billowing dome. At last it was finished, and there followed a triumphant week of procession and ceremony, chorus and sermon. Then silence fell. The next morning a child was praying in the crypt when a vision of Our Lady appeared. Smiling that most beatific of all smiles, She looked down and said, "Build a beautiful church on this site."[37]

That first time at Harvard was a happy one for the Moynihans. It took a lot of work for Liz to turn 19 Francis Avenue into the family home she had always wanted, but before long it was done. If Pat remained scarred by the reception of the Report, the wounds were healing. To be a professor at Harvard was not nothing. To have put himself at the center of one of the most significant intellectual and political debates of the time was just what he had wanted to do. Teaching Harvard students like Checker Finn and Ed Epstein was a pleasure. And Pat found time for an immense outpouring of work: op-ed pieces, reviews, articles, lectures in which he both hammered out his own position on a score of issues and did his best to convert others to his evolving views. From the point of view of his own career, the most important was a talk that he gave to the national board of the liberal pressure group Americans for Democratic Action at the Willard

Hotel in Washington on September 23, 1967.[38] That summer, as in every other summer except while they were in India, the Moynihans retreated to their rural fastness at Pindars Corners. There, while the country contemplated the consequences of the Detroit riot, Pat set out to challenge the cherished orthodoxy of those who had hitherto been his liberal allies.

He began his speech by saying that, from the "middling vantage point known generally as liberalism," two alternative views were possible: that the nation was entering a period of political instability from which it would not emerge intact; or that it would not only survive, but emerge having demonstrated anew the deep sources of stability in American life. The problem, violence abroad and violence at home, he considered, was clearly the doing of liberals. The Vietnam War was thought up by, and was being managed by, the men John F. Kennedy brought to Washington; it was liberals who put us "waist deep in the big muddy." And this was even more true of the violence at home. The riot-torn summer of 1967 followed one of the most extraordinary periods of liberal legislation, liberal electoral victory, and liberal domination of the media. Some of the worst violence occurred in Detroit, a city with one of the most liberal administrations in the nation. Both in Asia and in America, the situation was likely to get worse.

What was to be done? He offered his liberal audience three propositions for their guidance and labeled them "the politics of stability." His message was sharp and troubling. The country was falling apart. If liberals did not face realities and act to put things right, the job would be done by others in ways they wouldn't like.

First, liberals "must see more clearly that their essential interest is in the stability of the social order," and that, "given the present threats to that stability, they must seek out and make much more effective alliances with political conservatives." In passing, he mentioned the conservative Republican Congressman Melvin Laird of Wisconsin, to whose collection of *Republican Papers* he was to contribute another notable essay early in 1968.[39] It was just another sign that he was beginning to keep different intellectual company.

Then, he argued, liberals must get rid of the notion that the nation — and especially the cities of the nation — could be run from agencies in Washington. "The real business of Washington in our age," he said, "is pretty much to run the world." Given the priority that the United States government would always give to foreign affairs, a way would have to be found for keeping domestic programs going, and that meant decentralizing control of them.

Liberals, thirdly, "must somehow overcome the curious condescension that takes the form of defending and explaining away anything, however outrageous, which Negroes, individually or collectively, might do." And he went on to sketch a pessimistic picture of what was happening "within the black community." A vast underclass had grown up in the northern cities, "a disorganized, angry, hurt group of persons easily given to self-destructive violence." Alongside it was "a group of radical, nihilistic youth," not members of this underclass but identifying with it, able to communicate with it and determined to use it as "an instrument of violent, apocalyptic confrontation with a white society they have decided is irredeemably militaristic and racist." He did not mince his words. All the signs showed that violence had not ended. Worse, "We must prepare for the onset of terrorism."

He then launched a sharp attack on the liberals whose "board of directors" he was addressing, but with whom he still formally identified. For liberals, the onset of violence and the probability of terrorism posed "a special problem that derives in a sense from our own decencies." They had blamed themselves for the shortcomings of the poor. A "terrifying example" was the people who had called James Coleman a racist for concluding that low educational achievement by blacks was the fault, not of poor schools, but of their own family background and that of their classmates. It is not hard to guess that Moynihan was thinking, as he spoke, not only of Coleman, but of himself.

"The time for confronting the realities of black and white has come in America," he said. "It will not be pretty." There is an ambiguity in such language, and Moynihan must have been aware of it. At one level, he meant that liberals must work harder at understanding social realities and translating the politics of stability into programs. At another, he was declaring his independence from organized liberalism and proclaiming his availability to work with others who were willing to ignore the liberal pieties and confront what he saw as the dire realities of the American city in 1967. If so, the response was dramatic, and from an unexpected direction.

Over the next year, a strange courtship ritual unfolded between two of the unlikeliest political partners, the New York liberal Democrat who was teaching at Harvard and the man who New York liberals and Harvard professors most liked to demonize and who often repaid the compliment with interest: Richard M. Nixon.

No episode in Moynihan's life, perhaps, not even the Moynihan Report itself, has been so misunderstood as this crossover to the Nixon White House. It has sometimes been interpreted as an ideological conversion, a road-to-Damascus transformation from liberal into conservative. Alternatively, it has been presented as a cynical career maneuver. Moynihan himself, on the other hand, brushes aside inquiry as if it were a logical, almost inevitable move. If the president of the United States asks you to help, he says, you help him.[40] It is true that he had always respected the office with something close to reverence: many Democrats who were brought up when Franklin D. Roosevelt was in the White House felt that way. Another point he made in an interview was that, in late 1967 and early 1968, "There was no Democratic party."[41] That was an exaggeration. But this was the winter of the party's discontent. It was riven between the partisans of Lyndon Johnson and the adherents of Robert Kennedy. The president and his administration were distracted from domestic concerns by the war. The liberals themselves were bitterly divided between those who remained loyal to Johnson and those who were looking for more radical leadership. For someone like Moynihan, who believed that the country was in trouble, that something must be done, and who had come to believe that his liberal friends were not likely to do the right thing, it seemed logical at least to see what other alliances might be available.

One of the partners Nixon had acquired when he agreed, after his humiliating defeat in the California gubernatorial election of 1962, to move to New York and become the senior partner of the law firm that became Nixon, Mudge, Rose, Guthrie and Alexander was an ebullient young lawyer called Leonard Garment.[42] Jewish, brought up in the Crown Heights section of Brooklyn, the son of a small clothing manufacturer in Queens, Garment played saxophone for a while in 1944 with the Woody Herman Big Band.[43] He was a Democrat and thought of himself as a liberal. He had hosted a fund-raising party at his Brooklyn home for Bobby Kennedy.[44] Nixon, to his surprise, waved all this away. And, even more to his surprise, Garment found himself at ease with Nixon, with whom he shared a poor-boy-made-good mentality.

In September 1967, Garment read a newspaper report of Pat Moynihan's speech to the ADA.[45] It caught his eye because of its title:

After Detroit, "the politics of stability" sounded attractive. Nice work if you could get it. He wrote a letter to Moynihan, who sent him the reading copy of the ADA speech and a note.[46] The two men met and got on. Garment was the head of Nixon's small speechwriting team, and he sent the Moynihan ADA speech to Richard Whalen, one of Nixon's chief speechwriters until they fell out in 1968.[47] Both Garment and Whalen suggested that Nixon should use Moynihan's ideas as the basis for a big speech he was planning, to the National Association of Manufacturers (NAM). At that point, George Romney, the former Michigan governor who had been the head of American Motors, was leading in the polls for the Republican presidential nomination, but Nixon was at least as much concerned with Nelson Rockfeller, the governor of New York, who was hesitating: "In, out, in, out," said Leonard Garment.[48] The speech, Garment wrote, should summon the businessmen (Garment actually called them "fat cats") "to the mountaintop." It should be "a blunt hard-hitting message on the social crisis which confronts all America," which had been Moynihan's theme. Nixon agreed, and Whalen wrote a strong speech. After the speech, Nixon wrote personally to Moynihan, who in the meantime had written to Nixon, offering him an open invitation to speak at Harvard.[49] In the NAM speech, Nixon quoted directly the passage in which Moynihan had urged liberals to ally themselves with conservatives:

> In his eloquent address to Americans for Democratic Action last September, Daniel Moynihan held out a hand that true conservatives should be quick to grasp. He warned his fellow liberals that they should "see more clearly that their essential interest is in the stability of the social order, and that given the present threats to that stability, it is necessary to seek out and make much more effective alliances with political conservatives who share that concern, and who recognize that unyielding rigidity is just as much a threat to the continuity of things as is an anarchic desire for change."[50]

Nixon picked up that offer. "Let us not let that opportunity pass," he said.

There was still a long road to walk before Nixon asked Moynihan to work for him, and before Moynihan accepted. Moynihan spoke for Robert Kennedy in his brief, dramatic campaign. On June 4, he gave the commencement address at the New School for Social Research in Manhattan; it was a robust series of reflections on what he called "the new racialism," including a blunt warning that if ethnic quotas ever came to Harvard, something like seven out of every eight Jewish undergraduates and a higher proportion in the graduate schools would have to leave. After the lecture, he went to bed at the Harvard Club. He woke to find his talk on the front page of the *New York Times,* "above the fold," and Robert Kennedy dead.[51]

That same summer Melvin Laird published a similar piece written by Moynihan in late 1967 in his collection of essays. Laird justified his inclusion of a paper from a non-Republican on the grounds that Moynihan was a man prepared "to set aside the irrational argument as to who is most aware of the problems in our society and to turn instead to the more relevant questions of what to do about them." Interestingly, Moynihan was looking ahead, past the all-absorbing 1968 election, to the disaster that would be the election "next year or five years from now, of a determined right-wing President." That would actually take twelve long years.

In the course of the year, he continued to speak out. But by October 24, 1968, Moynihan was writing to Nixon, as a Democrat, but also as a volunteer.

Dear Mr. Nixon,

I was greatly impressed by your radio address on the subject of employment. It seems we are finally beginning to understand that employment is the key to stability, a fact which you made clear and explicit.

You hardly need letters from Democrats to tell you this. In truth, I am writing with something else in mind: the apparent intention of the Business Council to press for a 5.5 per cent unemployment rate. . . .

I feel that they do not understand what such unemployment rate would do to the urban Negro social structure . . . A rate of 5.5 per cent for the work force generally means 11 per cent for Negro males, and 35 per cent for Negro teenagers. It means more broken families, more welfare recipients, more persons sent to prison . . . more of all the problems you will be trying to resolve.

. . . If you like, after November (assuming everything goes well for you!) I should be happy to show this material to whomever of your advisers might be interested . . . they can make such use of it as they choose.[52]

As soon as Nixon was elected, Nixon's aide H. R. Haldeman, speaking for Nixon, told Len Garment to "Get Moynihan!"[53] A few days after the election, I had lunch with the Moynihans on Francis

Avenue. When Pat announced that he was going to work for Nixon in the White House, I almost fell off my chair. Many of Moynihan's friends tried with something close to despair to persuade him to change his mind. Blair Clark, for example, a prominent New York Democrat, recalls a "pub crawl" around Manhattan which failed to deter his old friend.

There are two interesting questions about that decision. The first, and the easier to answer, is why the victorious Nixon wanted to hire as his chief domestic adviser a Harvard liberal. For one thing, Nixon was more ambivalent than hostile toward Harvard. He saw Harvard as objectively a positive value, says Len Garment: he liked the idea that the two Harvard professors, Kissinger and Moynihan, would vouch for his administration's policies. For all his bitter fulminations against the East Coast, Ivy League elite, Nixon wanted to feel that he had "made it," that he had compelled even those who had once despised him as a crude outsider to recognize his merit. More important, Nixon was intelligent enough to realize that the racial anger of which the Detroit riot was a potent symbol would be the most important and dangerous domestic issue he would have to confront as president. Moynihan was the acknowledged expert on "urban problems," then the euphemism of choice for racial conflicts. He had said enough to make it plain that he was not one of those liberals who had retreated into a circle of wagons, but was prepared to work with Republicans. So it was entirely logical to "get Moynihan."

The much more difficult question is why Moynihan would want to work for Nixon. He was, after all, as he has said, "baptized a Catholic and born a Democrat." Even after deciding to take not one but a string of high-level jobs in Republican administrations, he never pretended to be a Republican. Moreover, he never ceased to be a liberal, at least in his own mind. He never wavered in his concern for black people, as indeed his October 1968 letter to Nixon clearly shows.

His motives for holding his nose and taking the plunge into the deep end of the Nixon administration were complex. He was resentful about the way in which, as he saw it, he had been unfairly attacked by some liberals, and genuinely convinced that liberals were making the nation's acute problems worse, not better. He was skeptical about the ability of the Johnson administration, or a successor Humphrey administration, given Washington's preoccupation with the war, to spare resources and attention for the domestic action he thought was desperately needed. He did think he had a duty to serve a president who asked for his help.

Above all, he had an idea. He thought it might work where the War on Poverty had failed. He referred to it in passing in his paper for Melvin Laird.[54] He saw in it the possibility of a simultaneous solution to two linked problems that had long preoccupied him: the destruction of the family, and especially the black family; and the creation of an underclass. He conceived it as a scheme for getting public money directly to the poor, unmediated by officious and uncomprehending middle-class professors and bureaucrats. It was still only little more than instinct, a strategy that had not yet been worked into a plan. But he was already thinking in terms of a family assistance program, even though it was others who gave it that name later. The point was that he thought there was more chance of Richard Nixon than of the Democrats doing what needed to be done. He was ready to gamble his career that salvation had arrived from such an unsuspected direction, and that his moment had come.

BOOK II

7

Tory Men, Whig Measures

WORKING FOR NIXON IN THE
WHITE HOUSE

A sound conservative government, I understand:
Tory men and Whig measures.

— Benjamin Disraeli, *Coningsby*

IN AUGUST 1971 a certain Richard A. Winter, a management educator, wrote to Moynihan saying that he had been so impressed
by something he had said to *Time* magazine that he had had part
of it cast in bronze and addressed to President Nixon: "The first
[thing] is to be of good cheer and good conscience. Depressing, even
frightening things are being said about this administration. They are
not true. This has been a company of honorable and able men, led by
a president of singular courage and compassion in the face of a sometimes awful knowledge of the problems and probabilities that confront him."[1]

Moynihan has written that his relationship with Richard Nixon
"was excellent indeed."[2] As late as the summer of 1972, long after he
had left the White House, he composed a glowing tribute to Nixon,
for *Life* magazine. Based on a conversation with the president, though
without quoting him directly, it praised his diplomatic achievements
and his steadfastness and even suggested that he represented a
"Stevensonian" concept of civility.[3] This was too much for many of
his correspondents. An old friend, Alan Pifer of the Carnegie Corporation, wrote that he found the article "nauseating" and said, "I hate
to see you write that kind of tripe."[4] Only the columnist Joseph
Alsop, unrelenting advocate of the Vietnam War, praised it. Yet if the
Life piece was a touch over the top, it was not mere flattery. Even

after the Watergate cloud had burst in torrents of abuse and disaster, Moynihan stuck by Nixon, and by his own coolly favorable judgment of him.

There were several reasons for Moynihan's indulgent, even quixotic attitude toward Nixon. One, certainly, was that he was prepared to give the benefit of the doubt to the ancient Middle Eastern axiom that the enemy of my enemy is my friend. He had, as he saw it, been bitterly and unjustly abused by a class of liberals who could be seen without too much exaggeration as the sort of people who defended Alger Hiss in the teeth of all the evidence that he was a Soviet spy. "There was a great deal of class and cultural conflict involved in that painful and protracted division," he has said.[5] Irving Kristol "got it right," he feels,[6] when he said of Joseph McCarthy that the American people knew he was against communism, but of American liberals they knew no such thing. Moynihan and his friends simply did not share the prevailing liberal judgment that the way Richard Nixon had behaved at the time of the great hunt for communists in the 1950s put him beyond the political pale.

There were other, more immediate factors, too. Moynihan had an agenda. He believed that the country was in a dire situation. In the course of the year 1968 he had seen Robert Kennedy, whom he admired and for whom he had campaigned, assassinated. After Martin Luther King's death, he saw American cities, starting with New York, about which he cared passionately, and Washington, where he lived, smashed and burned by rioting mobs. He believed that both the new radical black leadership and the white liberals who went too far, as he saw it, to meet and agree with the radicals were profoundly dangerous. He thought he understood what was happening, and what little might be done to improve a situation that he diagnosed as near desperate. And he understood, first, that the Democrats were out of power, perhaps for a long time, and then that, if and when they did come back, there was little hope that they would pay attention to him. "By the end of 1968," he told the author, "RFK was dead. Martin Luther King was dead. LBJ had abdicated. There wasn't a Democratic party!"[7]

There were, finally, human dimensions. Moynihan never developed any great personal warmth for Richard Nixon. But nor, on the other hand, did he have any personal quarrel with him. Nixon listened, often with flattering attention, to what Dr. Moynihan had to say. He encouraged Professor Moynihan to give him reading lists. At least at first, he seemed open to Counselor Moynihan's recommendations, even to some that seemed eccentric to the conservative Republicans who for the most part staffed the Nixon White House. But there were men in the Nixon White House, like William Safire and especially Leonard Garment, for whom he felt genuine affection and others in the wider Nixon administration, like Robert Finch and George Shultz, whom he admired.

Above all, Moynihan loved to be in the White House. It was the focus of power. He had watched it as it is obsessively watched in Washington, without ever working there as an insider. In personal terms, he was willing to pay a price for the power and the glory that go with a White House office. His wife refused point-blank to come down to Washington with him. She stayed in Cambridge with the children, and he lived a bachelor life in an apartment he rented from Sandy Vanocur of NBC, his old friend from London, now a star on-screen reporter. It was a modest place in Columbia Plaza, a vast warren of midpriced apartments between the State Department and the fancier Watergate in Foggy Bottom. That was where he slept. "So far as I know," his wife told me later, "he never ate there."

His life was lonelier than in the Tregaron years, not only because Liz was not there, but also because he was somewhat isolated in the Nixon White House. He had brought in personal staff who were devoted to him, including Stephen Hess, a liberal Republican and former Nixon biographer, and several of his Harvard graduate students, including Chester L. "Checker" Finn, Jr. But in those first two years there was an unmistakable state of siege about the whole administration.

Once, flying in to do a TV story myself on the 1970 Cambodia demonstrations, I made an appointment, without thinking, to see Moynihan in the bar of the Hay-Adams Hotel in Lafayette Square, opposite the White House, a place where we had had a few drinks in the past. I had not realized when I made the phone call that the White House was literally laagered by a ring of dozens of silver Metro buses. The square was full of half-naked students, longhaired and bearded. There were garish banners accusing the administration of every kind of bloodthirsty motive in Southeast Asia. Someone even produced the bleeding head of a lamb to make his point on the evening news. I watched Moynihan's head bobbing above the crowd of demonstrators, some of whom shouted obscenities at him, as he worked his way around the square toward me, unintimidated, but alone. He was conscious of the roiling rage on the Harvard campus, and of the potential threat of violence to his family. It was an eerie time for a Democrat to be working for Richard Nixon. For many of his students and even for some of his erstwhile friends, Pat Moynihan had gone over to the enemy.

From the beginning, he declined to be restricted to the narrow limits of his urban affairs brief. Even before Nixon arrived in the White House, Moynihan suggested to him that the White House floodlighting, which had been switched off as an economy-cum-public-relations measure by Lyndon Johnson, should be switched on again. "At a time when the most unassuming New England village floodlights its First Presbyterian Church as a matter of course, and most of the public buildings of Washington are brilliantly lit at night, the White House appears to be in permanent mourning." Nixon liked the idea.[8] In his personal contacts with the president, Moynihan, as ever, was not above a little judicious flattery. In September 1969, for example, he sent Nixon a memo congratulating the president on the worldwide response to a speech on a Nixon initiative, now long forgotten, called the "New Federalism." This idea, Moynihan somewhat implausibly reported, was "generally held" in London, where he had just been, "to be the most important domestic initiative since the New Deal."[9]

For all these occasional flights of hyperbole, however, Moynihan never left Nixon under any illusion that he had become his man. On two points, especially, he was very specific. He was a Democrat, not a Republican. And he was convinced that the Vietnam War was a mistake, and therefore, because of the price it carried, a crime.

One particular memo he wrote to H. R. Haldeman, the president's chief of staff and the stern guardian of his political interests, spells both points out in such a way that neither Haldeman nor Nixon could possibly have misunderstood his meaning.[10] It was hard for him to offer political advice, he said. "I have been an active Democrat and if they allow me (which alas I doubt) will be one again. But I do happen to know about serving a President of the United States." Last Friday, he went on, "I tried to state as clearly and openly as I could my feeling that the war is a political disaster which the president is not responsible for, and which in no circumstances should he allow himself to be labelled with."

There were, he said, two reactions in the room. "First, there seemed to be a number of people who quite clearly feel the American public is behind the war. Still. Second, there were at least a few persons who seem to think the war is some kind of presidential prerogative which we must not allow college boys or effeminate protesters to infringe. God have mercy if this mood prevails."

On this letter, Haldeman jotted "Not that but not cop out" and "only that P[resident] must make decisions — and staff must support." Not only was Moynihan being exceptionally blunt. He was doing so when, as he well understood, it would do him no good with the second most powerful man in the White House. Later, Haldeman dictated a note for his diary about how Nixon thought the only real enthusiasts in his White House were "Garment and Moynihan, and they aren't really on our side."[11]

The fact that Moynihan, as a Democrat, was never wholly trusted by Nixon's palace guard did not deter him from speaking his mind. After the revelation of the massacre at My Lai, for example, he wrote Nixon an anguished but subtle five pages. Vietnam, he said, was "the war of liberal anti-communism."[12] In personal terms, that meant it was "Johnson's war." That offered Nixon comfort. And Moynihan went on to suggest ways in which the nation could be led in a quest for "understanding." It could be argued, he said, that "the troops were worn out. They had taken too many casualties. Their lieutenant looks and sounds like a Southern psychotic. It is not the American character that came out at My Lai. It is what war can do to any character."

That might sound like the courtier providing excuses and rationales for his leader. But the memo went far deeper than that. "It has become obvious that we cannot 'win' the war," he said, something others, notably Henry Kissinger, did not have the courage to tell Nixon to his face. He dared to say that the reason he had spoken for Robert Kennedy (against Nixon) in 1968 was that he "gradually came to see what a disastrous mistake we had all made." He went on. "Something hideous happened at My Lai. . . . Look, if you will, at the pictures in *Time* this week. As a father of sons about the age of those lying dead in that Vietnam ditch, I shuddered." Moynihan feared, he said, that too many Americans would react by believing that "this is a hideous, corrupt society."

There is something in this memo, and in others that Moynihan wrote to Nixon, very different from what presidents are accustomed to receiving from their staff, something of authentic emotion, of Catholic ethics, of Moynihan's ever-present concern for the state of

America's reputation, even for America's soul. There is little flattery or even politic discretion. "K," Nixon scrawled on it with a thick pencil for his national security adviser, "what is your reaction to this memo?" One can imagine that both Nixon and Kissinger would have been taken aback by the fervor of its tone.

On May 9, 1970, at the time of the tumultuous demonstrations that followed the killings of students at Kent State and Jackson State, Moynihan sent the president an even more astonishing memo. The invasion of Cambodia had unleashed an extraordinary paroxysm of anger across the country, especially among students. On May 1, the president, in an aside heard and quoted by reporters, called the student demonstrators "bums." On May 4, four students were shot and killed by the National Guard at Kent State University in Ohio. Later two students were killed at Jackson State in Mississippi. "Yesterday in Cambridge," Moynihan wrote Nixon, "the SDS [the radical group Students for a Democratic Society] announced that my house would be burned during the night. The University asked my family to 'evacuate' and they, in effect, went into hiding. Six Divinity students guarded the house, and nothing finally happened. I don't know what will come tomorrow."[13]

Liz Moynihan remembers all too well what it felt like. There was a huge meeting at Soldiers Field, the Harvard football stadium, at which the radicals announced their plan to burn down the ROTC building. The "secondary target," they said, would be to trash the Moynihan home on Francis Avenue. "Trashing" was not a euphemism, not a joke. The demonstrators would smash someone's windows and pour the trash from the garbage cans into the house. One of Liz's neighbors, who worked for the university, stopped by to say he planned to take his family to their summer home on Cape Ann for safety. Liz called the schools and sent word for the children to go to a friend's house on the other side of the campus. Then she got hold of two of the babysitters, Harvard students who lived on their top floor. They pushed the furniture into the middle of the room and covered it with dust sheets. She grabbed the things that seemed most precious: three boxes of the manuscript of Pat's (never published) Negro family book, which she took to the Cambridge Trust Company for safety; photos of the kids and their favorite pets. Then she and the babysitters made a huge peace sign and left it on the pile of furniture. Finally she told the students to leave the house and mingle with the crowd.

She called Pat at the White House and was put through to him in the Oval Office. She told him not to come home whatever he did. Half an hour later, as she was contemplating defending her home with a baseball bat (and no one who knows her would doubt for a moment that she would have done so), she saw that a couple of black cars had driven up with four or five determined-looking guys in them. It turned out that Nixon himself had called and sent security. In the end, the Harvard Divinity School freshmen faced down the radicals, and neither the burning nor the trashing took place.

"Even so," Moynihan wrote, before he knew the family was out of danger, "I'm sticking here. I am choosing the interests of the administration over the interests of my children. But this would be the act of a fool if I did not feel free to tell you exactly what I think, and to feel that you at least were hearing me out."

He went on to say, "You were superb last night. What you said was masterful and truthful." Yet Nixon's aides, including Vice President Spiro T. Agnew, he thought, were "taking the low road." Moynihan went on courageously, "I don't think you can afford this. It seems absolutely necessary that you call a halt to . . . vulgar partisanship . . . and hysterical demagoguery (e.g. Agnew) of people theoretically on your team." And because there was "an air of national crisis," he asked, "should you not consider the possibility of a national [nonpartisan] government?"

Moynihan made no attempt to conceal his conviction that the Vietnam War was a disastrous error. "Unless I am mistaken," he wrote to the president in April 1969, "America has 'lost' its first war."[14] Worse, he went on, "the elite intelligentsia of the country are turning against the country — in science, in politics, in the fundamentals of patriotism. How can we not pay for this?"[15] Even some elements in the military were responding in the same way, he noted. They included, Moynihan pointed out, General David M. Shoup, former commandant of the marine corps, of all people, who had just written in *The Atlantic Monthly,* "America has become a militaristic and aggressive nation."

The truth was, and Moynihan was well aware of it, that the Nixon administration was deeply ambivalent in policy terms. The president genuinely believed that he could find better solutions than the Johnson administration and its attendant liberals for the country's deep social problems. He himself was considered to be free from racial bigotry, though the Watergate tapes would later reveal that, like many men of his generation, he used coarse and even at times anti-Semitic language. He was proud of the fact that more school desegregation took place under his administration than under Kennedy and Johnson.[16]

At the same time, Nixon had been elected president in part because of his "Southern strategy." In alliance with such a battle-hardened segregationist as Strom Thurmond, a leader of the Dixiecrat schism in the Democratic party and its presidential candidate in 1948, and other Southern Republicans, Nixon had offered the South reassurance and understanding. In the North, too, he had appealed subtly to those "ethnic" and other voters who felt that "things were moving too fast."

Moynihan played on this ambivalence, which divided not only the administration, but the president as well. No doubt he felt more than a slight echo of it in himself. From the start, after all, he was aware that it was abnormal that a birthright Democrat should find himself in such a key role at the elbow of a Republican president. He explained it to himself, in terms not of a conversion or a change of heart, but of his pragmatic desire to achieve certain policy outcomes he believed the nation needed. Certainly he used his place in Nixon's confidence to make some suggestions that no mere courtier would have made. In May 1970, for example, he brought to Nixon's attention that the widow of the great black writer and leader W.E.B. Du Bois, who had lived for many years with her husband in the Soviet Union, wanted to return to the United States "to visit, or to die, or whatever (she is now very old)."[17] She had been denied entry on the grounds that she was presumably a communist, Moynihan said. "I do not doubt that she was," he wrote airily. "But what possible difference could it make? Her husband was a truly great man who only very late in life became a kind of bitter Stalinist." And he added that he himself had recently tried to persuade a publisher to reissue one of Du Bois's books and had written an introduction to it. Nixon, known and feared by the entire Left as the remorseless scourge of communists, scribbled to his adviser John Ehrlichman "sounds like a good case for 'clemency.' Ask [Attorney General John N.] Mitchell to give me a recommendation." Mrs. Du Bois was duly admitted, visited the United States on two occasions, but chose not to return permanently and continued to make her home in Cairo.[18]

It was in this troubled and contradictory spirit, as the president's candid and unpredictable counselor on domestic affairs, that Moynihan wrote what became his most famous, or infamous, memorandum.

On January 26, 1970, having been in the White House for just over one year, Moynihan sent Nixon "a general assessment of the position of Negroes."[19] In quantitative terms, he proclaimed, "the American Negro is making extraordinary progress," and the same would appear to be true in political terms. In both cases, however, "there would seem to be counter-currents that pose a serious threat to the welfare of the blacks and to the stability of society, white and black."

The 1960s, he claimed, had seen the great breakthrough for blacks. One-third of all families of Negro and other races earned $8,000 or more in 1968, compared in constant dollars with 15 percent in 1960. Blacks were getting better jobs and more of them were staying in school and going to college.[20] In other respects, however, the situation of blacks was getting worse. Almost 30 percent of black babies, as against fewer than 5 percent of white babies, were born illegitimate. And antisocial behavior among young blacks remained extraordinarily high. "Apart from white racial attitudes," he suggested, "this is the biggest problem black Americans face, and in part it helps shape white attitudes. Black Americans injure one another."

So far, the memorandum was a factual summary of social data. Then Moynihan ventured, still in the same scientific tone, onto more controversial ground. "With no real evidence," he wrote,

> I would nonetheless suggest that a great deal of the crime, the fire setting, the rampant school violence, and other such phenomena in the black community have become quasi-politicized. Hatred — revenge — against whites is now an acceptable excuse for doing what might have been done anyway. This is bad news for any society, especially when it takes [the] form which the Black Panthers seem to have adopted. This social alienation among the black lower classes is matched, and probably enhanced, by a virulent form of anti-white feeling among portions of the large and prospering black middle class. It would be difficult to overestimate the degree to which young well-educated blacks detest white America.

Moynihan then moved on to the relationship between the black population and the Nixon administration. "There is a silent black majority as well as a white one," and politically moderate on all issues except racial equality.

It was Moynihan's second suggestion, though, that caused the trouble. "The time may have come," he wrote, "when the issue of race could benefit from a period of 'benign neglect.' The subject has been too much talked about. The forum has been too much taken over by hysterics, paranoids and boodlers on all sides. We may need a period in which Negro progress continues and racial rhetoric fades."

The administration should avoid "situations in which extremists of either race are given opportunities for martyrdom, heroics, histrionics or whatever." In particular, he suggested, it should ignore the Black Panthers, who were almost defunct as a group until the Chicago police raided their headquarters and turned them into heroes. He added one of those asides from the outside world in which his journalistic flair was always best displayed:

"You perhaps did not note on the society page of yesterday's *Times* that Mrs. Leonard Bernstein gave a cocktail party on Wednesday to raise money for the Panthers. Mrs. W. Vincent Astor was among the guests. Mrs. Peter Duchin, 'the rich blond wife of the orchestra leader,' was thrilled. 'I've never met a Panther,' she said. 'This is a first for me.'"

The president was ecstatic. Over the words "benign neglect," he wrote, "I agree." The whole page of his copy of the memo was ringed, underlined and marked in his handwriting. At the bottom he wrote, "K note?!" presumably to restrain any tendency Dr. Kissinger might have to gravitate to parties given by Mrs. Leonard Bernstein or her glittering ilk. And then he wrote, and it is hard to believe it was not with emphatic satisfaction, "The complete decadence of the American 'upper class' intellectual elite."

That memorandum was duly circulated around the White House staff and had comparatively few consequences at the time. Moynihan saw a copy of the memo with the president's excited scribbling on it and learned that it was to be sent to the cabinet.[21] He immediately saw the danger. He called Haldeman and said, "Get those annotated copies *back!*" So Haldeman sent out clean copies, and it was one of those that was leaked, first to a New Jersey newspaper. "P. [the president] also cranked up," Haldeman wrote in his diary, "about two major leaks in *New York Times* today, especially one of Moynihan memo about blacks. Wants complete freeze on *Times* etc."[22] To this day, it is not clear who did the leaking. Senator Moynihan thinks it was someone "who intended to show what bastards we were." His wife thinks it may have been an assistant to the White House economist Arthur Burns. With almost thirty years more experience of the nation's capital under his belt, the senator now comments with a single word: "Washington."[23] It was to do his reputation great damage. Yet it is absolutely clear from the text and the context that Moynihan did not mean that African Americans should be left in benign neglect, but that they needed a time when progress could continue and racial rhetoric fade.

This episode, the surfacing in a newspaper of a private memorandum, marked one of the chief milestones of Moynihan's career. Along with the reception of the Moynihan Report, it was the second of two incidents that hardened Moynihan and taught him how little consideration, let alone justice, a public man could count on receiving. If the accusations of racism after the publication of the Moynihan Report in 1965 scarred Moynihan's personality in certain lasting ways, the widespread misinterpretation of the "benign neglect" memo was just as painful.

Moynihan drew the conclusion that he couldn't win; that whatever he said was likely to be misinterpreted in an unfair and damaging way by a group of people he now thought of simply as "the liberals." His reaction may have been oversensitive but it was hardly surprising. He has remained tender on the issue. In private, he used to inveigh against the unfairness with which those two words have stuck to him like a tar baby. In public, he was and is generally stoical. But the response to the leaking of the "benign neglect" memo was a major event in his life. Privately, it toughened him against the unfairness of political life; publicly, for a decade or so, it widened the gap, fast becoming an abyss, between him and the liberals, his former companions.

Early in his time in the White House, Richard Nixon sent Moynihan a note asking him for a list of ten books to read. That says something about the president's lack of confidence in intellectual realms, more perhaps about his respect for his domestic counselor. The first book Moynihan chose was Robert Blake's biography of the great nineteenth-century British Conservative prime minister Benjamin Disraeli. He sent it along with a note suggesting that it was Tory men with Whig measures who changed England.[24] Nixon read the book all the way through, which, Moynihan admits, was more than he had done himself, and took the idea with great seriousness, at least for a time. At a critical moment in the greatest debate on domestic policy in his administration, Nixon quoted the words in the form in which Lord Randolph Churchill had used them in the book: "Tory men and Liberal measures have changed the world."[25]

That was a good, if minor, example of the role Moynihan played in the White House as an "ideas man." He used his journalistic flair for nosing out potential questions and issues that the administration would have to face, as well as making connections and coming up with graphic phrases to describe the administration's thinking.

A more significant example of this flair for spotting the issues of the future was a paper he sent to Nixon in August 1969, predicting that "female equality will be a major cultural/political force of the 1970s. We have educated women for equality in America, but have not really given it to them. Not at all. Inequality is so great that the dominant group either doesn't notice it, or assumes the dominated group likes it that way."[26]

Almost exactly a year later, he sent that memo to Nixon again, saying that it had been given greater topicality by the passage by Congress of the Equal Rights Amendment, and asking whether the president would like him to get a discussion group going. For a start, he said, "There ought to be more female appointments." As on many other subjects and occasions, Moynihan in this instance exaggerated Richard Nixon's openness to the sort of ideas that shocked traditional Republicans and overestimated his willingness to show political courage.

The supreme example of this willingness to think Richard Nixon a braver and more imaginative man than he was turned out to be the central drama of Moynihan's time in the Nixon White House. Nixon had hired him for his expertise on the racial divisions in American cities. But the main thing Moynihan hoped to achieve by his sojourn among the Republicans was to hammer out, and get Congress to approve, a bold new policy for dealing with the problem of welfare. The administration did not lose any time.

On January 23, 1969, only three days after his inauguration, President Nixon signed an executive order creating an Urban Affairs Council.[27] The idea, reflecting the widespread sense of a national domestic crisis focusing on racial conflict, urban disorder and social trauma evidenced by exploding welfare costs, was that it should be roughly equivalent to the National Security Council, set up in 1947 at a time of perceived international threat. The president was to be in the chair, and all the cabinet members except the secretaries of state, defense and the treasury were members. Moynihan was to be executive secretary to the council.

Eight days later, keeping to a tight deadline set by the president's chief of staff, "German shepherd" Haldeman, as he was known in Washington, Moynihan sent his first policy memo. It urged Nixon to send a message immediately calling for a national minimum standard for welfare payments. This approach to the welfare problem that was already emerging as one of the top items on the Nixon administration's agenda was extremely cautious. Within weeks, Moynihan was to be launched into one of the biggest political fights of his life, for what came to be called a Family Assistance Plan or, in other words, the policy of providing a guaranteed income to poor people. It helped to define his own political philosophy as well as his image in Washington and in the media.

Moynihan, however, did not come into the White House as the acknowledged advocate of such a plan. He became convinced only gradually that it was the answer — an answer that it would be practical to promote. The guaranteed income idea had a past. To be precise, it had two pasts: a conservative past and a liberal one. In the same volume of *Republican Papers,* edited by Nixon's defense secretary, Melvin Laird, in which Moynihan had made his first appearance in conservative company, was a paper by Milton Friedman, the great libertarian economist. In it, Friedman set out with his customary clarity the case for a "negative income tax" as an alternative to the sundry existing welfare programs.[28] (Friedman had first proposed this device as early as 1962.)[29] The essential idea, as he put it, "is to extend the income tax by supplementing the income of the poor by a fraction of their unused income tax exemptions and deductions." So, for example, if a family had a zero pretax income, it would have a negative taxable income of $3,000. With a 50 percent rate, it would be entitled to receive $1,500, leaving it with a posttax income of $1,500. Friedman claimed a number of advantages for this scheme. It would concentrate public funds on the poor who really need them. It would treat the poor as responsible individuals, giving them an incentive to help themselves. And it would help the poor more, while costing the taxpayer less, than current arrangements.

Throughout the 1960s, economists in Washington and in the universities kicked around the idea of a negative income tax. Already by

1966, an Office of Economic Opportunity task force was recommending its adoption. There was also increasing concern over the steep rise in the cost of welfare. In 1967, Nelson Rockefeller, as governor of New York, called a conference at the former Harriman mansion, Arden House, to plan "new approaches to public welfare."[30]

The idea was around, and the incentive to adopt it was becoming more pressing. And now it was the liberal Left that was taking it up. In early 1968, with Wilbur Cohen, the veteran advocate of welfare reform, newly appointed secretary of Health, Education and Welfare, the chances of a bold step toward some variant of the negative income tax looked good. Yet the Johnson administration, increasingly obsessed by the war in Vietnam, held back.

At first, the incoming Nixon administration, too, contented itself with a more cautious alternative: "national standards" to reduce disparities between Southern states like Mississippi, which were paying welfare recipients $20 a month, and Northern industrial states like New York or Michigan that were paying $100 a month. Early in November, however, right after his election victory, Nixon appointed Richard Nathan of the Brookings Institution as chairman of a new task force on welfare and poverty.[31] In the interval between Nixon's election and his inauguration, while the Nathan team was wondering how far to go, a welfare debate was beginning. At the same time, Moynihan's friends and colleagues on *The Public Interest* held a meeting at which the young Harvard political scientist Paul Weaver read out a long minute, which Moynihan subsequently showed to the president-elect.[32]

The social fabric of New York City, Weaver began by observing, was beginning to rip. In a "large and growing lower class, self-reliance, self-discipline and industry are waning . . . Families are more and more matrifocal and atomized; crime and disorder are sharply on the rise." Something comparable was happening in New York politics. Are we watching the "ultimate destructive working out of the *telos*[33] of liberal thought?" Weaver asked. The viability of liberal thought depended on "private subsystems of authority," notably the family. "Now, in parts of New York City, these subsystems are absolutely breaking down." So the liberal state "will no longer do."[34]

It was in this way, Moynihan commented,[35] that the subject of the family "forced its way on to the agenda of the American national government." In the end, Nixon, the Republican conservative, would choose to go with the most liberal of the options presented to him, a guaranteed family income without strings attached.

The Nathan report was leaked to the newspapers in early January. It was a cautious document. Nathan was aware that he and his team, mostly liberal Democrats, would be viewed with suspicion by the incoming Nixon administration. Nixon himself joked publicly that most of them had probably voted for Hubert Humphrey only a few weeks earlier. So Nathan's main emphasis was on saving money on welfare, and on introducing national standards, which had come to be seen as a minimalist reform. Meanwhile, Richard Nixon exploded when he saw a *New York Times* story headlined "Millions in City Poverty Funds Lost by Fraud and Inefficiency."[36] He shot off a memo to Robert Finch at HEW, Attorney General John Mitchell, White House aide Bryce Harlow and Moynihan, saying, "This New York welfare mess is probably typical of a problem which exists all over the country. I want a thorough investigation made. You will get a lot of nonsense from the establishment in the departments that this is 'chickenfeed' etc.," he fumed. "This whole thing smells to high heaven and we should get charging on it immediately."[37]

Moynihan saw himself as one of several advocates in the Nixon White House, competing for the president's attention and endorsement. He thought the most he could hope for at this stage would be implementation of the Nathan report and a commitment of something between $1 and $2 billion. Shortly after the inauguration, he assigned a staffer, John Price, to rewrite the Nathan proposals as a White House staff paper. Early in February, Moynihan sent the president a chart illustrating "Moynihan's scissors," the way the welfare caseload continued to climb even though unemployment was down.[38] Nixon was listening now, but he seems not to have understood how radical the plans being developed in the bureaucracy would turn out to be.

For at about this time, a crucial transformation took place in what was being proposed. On February 4, John Price finished his plan. It now guaranteed an income of $40 a month for all families with children and was to be called the Family Security System. When he showed it to Moynihan over veal scaloppine and red wine, Moynihan was excited. "You've got it," he cried. "That's it!"[39] And on February 6, the welfare subcommittee of the Urban Affairs Council discussed the Nathan-Price paper.

This, however, was too much for Dr. Arthur Burns, the arch-conservative Austrian-born economist who, immediately after the inauguration, had been appointed as Nixon's counselor. Moynihan's relations with Burns were friendly, and he went out of his way later to write a glowing tribute. "Burns was far more often correct in his forecasts than I was," Moynihan wrote. "An economist of formidable power, he is even more an intellectual in that singularly brilliant Middle-European Jewish tradition."[40]

That was handsomely said. The fact remained that Burns was a tree-sized hair in Moynihan's soup. Within weeks, he had assembled a staff, including the economist Martin Anderson from Columbia University,[41] which matched Moynihan's own staff for talent and exceeded it in experience. He fought Moynihan's ideas for welfare reform every inch of the way with dour tenacity and clouds of pipe smoke. In the end, he was largely responsible for Moynihan's failure to get a sufficiently strong commitment from Nixon, and, therefore, for Moynihan's departure from the Nixon White House. As a classic fiscal, small-government conservative who had been an economic adviser in the Eisenhower administration, Burns was much more on Nixon's wavelength, and that of his White House palace guard, than what seemed to them a half-converted liberal Democrat like Moynihan. Yet it was in a sense an accident that Burns had a job on the domestic side of the Nixon White House at all. The president wanted him to take over as chairman of the Federal Reserve, and the job as counselor was only a way of keeping him available until that job was open.

On the last day of January, Moynihan sent a memo to the president urging him to "send a message to Congress calling for national minimum standards in welfare . . . and [that] all states adopt AFDC."[42] So Moynihan was urging Nixon to make welfare reform a major plank of his domestic policy. But he was not yet overtly putting forward a Family Assistance Plan or a negative income tax. On the contrary, he was making the judgment that the Nathan report, with its modest approach and estimated cost of between $1 and $2 billion, was the most he could expect.

Even that was too much for Arthur Burns. On February 11, the economist wrote a memo expressing his reservation. "The answer is not to call for billions more in welfare payments . . . The American people are losing patience with our welfare system. They want and expect you to provide the leadership towards effective reform — that is, a reduction in the number on welfare, accompanied by an increase in the number on payrolls."[43] The Urban Affairs Council met the next morning, and on that afternoon the president told Burns, Finch and Moynihan that he wanted to set national standards for welfare payments.

While the new administration was thus inching its way toward a modest, but significant, welfare reform plan, the old-timers — holdovers from the Johnson administration and the bureaucracy at HEW — were preparing a much more radical proposal. The secretary of HEW was Nixon's friend Bob Finch, a liberal Republican from California. His undersecretary in charge of welfare, John Veneman, had set up a task force that in turn commissioned a paper from an outgoing Johnson administration official, Worth Bateman.[44] It was received with "red hot" enthusiasm, and on February 17 presented to Secretary Finch. By early March, when it was presented to Finch again in a refined form, the plan had become a negative income tax in all but name.

Moynihan continued to send the president long memos explaining the argument about caseloads and unemployment. He also explained (as if the president needed any reminder) that "there are some fairly clear racial overtones to attitudes toward welfare and poverty," or again giving his opinion that "welfare would seem to be less stigmatizing than in the past."[45] But in the meantime H. R. "Bob" Haldeman had recorded in his taped diary that the president's schedule was "screwed up because Moynihan had not properly staffed the agenda," meaning that he had not had his staff anticipate the implications of his policy. And he ended, ominously for Moynihan, "Hope our plan for [John Ehrlichman] to oversee domestic matters will overcome this."

Less than three months after he entered the White House, in fact, Nixon's men, while personally friendly with, even impressed by, Moynihan, were nonetheless scheming to strip him of the executive authority of his job. It would not be long before they had found a way of "kicking him upstairs" to a cabinet post with even less direct power.

This should not be misunderstood, however. "I had," Moynihan says, "and I am confident in this regard, a fine relationship with Haldeman and Ehrlichman. They were splendid staff people, with no agenda save the president's, and so long as he approved of me, they did." He tells a revealing anecdote about home rule for the District of Columbia, which he wanted Nixon to come out in favor of. Moynihan was summoned to the cabinet room one day early in the administration. Nixon came in. "Moynihan here," Haldeman said to Nixon, "wants you to propose home rule." Nixon replied, "Of course. I've always been for home rule."[46]

It was, Moynihan recalls, a maturing point in their relationship. They knew he was not one of theirs. Moynihan and Garment were not on our side, said Haldeman. But they were impressed by his intellectual powers and knew what he could do for the president. They were dismayed by his indifference to administrative procedure, but they were not against the Family Assistance Plan. It was just that the clashes between Moynihan and Burns were bad for good order and discipline.

On March 24, when the Urban Affairs Council's welfare subcommittee got the report from Veneman's task force, which recommended the Family Security System, Moynihan slapped the table, and said, "This is a great historic plan. I think we should go to the president with it immediately. If we worked on it for five years I don't think we could come up with a better plan."[47] Later he told Franklin Raines[48] that he understood the boldness of the HEW plan, but for tactical reasons made the decision to act as if it wasn't unusual, saying things like, "Well, this is our proposal. How do we staff it out now?" He hoped, he told Raines, that the conservatives within the White House wouldn't notice how bold it was. Moynihan may have been rewriting history here. The evidence suggests that, rather than coming into the White House with a ready-made plan for family assistance, he started from a sense of the urgency of the issue, then reached for measures to do something about it. Gradually he realized that the president might be willing to consider more daring policies than he thought at first.

If Moynihan's tactic was to lull his opponents by pretending he had not noticed what was at stake, Martin Anderson, who was representing Burns at the subcommittee meeting, wasn't fooled. Anderson first attacked by quoting a campaign speech in which Nixon had said he would never support a negative income tax. He said he believed in calling a spade a spade, and Moynihan quoted Oscar Wilde to him: "Those who called a spade a spade should be compelled to use one."

Such academic jousting was a mere diversion from what was becoming a serious fight. On March 26, seizing the opportunity offered by the HEW paper, Moynihan argued that the Family Security System, far from being the call, as Arthur Burns asserted, to spend billions on welfare, was really a bargain. He also shrewdly interpreted the politics of the proposal in terms that would appeal to Nixon.

"The essential fact about the Family Security System," he wrote,

is that it will abolish poverty for dependent children and the working poor. The cost is not very great because it is a direct payment system. The tremendous cost of the poverty program comes from services, i.e. year-round Head Start costs $1000 per child. Almost all of this money goes to middle-class teachers, and the like. The Family Security System would enable you to begin cutting back sharply on these costly and questionable services and yet to assert with full validity that it was under your presidency that poverty was abolished in America.[49]

The president decided to resolve these conflicting proposals from his advisers in one of his favorite ways. He asked Moynihan, Arthur Burns and Robert Finch, who showed signs of wanting to act as a mediator, all to prepare proposals and present them to him and to John Ehrlichman in his winter retreat in Key Biscayne, Florida. Moynihan wrote a cover memo to his paper in which he said that by adopting the Family Security System, "for two weeks growth in the Gross National Income" Nixon could "all but eliminate poverty in America. And make history." Burns, for his part, came up with a long paper that avoided the main issue. The president did not make up his mind in the Florida sunshine, but a few days after the party had trekked back north to Washington, Ehrlichman pulled Moynihan aside at a White House dinner and told him that the president had decided to go with the FSS plan. And on April 11, Nixon noted to Ehrlichman on a Moynihan memo that "In confidence, I have decided to go ahead on this program. Don't tell Finch et al."[50]

The battle was not won yet, however. Although Nixon loved to tell everyone how tough he was, his instinct was to surround himself with advisers and staff who represented differing opinions, to avoid direct confrontation among them and to play one group off another. Bob Haldeman confided to his tape recorder that "the real problem is the Burns-Moynihan dichotomy. . . . The problem for E[hrlichman] is to get control so White House speaks with one voice."[51] At first, Nixon thought he wanted strong, conflicting voices like those of Burns and Moynihan, but in practice it was not long before he confided to Ehrlichman that he was tired of "these two wild men on the domestic side . . . beating up on me all the time."

Welfare reform, that spring, was not the White House's only or even its most urgent preoccupation. On May 9, 1969, William Beecher revealed in the *New York Times* that the president and Henry Kissinger had secretly ordered bombing of Viet Cong sanctuaries in Cambodia.[52] It was that leak that impelled Nixon to call for the Tom Charles Huston security plan that led in turn to the Plumbers' Unit and to what Attorney General John Mitchell himself called the White House "horrors" that culminated in the Watergate break-in in the summer of 1972. Throughout his first spring in the White House, Nixon was preoccupied by how much harder it proved than he had expected to "bring the boys home." Frustrated in his attempts to get the Russians to put pressure on Hanoi, he began to move toward "Vietnamization," a euphemism for gradual withdrawal of American troops from South Vietnam. At home, the peace movement continued to build. It progressed in the Nixon administration through the Mobilization for Peace in the fall of 1969, to the huge, menacing demonstrations against Nixon's April 30, 1970, speech on Cambodia and the killings at Kent State and Jackson State.

So foreign affairs and the accompanying domestic turmoil were the background to the stubborn bureaucratic hand-to-hand fighting over welfare. Moynihan, too, encountered infuriating distractions. He was concerned over evidence that great American cities, caught between black anger and white backlash, might become ungovernable. Big-city mayors were bearing the brunt of the social crisis on the streets, and he asked Nixon to meet with eleven of them. It was an impressive group, including men of the caliber of John V. Lindsay of New York and Richard J. Daley of Chicago, Carl B. Stokes of Cleveland and Ivan Allen of Atlanta. Nixon, in a scrawled memo to Haldeman, agreed to spend one hour with them on April 24. The meeting went well until Nixon left. Then Vice President Spiro Agnew took the chair. Agnew had earlier successfully campaigned for governor of Maryland by portraying himself as tough on crime, not without some race-conscious undertones. He "proceeded to antagonize all the mayors completely," a furious Haldeman recorded, "and undo all the good of [the president's] time. . . ." Moynihan, he added, was "frantic."[53]

The welfare reform battle was still joined throughout May and on through June and July. Moynihan showered Nixon with memos, while Paul McCracken, chairman of the Council of Economic Advisers, proposed a compromise that leaned toward Arthur Burns's position. Moynihan, always adept at seeking support from those who might have been thought to be his opponents, countered by lobbying the politically conservative William F. Buckley, Cardinal Cooke and even David Rockefeller.

On June 6, he produced his most urgent and effective advocacy to date in a memo to the president.[54] He dismissed McCracken's arguments as merely technical. "I feel the issue before you," he told Nixon, "is not technical but political. . . . If you move now, you will dominate the discussion. Congress will be discussing your plan." Congress was almost certainly going to have to hammer out a major change in the welfare system, he argued. "It is up to you to dominate and direct this social transformation," he said. "This is an idea whose time has come."

It was a gambler's throw. Moynihan was now openly advocating that Nixon reject the ideas of all his other advisers, and adopt his own. As he must have understood, he was risking his whole position at the White House by his outspoken advocacy of the Family Security System. John Ehrlichman had already brought in George Shultz, the secretary of labor, to take an independent look at the rival proposals. Shultz delegated the assignment to Jerome Rosow, assistant secretary for planning, a labor relations expert whose strategy was to keep the family security approach but to strengthen the incentives for welfare recipients to find work. Shultz sent to the White House a revision of FSS that would exclude the first $20 a week in earnings when calculating how much money families would receive. That would cost another billion dollars, but it was "a fundamental girder in building a solid bridge from welfare to work."[55] Haldeman noted that Ehrlichman would have to drop all his other assignments and concentrate on creating a more orderly White House, with Ehrlichman "in actual charge and Burns and Moynihan as the planning units,"[56] a bizarre idea given that the whole problem was the near impossibility of getting the two men to agree about anything. It looked as if Moynihan's ideas were winning, but he was in danger of being pushed out altogether in the process. Unbeknownst to him, Ehrlichman asked Bob Finch to send someone over to prepare legislation. Finch sent over one of his deputy assistant secretaries, Robert Patricelli. On Ehrlichman's orders he began to draft legislation, but he was not allowed to tell anyone that he was doing so.

There was a showdown on June 30 and July 1 on the question of whether the plan should be sent to Congress. On June 30, Nixon decided to send it up to the Hill, and Ehrlichman told a staff meeting of the decision. Martin Anderson rushed to his patron, Burns, to rally opposition, and Anderson was added to the team drafting the presidential message. The next day, Haldeman said, "Moynihan was also furious, and was in and out of my office all day fuming."[57]

There was another heavy engagement in mid-July. Nixon, who had promised to send the Family Security Plan to Congress at the beginning of the month, was talked out of it by Burns and his allies. Moynihan countered by appearing at a press conference and saying that before Congress recessed the president would propose a total change in the welfare system.

The same day Haldeman reported in his diary that Nixon was "really rolling on the new domestic plan."[58] He was also beginning to roll with Henry Kissinger's innovative foreign maneuvers. Early in June, he sent Kissinger a note suggesting "we could needle our Moscow friends by arranging more visits to the Eastern Europe countries."[59] At first he was thinking of sending cabinet officers. Then he thought of a masterstroke; he would go himself. The president was scheduled to be present for the splashdown in the Pacific on July 24 of *Apollo 11*, the capsule that held the three astronauts involved in the first moon landing (Neil Armstrong, Buzz Aldrin and Michael Collins). On June 28, the White House announced that Nixon would visit Romania on his way back from the Pacific. The visit to Romania would be the first time any American president had traveled behind the Iron Curtain.[60]

Nixon, and of course Moynihan, wanted the Family Security Plan sent to Congress before the trip. Haldeman, the public relations man, was against such a move, afraid that it would "lose a lot of impact, overshadowed by moon shot plus trip."[61] So on July 19, the White House announced that the president would reveal his new welfare plan on August 8, immediately after his world tour. On the last day in July, Erlichman summoned the drafting team to Camp David, for what was supposed to be a short meeting. It went on for six hours because of a last-ditch attack on the whole concept by Martin Anderson. So when Ehrlichman flew to Romania the next day to meet with Nixon, he took with him protests from Burns, McCracken and David Kennedy, the treasury secretary.

On August 4, Nixon went over the whole subject from first principles one last time. He had already decided, Moynihan said, but he needed to know why he was taking this dramatic and potentially dangerous step. Moynihan characteristically drew him up to the high ground. There were three reasons. The poor, especially the black poor, were being destroyed by the welfare system. It was time to bring the South back into the mainstream of American life. And it was necessary to prove that government could work. "The moonshot had been one kind of success," Moynihan argued, "a guaranteed income would be another." America, he said, sounding what was to be a refrain almost obsessively repeated in the 1970s, needed some successes.[62]

August 6 brought what would prove to be, at least as far as the internal workings of the executive branch were concerned, the decisive meeting at Camp David. Moynihan flew up with the cabinet and the bureaucrats who had worked on the welfare plan to the presidential retreat in the Catoctin Mountains, seventy miles north of Washington. Moynihan said later that as the helicopter carried them to Camp David, he knew that he had the winning hand. But if so, he did not act like it. Bob Finch, too, said that "Moynihan was really uptight. Three or four times he came up to me at Camp David, and said, 'You really think he's going to go through with it?' "

The meeting took place in Laurel Cottage. Robert Patricelli made a brilliant presentation: after he had explained one particularly complicated point, Nixon turned to Melvin Laird, and said, "How do you get to be that smart?"[63] There was a consensus among the cabinet members, staunch Republicans all, that the name of the program was wrong. It was too "New Dealish." Moynihan recalls that they took paper and pencil and tried to think of a more conservative name.[64] The next day it was the speechwriters who came up with the name that stuck: the Family Assistance Plan.

The plan was complicated. The whole idea of a negative income tax is difficult to grasp in the first place, but the FAP was more complex than it need have been, in part because of the White House's political concern that the plan should be all things to all men. The plan had two main parts, aid for families of the unemployed and for the working poor. The unemployed would be paid a basic $1,600 a year for a family of four, plus food stamps at the rate of $500 per head for the first two and an additional $300 each for family members up to seven. That added up to $3,200 for a family of four. The working poor with incomes up to $3,920 would be given a subsidy calculated according to a formula. The working head of a household would keep the first $720 of his earnings, then half of his income above that level and still receive welfare payments until his income reached $3,920.

Nixon went public with it in a television address on August 8. His speech was not written by Pat Moynihan, but — like Lyndon Johnson's speech at Howard University just over four years earlier — it was largely inspired by Moynihan's social ideals and political assumptions. America faced an "urban crisis, a social crisis," the president said, exemplified by welfare. "What began on a small scale in the depression thirties has become a huge monster in the prosperous sixties."[65] Welfare broke up homes. It penalized work, robbed recipients of dignity and because benefits varied so much from state to state, it lured people into overcrowded cities and created an incentive for desertion. "A father is unable to find a job at all or one that will support his children. So, to make the children eligible for welfare, he leaves home — and the children are denied the authority, the discipline, and the love, that come with having a father in the home. This is wrong."[66]

The words might be the words of Nixon, drafted for him by Raymond Price or William Safire. But the thought is pure Moynihan. Indeed, it is the essence of what he had to say on the subject of welfare for a third of a century, distilled from years of study and countless statistical tabulations, but also from bitter childhood experience.

Nixon was proposing to abolish the existing welfare system, including Aid to Families with Dependent Children. In its place, he would put a new system based on three principles: equality of treatment in every state, a work requirement and a work incentive. The government would recognize that it had an obligation to the working poor, as well as to the unemployed, and set benefits so that it would always pay to work. He tried to draw a distinction between a guaranteed income (which he had opposed in his campaign speeches) and this new Family Assistance Plan, because it recognized the responsibility of the poor to seek work. "There is no reason why one person should be taxed so that another can choose to live idly."

From the beginning, the program was not understood — it was not easy to understand, and if truth were told the administration did not particularly want it to be fully understood. For it was of its nature a compromise, not just in the usual sense that most political programs have been cut and hammered to accommodate different interests.

The Family Assistance Plan was a compromise at a deep, philosophical level, between the liberal and the conservative sides of Richard Nixon's nature, as well as between his liberal and conservative advisers. It was shaped to appeal to both the liberals and the conservatives whose votes it would need to become law. It was sold as a measure for pushing poor people off welfare and back to work; yet it was also a potentially hugely expensive proposal to raise the incomes of working and dependent poor alike. Pat Moynihan called it "the most startling proposal to help poor persons ever made by a modern democratic government," and he was not wrong.

He has repeatedly presented the FAP as inspired by benevolent guile on the part of the president. It was at this point, between the Camp David meeting and the television speech, that he attributes to Nixon the phrase that stands as an epigraph to this chapter, about "Tory men and Liberal policies." He quotes with approval the remark of William Safire, to one of his more conservative speechwriting colleagues, that "you miss the president's main point, which is to make a radical proposal seem conservative." And he quotes Nixon as saying, "I don't care a damn about the work requirement. This is the price of getting the $1,600."

Perhaps that is what Nixon thought at the time. Certainly it is what Moynihan believed, or hoped Nixon thought. But if Richard Nixon was not a firm conservative ideologue, neither was he a bold liberal reformer. He was a neurotic tangle of conservative instincts and liberal aspirations, wrapped in cynical political calculation that was not so much second as first nature. The fate of the Family Assistance Plan eventually showed that Moynihan had placed his trust in a president who did not deserve it. Moynihan preferred to blame the Congress for the legislative tragedy that ensued and not the president who — as the record shows — never quite gave this bold but almost incomprehensible package of compromises his unqualified commitment. His biographer Stephen E. Ambrose, certainly no Nixon hater, commented on Moynihan's optimism about the plan, writing that Nixon "had what he wanted out of FAP, a great PR triumph. He wasn't all that sure he wanted it passed anyway. After all, what kind of a Republican President would he be if he added six or seven million people to the welfare rolls?"[67] When liberals and conservatives finally joined forces to destroy the FAP, Moynihan chose to blame the liberals more than the conservatives.

When hearings began on HR-1, as the FAP legislation was called, it was indeed a liberal who led the assault. Congress Al Ullman, Democrat of Oregon, professed that he was "shocked . . . almost to the point of being rendered speechless by the plan. You are opening the Treasury of the United States as it has never been opened before," he charged. But by mid-November, the Ways and Means committee, under its formidable chairman Wilbur Mills, began executive sessions. In the State of the Union address in January, Nixon made welfare reform the top domestic priority. Late in February, Ways and Means decided to report out a bill, and on March 5 the committee voted 21 to 3 to send the Family Assistance Act of 1970 to the House. On April 16, 1970, the House of Representatives passed HR-16311, essentially the Nixon-Moynihan Bill, on a 243 to 155 roll call vote.

That, however, was the high point both of the FAP's legislative fortunes and of Pat Moynihan's career in the Nixon White House. On November 1, 1969, less than ten months after Nixon's inauguration, Haldeman succeeded in "promoting" Moynihan and another White House aide, the veteran Bryce Harlow, to counselor. The catch was that Moynihan had lost all executive authority. Haldeman "had to sell the promotion to Harlow," he noted.[68] Moynihan, at least to Haldeman, appeared content, and for a time both the Haldeman tapes and the Nixon papers show Moynihan as much in favor as ever with Nixon as an adviser. Then, in April 1970, came the Cambodia crisis. That stretched unbearably tight the tension between Moynihan's instincts and the pugnacity of his new allies, between his deep opposition to the war and Nixon's determination not to be the president who "lost" Indochina.

Nixon had been in a tense and frustrated mood all spring. What no document can reveal, commented Henry Kissinger, is "the accumulated impact of accident, intangibles, fears, and hesitation."[69] He was furious with the Senate for blocking his nominations of Judges Clement F. Haynsworth and G. Harrold Carswell, both Southern strict-constructionists, to the Supreme Court. He was humiliated when his daughter Julie pleaded with John Ehrlichman to dissuade her father from attending her graduation at Smith because of the strength of feeling against him.[70] Nixon had gained personal satisfaction as well as political strength from *Apollo 11*'s triumphant voyage to the moon, so it was a bitter blow when *Apollo 13* was disabled en route and that lunar landing had to be aborted. The event, Henry Kissinger remembered later, "took a heavy toll of Nixon's nervous energy."[71]

The frustration and irritation welled up into rage in Nixon. He decided to "drop a bombshell" on the peace movement by announcing that 150,000 American troops would be pulled out of Vietnam. But there was pressure from the Joint Chiefs of Staff, and from Vice President Agnew, to take drastic action. The sequence of events shows Nixon overwrought, full of aggression against the enemy in Southeast Asia, but nervous and indecisive about his opponents at home. At 5:00 A.M. on April 12 he dictated a memo to Kissinger, beginning, "I think we need a bold move on Cambodia,"[72] where there had been a coup. On April 23, according to Kissinger, "Nixon flew into a monumental rage"[73] over Cambodia and the Supreme Court nominations, shouting, according to one source, "I'll show them who's tough!"[74] The next day the president, his voice slurred, called Kissinger and put on his Cuban crony Bebe Rebozo, who said, "The President wants you to know, if this doesn't work, Henry, it's your ass."[75] The day after that, paddling in the Camp David pool with the faithful Kissinger walking alongside, Nixon said he wanted "a big play," because there would be "a hell of an uproar at home"[76] whatever he did. And on April 25, when the president was joined by Rebozo, Kissinger and Attorney General John Mitchell for a cruise down the Potomac in the presidential launch *Sequoia,* there was so much heavy drinking that as the presidential party passed Mount Vernon they tried to stand to attention to salute George Washington, but not all of the party managed to stay upright.[77]

On April 30, Nixon made a speech that set off a firestorm of protest and incidentally produced a crisis in his relations with Daniel Patrick Moynihan. He announced that American and South Vietnamese troops were jointly attacking the Parrot's Beak and would soon be attacking the Fishhook (U.S. military code names for salients that brought the Cambodian border, and therefore Viet Cong refuges, close to Saigon). Then he added that "if, when the chips are down, the world's most powerful nation, the United States of America, acts like a pitiful helpless giant, the forces of totalitarianism and anarchy will threaten free nations and free institutions throughout the world." He added that he would rather be a one-term president and do what he believed to be right than be a two-term president at the cost of seeing America become a second-rate power.

This was the time when Moynihan's home and family were threatened. Moynihan himself was sufficiently out of sympathy with the administration's course in Indochina that he asked for a meeting with the president. Nixon saw him on May 13, and Moynihan said that he wanted to leave on July 1. "I know what you're going through," said Nixon, but persuaded him to stay until August. "We'll get the FAP," he said.[78] Moynihan agreed to stay on, but he wanted to start the fall semester at Harvard. Nixon was quite insistent, and there is no doubt he appreciated Moynihan's enthusiasm for the administration's projects, his constant fountain of ideas and his wit. Yet Haldeman recorded that "P," the president, "seems more relieved than concerned to have him go."[79] Moynihan's motives, too, were probably mixed. He was disgusted with the Cambodian operation and perhaps even more with the gung ho mood and superpatriotic style that the war and his other frustrations had produced in Nixon. This was the time when the president was forever looking for someone to watch *Patton* with him in the White House movie theater for the umpteenth time.

Moynihan was also deeply troubled about what the war was doing to the country, and particularly to two groups: students and the military. He arranged for a number of younger White House staffers, including Checker Finn, his former Harvard education student, now on his staff, to go out and report to the president on the mood on the campuses. On August 3, he wrote to Nixon saying that he had begun to fear "the prospect of symbolic mutiny in the Armed Forces."[80] He had talked "with careful men like Irving Kristol," he said, and found they shared his fears. "Almost the dominant fact of the United States at this time," he wrote, "is the rejection by youth of adult managed authority systems. This rejection began in elite circles, as is usually the case with big cultural changes. But it would be profoundly mistaken to suppose it has been confined there. In the form of intense fear and distrust of the government, and detestation of the war in Vietnam it is present on every campus in the nation, and has made astonishing inroads into the high schools."

The drug culture was well established in the armed forces. He dreaded the costs of public refusal to obey orders by even small units. This raised the question of the draft. Should the president go to the people, Moynihan asked, with the argument for an all-volunteer service? Should he consider announcing that he would veto next year's selective service legislation? Next to which Nixon wrote "not possible" in bold letters and underlined the two words.

The two years' leave of absence from Harvard would run out at the end of 1970, and Harvard, quite apart from any distaste for one of its faculty working for Nixon, was rigid in enforcing the two-years rule. Then there was Liz to think of. Her husband was coming up to Cambridge most weekends, but she was tired of not having him there, especially with the campus in chaos, and the children were missing their father too.

The lure of high office, and the yearning to achieve great things on the political stage, was strong, too. On June 5, Haldeman recorded that he was to dine with the president, John Ehrlichman, Henry Kissinger and Bebe Rebozo aboard the *Sequoia* for "a good chat, about all sorts of things, especially people." Nixon was excited about the prospect of moving Robert Finch and replacing him as secretary of health, education and welfare with Elliot Richardson. There was one interesting problem, Haldeman said: John Ehrlichman had already asked Moynihan if he wanted the HEW job, and Moynihan had said yes. "Now have to turn him off," recorded Haldeman laconically.[81]

The next day Nixon, who had gone up to Camp David with his family, had a brain wave. He called Haldeman to suggest considering Moynihan as ambassador to the United Nations. Haldeman called him into his office, where Ehrlichman and a few others gathered. They asked Moynihan if he would be interested in going to the UN. "But you don't understand," Moynihan replied, "I've resigned!"[82] On Monday morning, June 8, Nixon had Moynihan in at the end of a full morning schedule and asked if he would like to go to the UN. The president had his feet up on the desk. At one point he suddenly said, "You're a Catholic, aren't you! Do you believe all that stuff?" (Moynihan kicked himself afterward for not saying, "Well, Mr. President, I even believe in doctors," because Haldeman, a Christian Scientist, was present.)[83] But he was pleased, Haldeman reported, and would consider the offer. George Shultz thought it was a "masterstroke."

All summer, Moynihan had been involved in a committee (nominally chaired by Agnew, who rarely bothered to attend) to prepare for the ending of dual school systems in the South. There was a long series of biracial meetings in the executive office building.[84] Then the Southerners, black and white, would be ushered over to the Roosevelt Room, across a narrow hall from the Oval Office. The star turn was the postmaster general, Winton "Red" Blount, a jovial construction tycoon who would greet everyone with a huge "hell-oo!" Uniformed stewards would hand around drinks on silver trays and ply the guests with cuff links and golf balls stamped with the presidential seal. Finally, in a supreme act of presidential condescension, they would be ushered into the Oval Office to see the president himself.

As a culmination of this process of wooing Southern elites to ensure a peaceful conclusion of the long and stormy process of Southern school desegregation, the president visited New Orleans, and Moynihan went along in his party. The president announced to a great gathering of Southern school officials that with the opening of schools in a few weeks' time the segregated school system was finally over. Moynihan was impressed.[85] No doubt he had his own, political motives for seeing an end to the painful process that had started with the Supreme Court's decision in *Brown v. Board of Education,* sixteen years earlier. But Nixon had done it. On the plane on the way home he told the president he would take the UN job.

So all through the fall of 1970, it was taken for granted within the administration that Moynihan would not return to Harvard, but would go to the United Nations as ambassador.[86] The 1970 midterm elections came and went. News of the appointment was even leaked to the newspapers on November 21. Two nights later, Moynihan took Steve Hess to dinner at a French restaurant and asked him whether he would go to New York as his deputy. Hess said he would. Moynihan returned to his digs in Columbia Plaza. Between getting into the elevator and getting out, he changed his mind and decided he would not go. He called Liz, and said, "I'm coming home." She cried with relief.[87]

On November 25, Bob Haldeman noted that Moynihan "wrote P. yesterday to say he couldn't take UN job. Gave whole range of reasons. In talk however he said it boiled down purely to family. When faced with it Liz just wouldn't go and said they would have to have a separation. So he's going back to Harvard." Moynihan does not recall now that there was any talk of divorce or separation. He was well aware that Liz wanted him home, and it may be that he found family values a convenient way of summarizing to the straitlaced Haldeman what were indeed complicated motives.

He certainly had mixed feelings about the Nixon administration and about working for it. "I was getting worried about the Nixon White House," he said in an interview. "The basement of the Executive Office Building was full of soldiers." The implication was that they had been deployed to protect an unpopular president. In a November 5, 1970, letter to Finch, Haldeman and Shultz, Moynihan asked, "Why are we so detested?" in the universities, given that the Nixon administration had made exceptionally enlightened proposals for higher education. He answered his own question: "For all the proprieties of our formal positions, we have simultaneously been sending out signals that *we* detest *them.*" He quoted a letter he had received from Alan Pifer, the head of the Carnegie Corporation, who, though a liberal, had served as chairman of Nixon's task force on education not two years previously.

"What you have to realize, however," Pifer wrote,

> is the utter lack of credibility the Nixon administration has with the educational community at all levels. I'm not talking about militant students and radical young faculty. I'm talking about millions of intelligent people who feel that the President and his administration have downgraded their profession, disregarded them and let the Vice President ridicule what they stand for. They are deeply affronted. . . . It has left a residue of bitterness among intelligent and informed Americans that will not disappear as long as these men are in office.

Moynihan went on to argue that there was, whatever Nixon and Agnew might imagine, a "fundamental community of interest" between the administration and the higher education system. There was the matter of financial support, of course. But the universities had "an urgent and increasingly perceived interest" in diminishing the power and the attraction of the "authoritarian left" and of the groups that might join with it in moments of crisis. Nothing would do more to reduce the power of the Left than "the continued success of a respectable conservative Administration winding down the war, winding up the economy, easing group relations, looking to the future."

That was a blunt statement, to three of those in the administration whom he found sympathetic, of his fears about the darker angels of the president's nature and the men who appealed to them. It was also a revealing statement of his own fears and of his evolving political orientation. He was afraid of what the radical movements shaking the country could do to it. And he was prepared to admit that his own preferred alternative course could be called "conservative," at least to win the approval of conservatives. With his keen political antennae, he had some premonition of where a paranoid, embattled mentality and a culture of Prussian obedience and the will for victory at all costs might take an administration he had once been proud to serve. But he remained on good terms with the president himself, not only after he left the White House, but even after the Watergate storm had broken.

He asked for, and was given, the status of a consultant to the White House. Although he duly returned to Harvard, he continued to advise the administration. He was made the "public delegate" of the United States to the United Nations, supporting the ambassador. On December 13, 1972, he wrote Nixon from Harvard in joshing, if respectful terms:

> Dear Mr. President,
>
> As perhaps my last act as Consultant to you on domestic affairs, I would call your attention to the fact that the cover of the current United States Government Organization Manual features a maze with the unique feature that there is one way in but no way out. It suggests that your reorganization efforts have come not a moment too soon.[88]

Pat Moynihan's greatest claim to fame in the Nixon White House was the Family Assistance Plan. It was a legislative tragedy, a glorious attempt, but a long, drawn-out, tormenting failure. Briefly, the bill was in trouble almost as soon as it reached the Senate Finance Committee, whose chairman, Russell B. Long of Louisiana, sent it back to the White House. The plan went back to the Hill in June. Grimly, the Senate chopped it to pieces. On December 29, the Senate voted 49 to 21 to delete the Family Assistance Plan from an omnibus bill. The Ways and Means Committee refused to take the mutilated bill to a conference.

In 1971, Nixon tried again. In his State of the Union message he listed six legislative priorities, of which welfare reform was the most important. In June, he urged passage of the bill, saying it was "the most important social legislation in thirty-five years." But it was too late. At the end of July, the bill reached the Senate, but in August President Nixon announced a new economic policy aimed at fighting inflation. That included a decision to postpone welfare reform for one year. The opportunity had passed. The political circus moved on.

Pat Moynihan had long given up on enactment of the plan he had advocated with such enthusiasm. He applied to its fate Karl Marx's celebrated dictum that history does repeat itself, the first time as tragedy, the second as farce. In 1970, he meant, it was a tragedy that welfare reform did not pass. By 1971, farce was the appropriate term. There were those who pretended that the proposal was still a serious one, he wrote acidly, "but these were few."[89]

He understood that the administration had been trapped. The Family Assistance Plan married two ideas, one essentially of the Left, namely a guaranteed income, the other, welfare reform, essentially of the Right. It ought, therefore, to have been possible to construct a coalition for it, but it was not. Instead, liberals concentrated on attacking it for guaranteeing too low an income, while conservatives focused on the extent to which the plan would add to the welfare rolls, on its large and open-ended cost and on its excessive tenderness to the poor. All of this, he understood as well as anyone.

Moynihan was also unwilling to blame Richard Nixon personally. In his own subsequent account of the sad story, he made a point of citing Nixon's moving speech on behalf of the plan at the end of 1970. He was reluctant to believe that Nixon would in the end, with a pragmatism that was akin to cynicism, drop the whole thing when it was no longer good politics. When the *New York Times* wrote that "even Richard Nixon came out for income maintenance payments for desperately poor families," Moynihan commented, "Not 'even,' among presidents 'only.' "[90]

The experience of the Family Assistance Plan, like the Moynihan Report, led Pat Moynihan to think again about a political scene that was increasingly a conflict between liberals and conservatives, an opposition he had always instinctively resisted. Later, there would be issues that would show up the limits of his willingness to be counted among the conservatives. But in 1971, as he returned to Harvard licking the fresh wounds of the family assistance battle, his animus was directed not so much against the conservatives, from whom he had expected little, but toward the liberals, whose opposition felt like a betrayal. For the next five years, he gave up the thankless struggle for domestic reform. Through more of those chance encounters and random walks, he began to look outward again to the world, and to America's place in it.

8

Watergate from Afar

RETHINKING NIXON, AMERICA
AND THE WORLD

> Parnell came down the road, he said to a cheering man:
> Ireland shall get her freedom and you still break stone.
>
> — William Butler Yeats, "Parnell"

EARLY IN 1973, Moynihan's next "random walk" took him to New Delhi. Several weeks after he arrived there, Ambassador Moynihan was summoned to a regional meeting of U.S. chiefs of mission held, as it happened, in Tehran. It was Easter Sunday 1973, just one week before Bob Haldeman and John Ehrlichman announced their resignations from the White House. Moynihan sat down and wrote a declaration of personal loyalty to Richard Nixon. It is an unexpected document in many respects. It would certainly have surprised most of his friends in Washington and Cambridge to learn that he had written in this vein to or about Nixon even a year earlier. One suspects it would have surprised his wife. But such a letter to the president, now at bay and snarling in the White House, can best be described as quixotic. It was not only politically unexpected, but it reveals a personal morality that has perhaps always been more important to Moynihan than either politics or ideology. It is certainly worth quoting at some length.

He had, Moynihan wrote from Tehran, "been thinking of you almost continuously this past week."

> I wonder, now, how well I served you. From almost my first day in the White House I sensed that the greatest danger you faced would be from the kind of misjudgements and misdeeds of which disclo-

sure now is mounting. I never bluntly said so. I hinted, I alluded, I inferred, I groused even, but I never straight out said what I thought, which was that such things were going on, and would go on, and would come to grief . . . For things undone, I ask — what? — forgiveness, I suppose.

But I write not for this purpose, nor to declare my own unshaken loyalty, and not at all to strengthen you, for you seem to find resolve in crisis. I write, rather, with a simple thought, which is that it has not really been evil that has brought on the present shame, but innocence. What struck me most, and alarmed me most, about the almost always decent men who came to Washington with you, or in your train, was how little they knew of government, and especially of the standards of personal behavior required of men in power.

They had acquired in their youth, or as was sometimes the case, in long years excluded from national affairs, an oppositional frame of mind which much too easily assumed that squalid behavior was common rather than rare in Washington, and they were all too ready to judge what would be required of them by reference to what they thought others did, rather than what they knew ought to be done. There was a failing of education and imagination. As a teacher [on leave from] an elite school I live with it daily from the opposite political perspective: The government is fascist; what then is wrong with *us* blowing up a building? But this is innocence, not evil . . .

I have no way of knowing what you are thinking, or what you will do. But if you think there would be any use in my returning to the White House, you have only to ask.[1]

On June 13, Moynihan noted laconically in his diary, "I had an answer to my Easter letter. Robotyped." Nixon's letter read in its entirety:

Dear Pat

Of the many messages I have received in recent weeks, I particularly welcomed those which have come from members of this Administration. To know I have your continuing loyal support and trust means a great deal to me, and I want to tell you of my appreciation.

Although developments in recent months have posed a great test of our administration, your words of understanding renew my faith that, working together, we can achieve the great goals of peace and progress all Americans seek.

With kind personal regards,
Sincerely.[2]

And then this embattled man, too proud and mistrustful to ask for help, much less to accept it when it was offered, scrawled his initials. "Well," Moynihan wrote. "I tried. Rose Woods read my letter. So, I am sure, did he. But I was the only one he ever had around who knew how to draft a reply to professorial homilies."³ Or, he might have added, to paladins volunteering to throw away their careers on his behalf.

The scant two years Moynihan spent in Delhi were an exile from the main focus of his interests and ambitions, in Cambridge, in New York and in Washington. He used them for several purposes. He performed one great service and several smaller ones to India: his role as ambassador will be described in more detail in the next chapter. He formulated a theory about how the United States was being isolated and outmaneuvered by the Soviet Union's ability to take advantage of the devotion of Third World elites to European ideals of socialism. Then he used that theory to negotiate his return to a Republican administration in a way that opened up new prospects for his own career and also transformed the way the United States talked to the rest of the world. That too will be described in Chapter 9. Above all, perhaps, the Delhi years enabled Moynihan to step back and to look at Washington, and his own career, with a new detachment; or at least — because he flew back there quite often and was never altogether detached even when he was in Delhi — with a new understanding.

They were also, however, the Watergate years. When Pat Moynihan agreed to go to Delhi, it was possible to dismiss the Watergate break-in as a second-rate burglary and the *Washington Post*'s reporting as irresponsible and politically motivated. Not that Moynihan was unaware of a disreputably partisan, even gamy side of the Nixon White House, as his Tehran letter hinted.⁴ But, as he put it himself in a long letter to Nathan Glazer: "I left Washington for India in quite a good mood. One recalled Watergate, if at all, as an event that had *preceded* the campaign."⁵ In his letters to old friends and in the diary he kept while he was in Delhi, one can see how he responded to the gradual unfolding of his worst nightmares about the administration he had served. And one also catches a glimpse of his own worry about what this most extraordinary political crisis might do to his own prospects.

"All indicted," he wrote in his diary on March 1. "Mitchell, Haldeman, Ehrlichman, Colson . . . and with the awful language of the

Common Law in Arms: 'as they did then and there truly know.' "
Will they break? he asked, and added, "It hardly matters. The presidency has departed Richard Nixon as the Mandate of Heaven was
withdrawn from Chinese emperors."[6]

As Watergate unfolded, one of Moynihan's instincts was to blame
the liberals for the transgressions of their enemies. Almost without
exception, the close friends from whom he learned about the mood
in the United States, and with whom he tried to work out a response,
were people who, like Moynihan himself at the time, had gone
through the neoconservative experience. Irving Kristol, Norman
Podhoretz, Nathan Glazer and Edward J. Epstein, all of whom are
quoted in the diary, visited Delhi or corresponded with him, were
very different men. They by no means automatically agreed about
politics, issues or anything else. But they had — with the arguable exception of Irving Kristol — all started out more or less on the Left.
They had all invested some degree of hope in the Nixon administration. None of them was disposed to be very sympathetic to Nixon's
enemies, let alone to the *Washington Post*. Like them, Moynihan
struggled to know what to think about Nixon and his fall from grace.
And in his diary and the letters he gradually comes to terms with the
sheer scale of the disaster that had overwhelmed the man he had chosen to work for. Moynihan on Nixon, Watergate observed from afar,
says a lot about both men.

In May, he wrote to Glazer that he had been thinking of little but
Watergate, and quotes Glazer's letter back to him: "Is Watergate a
difference in the quantity of political skullduggery, promoted into the
disaster it is by a special relation to press or media, or a difference in
real quality, which reflects some basic moral and political failing both
of Nixon and those of us who saw him in the mainstream of American politics, rather than as some cunning aberration?"[7]

Glazer had said he couldn't answer that question, and Moynihan
replied that thirty years of reading and forty years of going to Catholic churches left him with no preparation for putting the question,
let alone answering it. The departure of Charles Colson had been
a matter of rejoicing among the "decent, honorable, competent public men" in the White House, he wrote. He thought these men
knew little or nothing of Watergate. "And yet," he went on, "what
cringing animals this makes of us all. 'I knew nothing.' It makes us
not only animals but liars." Of course they knew, he said, and "there

is a sense in which all 'knew.' " He liked to think that people like John Ehrlichman knew he wouldn't go along, but he expected it was simply that they didn't trust him. He pointed out in self-justification that he refused to join Democrats for Nixon in 1972. "I made no speeches, signed no statements, took no position." He did write the tribute to Nixon for *Life* magazine. "Yet neither did I protest. I wanted no part of that administration, yet I did not break with it. Next, I voted for it — privately, to be sure, but I did vote for it. Finally, I returned to it. What do you call such a person? A Moynihan, I suppose. A term suggestive of moral and political failing."

He then launched into a detailed account to his friend of how he saw the Nixon administration's failings. It is at once a self-justification and a remarkably frank account, after the event, of how his feelings about the administration evolved. He and his friends, he wrote, spent much of the 1960s being appalled at the decline of the liberal Left's intellectual and moral standards. "We saw this as a phenomenon of ideology, when in fact it was increasingly a function of what American government was becoming." When a conservative government came in we were too grateful by half and too willing to supply arguments. "We were willing to be used."

He and his friends saw the voters drifting to the Right, while the Left had the smarter minds. "They" — all the president's men — never got it. But this was understandable, for "what was I saying but [that] they were not smart enough to follow what it was I was saying?"

Watergate itself was a result of their stupidity. How would they use any information they obtained? Why break into Ellsberg's psychiatrist's office when they could have found out all they wanted about Ellsberg by talking to his friends in Cambridge? They were "so straight they are deviant." Moynihan blamed himself. "In a sense I introduced the Nixon administration to you all, and did so on much too favorable terms. Or rather, I never made clear, later, how much I had soured."

His disillusion began with the first big peace demonstrations in 1969. Most of the Moynihan staff, young men like Checker Finn and Richard Blumenthal,[8] made contact with the marshals at the protest. But Attorney General John Mitchell thought the demonstration "looks like the Russian Revolution," and he tried to get Blumenthal fired for being in cahoots with the organizers. Moynihan claims he was able to protect Blumenthal. But by October 1969, he himself was on his way out, kicked upstairs, as has been noted, to be a counselor to the president. Domestic policy was to be run by "the balloon men," as Moynihan called those on Ehrlichman's staff whose duty during the campaign had been to arrange for the balloons to drop at the end of rallies.

"I dropped out," Moynihan admitted. He stopped going to morning meetings and opted out of operational activities. The atmosphere worsened, though not for him personally. "The kind of upper and lower class nihilism of which we spoke so often in those days was mounting, and with it alarm and a kind of political vengeance in the White House." Moynihan became very concerned about the Black Panthers; it was in that context that he had written the "benign neglect" memo. When it was published, suddenly he found himself branded as a reactionary in the *New York Times*. "The real reactionaries [were those in Nixon's inner circle] — and there were some — delighted at my disgrace." Then came Cambodia. And one morning a "shaken" Egil "Bud" Krogh, one of Haldeman's aides, later implicated in Watergate, opened Moynihan's door in the White House basement to say there had been shooting at a place called Kent State. What should the president say? Moynihan wrote a "compassionate and placatory"[9] response. Krogh took it, but the president issued just the opposite kind of statement. Moynihan became more distant. He asked the president if he could resign. Nixon asked him to stay on to work on the Family Assistance Plan. He did, and he also got caught up in Southern school desegregation.

Moynihan offered Glazer a summary. Nixon's cause was getting weaker. They were on a slippery slope. They betrayed us, he said, but there is a sense in which they were also betrayed. Nothing they could have done would have won the approval of some people and some newspapers. "They were not berserk. They merely let themselves get involved step by step into something that got out of control, whereupon they tried to cover up and thereupon came catastrophe. They were not evil so much as innocent: they believed what they told one another about the degraded standards of behavior in Washington. Much as do the elite leftists of Cambridge."[10]

Impossible, at that time, for Moynihan to resist an opportunity to take a swipe at Cambridge leftists. To some extent he was still looking for justification for Nixon and the people who had led him into

Watergate. But he did not shirk his own responsibility. And he closed his letter to Glazer with the guess that he personally was in more or less irrevocable trouble.

A little more than a month after writing that letter, Moynihan actually saw Nixon. To be exact, he contrived to see Nixon, in circumstances he described in his diary with a delicate sense of the absurdity of power. Moynihan flew to San Clemente, where President Nixon had installed — at considerable public expense — what was somewhat grandiosely known as the Western White House.[11] The hearings were already on, and at San Clemente, as everywhere else across the nation, men who had worked for Haldeman and Ehrlichman could watch them accused of "deed after deed after deed" by John Dean.

"They are glad to see me," Moynihan wrote in his diary. "This is real, I think." And he explained that while Nixon's Republicans did not have the pride in government which Democrats had in the 1960s, they looked back with nostalgia to the "grand old days when [Arthur] Burns and I got at each other with great clubs and huge joy." For them he supposed, it was rather as "the Kennedy days were for us."

He quoted his favorite lines from Yeats:

> Parnell came down the road, he said to a cheering man:
> Ireland shall get her freedom and you still break stone.[12]

He ran into Nixon's speechwriter Ray Price, the liberal foil to the conservative Pat Buchanan, and found that, setting aside his hopes of writing a philosophical work, he was back to writing statements that were all denials. How did it all happen? Price asked. Moynihan came out with a formula that he got from Theodore H. White: "whilst becoming a great President he remained a vicious politician."

Not for nothing, reflected Moynihan, "have I been in the business a long while." One of the things he learned was: "Never Forgo a Chance Encounter with the President . . . Appointments he [the president] had with anyone; corridor talk is the mark of the initiate." So Moynihan jumped up and ran in one door and out the next into the alley between two prefab buildings.

Missed! His outside door is closing behind him. Press on! Remember you are a man the Secret Service will not shoot at. Into the reception room. He is just disappearing behind the door to his inner office. Not too late. He is alone. You can shout!
"Mr. President!"

"Pat!"

"How are you, Sir?"

"Good, good. How are you? Do you like your job?"

"No."

"Those people."

"That land."

"That woman."

"Can we meet?"

A small hesitation. Then, just as the budget director, Roy Ash, was coming into the room, "Yes."

"I belonged with this crowd," Moynihan wrote, without revealing whether the reflection gave him pride or shame.[13] Haldeman's aide Steve Bull came by. "There have only ever been three men he has ever felt easy talking to," said Bull. "Haldeman, [Treasury Secretary John] Connally and you." (He omitted Bebe Rebozo.) Bull urged him to talk to Nixon.

He wanted nothing else. While waiting for Nixon's promise of an audience, wrung from a tenuous opportunity by experience and determination, to be transformed into an appointment, Moynihan went to discuss India with Henry Kissinger. He found him "overwrought, overbearing, overextended," but serious. "Foreign policy is not for him a casual exercise of the personal power he has . . . It is commitment." Kissinger was a queen bee: on emerging from the cell "he/she systematically kills all the other cells that might contain another queen bee." Moynihan read through the list of Nixon's enemies and found there the names of Derek Bok, the president of Harvard, and Kingman Brewster, the president of Yale. He knew he ought to tell Nixon that it was an honor to be on that list, but he knew he wouldn't say it when it came to the point, and he didn't. Yet "I've not an ounce of fear of the man. Never have. His favor can only do me disservice. I don't want his job, and expect not to see him more than perhaps three times in my life. And yet he is President."

After Moynihan had spent three-quarters of an hour with Kissinger, the president was ready. Moynihan observed that the American flag was flying upside down on his lapel, the navy distress signal. Moynihan complained that the State Department had cut his pay. Nixon said we have too many embassies in countries where the population is two million. Moynihan countered that the population of India is equal to those of Africa and Latin America combined.

"How are you?" Moynihan asked. "He doesn't say, but he answers." Life is a battle. There have been battles before. Kent State. We will get through it. He was not what Moynihan feared: not hurt, coiled, venomous. He was going over his history but more concerned with his triumphs than with his grievances. He, Richard Nixon, had made the great breakthrough with the Communist world. He was the man the Communists feared most. Mao's China was a Stalinist regime. But he had to deal with it. China now looked on America as a friend, the only friend it had among the countries that mattered. It was a glimpse of Nixon at bay, bloody but unbowed.

Within the week Moynihan was back in Delhi. At an American-style July 4 picnic at the embassy's ballpark, there were "hotdogs, beer, fireworks and a patriotic speech by me."[14] There was also a speech by John Connally, Nixon's secretary of the treasury, who was visiting Delhi at the time. Diversion was supplied by "a couple [who] fornicated on second base to the general wonder of his Secret Service agents." The ambassador commented that this was better than the previous year, when fighting broke out between marines and Peace Corps men. He blamed the weather, which was sultry, and the local cannabis, stronger than Americans were used to. Liz, the lifelong Democrat, was furious when her husband offered a toast to the president of the United States. He explained that it was impersonal, "the precise same thing as toasting 'the Queen.' " Curiously, he added, "she did not know this. We have not much ceremony in America, and women generally are not so much left out as excluded."

Two weeks later came the news of Alexander Butterfield's testimony to the Ervin committee, revealing that Nixon had taped conversations in the Oval Office (as had, under certain circumstances, his two predecessors). Moynihan commented with bleak prescience that the tapes would have to be given up, or the president would be presumed guilty. "What a calamity those men were," he added. "Butterfield the best of them: gave up a first rate Air Force career to work for Ehrlichman as a man with no politics and no ambition. And that was his weakness. The others: theirs was the politics of playing on 'the worst side of Richard Nixon's character.' " He noticed, too, on the part of Nixon's aides, what he called "a curious mania for getting everything recorded and written down," and proposed, in the privacy of his diary, a constitutional reform: abolish presidential libraries. It was clear enough to him already that the hounds were closing in for the kill.

A week later, Moynihan noted that the president had agreed to abide by the Supreme Court's decision on making publicly available the tapes, whose existence had just been revealed by Butterfield. In fact, Moynihan was overly sanguine. Nixon fought for a year to prevent the tapes being made public, and it was the Supreme Court's decision, a year later, to overrule his reluctance, that led directly to his resignation. Sitting in Delhi, however, Moynihan launched into a sardonic reflection on the class politics of Watergate as he saw them. It is a curious, characteristic and revealing example of his sensitivity to the taboo subject of social class in America.

Ehrlichman had been testifying, he noted. Among the counsel to the Ervin committee was a certain Terry Lenzner, "an attractive young Republican who headed the legal services department of the Office of Economic Opportunity," that is, of the so-called War on Poverty, "and then was fired because he got into a scrap with Governor Reagan." His rise thereafter, as Checker Finn pointed out, was meteoric. First he was elected to the Harvard Board of Overseers, "as will anyone fired by the Nixon administration." Next Lenzner appeared as counsel for Daniel and Philip Berrigan, two Catholic priests, then serving prison sentences in a federal penitentiary for destroying draft records, and additionally accused by J. Edgar Hoover of planning to kidnap Henry Kissinger.[15] And now Lenzner was of counsel for the Ervin committee. "Revenge," Moynihan commented in his diary, "best eaten cold."

He then propounded "a theory." He identified the Nixon Republicans with the old city machine bosses. They have, he said, "or had," a solid hold on a sizeable majority because of a "thoroughly unsentimental attention to its material needs and its plebeian taste for despising the toffs." But the Nixon administration, like the wicked city bosses of old, was too "vulgar and at times criminal." Repeatedly the "better classes" find them out and drive them from office for a while. You cannot govern successfully any longer in America, Moynihan mused, without the educated classes, "and they increasingly withhold their co-operation from social inferiors." Lenzner went to work for Nixon, but poor Ehrlichman was "too lower middle-class to appreciate his importance," and in any case he probably didn't recognize his old colleague through the klieg lights at the hearing.

The Republicans, he went on, had some Lenzners, but Moynihan imagined that they would not have any again for a generation. Would this break the Republican party? Possibly, he answered his own question. More likely not. "Colson[16] and Phillips[17] and such were moving to a radical redefinition of the party," he wrote, "bringing in a working class cadre organized around fear and resentment of the militant blacks and the radical rich."

There could hardly be a better example of the way personal experience, political insights and class attitudes could be stirred together in Moynihan's mind to emerge as a precise and rather accurate prediction. The somewhat obscure Lenzner was typecast as the representative of "the radical rich." What he would perhaps have portrayed as his own "radicalization," as a result of an encounter with conservative responses to the War on Poverty, was interpreted as an example of the class panic of the limousine liberals. Perhaps Moynihan also elided Lenzner in his own mind with those liberals, like William Ryan and the Reverend Robert Spike, who had done him such an injustice over the Moynihan Report. Perhaps, too, he identified him with John Oakes of the *New York Times* and other wealthy, socially influential liberals, who had misinterpreted his memo about "benign neglect." A few weeks later, he noted in the same diary that both *Time* and *Newsweek*, referring to him, would not resist leading with a reference to "benign neglect," and *Newsweek* headlined its article "Benign Reject." Moynihan commented, "It won't ever go away, will it?" The media reaction was just another proof, if any were needed, of how the unjust lashes of the liberal press still hurt.

There was more to it than raw personal resentment, though, as he sat there in Delhi, occasionally descending on Washington. He was mostly preoccupied with ambassadorial duties, but these left him with plenty of time for reflection on the kaleidoscopic change that was taking place in American politics; and for trying to work out where his own place could be in the evolving system. The hapless Terry Lenzner, in that context, was merely a specimen of those moderate Republicans, prosperous and Protestant, the John V. Lindsays, Bradford Morses, Charles Mathiases and the like, who were being swept from the Republican party their forebears had once controlled.

Late in November 1974, as he was getting ready to leave India, Moynihan developed a theory of his own about the origins of Watergate. On November 19, he opened a conference about the international drug trade in Delhi with his own history of the Nixon administration's antidrug activities, "throwing in the Liddy/Watergate theory at the end, to wake up the audience." At the end, his former White House colleague Geoffrey Shephard came up and said Moynihan was "five percent off." Over drinks on the following day, Shephard told Moynihan where he thought he was wrong, with the result that the ambassador confided to his diary that "I now have, I think, a political science of Watergate."

Egil Krogh, the Nixon aide entrusted with the antidrug operation, thought the bureaucracies would not work for the president to combat heroin. The Bureau of Narcotics and Dangerous Drugs was too slow. The State Department was afraid of the diplomatic consequences of tough campaigns in countries like Colombia or Turkey. "Liddy appeared." This was G. Gordon Liddy, who had been working "on gun control — for which read against gun control" in the Justice Department. Officials at Justice were determined to get rid of him, so Liddy turned up on Krogh's payroll. "Then it began," wrote Moynihan. "Evidently they went quite wild, talking of assassination squads, to get Mafiosi. Talking of buying off Cambodian chieftains."

Then — Moynihan theorized in his diary — came the leaks, including that of the Pentagon Papers by Daniel Ellsberg. The president believed that J. Edgar Hoover was a friend of Ellsberg's father-in-law. He assumed the FBI would not even try to stop the leaks. So he concluded the White House would have to "do it yourself." That was how the Plumbers' Unit came to be set up, under Ehrlichman, who gave it to Krogh to run. Liddy offered to set about the task in a way that simply would not have occurred to a West Coast Christian Scientist lawyer like Ehrlichman. All too easily, the campaign spread from fighting drugs to combating disloyalty. It remained only for the operation to be transferred to the Committee to Re-elect the President, the notorious CREEP, and the "institutional setting" for Watergate was in place.

This explanation appealed to Moynihan for several reasons. He preferred it to the psychological explanation "Nixon was paranoid" and to the ideological theory that Nixon was "authoritarian, even fascist" and even to the political explanation that once Edward Kennedy had been discredited by the Chappaquiddick incident, Nixon was free to behave as he pleased. Best of all, from Moynihan's point of view, the drug-war theory countered the theory of the "imperial presidency." Far from being the result of an overpowerful presidency, Moynihan commented in his diary, "Watergate is the result of a presidency with too little power with respect to the major institutions which are supposed to support the president and obey his orders."

This was not mere idle musing in the privacy of his own diary. On

November 22, he wrote to his old editor, Robert Bingham, at *The Reporter,* asking, "Have you ever wondered how Watergate happened?" and producing his theory. The real question, he said, was how it came about that the president had "on his own staff," and he underlined those words, "men who would do the things that G. Gordon Liddy and E. Howard Hunt did." The answer was, he suggested, "that they were there as part of the White House drug operation which Egil Krogh ran." And he offered Bingham an article that would argue that Watergate was a consequence of the malfunctioning, not of the political system, but of the bureaucracy. Nixon's mistake in setting up an espionage-style operation inside the White House was profound. But it stemmed not from the imperial pretensions of the presidency, but from its weakness.

Between the lines of these diary jottings it was plain that, however disillusioned their author might be with the orthodox Democratic liberalism of Harvard and the Manhattan Democratic clubs, however wounded by the way that world had misinterpreted his best efforts to understand what was happening in American society, he was not going to die in the last ditch with Nixon and his men. However anxious to find villains other than Nixon at the root of the Watergate disaster, he was not a willing recruit to the project he attributed to Colson, of directing a resentful working-class Republicanism against "militant blacks and the radical rich." That left one natural group of political friends: the neoconservatives, still for the most part clustered around the conservative wing of the Democratic party and the labor movement. It would not be long before the ambassador, almost as if by elimination, identified himself publicly with a group who already numbered some of his closest friends among them, and we shall return to how that political and intellectual affinity developed. But not all of the ambassador's energies were devoted to watching the annihilation of his former colleagues in the Nixon administration, nor even to reflecting on how he could restore his own political future. In the meantime, hard as it might be to get anyone in Washington to show any interest, with the political roof there falling in, there was work to be done in India.

torships. . . . We have an open society, a multi-party government, an independent judiciary, a free press. They do not. Our problems are matters of public inquiry and debate. Theirs are not. There is nothing more to say."

Moynihan spoke up for the Soviet Jews, an issue that looked back to his first venture into international affairs in Ljubljana in 1965, but more importantly looked forward to his own term as ambassador in 1975. But he also supported Ambassador Bush when he denounced Rabbi Meir Kahane and his associates, who had shot up the Soviet embassy residence and who demonstrated against Bush in the lobby of the United States UN embassy offices.[5] In his part-time first foray into diplomacy, Moynihan was sketching a new style in which the United States could be represented: fair and fraternal toward nations of good will, but proud and contemptuous of those who used the processes of international relations in bad faith to undermine America's reputation or interests. He would soon have an opportunity to put these ideas to work in another field. But before that he went to India, to New Delhi, as Richard Nixon's ambassador to what was still, for all its gathering political and economic difficulties, the world's largest democracy.

In late 1970, a chain of circumstances began to unfold that, while comparatively little noticed in the United States, was to have tragic and lasting consequences for the billion people and more of the Indian subcontinent. Since Pakistan, along with India, had won independence from Britain in 1947, there had never been democratic elections there. Pakistan was a divided country. West Pakistan had a near monopoly of political and, more to the point, given the long series of coups, of military power. But East Pakistan, meaning the eastern, Muslim half of Bengal, had more people. So democratic elections were finally held in December 1970. The Awami League, the political expression of Bangladeshi nationalism, won the election not just in Bengal, but in the whole of Pakistan. The league's leader, Sheikh Mujibur Rahman, should have become prime minister. Instead General Yahya Khan, to all intents a military dictator, refused to honor the election result. Sheikh Mujib, as his followers knew him, demanded what amounted to independence for Bangladesh, the land of the Bengalis. Yahya Khan ordered a brutal repression. Mujib called on his people to rise and fight for their independence. Forty thousand troops, largely recruited from, and overwhelmingly commanded by, men from the western half of the divided country subdued the rebellion in Bengal with brutal violence. Mujib was secretly put on trial for his life.

Bengalis fled from the army's cruelties. By October, more than nine million had crossed the frontier to India. The predictable result was a cholera epidemic. As soon as the monsoon was over, in late fall, the Indian army seized the opportunity and invaded Bangladesh, capturing the capital, Dhaka. Indian forces also won an easy victory in the west. These events might have been ignored in the United States, had it not been for two circumstances. In 1971, Henry Kissinger was engaged in a deeply secret diplomatic maneuver of vital importance to his hopes of successful negotiations to end the Vietnam War, to transform relations with the Soviet Union and, in the process, safeguard his own somewhat endangered career. The key move was a secret contact with China, arranged and concealed through the good offices of Pakistan. Through this bold move, Kissinger hoped to bring the Chinese to put pressure on the Soviet Union, which in turn would put pressure on Vietnam. Suddenly, this delicate exercise in pressure and deception was threatened by events he could scarcely bring himself to take seriously even when he sat down to write his memoirs years later. And what eventually became a fully developed international crisis was complicated by the mutual dislike and suspicion between Nixon and Kissinger, on the one hand, and the Indian prime minister, Indira Gandhi, on the other. They, and many other Americans, saw Mrs. Gandhi as arrogant, though she was hardly uniquely so when compared with, for example, Pakistani generals.

What they saw as Mrs. Gandhi's alleged arrogance might still have been forgiven, though, had she not chosen, on August 9, 1971, at the height of the crisis, to sign a treaty of friendship with the Soviet Union. (It did not help that Kissinger, for all his legendary mastery of intelligence, had no warning whatsoever of this cardinal development; he read about it in the newspaper.)[6] She saw it as necessary to protect her country against China (which had invaded India in 1962) and against the United States (which appeared to be the ally of her bitterest enemy, Pakistan, and was to send an aircraft carrier as yet another pressure move before the crisis was over). But to Nixon and Kissinger, the move was explicable only in terms of the deepest ingratitude and treachery. In a recent interview, Kissinger maintained that in late 1971 and 1972 "we were obliged to make a demonstration that we stood by our friends." But he also maintained that it was always the intention to "tack back towards India."[7]

Pat Moynihan was not directly involved in these events. But as a delegate to the United Nations he followed them closely. His papers show that he read the cable traffic and the intelligence reports.[8] And he totally disagreed with Kissinger's analysis, perhaps because his years at the LSE had given him more background understanding of the subcontinent, perhaps because he did not have Kissinger's personal and policy investment in the "tilt towards Pakistan," as Kissinger ill-advisedly called it,[9] perhaps because the chemistry between him and Nixon's national security adviser had been abrasive from the start. Right at the beginning of the Nixon administration, Moynihan was told by Nixon that Kissinger had warned the president against him, saying, "Moynihan will only go off and write a nasty book about you."[10] Whatever the reason, he thought President Nixon was making a mistake, and he said so. In a phone call from the New York hotel where he was staying to attend UN meetings, Moynihan asked bluntly of Nixon: "What the hell are we doing backing a military regime and a losing one at that?" Nixon replied guardedly, "I can't tell you that on the phone." The reference, of course, was to Kissinger's back-channel commitment to Pakistan and to the China trip; the remark was also, though, an implicit admission that China, the communist dictatorship, bulked much larger in Nixon's (and Kissinger's) calculations, than democratic, if ornery, India.

Public Delegate Moynihan's term ended with the year 1971, and during 1972, the year of President Nixon's triumphal visit to China and Henry Kissinger's coronation as the American Metternich, Professor Moynihan was back teaching his students at Harvard, until another Nixon phone call interrupted his Thanksgiving meal.

By January 2, 1973, Henry Kissinger was writing,

Dear Pat,
. . . We are moving ahead on India and the main question is almost ready for Presidential decision. Please write or cable in backchannel. The president will want your judgment. This is no time for uncharacteristic modesty.[11]

Two days later, the nomination of Daniel Patrick Moynihan to be ambassador to India was sent to the Senate. As it turned out, the timing was nearly disastrous. On February 5, the ambassador designate testified before the Senate Foreign Relations Committee. He told the committee that the president and Mrs. Gandhi had recently exchanged pleasant notes, and that the administration had decided it was time to improve relations between the two countries. The very next day, at a gathering called the One Asia Assembly in Delhi, Mrs. Gandhi chose to criticize U.S. policy in Indochina. Nixon and Kissinger were furious. The State Department duly expressed shock. The flap did not prevent Ambassador Moynihan's confirmation, which was approved by the Foreign Relations Committee and by the Senate two days later, on February 8. But it did delay the new ambassador's arrival in Delhi by a few days. He reached his new post on February 20.

Moynihan's feelings about the place, the job and his hosts were and remain complex. If time has softened some of his dislikes and irritations, it is also true that he was from the first more sympathetic toward the (often British-educated) Indian governing class than one might have expected, or than it sometimes suited him afterward to admit. The Moynihans remain Indophiles. India is an important part of their lives. They go there whenever they can. Their daughter, Maura, speaks three Indian languages and is deeply committed to the cause of Tibet and of the Tibetan refugees in Nepal and India. Liz has written several books about India. The first, *Paradise as a Garden,* is a study of the gardens of Mughal palaces for which she received an honorary degree from New York University. She has subsequently written a biography of Babur, the first Mughal emperor, and tramped over large parts of the empire's mountain frontiers in her search for atmosphere and evidence. She has also located the gardens built by the Emperor Shah Jehan across the river Jumna from the Taj Mahal.

The joke goes that the Moynihans fell in love with three different Indias: Liz with Mughal India, Maura with Hindu India and Pat with British India. It contains a smidgen of truth. But it was not love at first sight. "They only fell in love with India retrospectively," says Checker Finn, who went with the family to India as an aide and friend. "Liz hated it the whole time she was there. She came to love it when it was getting time to go. Maura didn't specially like it while she was there."[12]

Liz did hate Roosevelt House, the great white marble embassy built by Edward Stone so that no one in India might mistake the power and wealth of the United States; it was hot and drafty, and there was pomposity but no privacy there.

For the whole family, it was the first contact with the Third World. There is a culture shock, compounded of pity, shame and rage, that comes for most Westerners from the first encounter with stinking shantytowns, the first sight of hideously deformed beggars and children with glaucoma. Few are unaffected at first exposure to the poverty and squalor that go hand in hand with the beauty and glamor of India, and the Moynihans were not among those few. Catherine Galbraith, the wife of John Kenneth, who loved her time as the ambassador's wife in Delhi, was disappointed to find that Liz was not happy there at first. But after a year, Liz said she was loving India.[13]

It was also the first time the family had been so far from home. Liz's mother had to have a mastectomy, and Tim, still in school in New England, went to see her. Mrs. Brennan and Mrs. Moynihan, Pat's mother, made plans to go to Tim's graduation at Phillips Exeter. There was a flap and more severe letters from the ambassador when Harvard decided to take the management of the Moynihans' residence in Cambridge, along with all its other house property, into its own hands. The first that Pat and Liz knew of it was when they received a letter from Harvard's agents "notifying" them that their lease on Francis Avenue would be terminated while they were in India. The ambassador wrote back telling the agents that their letter "is not a little abrupt." The agents "can do better than this and had damn well better." It turned out that "by some oversight" the Harvard real estate department had mistakenly informed the Moynihans that their lease was going to be terminated, when instead it would simply be managed directly by the university. As always, the ambassador wrote witty reproof, the ambassador's wife sorted things out.

The Moynihans were not spared the tribulation most Westerners experience in India: gastroenteritis in all its myriad forms. "A howling night of bacillary," Pat recorded one night in his diary.[14] He had been up until dawn, slept all the next day. "We are all sick here all the time," he complained in his diary. "I have been sick for two years, and it has begun to get to me. Our talk is mostly of sickness, of miscarriages, of hepatitis, of abortions following hepatitis."

And then there was the heat. At noon in Delhi, before the monsoon, when it can reach 125 in the shade, it is so intense that one has to play games to hang on to his sanity. One of the games the American ambassador used to play was to picture that it was 1:00, lunchtime, at the farm, time to stroll down the hill from the white wooden schoolroom in the shade of the roadside trees, with lunch waiting, a nap and a swim in the pool. He would imagine the wooded crest of the hill behind the farm, and the stream at the foot of the gentle downward slope where he would fish in the cool of the evening. Lush foliage lined the country road: maples, self-seeded apple and wild cherry, locust and hemlock. As the pitiless Indian sun beat down, he would dream above all of shade. All the Moynihans took every opportunity to cope with the heat in the traditional way: by fleeing to the hills. It was then that Maura discovered an enduring passion for Nepal and Liz began to explore Mughal architecture, and to the hills that the ambassador traveled on the rare occasions when events in Delhi allowed.

There were aspects of India that appealed, however. Checker Finn believes Moynihan's Anglophilia helped. "He wore his LSE blazer," he jokes, "even while he was denouncing the influence of the LSE on the Indian elite." About that elite, too, he was ambivalent. He was irritated, as most Americans were then and perhaps still are, by the airs of moral superiority with which some Indian intellectuals denounced American "crimes" while expecting the United States to operate a double standard in India's favor. But he understood better than many Americans the deep roots of such Indian attitudes in a sense of shame and impotence toward the desperate poverty, the legacy of caste and religious prejudice and the psychology of the colonized. For a social scientist with an interest in the politics of ethnicity, India was a vast and tempting laboratory. And he certainly found the Delhi officials and intellectuals, for all the anti-American prejudices of some of them, attractive to spend time with.

Of a lunch given to him by the foreign ministry in January 1974, he wrote, "and a very good lunch it was . . . the women as handsome as the men." If Kewal Singh (the senior permanent official at the foreign ministry) "is not a good man, I have no sense for the matter and should be got out of this business." They were a bit at home in Moscow now, he guessed, "but London and Washington come much easier to them, and I would dare to think they were more comfortable there than in Delhi." Gopi Kaul (another official) "was wearing a particularly handsome houndstooth jacket. Woodward & Lothrop."[15] He found their worldly, slightly malicious conversation just to his taste. He paid a mock solemn compliment about the sacrifices one Indian diplomat had made. "Exactly," came the reply from his colleague. "He has even sacrificed his opinions." He records another conversation with a senior Indian official in which the unstated assumptions of the Indian and the American were taken for granted.

"What does she think?" Moynihan asked, meaning she who must be obeyed, Mrs. Gandhi.

"She is not a communist."

"Ought I not to be offended that you would feel it necessary to say that. Of course she is not a communist. She had her leftist days at Oxford, but who did not?"

No answer, Moynihan wrote: only a quotation from George Bernard Shaw: "Everyone over forty is a rascal." It reminded Moynihan of a conversation in Chekhov. "Somewhere off stage the cherry trees are being chopped down to make room for a new Asia neither of us dreamed of."

In truth, the ambassador often found the Americans in Delhi more irritating than the Indians. The embassy was huge and overstaffed, and though some of the officials, such as David Schneider, the deputy chief of mission, were of the highest quality and devotion, others were not. Moynihan was particularly displeased by the three semi-independent agencies, the CIA, the Agency for International Development (AID) and the Peace Corps.

The Indians were paranoid about the CIA. This was admittedly the time of CIA covert actions in Indochina, Chile, Italy and many other places. Investigative reporting, in the United States and abroad, was beginning to reveal just how widely and unwisely the agency had neglected its intelligence-gathering responsibility in favor of clandestine interference in many countries. The Indians assumed that it was happening in their country too, and they were not entirely wrong. On two occasions, the CIA had given money to Mrs. Gandhi's Congress party to use against the communists in elections in West Bengal and Kerala. Indeed, on one occasion the money was given to Mrs. Gandhi personally.[16] Soon after he arrived in India, Moynihan learned that the CIA had installed equipment high in the Himalayas to monitor Chinese nuclear tests: On October 16, 1964, the Chinese detonated their first nuclear device at Lop Nor on the edge of the Gobi Desert in Sinkiang. Relations between India and Washington had improved. Just before the assassination of President Kennedy in November 1963, the then Indian prime minister, Jawaharlal Nehru, the high priest of nonalignment, terrified by the Chinese military successes against

India on the Himalayan front in 1962, sent him a desperate message, asking for help in the concrete shape of U.S. military aircraft. U.S. intelligence personnel, under the most varied forms of cover, began to appear in India.

In 1965, the Indian Intelligence Bureau (IB), acting on behalf of the CIA, recruited four Indian mountaineers, members of the 1962 Everest expedition. They formed part of a twenty-one-man Indo-American team, which was to climb Nanda Devi, a peak over twenty-four thousand feet high, to put equipment in place to monitor Chinese tests. The power pack needed to activate the sensors consisted of an aluminum cylinder, thirteen inches long and fourteen inches in diameter, containing tiny tantalum pods to shield some three pounds of plutonium 238 isotopes. They were forced by the weather to abandon the attempt, called Operation Blue Mountain, and left the cylinder about one thousand feet below the summit of Nanda Devi. When the team returned in May 1966 to retrieve the plutonium pack, it had been lost in an avalanche.[17] A small but radioactive quantity of plutonium was lost in the snowpack at the headwaters of the sacred Ganges. The U.S. ambassador at the time, Chester Bowles, informed Mrs. Gandhi, no less, and a second Indo-American expedition installed the instruments on top of the nearby, slightly lower peak of Nanda Kot. Altogether, four Indian prime ministers — Nehru, Lal Bahadur Shastri, Indira Gandhi and Morarji Desai — were aware of the plan to put plutonium in the high peaks of the Garhwal Himalayas.

Moynihan knew enough about the mythic power of Mother Ganga as a symbol of India's inviolability that he could imagine what the Indian press, with the communist papers setting the pace, would make of the idea that the Americans were poisoning the holy river of the Hindus with nuclear radiation.

The whole episode did nothing for the CIA's reputation with those who knew what had happened. Nor did the fact that one of the biggest CIA stations in the world totally failed to give the embassy or the government in Washington any warning when, on May 17, 1973, India exploded a nuclear device under the Rajasthan desert, near the country's western border with Pakistan, and so became, at least potentially, a nuclear power.

Moynihan's experience of the CIA in India influenced his later attitudes as a member of the Senate Intelligence Oversight Committee and as the chairman of a Senate committee investigating excessive government secrecy. "CIA is not dead," he wrote in his diary, "but dying, I should think."

> Killed by Howard Hunt.[18] Too much white shoe fun in an unfunny world. They have just mercilessly ["fouled" crossed out] fucked up in Thailand . . . a cease fire from the Communist insurgents in the North. Object psych warfare. Make insurgents give up because they think it is all over. Alas, the illiterate youth who was given the letter to mail registered it with the home address of the agent who had given it to him.
>
> Result, black wreaths hung on the Embassy gates, apologies, silences. . . .[19]

Another result, he pointed out angrily in his diary, was that when he, as ambassador, was about to raise hell with the Indian government about a pronouncement by the prime minister's own party in Uttar Pradesh (the most populous state in the country), asserting that the CIA was behind the parties of the Right, he decided instead to say nothing. "They know that we have done such things in India. Never mind on their behalf. They know we are doing them in Thailand. Why should they take my word that we are not doing them in UP?" The station chief in Delhi, R. Jack Smith, was "a sensitive and superbly prudent and patient man." And yet, Moynihan said, "in a year of trying to get them to *think* about Indian communism for me, they have not been able to do so. At best I get a list of suspect party members compiled at about the level the FBI used to do such things." The ambassador's personal mail, meanwhile, was routinely opened and resealed with government-issue glue of approximately the color and texture of shoe leather. Liz, he said, was treasuring a note from Jacqueline Kennedy Onassis written on flimsy paper and sealed, as it were, "with babies' breath," then resealed in the Delhi central post office.

The ambassador was even more severe on the other agencies. He called them "the three dead bureaucracies," all killed by the Vietnam War. "Apology became their primary mode. Having once become ashamed of their country, they cannot now serve it," he felt. "All should be disbanded."

His young staffers, for instance, called the Peace Corps the "Peace Corpse." The volunteers were all right, but the bureaucracy indeed was dead. "It died that day of the Cambodian protest when they flew the Vietcong flag from the pole of their headquarters in Washington. You don't get over such things." The Agency for International

Development was "pathetic." Asked for $75 million in assistance for India, they came up with $500,000. AID, said Moynihan, will not forgive the Indians. AID existed primarily — such, said the ambassador, seemed to be the bureaucrats' conviction — "to sustain and enhance the self-images of the administrators as benefactors of the unfortunate and the fallen. When the unfortunate and the fallen used bad language they were cut off . . . [i]s there anything so malignant as an American do good enterprise turned bitter?" The United States Information Agency, the ambassador confided to his diary, was "bigger and worser. They have no idea what they are doing in India, and do nothing." He diagnosed weakness of mind, the "liberal disease."

In these jaundiced musings, the thoughts of a far from dry mind in a far from dry season, Moynihan was formulating some of the thoughts he would carry back like banners into the stricken field of post-Watergate American politics. His brutal judgments of the bureaucracy's shortcomings were not aimed at government as such. He was demanding that the American Raj, like Harvard's real estate agent, "should damn well do better."

What he saw, too, was that the problems were not just on the farther shores of the American imperium. They were in Washington, too. The American business community was utterly uninterested in India, in spite of the size of its population and of its economy; in an interview with Patricia J. Sethi of *Newsweek,* just before he left Delhi, Moynihan said, "There are about 40 American businessmen in this country and even that number is going down." Congress was eerily indifferent to so large and important a country. "It is more than a year since a live Congressman set foot on Indian soil," Moynihan wrote in his diary in January 1974. He would have settled for Michael Van Dusen, staff director of the House Subcommittee on South Asia, who had been writing reports that were "the only visible sign from Congress that India exists." But even Van Dusen cabled that he would not be able to make it to Delhi from Pakistan.

But if Congress was indifferent, the executive branch of the U.S. government, in the shape both of the State Department and of Henry Kissinger, was actively unsympathetic to India and its problems. The American ambassador to India was forever stressing the importance of India, with its gross national product, tiny in proportion to India's huge population, but absolutely large, and its formidable military forces, now strengthened by at least the prospect of acquiring nuclear weapons at an early date. When Washington proposed an international conference to discuss the oil crisis, for example, Moynihan asked his diary, "Why not invite India — one (if to be sure the last) of the ten nations with the highest GNP?" The image of India as a land of fakirs and oxcarts, boundless poverty and timeless languor, was too deeply embedded in Washington to be eradicated.

Early in 1974, there were reports that Henry Kissinger himself would be visiting India in March. In the event, the visit was postponed until the fall. The news that Joseph Sisco had been promoted to undersecretary of state for political affairs by his mentor, Kissinger, set off a diatribe in Moynihan's diary against Sisco, the State Department and Kissinger. Moynihan declined to come back to a job in Washington as counselor to the State Department, offered by Kissinger, he said, because India "was too important to leave this soon." But Sisco knew better. His attitude, and Kissinger's, Moynihan thought, was "Screw India. Who needs it?" Washington has no ideas about this place, he added, and no interest. Moynihan was aware that he was up against the age-old American preference for China over India. Americans had long seen China as an opportunity for American salesmen, American missionaries and American diplomats, while the Indian subcontinent, with almost as large a population as China, democratic as opposed to Communist, and to a considerable extent English-speaking, was seen as inaccessible or insignificant. This historic antipathy to India was reinforced by Nixon, Kissinger, and their colleagues with their investment in the new opening to China.

Up to the point in early 1974 when he wrote those disillusioned words about his superiors in Washington, Moynihan had in fact been a highly successful, if distinctly unorthodox, ambassador. His great achievement involved the writing off of two-thirds of the rupee debt, or "counterpart funds," which India had contracted to pay for foodstuffs before, as a result of the "Green Revolution," it became virtually self-sufficient in food. At the conclusion of the negotiation it fell to him as ambassador to write a check to the government of India for $2.2 billion. It was, he maintains, the biggest check ever written up to that time. Framed, it still occupies a place of honor on the wall of his Senate office.

From the moment he was appointed ambassador, Moynihan made the "rupee problem" one of his two first priorities in India. The problem arose because in 1954 the United States Congress, with memorable generosity, passed Public Law 480, enabling Third World countries to buy American wheat and other foodstuffs for local currency. In the 1950s and 1960s, India bought a total of about 60 million tons of food. The government of India, by 1973, had repaid about $900 million for food and other aid, and the balance was deposited in a special U.S. government account in the Reserve Bank of India, accumulating interest at the concessionary rate of 1.5 percent. The money was supposed to be used for supporting the U.S. embassy and other activities in India. But the United States could not spend more than a fraction of the money for that. Instead, large sums were lent back to the Indian government in the form of interest-bearing paper for development projects. By the time Moynihan arrived, the Indian debt had snowballed to $3.2 billion and, if not canceled, would nearly double by the turn of the new century. As Moynihan argued forcefully, the mere fact that a substantial part of the economy — perhaps as much as one-fifth — was controlled, even if only on paper, by a foreign power troubled the Indian government and many ordinary Indians. The American debt reinforced Indian paranoia about the alleged greed of Western capitalists. It also touched raw nerves in a country where most farmers struggled with extortionate debt repayments to the *bania*, the village moneylender.

Moynihan's mind may have been set on the track that led to this bold policy initiative by a chance letter from a Dr. Kevin Cahill, of the tropical diseases center at Lenox Hill Hospital on Manhattan's East Side. Cahill wrote him on July 25, 1973, when he was getting ready to go to India, asking Moynihan if it would be possible to use some of the blocked rupees for a scientific conference in Bombay. Moynihan saw the defensive potential. By settling the rupee debt question, it might be possible to remove a dangerous source of potential future resentment in India against the United States. Afterward he wrote:

> ... the grain was eaten and soon forgotten. The debt remained, equal to a third of the Indian money supply, to be paid, if ever, by great-great-grandchildren. Already it was being put about that far from being an act of generosity, the wheat had been "dumped" on India to sustain American farm prices. Soon, surely, it would be "discovered" that the larger purpose had been to injure Indian agriculture.
>
> At that point, demand for repudiation of the debt would not be far off. What else was to be expected? The United States ought either to have given the Indians the food or summoned the nerve to let them go hungry. We chose instead to feed them and to humiliate them.[20]

So on this logic he set out on the path, not an easy one, of persuading the Nixon administration and Congress that the political and diplomatic advantages to the United States of forgiving the debt far outweighed the advantage of enforcing it. After all, the debt was repayable in rupees, not dollars, and the U.S. government not only didn't want so many rupees; it would find it impossible to exchange them into dollars without upsetting the Indian economy.

By the end of his first year in the embassy, Moynihan had broken down this resistance. He succeeded in persuading the Congress to go along with what was, after all, a gesture of historic magnanimity, especially in view of the Indian government's friendly relations with the Soviet Union, the United States's most dangerous adversary. He made a whole series of trips to Washington. Legend has it that on one occasion he sent a cable to the State Department, then flew to Washington and composed a favorable answer. He was back in Washington in June for consultations with the State Department and Treasury and then flew out to meet the president at the Western White House at San Clemente, California, to discuss the rupee debt issue and other matters. In meeting with Mrs. Gandhi in mid-July, he stressed his closeness to Kissinger, Secretary of State William Rogers and Treasury Secretary George Shultz as a means of gaining leverage.[21] Deal with me while I'm still here, he was saying. I may not be here forever. His personal commitment was beyond doubt. He recalled to Tony Clifton of *Newsweek* how at his final, as it turned out decisive, appearance before the Senate Foreign Relations Committee, the chairman, Senator J. William Fulbright of Arkansas, asked him, "Do you think what you propose is in the best interests of the United States?"[22]

It was, he thought, "the most solemn moment in my life since I made the same reply at my wedding."

The breakthrough in negotiations came in September. The agreement as it was finally worked out was ingenious. India prepaid all outstanding rupee debt obligations due over the next forty years, a total of over sixteen billion rupees, thus getting rid of all future interest payments. In a paper transaction, the United States would then "grant" India the money, which India would be able to use for development under a new five-year plan. Moynihan and the Indian finance minister, T. R. Kaul, initialed the agreement on December 13,[23] and Moynihan signed the check. On December 19, President Nixon wrote Indira Gandhi that a "resolution of this long-standing and extremely complex issue will mark an important new step forward in our relations," and in early January, Mrs. Gandhi cabled back her appreciation of Ambassador Moynihan's "tireless efforts" and agreed that the two countries were poised to "build forthwith a new relationship by constructive dialogue and mutual co-operation."[24] Later that month, the ambassador was back in Washington lining up support in Congress for the agreement, which was finally ratified in the middle of February.

Before Moynihan could test the sincerity of Mrs. Gandhi's sentiments, indeed only two days after the rupee agreement was initialed, he and Liz went through an extremely unpleasant personal experience. On August 5, 1973, "Black September" terrorists threw grenades and sprayed gunfire into lines of passengers waiting to check in at Glyfada Airport in Athens. Four died. According to Israeli intelligence, passed on to the United States, Black September, responsible for the attacks on Israeli athletes at the Olympic games in Munich the previous year, was part of Al Fatah, the Palestinian movement led by Yasser Arafat.

On December 15, the Egyptian ambassador in Delhi contacted Moynihan.[25] The two ambassadors met at a New Delhi hotel. The Egyptian came to the point. He had been instructed by Cairo to warn Moynihan that Arab terrorists wanted to prevent the planned Middle East peace conference taking place in Geneva, due to start in a couple of weeks, by a series of terrorist attacks. One was a hijacking at Rome's Leonardo da Vinci Airport. That duly took place on December 17. So one of the Egyptian's tip-offs checked out. The other was that the terrorists planned to assassinate Daniel P. Moynihan.

Moynihan went back to the embassy and told his aides. They contacted the government of India, which confirmed that there was a PLO office in Delhi and, more to the point, confirmed the Egyptian intelligence report that there was a plot against Moynihan. The Indians advised him to stay inside the embassy compound over the Christmas holiday, and Liz Moynihan remembers that there were Indian soldiers deployed around the perimeter.[26] "Roosevelt House," wrote Pat in his diary, "was turned into a fort at Christmas. Security men at midnight mass." He remained skeptical about the reliability of the Egyptian ambassador's dramatic warning.[27] True or not, the experience was alarming, and one that may well have colored subconsciously Moynihan's attitude to those countries that helped the PLO.

The second task he set himself, and it proved even harder than giving away more money than anyone had ever given away at any single time, was to improve relations with the imperious and mysterious Mrs. Gandhi. They had not started well. There was the speech attacking U.S. policy in Vietnam. In the recent past, there had been the war with Pakistan, ending in comprehensive defeat for Henry Kissinger's new friend, General Yahya Khan. There was the fact that Richard Nixon, however much he might have decided to improve U.S.-Indian relations, just didn't like the woman. There were personal, cultural, diplomatic and geopolitical obstacles to be overcome, and deep reciprocal suspicion, as was graphically brought home by a rather trivial incident early in Moynihan's time in Delhi.

A young foreign service officer, A. Peter Burleigh, who had previously been in the Peace Corps, got on a bus and went back to the remote district in Bihar where he had served, and was blamed for an attack on a *harijan,* or untouchable. A communist paper in West Bengal picked up the story. It said Burleigh was a CIA agent come to stir up communal unrest. Mrs. Gandhi believed it, and the Indian government prepared to declare the young American persona non grata. Moynihan called on Kewal Singh, and announced bluntly, "If you send him home, I will go with him and I don't know when anyone will be back."[28] Moynihan could take as high a view in his way of what was due to the honor and dignity of the American Republic as any proconsul of the Raj could have taken of the majesty of the queen-empress.

The rupee debt negotiations improved relations noticeably, though Moynihan was disappointed by Mrs. Gandhi's unwillingness to release publicly the text of the letters exchanged between the two governments on the subject. She was no communist, true. But "she is in an electoral alliance with the Communist Party and this comes first in her mind."[29]

U.S.-Indian relations were to be more severely tested by the explosion of an Indian nuclear bomb in the Rajasthan desert. On June 19, Moynihan wrote that he had enjoyed a "friendly, easy talk" with Mrs. Gandhi.[30] In it, however, she pointed out that the United States had not objected when France and China had both set off larger nuclear explosions than India's, and that her father had been ridiculed when he had proposed a nuclear nonproliferation treaty of the kind the United States was now pressing India to sign. The previous day, the ambassador had a long conversation with Mrs. Gandhi's private secretary, Professor L. K. Dhar. "Surely now," Moynihan said, "is the time for India to move. Now! Under cover of the energy crisis." He meant that India should abandon the socialist path and the Soviet connection. "There will be no aid," he told Dhar. "Oil prices have killed it." Instead India should rely on engaging with the economies of the West, selling coal, oil, raw materials. Three weeks later, he wrote an eight-page paper for Kissinger called "A Strategy to Prevent the Indian Nuclear Explosion Leading to General Nuclear Proliferation."[31]

So long as Mrs. Gandhi remained prime minister, he conceded, no "conversion" was likely. But events would persuade Delhi that if the United States "will help, it can." He argued that Henry Kissinger's visit to Delhi, scheduled for September, was an opportunity that must be seized to prevent the Indian nuclear explosion from leading to a general proliferation of nuclear weapons. He spelled out his thinking even more frankly in a long, racy cable to Kissinger's aide Lawrence Eagleburger. The worst India could do to the United States, he argued, was to collapse, and the Indian economy would be hard-pressed by the rise in oil and wheat prices. "There is an American interest in the economic success of India," he said, but it was not clear what course of action followed from that conclusion. The aid programs of the 1960s were no longer workable. He pointed out that the United States gave India less money than other countries, such as the United Kingdom, Germany, Canada and Japan, and argued that the rupee agreement should be followed by further "debt rescheduling amounting to outright forgiveness."

Moynihan was laboring in the vineyard to improve relations with India and at the same time to draw India out of the Soviet orbit and into that of the United States. To that end, he wanted Kissinger, now secretary of state, to visit Delhi and make a speech full of "praise for India. Praise for its leader. Praise for great future." He should praise nonalignment, for the simple reason that nonalignment, after the oil price rise, was dead. India was already the tenth industrial country in the world, "a great nation and will be greater still." The real crisis in India was a crisis of confidence, and Kissinger should tell the Indians they need have no fear.

On August 8, Nixon resigned. On August 9, Moynihan submitted his resignation as ambassador, which the incoming President Ford ignored. Washington had more immediate things to think about than India. Long before Nixon resigned, however, Moynihan had decided that it was only a matter of time before he too would be leaving New Delhi.

———

On July 8, 1999, Hillary Clinton came to the Moynihans' farm to launch her campaign for the U.S. Senate. When she and Moynihan emerged to meet the media, the senator joked, "My God, I almost forgot! I'm here to say I hope she'll go all the way." *Keith Meyers/NYT Pictures*

Ensign Moynihan in June 1946, after he graduated from Tufts and was assigned to the USS *Quirinus*. Gloria Greenley, a student at Middlebury, was Moynihan's girlfriend. *Courtesy Daniel P. Moynihan*

Moynihan skiing with his boss, New York Governor Averell Harriman, at Whiteface Mountain in the Adirondacks in April 1955. Harriman was running for president and wanted to look young and vigorous. Pat, then twenty-eight, simply did look that way. *AP/Wide World Photos*

The caption Moynihan wrote for this photograph, which is on his office wall, reads: "This portrait was taken by me from Mrs. Lincoln's office at about midnight on November 22, 1963. The photograph was the only thing she'd left behind. I took it, went round to the center door of the Oval Office, saluted and left." *Courtesy Daniel P. Moynihan*

Moynihan played an important part in shaping Lyndon Johnson's War on Poverty. Here he is with LBJ at a Senate hearing before Johnson became president. *Courtesy Daniel P. Moynihan*

When President Johnson spotted Moynihan in a receiving line in the early days of his presidency, he wheeled and shouted, "Moynihan! Moynihan! That's my man!" But when he suspected Moynihan of being a Kennedy man, he wouldn't even write him a letter of thanks. *Courtesy Daniel P. Moynihan*

In Rome in June 1965, the Moynihans had an audience with Pope Paul VI, who became agitated when Pat asked, "What about our friends the Jews?" *Fotografia Felici*

The refurbishing of Pennsylvania Avenue was one of Moynihan's lifetime projects. He first proposed it to President Kennedy and was still fighting for it under President Clinton. Here he is showing a model to President Nixon. Moynihan now lives on the avenue. *Courtesy National Archives*

UNITED STATES

As U.S. ambassador to the United Nations, Moynihan was contemptuous of the 1975 resolution identifying Zionism with racism. After one vote, he embraced the Israeli ambassador and was heard to say, "Fuck 'em." *Courtesy Daniel P. Moynihan*

When the Erie Canal was reopened in 1983, Moynihan, now a United States senator from New York, went for a boat ride with his wife. *Photograph by Joe Traver from the Courier Express Collection, courtesy of E. H. Butler Library Archives, Buffalo State College and the Buffalo and Erie County Historical Society*

Three hundred yards up the hill from the Moynihan farm is an old white wooden schoolhouse with a potbellied stove where Pat has written eighteen books on a Smith-Corona electric typewriter.
N. Boenzi/NYT Pictures

Moynihan soon became a critic of President Reagan's economic policies and later of his staff's foreign adventures. But he retained great affection for Reagan personally.
Courtesy Ronald Reagan Library

In November 1992, with his friend Peter Galbraith, son of John Kenneth, Moynihan visited Sarajevo, then the scene of "the most intense urban warfare in the world." While there he had dinner with the French Foreign Legion, who "have a thing about dining well under fire." *Picture by courtesy of Reuters*

Moynihan called President Clinton's health care reform "boob bait for the bubbas," but that didn't prevent him from enjoying Clinton's black tie hospitality with his daughter, Maura. *White House Photo*

The senator reads to his grandson Michael Patrick Avedon, Maura's son. *Courtesy Daniel P. Moynihan*

The Moynihans' apartment overlooks both Pennsylvania Avenue, rebuilt largely as a result of the senator's faith and works, and the U.S. Navy Memorial, where he likes to attend band concerts. © *John McDonnell, Washington Post, reprinted with permission*

On January 9, 1974, Moynihan anticipated his own end as ambassador to India in almost boisterously cheerful terms. It had been an agreeable day. He had risen at five to see off Liz and her old friend Margaret Bright, who was in India to give some lectures on population. Off they went, "being girls again. Bottle of sherry in the hamper. Wot the hell." Then he described how the cables delivered blow after blow. Sisco's promotion. Only $500,000 in aid. His colleague Henry Byroade in Pakistan "has gone over completely to the enemy." And so on.

In some MGM movie of the 1930s, he remembered, a group of British officers were examining "a peach-bottomed youth seeking service in her Majesty's dominions." What would happen, the senior officer asked the boy, if you were struck on the arm by a king cobra?[32] "The youth hesitates, rejects a sequence of desperate moves and then stammers, 'I'd . . . die, sir.' 'Exactly,' says the old gentleman." Let it then be recorded, Moynihan wrote in his diary that day, "that my embassy died on Wednesday, January 9, 1974. Rather with the young man it was a decision not to struggle against the inevitable."[33]

He then proceeded to list a dozen reasons why he despaired of achieving what he wanted in Washington. Checker Finn said recently that Moynihan realized there wasn't much work for him in Delhi, and used his time writing. In the spring of 1974, for example, he received a long and thoughtful letter from Irving Kristol, to whom he had sent a critique of an issue of *The Public Interest* on the Great Society. The key issue, Kristol wrote, is "Social democracy — why doesn't it work." It is not too early, Kristol went on, to draw conclusions from the social democratic experiments of Western Europe and the United States. They had degenerated into "a barren and quite squalid form of paternalism-egalitarianism, in which the nation is convulsed by the issue of why, if one batch of people are getting false teeth free of charge, some other group should not." Almost six weeks later, the ambassador wrote back that he was hard at work on two pieces for Kristol. He added, in response to Kristol's letter about social democracy, merely, "there is something there."

The evidence of his diary suggests, however, not that he was uninterested in his embassy, but something rather different: that he set out with the two objectives of settling the rupee debt problem and improving relations with Mrs. Gandhi. Only when one goal had been reached, and the other began to look elusive, did he begin to use his time in Delhi, away from the increasingly strident politics of post-Watergate Washington, as a time for some fundamental reflection about both America's place in the world and the strange death of Great Society liberalism.

By February 1974, the rupee agreement was in the bag, but relations between India and the United States were showing no signs of serious improvement. In Washington, this stalemate was put down to the impossibility of the Indians. As Moynihan memorably described the Pentagon's attitude in his cable to Eagleburger, there was in some parts of official Washington "a kind of John Birch Society contempt for the views of raggedy ass people in pajamas on the other side of the world."

That was not Moynihan's attitude. He respected Indians, liked some of them and always treated India as a great nation with problems that just might overwhelm it, even while he was as irritated as most by the pretensions and the self-deceptions of Indian politicians and intellectuals. When asked whether the Indians he had known at LSE irritated him, he answered simply, "No, attracted." His attitude to Mrs. Gandhi, too, was very different from that of Richard Nixon, who called her "hypocritical" and "duplicitous" and saw her as little more than a cat's-paw for the Soviet Union.

Henry Kissinger's attitude was somewhere between Nixon's and Moynihan's. He agreed in an interview that he was "not fantastically interested" in India.[34] He was not fond of what he called "the Harvard interpretation" of India and its policies. He felt the Indian government was full of "cold-blooded manipulators" who were trying to recreate the British Empire east of Suez. Even so, the last great public event of Moynihan's time in Delhi was Kissinger's official visit in late October 1974.

Moynihan flew to Moscow to meet Kissinger and accompany him on his flight to Delhi. He was unimpressed by Moscow. The Kremlin, he thought, was "a cross between Pall Mall and the Ohio State University campus" and "any dusty Rajasthan town has ramparts twice the size of the Kremlin's."[35] He recorded with pleasure a conversation at the Soviet Institute for the Study of the United States. Did he know the Russian novel *Peace and War*? he was asked. "It is like your novel *Gone With the Wind*."

He composed for his diary a memorable description of Henry Kissinger's flying circus. "The secretary sat in splendor up front, while in the middle cabin, or middle passage as it might better be known, is a horror of human cargo . . . [sundry famous diplomats] and me on the port benches, [other diplomats] and a change of secretaries to starboard. A Xerox machine, an IBM typewriter, briefing books, cameras, clothes, old meals, attaché cases, attaché cases, attaché cases, attaché cases. There is no stench as such. These are scrubbed and laundered Americans. But somewhere under the detritus is the last press spokesman but four. The football scores go round. Yale won again."[36]

The diplomats told stories of the lashes their master inflicted. They recalled with horror the time in Cairo when he had stormed out of a meeting with Anwar Sadat. Where was the paper he needed? In his briefcase, he was told. "Kindly recall," said the secretary, "that it was I who was meeting with the premier, not my briefcase."

At the last minute, Kissinger even made a halfhearted attempt to get out of going to Delhi altogether, but Moynihan easily persuaded him that he had no alternative but to go through with the visit. But at the airport, Kissinger, putting aside several drafts of his arrival speech, supplied by his staff, was "superb." He ad-libbed three paragraphs of his own, saying that the two greatest democracies in the world had rediscovered their common purposes.

To discover whether or not they had truly done so was the purpose of the visit. Kissinger had two meetings with Mrs. Gandhi on the Monday, with no holds barred. Moynihan noted that Kissinger's style in summit meetings seemed to be to move from "the pretty to the real." Mrs. Gandhi complained about CIA operations in India, and Kissinger lectured her about the new Indian nuclear bomb. That evening Kissinger made a major speech, assuring the Indians that "the United States accepts nonalignment." It was, as Moynihan pointed out crossly to his friends at the *New York Times*, who had not seen fit to report it, a major departure from twenty years of the foreign policy of John Foster Dulles. Only Murrey Marder of the *Washington Post* had seen how important that was. Kissinger was a little bored by Delhi, he admitted that night. He preferred Beijing, where he and his Chinese friends could philosophize together all night. It was true, Kissinger reminisced twenty-five years later. With the Chinese, you could talk eighteenth-century balance-of-power politics. You couldn't talk about trade, or arms sales. "We had no questions to talk about except the important ones."[37]

After tough talks with various top Indian officials, Kissinger had been looking forward to a dinner planned with Indian "intellectuals," but the event was something close to a disaster. The intellectuals produced what Moynihan called "one dreary hack communist question after another."

There was time for some straight talking between the ambassador and the secretary. Moynihan tackled Kissinger about why Nixon had sent the U.S. aircraft carrier *Enterprise* to the Bay of Bengal during the 1971 crisis over the creation of Bangladesh. Kissinger admitted that one reason was that Nixon wanted to impress the Soviet leadership with his "brass balls," even to appear "trigger happy," in order to intimidate them. Kissinger volunteered that Moynihan had been right not to go back to Washington to work for him, as he had asked. All in all, Moynihan reported to India hands in the United States, the visit had been a great success.[38] Kissinger had been "simply brilliant." When the time came to say goodbye to the secretary at the airport, "we hugged each other. Felt like it."

Moynihan was fascinated by the elusive personality of Indira Gandhi. Her exceptionally complex as well as rather devious character not only challenged his own subtlety; it reflected his ambivalence about India as well. Her charm in personal relations contrasted with considerable ruthlessness. She also changed her political line, in particular toward the United States, in accordance with what she saw as the needs of India, with which she had a strong tendency to identify herself. (She once told me that as her father's representative, she had perhaps visited more of the reputed half million villages in India than anyone else in history.) Letting off steam in an interview with his friend Richard Meryman, Moynihan said that Mrs. Gandhi "acquired a very, very vague left view of the world in which the U.S. was seen as an ominous power, acting out of capitalist, imperialist racist motives. She just trundled that junk home with her and nothing much was added later."[39] That interview was given in early 1977, after Moynihan's time at the United Nations, and when he was considering whether to run for office. Earlier, and later, his views were more complex. In his book *A Dangerous Place*, he claimed to have anticipated that she would abolish democracy, and that he was talked out of saying so publicly at a press conference only the day before he left Delhi by David Schneider, his deputy chief of mission.

Shortly after he left Delhi, he received a dignified and friendly letter from Mrs. Gandhi. She began by thanking him for "speaking up for India" on his trip to Beijing. However, she rejected Moynihan's suggestion that her father had been anti-American. "There were elements in America of which he certainly disapproved. But he did realize that these attitudes were not confined to the U.S. We find them amongst the people of other affluent countries and indeed in some sections of our own people . . . But he had the greatest admiration for the vision which guided America's Founding Fathers."[40]

Years later, Moynihan put down some of his feelings about Indira Gandhi. In 1975, he recalled, an Indian magistrate found her guilty of violating election laws, declared her election invalid and banned her from public life. "That sort of thing happens in India, much as it does here. It is called democracy."[41] Her response was to declare a state of emergency, which was constitutionally proper, and to put two hundred thousand opponents in prison, which was not. For two years she ruled by decree. Then she called a national election, confident that it would legitimate what was an illegitimate government. The Indian people voted no. "And?" Moynihan wrote. "And Indira Gandhi turned over the prime ministership, the Treasury, the Army, the Great Seal, to her successor, and went off to live in a bungalow. In that moment, she put herself at the greatest risk of arrest and retribution. Simultaneously, she established Indian democracy. I could not always agree with her, but I flew 7,486 miles to her funeral." It is hard to avoid the judgment that Moynihan's estimates of Indira Gandhi were as political as her own shifts of tone toward the United States. In early 1975, as he prepared to go to the United Nations to reassert American self-belief, and in the winter of 1977 to 1978, when he wrote his own often angry account of the nonaligned nations in general and India in particular, he was caustic about Mrs. Gandhi. Later, when she had voluntarily surrendered power, he took a more admiring view.

It was, in any case, in an ambivalent mood, despairing at what he saw as folly and intellectual laziness in Washington at least as much as he was motivated by hostility to what he saw in Delhi, that he sat down to write an essay that can be said to have transformed his life.

Pat Moynihan had written for *Commentary* magazine since the early 1960s, and had a very high opinion of its editor, Norman Podhoretz. He wrote from Delhi to Bob Christopher of *Newsweek,* "Norman Podhoretz is very simply the finest literary-intellectual editor of this age."[42] He added, characteristically, "and he has, of course, paid for it." By the time they went to India, the Moynihans were very close socially as well to the Podhoretzes — Norman and his wife, Midge Decter. Late in 1973, for example, the Moynihans offered to lend the Podhoretzes the farm. Later that year, Podhoretz, "not without misgivings, after all I've said about the Wasp patriciate," asked Moynihan to write a recommendation on behalf of his son John to Exeter and Andover. Moynihan responded in glowing terms. In August 1974, Podhoretz, on a world tour, relayed "the splended news" that he would be coming to lecture in Delhi, which he did, on "The Crisis of the American Elite," on September 5.

On November 24, Podhoretz received a letter from a friend at Berkeley, Paul Seabury, suggesting a *Commentary* piece. "Moynihan ought to write it, after he escapes India."

> The idea is this: what is it that accounts for the powerful upsurge of the so-called Afro-Arab-Asian-Communist bloc, and the passivity of so many Western countries in responding to it? It would be mistaken to think of it only as it affects Israel; in fact, Israel may be only a current pressure point for it. In actuality it operates on many fronts . . . Putting all of the pieces together it is clear that the coalition is unified on an anti-Western theme . . . What is unusual now is the snowball effect of it, and its essential cynical disregard of some basic groundrules in international organizations.[43]

Podhoretz forwarded this letter to Delhi, adding only, "Dear Pat: I think this is a good idea. What do you think?"

He thought it was a good idea, too. By the end of the year, he was able to report "paper going well" and that it was tentatively called "The Revolution of the Second International." (Moynihan confused it with the Socialist International, which brought together the anti-Communist social democratic parties of Western Europe, including the British Labour party, the German SPD, the French socialists, the Israeli Labour party and their allies across the world, many of them in former colonial territories.) The ideology of the Second International, Moynihan wrote to Podhoretz, had a powerful British base. What Americans had failed to understand, he went on, was that "there is an ideological coherence to the Group of Seventy-seven, now Ninety-six" (that is, to the "non-aligned movement").[44] "Upon their becoming independent," he wrote, "we saw them as candidates for the American tradition or the Russian, not perceiving that they already had one of their own." It had taken over from British socialism the "master concepts" of having been exploited and having been discriminated against. "We can't deal with this world," he ended, "unless we recognize its ideology."

At this stage in his thinking, Moynihan's interest seemed to have been in understanding the Third World's socialist ideas. By the time he had developed these ideas into the March 1975 *Commentary* article, which carried the shriller and at the same time more defensive headline "The United States in Opposition," analysis had been made to lead into something close to polemic.

Moynihan began by pointing out that the United States, which had taken the lead in creating the United Nations, often found itself in 1974 in a minority, often of at most half a dozen, out of 138 members. The explanation, he suggested, was that the world was beginning to experience "what for want of a better term I shall call the British revolution," which began with the granting by socialist Britain of independence to socialist India in 1947. Since then, all the European empires had broken up into independent nations that varied in many ways, but were "to a quite astonishing degree . . . ideologically uniform," having "fashioned their polities" in accordance with the beliefs of British socialism of the first half of the twentieth century. Moynihan singled out two aspects of this tradition. British socialism was more concerned with redistribution than with production. And, second, he said, it was anti-American.

These ideas, Moynihan said, were spread in the first half of the twentieth century by oppositional British intellectuals to the whole of the British Empire, which, as he wittily put it, "an inspired cartographic convention had long ago decreed be colored pink." Four particular ideas of British socialism had spread to the newly independent countries. One was the idea of independence itself, and that peoples had a right to independence. The second was the idea, the metaphor, almost, that the colonial peoples had been exploited, just as the working class in Britain had been exploited. And the third was that they had suffered ethnic discrimination analogous to the discrimination and inequality visited on the working class. Finally, British socialism had taught that the way these evils could be cured was by legislation. After all, as Moynihan pointed out, a third of the world's nations had come into existence by a Westminster statute, and most of those that had formerly been French, Dutch or other European colonies, had come into existence with much the same ideology and in much the same way.

How had the United States dealt with the new nations and their ideology? Not well. There had been massive diplomatic failure, Moynihan concluded. He devoted some space to showing how the "non-aligned" nations had taken an anti-American position on new issues — population, the environment — and to the "wild energy" of Chinese attacks on the West.

If the beginning of wisdom was to recognize the ideological coherence of the Third World countries under the influence of British socialism, Moynihan argued, there was every reason to welcome its influence, because as a result "the prospect [was] that the world would not go totalitarian." Things could go wrong. "The great darkness could yet consume us." But in any case, political gains, the survival of some form of democracy in countries like India, had been purchased at the cost of economic losses. In 1947, for example, India produced 1.2 million tons of steel, Japan 900,000. By 1972, India produced 6.8 million tons, Japan 106.8 million. Indian socialism had produced Calcutta's urban environment, with perhaps the lowest standard of living in the world, while capitalist economic policies had produced one of the world's highest in Singapore.

What should the United States do? It was time, Moynihan said, for the United States to "go into opposition" to the prevailing beliefs of the Third World ideology. This would not mean being "uniformly scornful." There were attractive regimes in the Third World, and attractive features to even the most misguided. "Half the people in the world who live under a regime of civil liberties," he reminded his readers, "live in India." But the anticapitalist, anti-imperial ideology was itself "the last stage of colonialism."

The countries that have put liberty ahead of equality, Moynihan quoted an unnamed Israeli socialist as saying, had done better by equality than those who had put equality first. He then cited Ralf Dahrendorf, newly designated as head of the London School of Economics: "the equality party has had its day. The liberty party's time has come." The United States had learned to deal with Communism. The task now was to deal with socialism. "It will not be less difficult a task, it ought to be a profoundly more pleasant one." The United States must speak out for political liberty. If an Algerian were to assume the presidency of the United Nations General Assembly, for example, how interesting it would be to pay an informed tribute to the career of the liberator Ben Bella, still rotting in an Algerian prison cell. It is time, he said, in the most influential sentence of the whole article, "that the American spokesman came to be feared in international forums for the truths he might tell."

By the time that article was published, in March 1975, its author was again teaching at Harvard. Then one day Henry Kissinger got into a State Department limousine. His office had packed his briefcase with papers for him to read. One of them was "The United States in Opposition." He read it in the car, from end to end. Then he called Moynihan on Francis Avenue.

"That's superb," he said. "I'll pay you the highest compliment. I wish I'd written it myself."

"And the next thing I know," Moynihan said, "I'm going to the UN as ambassador."

Before that happened, however, Moynihan made another journey that was to confirm his view that American political civilization was indeed on the defensive in the world. He went to China, with his children John and Maura, and with Liz, who was on her way to work on her biography of Babur in the British Museum Library[45] in London. He was given introductions to George and Barbara Bush, then in the embassy in Beijing.[46] Unofficially, Moynihan was accorded the honor of an in-depth conversation with Chiao Kuan-hua, the minister of foreign affairs of the day.[47] Unreported and therefore unknown to him, the National People's Congress was in session during his visit, for only the fourth time since the Revolution, to choose a head of state and adopt a constitution. No fewer than 2,864 delegates assembled in the Great Hall of the People, which however, Moynihan reported, "maintained throughout the inert external appearance of a post office on Sunday morning."

In Beijing, Moynihan was only partly a diplomatic visitor. He was chiefly there as a journalist, and in fact he wrote a long "Letter from Peking" for *The New Yorker*.[48] The piece was never published. Such was the magazine's publishing schedule that by the time the article was ready for press, Moynihan was already UN ambassador. The essay had to be pulled due to the possible perception of conflict. The "Letter" was largely concerned with what Moynihan himself told Elliott Abrams a few years later about his two main interests: architecture and communism. A large part of it was taken up with a description of the public housing of Beijing, which he compared rather favorably with that in New York, London, Hong Kong and other cities. He found the city's monuments disappointing, asking whether there was anything authentic and different in it. Then, by chance, he wandered off the shopping streets, and found just what he was looking for in the alleys. He was specially taken with the *sze heh yuan*, or yards, "as standardized as the Charlestown three-decker or the Manhattan railroad flat," uniform, but not dispiriting, rather as the sober Georgian squares of London were not improved by Victorian embellishment. Moynihan saw the *sze heh yuan* as the adaptation to urban conditions of the family farm, and as such as the shrine and home of the family, and he approved. He contrasted them with the new blocks, five stories high, that the government was building in the sprawling new suburbs, which he saw as dedicated to man in the mass.

Where Tammany, as he put it, "gave power to the people," the Beijing Neighborhood Revolutionary Committee takes it away. He was allowed to meet one such committee, consisting of a blunt-featured retired worker in his sixties, a young theoretician and apparatchik and a woman who said "as near to nothing as words permit." He was taken to see three-year-olds, singing little songs about how "We will grow up quickly to settle the border regions" — Tibet, perhaps, or Taiwan — and "We each will grow a pair of industrial hands." To a Western sensibility, he concluded, the control seems too intense. Yet he conceded that "one leaves China with no sense of a people groaning under oppression." Unlike Henry Kissinger, Moynihan found it easier to engage with India, and that China was too remote and mysterious for him. He was in any case about to engage, not with China, but with Russian communism and its allies in the countries that called themselves nonaligned.

10

The Other End of 42nd Street

AMBASSADOR AT THE UNITED NATIONS
AND THE ZIONISM RESOLUTION

> Few ideas are correct ones, and which they are none
> can tell, but with words we govern men.
> — Benjamin Disraeli

D EBATES IN THE THIRD COMMITTEE of the United Nations
rarely attain the quality of great theater; but the debate
on October 17, 1975, was an exception. Great issues and potentially great interests were at stake, and so were great moral principles. The resolution before the committee, which has jurisdiction
over human rights, affirmed that Zionism, the ancient striving of
the Jewish people for a homeland, was a form of "racism and racial
discrimination."

In spite of efforts to table or deflect it, this resolution reached
the Third Committee. If it passed there, it would go to the General
Assembly, where on form it would almost certainly pass. A bloc of
Muslim countries actively promoted this attack on Israel, led by the
radical Arab states and by allies of the Soviet Union. The newly independent states of sub-Saharan Africa, two years after the oil boycott
and price rise, were dependent on the Arab countries for fuel and
money. Behind them again stood the larger, looser alliance of the so-
called Non-Aligned Nations, generally whipped along by Cuba. And
in the background, shadowy but unmistakable, was the bulk of the
Soviet Union. If the closest thing to a world parliament could be prevailed upon to vote that Zionism was a form of racism, the stage
would be set for further resolutions to strip Israel of its legitimacy and
perhaps of its membership in the United Nations, and in the end to
furnish justification for its destruction.

So on the afternoon of October 17, 1975, the Israeli representative rose to oppose the resolution, knowing that, barring a miracle, it would pass and move on to the General Assembly. He was no ordinary diplomat, but a soldier, a scholar and a lawyer of high achievement, and he was later to be president of Israel. Born Chaim Herzog in Belfast, his father moved to Dublin when he became chief rabbi of Ireland. He studied at London and Cambridge universities as well as in Palestine, and was called to the bar as a lawyer in Britain. He served both in the Haganah, the Jewish secret army under the British mandate, and as an officer in the elite British Guards armored division in France, Holland and Germany. In the Guards, he was known as Vivian, after a corporal found that Chaim sounded too foreign, and the nickname stuck with his friends.

"We are a small people with a long and proud history," Herzog ended on a sustained note of controlled emotion. "We have lived through much in our history. We have survived all our oppressors and enemies over the centuries. We shall survive this shameful exhibition. But we, the Jewish people, will not forget. We shall not forget those who spoke up for decency and civilization; and I thank the delegations who expressed themselves against this pernicious resolution. We shall not forget those who voted to attack our religion and our faith." And he shouted the last words: "We shall never forget!"[1]

Then came the vote, registered on computer screens. Seventy countries, from Afghanistan to Yemen and Yugoslavia by way of the Soviet Union and its clients and satellites, Muslim nations like Indonesia and Turkey but also India and Brazil, voted that Zionism was racism. Twenty-nine countries, including the United States, the member states of the European Community, Britain, Ireland, some non-African members of the British Commonwealth and a few others, voted for Israel. Forty-three countries abstained or were absent.

When the result was announced, the Arabs broke into long, mocking applause. It seemed to Herzog that they were about to break into a war dance.[2] As the Israeli delegation gathered its papers together, his excellency, the representative of the United States, straightened his tie and buttoned his jacket. The blood rushed to his face. He rose and pushed his way through the hubbub. When he reached the Israeli representative, he shook his hand, then pulled him toward him and embraced him in front of the whole hall.[3] "Fuck 'em!" said his excellency.

———

Pat Moynihan's time at the United Nations was relatively brief: only eight months. It was a time of intense work and passionate feeling, a sort of switching point. Many of the lines of his past life converged on that short, angry time; many of the tracks of his future work fanned out from there. Some accused him, more suspected him, of campaigning for the Senate from the United Nations. He denies it. Certainly if the charge that he was campaigning for office while he was ambassador implies that he said or did anything in that role only for political reasons, that is false. It was a time of unfeigned fervor and passionate commitment.[4]

It is true that there was something about his time at the UN, and even more something about the tone of the book in which he gave his own account of that time, that is stressed, febrile, suffused with uncharacteristic rage. The immediate explanation, as we shall see, lies in the fact that Ambassador Moynihan felt himself to be in crossfire. In front of him were the massed ranks of the enemy: the Soviet Union and its witting or unwitting tools in a disgraceful but seriously dangerous assault on the reputation, the beliefs and the interests of the United States and its ally Israel. That was fair enough, he expected that. It was to do battle with the hosts of the ungodly that he had taken the job. What was less fair, and far less easy to handle, was what he saw as a series of treacherous assaults from behind. As he charged the enemy, he felt, he never knew when he was going to come under sniper fire from his own trenches. Sometimes it came from the State Department. On one painful occasion it came from his British colleague. But the most dangerous of the enemies on his own side, he sensed, was the man who had hired him and perhaps in the end would fire him, his old colleague from Harvard and from the Nixon White House, Secretary of State Henry Kissinger. Moynihan's feelings about Kissinger were complex. They included admiration, rivalry, suspicion, deep intellectual disagreement, a dash of contempt and occasional affection. But he chose to sum them up in the old story of the frog and the scorpion.[5]

The scorpion wanted to cross the river, and he asked the frog to ferry him.

"No way," said the frog. "If I take you halfway across you'll sting me."

"Why would I sting you?" said the scorpion. "If I stung you, I'd drown."

So the frog agreed, and the scorpion climbed on his back. Halfway across the river, the scorpion stung him. As he went down, the frog said, "Why did you do it?"

"It's not in my interest," said the scorpion. "It's in my nature."

There is another, more serious explanation for Moynihan's controlled rage at that time. Things were not going well for the country or for the causes he believed in. He had always identified with the fortunes and, to use an old-fashioned word, the honor of the United States. The middle years of the 1970s had been neither fortunate nor especially honorable. He was clear in his own mind that the Vietnam War was a profound mistake, and had shown the courage to speak out to that effect to Nixon more than once. Still, he had no sympathy with the Left. He had gone to work for Nixon in part, he said, because there was no Democratic party. At the Democratic National Convention in Miami that year, the McGovernites all but drummed Moynihan's old friends in labor and in the regular organizations out of the party.

When he first contemplated going to India in the summer of 1972, it was as the representative of a president he respected, who looked on the point of reordering the world's affairs in a masterly fashion, and who had been reelected by a landslide. By the time he arrived at the UN, Nixon had departed in ignominy. The United States was on the eve of losing the Vietnam War. The Soviet Union, with Leonid Brezhnev on the rampage, was challenging the West from Angola to Yemen, and had backed the Arab nations in a series of attempts on the territory and ultimately even on the survival of Israel. Those same Arab countries, with their other oil-producing allies, seemed for a time to have transformed the economic balance of power in the world. "Vietnam," Moynihan wrote in his diary in far-off Delhi, "has diminished and soured our relations with most of the non-communist world, and by a curious dynamic, two weeks of the Middle East war took the process farther than Vietnam had done. The easiness has gone, even, say, with the British. We shall at best become what the old sailors called spliced rope."[6] In the lonely days of Cambodia, he reminded himself, and in "the still more awful ones" of Watergate, "the one embassy in Washington which stood by Richard Nixon — the *one* — was that of Israel. Not India."

This sense of the isolation of the United States "in opposition" was one of the sources of his *Commentary* article. It was reinforced by the fact that he was sitting in Delhi observing the sheer foolishness of the things people believed to the credit of the Soviet Union and to the discredit of the United States. But the other big idea of the article was that the United States had no need to stand on the defensive, that its ideas were correct. The United States should stop apologizing for its own beliefs, and instead should shout them from the rooftops.

This upbeat, optimistic side of Moynihan's temperament was, however, in conflict — at this stage of his life as well as at others — with a deep psychological pessimism. What was the point of being Irish if you didn't know the world would break your heart? So, even in the act of wanting to accentuate the positive side of the United States's message, he saw everywhere the possibility of catastrophe, and in particular the danger to Israel.

The threat to Israel came, through a set of historical accidents and even paradoxes, to mesh with Moynihan's suspicion of Henry Kissinger. As a Jew, albeit a distinctly secular one, Kissinger was at first deeply reluctant to get involved in the politics of the Middle East. In his memoirs, he explains that he knew little of the Middle East when he arrived in the White House. Moreover, he speculated that President Nixon "suspected that my Jewish origins might cause me to lean too much towards Israel."[7] It is easy to guess that a man of his insecure temperament might have leaned over backward to assure his boss that he was not too close to Israel. It was only after Nixon was politically crippled by Watergate that Kissinger plunged into his famous Middle East shuttle diplomacy.

Almost by accident, though, right from the very start of his time as national security adviser, he became involved in another issue of deep importance to American Jews. Ironically, it was to make them at best highly suspicious of him and his motives. This was the issue of the emigration of Soviet Jews. After the Holocaust, the largest single national group of Jews, five million, lived in the United States. The second largest, over three million, lived in Israel. But even after centuries of anti-Semitism, decades of pogroms, the Nazi invasion and Stalinist oppression, there were still three million Jews in the Soviet Union. They were discriminated against by being treated as a separate nationality, so designated in identity documents, for example. Occasionally they were the victims of overtly anti-Semitic campaigns like that at the time of the "doctors' plot" in 1953, in which a number of Jewish physicians were falsely accused of a plot against Stalin. Many Soviet Jews had lost much of their Jewish identity. Some, not without justification, feared the consequences of proclaiming their Jewishness, let alone Zionism. Others identified in spite of everything with the fight against Nazism and the hopes of building a socialist society. Natan Sharansky, in his moving memoir, *Fear No Evil*, says that, growing up as a Jew in the Soviet Union, he had never heard of the Talmud or of Passover.[8] In the 1960s, after Stalin's death, this began to change. The revelations of Stalin's anti-Semitism in Khrushchev's speech to the Twentieth Party Congress in 1956 virtually ended Jewish opposition to Zionism,[9] and in the 1960s, as Sharansky has described,[10] there was a widespread revival among Soviet Jews both of Jewish consciousness and of a renewed desire to emigrate, in the first instance to Israel. Moreover, in late 1969 the government of Israel, which had not been keen on immigration from the Soviet Union in the past, changed its mind. Under Golda Meir, it decided that Soviet Jews were not only entitled to make their *aliyah* like any other Jews, but would also be a valuable reservoir of manpower, and should therefore be encouraged to move to the Jewish state.

Henry Kissinger raised this matter with his friend the Soviet ambassador Anatoly Dobrynin through his prized "back channel" as early as 1969. By 1973, Kissinger was proud that the number of Soviet Jews allowed to emigrate had risen from four hundred to thirty-five thousand a year.[11] Unfortunately for Kissinger, however, the question of Jewish emigration became mixed up with his plans for détente with the Soviet Union, and in particular with the question of whether the Soviet Union should receive "most favored nation" treatment: MFN. The phrase is unfortunate. It suggests some special favor for the Soviets. In fact, all it meant was that the Soviet Union should be treated the same as any other country.

In August 1972, shortly after negotiating most favored nation treatment with Henry Kissinger, the Soviet government imposed an "exit tax" on emigrants, most of them Jews. That October, Senator Henry M. Jackson of Washington State, universally known by his boyhood nickname "Scoop," introduced an amendment denying MFN to any Communist country that restricted the emigration of its citizens. A few days later, a similar amendment was introduced into the House of Representatives by Congressman Charles Vanik of Ohio, so the proposal to link MFN and, more broadly, détente to emigration for Soviet Jews came to be known as the Jackson-Vanik Amendment.

Senator Jackson had by 1972 acquired both seniority and powerful committee assignments in the Senate, a formidable reputation, an interestingly mixed constituency and an unusually able team of staff and advisers. Jackson was a keen supporter of the antiballistic missile, and he did not like what he heard of Kissinger's détente negotiations, either in respect to arms control or to trade.[12] Still less did he like the fact that even ranking members of the committees with jurisdiction over any treaty that might emerge from Kissinger's activities in Moscow had been kept almost wholly in the dark. He also had presidential ambitions for 1976.

The first effect of Jackson's opposition was to cloud the new atmosphere of détente which Kissinger had worked so hard to achieve. Early in 1973, Ambassador Dobrynin told Kissinger that his government had decided to lift the exit tax. But this move did little to appease Senator Jackson. Instead it encouraged him to push for further concessions. At a White House meeting, he demanded that the Soviets guarantee a minimum number of visas each year. By the end of 1973, the trade bill with the Jackson-Vanik Amendment tacked to it had passed the House of Representatives. Kissinger, desperate to preserve détente, met first with Jackson, then with both Jackson and Senator Abraham Ribicoff of Connecticut. Later Senator Jacob K. Javits of New York joined them. Jackson demanded a hundred thousand exit visas a year. Kissinger put this to the Soviet foreign minister, Andrei Gromyko, who was at first "opaque," then hinted that forty-five thousand a year might be the trend. In January 1975, the Senate passed the trade bill, with Jackson-Vanik, 88 to 0, and President Ford signed it. But, even before that, Kissinger announced that the Soviet Union had repudiated the 1972 trade agreement. Détente, for many reasons, was in ruins.

Henry Kissinger was "stunned" to come under attack from the neoconservatives.[13] As he saw it, he had just emerged from fierce criticism from the Left, only to come under equally heavy fire from the Right. He had been through the long agony of Vietnam. Then there had been détente, the nuclear alerts when Syria attacked Jordan and the crisis in Chile. His explanation is that the neoconservatives, Moynihan's friends and the supporters of Scoop Jackson, were coming over from the Left. "They needed space," he has said. "If they weren't going to be disciples, they had to be critics." And they believed Israel had to be defended by more aggressive tactics.

Senator Jackson's constituency was an unusual one. His original power base was the unionized workforce at Boeing in Seattle: he was often called "the Senator from Boeing." As a result of his loyal pro-union voting record, he became one of the AFL-CIO's favorite members of Congress. He shared the patriotic, strongly anti-Communist instincts of conservative labor leaders and intensely disliked the new elements in the Democratic party that supported Senators Eugene McCarthy and Robert Kennedy in 1968 and George McGovern in 1972. Relations between the Right and Left of the Democratic party from 1972 through 1975 were bitter.

Jackson's ideas and voting record commended him to many conservative Democratic intellectuals who were beginning to find the new liberalism shocking and foolish, including the group who became known as the "neoconservatives." Many of these, especially after the "community control" conflicts in New York and elsewhere, were Jews, some with strong ties to Israel. Two of Jackson's aides, in particular, took a strong anti-Soviet line in foreign affairs, were fiercely pro-Israel and intensely disliked détente. One of these was Richard Perle, later as an assistant secretary of defense a key architect of President Reagan's hard-nosed strategy for dealing with the Soviet Union. The other was Ben Wattenberg, an old liberal who had published, jointly with the pollster Richard Scammon, an influential book, *The Real Majority,* which ridiculed the McGovernite liberals.

Wattenberg and Penn Kemble founded the Coalition for a Democratic Majority. This was an activist political group, backed by labor, which aimed at recapturing the Democratic party from the McGovernites, and some of its members began to see Scoop Jackson as a future presidential candidate who would bring the lost party to its senses.

One intellectual, whose influence was perhaps at its zenith in the early 1970s, was Norman Podhoretz, whose son-in-law, Elliott Abrams, went to work for Scoop Jackson. The political climate of the early 1970s, in other words, had begun to produce a reaction to the counterculture liberalism of the McGovern campaign. The new aggressivity of the Soviet Union under Leonid Brezhnev, the dangers of détente, and in particular the dangers to Israel, were the focus of this group's foreign policy.

After the Six-Day War of 1967, started by Arab sneak attacks, encouraged by the Soviet Union and decisively won by Israel, there was a sharp increase in anti-Semitism in both the Arab world and in the

Soviet Union. The Arabs seethed with the desire for revenge. The Soviet Union chafed at the increased strength of America's chief ally in the Middle East. This Soviet-Arab alliance led to a new and even more dangerous war in 1973. Once again, Israel won, though less easily than in 1967. Once again, the Soviet Union lost face and influence. Defeated on the battlefield, the Soviet Union and its Arab allies turned to diplomacy, which, inverting the formula that Clausewitz pronounced in Napoleon's day, is now the continuation of war by other means. The particular device they put their faith in was an attempt to delegitimize Israel. One tactic was the attempt to have the United Nations accept the Palestine Liberation Organization as a member of the UN. Another was the campaign to equate Zionism with racism.

By the early 1970s, the bloc of Non-Aligned Nations, urged on by Cuba to follow the Soviet line, enjoyed a permanent majority at the UN. In December 1973, for the first time, ominously, the General Assembly adopted a resolution that condemned what a writer in the *Washington Post* called the alliance between "Portuguese colonialism, South African racism, Zionism and Israeli imperialism."[14]

Even the Israelis had been slow to recognize the danger implied by this campaign. Most Israelis, and most American Jews, regarded it as a pathetically implausible lie. They did not appreciate either the popular passions that Arab leaders had stirred up, or the extent to which political leaders in black Africa, stimulated by skillful Soviet and Cuban propaganda, bought the anti-Israeli case. The American State Department was apparently oblivious of the potential danger to Israel and to American interests.

To this gasoline-laden atmosphere, Pat Moynihan intended to set a match. His *Commentary* essay had received wide coverage. For the first time ever, the magazine held a press conference to introduce one of its articles. Rather than simply covering the conference, the *New York Times* sent its United Nations correspondent, Kathleen Teltsch, to interview the author. There was much hypocrisy at the UN, Teltsch told Moynihan. Delegates of countries that routinely tortured their own citizens would accuse Israel of human rights abuses. "We should rip the hides off everybody who presumes to talk about prisoners," Moynihan said, "— shame them, hurt them, yell at them."[15]

In the spring of 1975, soon after Moynihan confided these angry reflections to the *New York Times*, Henry Kissinger was in need of a new act to impress a world audience that, having long watched open-mouthed as he pulled off one prestidigitation after another, was beginning to ask how the tricks were done. First Cambodia fell, then Vietnam. In late March, Kissinger's Middle East shuttle collapsed. On March 23, he returned to Washington. Three days later, Moynihan went to his office for an early-evening drink and was invited to go to the UN as ambassador.

In his book *A Dangerous Place,* Moynihan said that he was "without illusion about Kissinger or without much." He interpreted the secretary of state's motives with ruthless realism. His center was giving way, he said, paraphrasing Marshal Foch, his right was in retreat; "it was time to attack." Kissinger never gave a thought to the UN except when it gave him trouble. He understood that he needed some successes, that Moynihan had written his article in the belief that the United States needed some successes. So for the time being his interests and those of his new ambassador coincided. Moynihan had said on television, not without a touch of patronizing, that Kissinger needed a little love, and that his new wife, Nancy, would help. But in retrospect, when he came to describe his feelings in his book, he added phrases of deadly moral contempt: "His problem was that he was dangerous to be close to . . . With Kissinger the risk was to end up destroyed. He could not help this."[16]

On April 12, Moynihan saw President Ford and formally accepted the United Nations job. On May 3, the *New York Times* published an editorial reminding its readers of the Kathleen Teltsch interview and asking whether the Ford administration saw the UN as an arena for constructive collective diplomacy or simply as a place to respond in kind to wounding and unfair criticism. It was a question that was to be asked again, but Moynihan reacted to it with anger. He told Donald Rumsfeld, Ford's chief of staff, that he could not take the job after all. Moynihan sent the same message to Kissinger, then sent telegrams to both men, saying, "I WON'T TAKE THE JOB." But in the end, he did. There was a friendly hearing, conducted by Senator Charles Percy of Illinois. There was a swearing-in ceremony in the White House Rose Garden, where Gerald Ford made himself very agreeable to Liz and to the children.[17]

On July 1, barely stopping by his new office in New York, the ambassador was on his way to Geneva for the UN Economic and Social Council (ECOSOC) meeting. He knew he would need a team who understood what he was about, and did not entirely trust the career foreign service people to back him up. He lost no time in recruiting two key staffers. One was Leonard Garment, his fellow liberal from the Nixon White House. At loose ends, Garment had drifted back to New York. He went to work for a law firm, but it wasn't long before he realized that he had "made a mess of my return to New York."[18] Earlier that spring, Moynihan had asked Garment's advice about taking the UN job. Now, having heard that the law firm was not working out, he had dinner with him and asked him to join his staff. The other key member of the team was Moynihan's former teaching assistant from Harvard, Suzanne Weaver, now on leave from a job in the political science department at Yale. Diminutive, intelligent and with extraordinary warmth, she was then married to Paul Weaver, a Harvard political scientist who was a member of the editorial board of *The Public Interest*. She moved out of her office, next to Moynihan's, to make room for Garment. Later, Moynihan recruited to his team the former civil rights leader Clarence Mitchell, and Thomas O. Enders, a forceful diplomat who, at six feet eight inches, towered even over Moynihan's six feet five.

Henry Kissinger now threw himself into the new, Moynihan-charted oppositional diplomacy. At the same time, he was aware of the importance of economics — a discipline he had tended to ignore in his dazzling flights of diplomatic élan — in the new world of interdependence. He was beginning to target the UN Special Session scheduled for September to confront the energy crisis, food shortages, inflation and recession.

He planned to expound the new line in a series of speeches. The first was in Milwaukee on July 14. It was a fairly blunt attack on the "bloc politics" of developing nations, a clear warning that if the United States was to help them, they must expect the Americans to say what they believed would work. There were broad hints that the United States would reward its friends, and punish its enemies, but it was up to other countries to decide into which category they wanted to fall. "Those who do not wish investment from abroad," he warned, "can be confident that they will not receive it."[19] The bloc voting in the General Assembly, he went on, coming closer to Moynihan's point, "did not reflect economic reality."

From the start, says Suzanne Garment, the State Department bureaucracy was unhappy. After all, what Moynihan was saying was that they were morally and intellectually derelict. "They were wary," she recalls. "I was too naïve to know it at the time, but there had been a lot of backchat."[20] The first piece of serious business was when Ambassador Barbara White, who had been representing the United States at a United Nations international women's year conference in Mexico, sent a cable announcing the conference's success. The group had, however, adopted a final resolution by 89 votes to 3 (Israel, the United States and Denmark voting against, with the major European nations abstaining), which called for "the elimination of . . . Zionism, apartheid, and racial discrimination." This was only the second time that the UN had formally equated Zionism with racism.

The response was vigorous. On July 17, the European Community hinted that it would oppose an abridgement of Israel's rights as a UN member. The next day the U.S. Senate adopted a resolution stating that if Israel were to be expelled from the UN, the United States would reassess membership. And Henry Kissinger warned of dramatic consequences if Israel were to be so much as suspended.[21] But the episode brought home to Moynihan, Garment and Weaver just how late the hour was in terms of the assault on Israel's legitimacy, and just how little the State Department professionals were attuned to their way of seeing how the nonaligned bloc of nations thought and behaved. On July 9, White cabled that it was "unfortunate" that the United States was "isolated in company only with Israel." She did not, she said, "consider it of great importance to the outcome of this conference."[22]

Moynihan did not agree. He cabled back asking acidly how, if the declaration was so inspiring, we had voted against it, and alternatively, if we had voted against it, how could it be so inspiring. And he ended with Disraeli's words: "Few ideas are correct ones, and which they are none can tell, but with words we govern men."[23]

In September 1975, the United Nations General Assembly was scheduled to hold a special session, its seventh. The reason was the widespread perception that the rise in oil and also in food prices had created a world economic crisis: the worst recession since the 1930s, coupled with inflation.

The question for Moynihan and his team was how to respond to a world in which suddenly both the Soviet Union and the developing nations, caucusing as the Non-Aligned, but in truth influenced to the point of manipulation by the Soviet Union, were both on the attack. The United States seemed to be not just in opposition, but on the defensive. Complex economic issues were involved. Enders was working on an elaborate plan for international income stabilization, a sort of international New Deal. There was a split between those Third World countries that produced oil, the price of which had just more than doubled, and those that did not. But Washington, and especially Kissinger, were also concerned with the split that seemed to be developing between the United States and the other countries in the developed world, a split that went back to differences about Vietnam and détente, but was sharply exacerbated by the worry of Western Europe and Japan about the impact of the oil price rise on their economies, and their fear that the United States, now itself dependent on Middle East oil imports, would leave them without supplies. There was a — generally unvoiced — fear that the United States, in its determination to back Israel against its Arab enemies, might provoke the Arabs to further hostile action against European and Japanese oil supplies. And there was a fear in Washington that the European Community, which had just signed the Lomé package of agreements on trade, aid and commodities with forty-six countries, mostly former colonies, might do their own deals with the oil-producing countries. The European motive was largely to help countries with which they had close historical and economic ties. But Moynihan, in his account of this period, took an uncharacteristically cynical view. Indeed, throughout this whole period of his life he worked himself up into a bitterly anti-European mood. "[O]ur erstwhile allies, far from merely defecting on the occasional vote, were in the process of negotiating something very like a separate peace with the developing nations . . . Were the Europeans reconstituting the old colonial system," he asked. "Minus the bother of maintaining a navy?"[24]

As he reflected on how best to put the American case in such a way that it would not increase American isolation, Moynihan received a long critique of his *Commentary* article from W. Scott Thompson, of Moynihan's own alma mater, the Fletcher School at Tufts. Writing after Mrs. Gandhi had temporarily suspended democracy in the emergency, Thompson pointed out that the dominant tradition in the Third World was no longer that of democratic British Fabian socialism, but dictatorship disguised with Marxist rhetoric about imperialism. Anticolonialism was deeply rooted in American tradition, Thompson reminded Moynihan. "Our foreign policy elite lectured Britain and France about the evils of colonialism for a critical generation."[25] So the Third World was given its independence, and the United States "cultivated relations with wretched dictators." Now battle was joined in America between the successors to the Cold War liberals, muckrakers who wanted to expose the evils of American interference in the world, and realists who wanted to take the Third World seriously. But it was too late, because the dictators of the Third World were not interested, as they said, in liberty. They were interested in ruling. That was what they understood by the socialism they were forever talking about.

Moynihan knew little about Africa. He thought he knew something about India, but India had now ceased — for the time being — to be the world's most populous democracy. In his perplexity, and in long discussions with his friends and particularly with Norman Podhoretz, there was one principle he clung to. "Podhoretz and I had agreed," he wrote, "that, come what may, we would not plead guilty." In this resolve, he felt let down by the State Department. In August, he pointed out to Henry Kissinger, who had called him on some robust remarks he had made, that if it hadn't been for him, the department would have done nothing to prevent the UN from recognizing the diminutive Communist party of Puerto Rico as a "national liberation movement." Moynihan reminded Kissinger tartly that the United States had described a similar proposal to help a liberation movement in Portuguese Africa as "a hostile act." He asked, "Why are we so unprepared to do for ourselves what we are willing to do for others?"[26]

He was fortified in his determination to treat such undermining attempts with defiance by the news that, at the Non-Aligned meeting in Lima, which was a kind of caucus for the UN special session, the Third World countries had once again identified Zionism with racism. The conference's official report was blatant propaganda. It made no attempt to conceal Soviet influence and went out of its way to link the United States with Israel.

"This massive support to the Zionist regimes," it said, "eliminates all doubts as to the deliberate intention of the United States and other imperialist powers to make Israel a base of colonialism and imperialism within the Third World, and use it to break the liberation movements, consolidate racist regimes, threaten peace and security in the developing countries and plunder their natural resources."[27]

Henry Kissinger had been due to give a major speech to the Special Session, but he was delayed in the Middle East, and Moynihan read the speech for him. It made bold proposals for international economic cooperation. Moynihan followed up with an ingenious tactic.

The chief obstacle, as he saw it, to agreement in the Special Session was the deeply offensive tone of the draft resolution from the Non-Aligned meeting at Lima. In forty hours over a weekend, Moynihan and Leonard Garment completely rewrote the document, "conforming to their format and using identical language, while changing the meaning of every sentence in ways that we hoped would take time and some wit to recognize."[28]

The Special Session had been due to end on Friday, September 12. Its closing was twice postponed. That day, Moynihan and Garment tried to go even further. Although the United States was the largest aid donor absolutely, it was not by any means as large a donor proportionately as many European countries. The United States had always refused to commit itself to the target of 0.7 percent of gross national product set in the 1960s for developed countries to give to the Third World. Calling on their friendship with Donald Rumsfeld, Moynihan and Garment persuaded him to say on his own initiative that the United States would commit itself to the 0.7 percent goal. But Henry Kissinger called back within two hours and turned the idea down flat.

By early Sunday morning, led by Tom Enders, the United States had negotiated an agreement with the Non-Aligned countries. Moynihan was sitting in an NBC TV studio in Rockefeller Plaza, ready for the beginning of *Meet the Press,* when news came through that Abdelaziz Bouteflika of Algeria, the president of the General Assembly, had after all rejected the agreement. The ambassador was handed a piece of paper. The journalists on the panel could tell that it was bad news. Moynihan replied in diplomatic parlance that "the other side has put in new language now, just a few moments ago, and I don't want to say an agreement is in jeopardy, but agreement has not been reached, and the clock is running."

He himself later glossed those words as meaning that the Special Session was about to collapse, and we didn't much give a damn. Paul Hofmann of the *New York Times* asked him about a story that had circulated at Lima. A newspaper in Tanzania had apparently printed a supposed diplomatic note from the government of the United States to the government of Tanzania saying that if Tanzania voted against the United States on the issue of Puerto Rico, then before the Lima meeting, the Americans would consider this interference in their domestic affairs, and an unfriendly act, heavy language in diplomatic discourse. The Tanzanian paper, Hofmann said, had called the note rude and intimidatory. The paper was right, Moynihan said; the United States had meant to be rude. He added that the UN's committee on decolonization consisted of sixteen police states, four democracies and four others. "We are not about to be lectured by police states on the processes of electoral democracy." And he went on to expound his own belief: that "an awful lot of these countries" seemed to want a symbolic admission of guilt from the United States. "But we aren't guilty any more than any other nation, any other people in the world, and we are not plea bargaining." What America was not going to do was assert that the present condition of the developing nations has been caused by the advanced nations and by the Americans.

That was the kernel of what Moynihan wanted to say. He had grasped that it was also what Americans felt in their heart of hearts, and what they wanted their diplomatic representatives to say to the world. He had understood the politics of the situation. Americans felt it was past time to stop apologizing for crimes they had not committed. His position, even in the robust language drawn from him by the bad news of Bouteflika's wrecking tactics, was less aggressive, more subtle, than it perhaps sounded. He had not lost his temper. He had calculated that the United States's position was stronger than it looked, or than American diplomats, used to years of apologetic policies, understood. For one thing, the world's poor countries knew that if they were to get help, much of it would have to come from the United States. For another, he had guessed correctly that however much they might share the ideology of anticolonialism, they were by no means all enchanted with heavy-handed Soviet bullying. He was proved right, and sooner than he expected.

Because the regular General Assembly meeting was due to open that afternoon, there was no alternative but to end the session formally on Tuesday, September 16. The previous evening, as Moynihan was hosting a reception for the delegates arriving for the regular General Assembly meeting in his sumptuous official apartment on the top floor of the Waldorf Towers, he was handed a copy of a resolution just passed by a Non-Aligned caucus, formally denouncing him by name. The next morning the *Times* duly reported that the Special Session had failed to reach agreement. It had gone to press too early. The Special Session had reconvened at 2:50 A.M. The record shows that "the meeting rose at 3:50 A.M." At the last possible moment, the Special Session had reached agreement on a major program of economic development. Moynihan could not resist the temptation to tweak a tail. "Perhaps never in the history of the United Nations," he said, "has there been so intensive and so genuine a negotiation among so many nations on so profoundly important a range of issues." And then he turned to Bouteflika, the presiding officer, and said, "This system works!"

Moynihan was cockahoop. He felt he had called the bluff of the Non-Aligned caucus. He had matched their proposals, and what he called the "genuinely poor nations" had responded as he had predicted. The game, however, was not over. The roughest exchanges were still to come. Even at the closing meeting of the Special Session, the representative of the Syrian Arab Republic could not resist dragging in the issue that was to bedevil the General Assembly's meeting. The Zionists, he said, represent a regime that is racist and aggressive, and they should be "banished" from the General Assembly. Chaim Herzog, for Israel, could handle that sort of stuff. He replied sharply that he rejected the "unwarranted and ill-conceived intervention of the Syrian delegation, injecting, as is its wont, a discordant note" into a session characterized by consensus. But the Syrian raspberry was a warning that the Arab delegations and their African allies would go for Israel before the main session was over.

In the meantime, a number of delicate questions of membership had arisen. Should both Vietnams be admitted to the General Assembly? Then what about both Koreas? Here, too, the clouds on the horizon would get bigger and more ominous. Moynihan was firmly of the opinion that the United States must accept the membership of both Vietnams. He sent his first long cable to Washington. To do otherwise, he argued, would be to seem to act "out of bitterness, blindness, weakness and fear."[29] The overwhelming response would be contempt. As a result, Chile, South Africa and then Israel would be expelled. If, on the other hand, the United States voted for acceptance of the two Vietnams, it might be possible to get membership for South Korea, which the Soviets had vetoed for twenty-six years.

This was Moynihan at his most magnanimous, arguing that meanness of spirit would be contrary to U.S. interests, but generosity would be politically expedient. Where the Vietnamese were concerned, however, Henry Kissinger was not in any mood for magnanimity. "He had no intention," Moynihan commented, "of letting in . . . a government that had betrayed him, outwitted him, beaten him."[30] But Kissinger did allow him to take his case to the president, who agreed with Kissinger. Moynihan, however, wanted at least to make a speech arguing that the United States would veto North Vietnam's admission, but would do so only because South Korea had been vetoed by the Soviet Union. The United Nations should be "as near as possible to universal in its membership," and the United States would not help to bring about a one-party world. That, too, was thought to be too contentious.

From the beginning of October on, that was in any case hardly the problem. On October 1, Field Marshal Idi Amin Dada, president of Uganda and also the incumbent chairman of the Organization of African Unity, arrived to speak at the General Assembly. From the moment of his arrival, Moynihan noted later, "the party was over." From a distance of almost a quarter century, Idi Amin may seem a comic figure. But if he was pompous and semiliterate, a caricature of the stereotype of the African leader as buffoon, there was nothing funny about him for those unfortunate enough to live in Uganda and in his power. He was in fact a highly sinister buffoon, cunning and cruel, who brought terrible suffering to his own country.

In his speech to the General Assembly, Idi Amin began with boilerplate anticolonial rhetoric, but then began to rave about the United States and Israel. "How can we expect freedom, peace and justice in the world," he asked, "when such a powerful nation as the United States of America is in the hands of the Zionists," and he called for "the expulsion of Israel from the United Nations and the extinction of Israel as a state." For good measure, he opined at a press conference that New York City was bankrupt because "the United States must send arms to Israel to murder the Arabs."

Moynihan decided this attack could not be allowed to go unanswered, that it would be good politics, in the United States and he hoped even in Africa, to take Amin on. The next day, October 3, he flew to San Francisco to speak at the annual AFL-CIO convention. He wrote his speech on the plane. He began by quoting George Meany, the staunchly anti-Communist president of the labor movement, that "Democracy has come under increasing attack," and added, "I see it every day at the United Nations. Every day, on every side, we are assailed. There are those in this country whose pleasure, or profit, it is to believe that our assailants are motivated by what is wrong about us. They are wrong. We are assailed because of what is right about us. We are assailed because we are a democracy."

Then he came to the phrase by which his speech was to be remembered. "It is no accident," he said, that on Wednesday "His Excellency

Field Marshal Al Hadji Amin Dada, President of the Republic of Uganda — to give him his UN title — called for 'the extinction of Israel as a state.' And it is no accident, I fear, that this 'racist murderer' — as one of our leading newspapers called him this morning — is head of the Organization of African Unity." Democracy was under attack, he said. "There is blood in the water, and the sharks grow frenzied." What was going on was a "systematic effort to create an international society in which government is the one and only legitimate institution."

The response was an explosion. The next morning the story appeared on page one of the *New York Times,* with the headline: "Moynihan Assails Uganda President — Delegate to UN Endorses Description of Amin as 'Racist Murderer.' " The following day the *Times* ran an even longer story, by Paul Hofmann. Though generally sympathetic, it did mention "benign neglect." And it ended with a note that annoyed Moynihan at the time, and has not entirely died away. "One American," Hofmann reported, "said, 'What is Pat Moynihan running for?' thus implying that by his public criticisms of the third world and other attitudes, he was building a personal constituency that could become the basis for some future quest of elective office." The reporter had managed to convey subjective judgment as if it were incontrovertible fact. But it was true. There were indeed many, in many places, who did draw the conclusion from the ambassador's undiplomatic manner and the undeniable fact that he was speaking to a domestic political audience as well as to an international audience that he was indeed running for office.

Moynihan had, as he later admitted, made a small but significant mistake. He had said that it was "no accident" that Amin was the president of the OAU. He meant it as a rhetorical sarcasm, a satire on the Marxist habit of saying that things were "no accident." But unfortunately it was an accident, in the strict sense of the word. The presidency of the Organization of African Unity (like, for example, the presidency of the European Union) rotates. It was therefore by sheer chance that, Uganda's turn having come around, Amin held it at the time of this debate.

There was a feeling in several quarters that Moynihan had gone too far. His own mission was getting ready to put out a statement saying that while some of Amin's remarks were morally offensive, others earned wide approval. The ambassador, as he put it later, "let it be known that not one goddamn thing Amin had said had won my 'wide approval.' " A press guidance sheet was prepared by the State Department. "Our positions on certain policies and actions of Amin are well known," it said. "Ambassador Moynihan's words are his own."

In his memoir, *A Dangerous Place,* jointly written with Suzanne Weaver, Moynihan did not directly tax Henry Kissinger with undermining him after the Idi Amin speech, but that is the impression his account gives. Kissinger did not welcome these developments, he says. "I was his ambassador. What was I doing on the front page of the *Times?*" The clear implication is that Moynihan thought that Kissinger was jealous of Moynihan's celebrity. He also implied that Kissinger's overwhelming concern was with Israel.[31] Vietnam, he says, had never absorbed him. He quoted Nathan Glazer as saying that Israel had become the religion of the Jews, and added, "and I believe it was Kissinger's as well." But it was not his own religion, Moynihan went on. "[I]t was not the Jews that were in my mind as the crisis of the Thirtieth General Assembly took form, nor yet Israel." What concerned Moynihan in the last analysis, he suggests, was "not the accused but the accusers," and not the Arabs or the Africans, but Moscow.

Moynihan has always contended that he did not plan his career, that it evolved from "chance encounters, random walks." The accusation has often been made that he took a hard line over the Zionism resolution because he was already planning to use the United Nations job as the launch pad for a run for the Senate, or for some other high political office. If it is suggested that he did not mean what he said, and that he was not sincere in his revulsion at the attack on Zionism, that is absurd. On the other hand, he surely sensed that there was a yearning in America to hear someone stand up and denounce the attacks that were being made on the reputation of the United States, and on Israel. His instincts coincided with those of the American majority.

In his account of the Amin episode, he hints that this was indeed the moment when he realized the political potential of what he was doing. "There are morals to be drawn from this," he wrote.[32] "The first is to avoid writing speeches in airplanes. Another, translated from the Gaelic, is that if you want an audience, start a fight." No one was closer to him professionally during the whole UN period, except perhaps Leonard Garment, than Suzanne Weaver. In an interview, she spoke very frankly about the Idi Amin speech. In the deepest sense, "We knew that we were doing the right thing. He had the strength to do it. The rest of us got strength from him." She saw the speech in political terms as aimed not so much at Henry Kissinger as at the State Department. "They did all they could to humiliate him. That was very embittering." But she added something else: "That was the pivotal moment," she said. "This was the moment when he took control of his public life."

In the meantime, helped by Weaver, Leonard Garment and Norman Podhoretz, Moynihan began systematically to research Zionism. They were helped by an article by the great Princeton scholar Bernard Lewis, which analyzed how Soviet propaganda had described Zionism as racist for years. And he commissioned a paper on the subject from Charles Fairbanks, a young political theorist at Yale. Fairbanks demolished the equation of Zionism with racism. And he also went on to argue that this equation would be disastrous even from the point of view of those who were pushing it. If racism is no worse than Zionism, many would ask, how bad is it? Many new nations owed their very existence to the idea of human rights. How good would it be to devalue that concept?

That, nonetheless, was precisely what the Non-Aligned countries, or rather the representatives at the United Nations of their predominantly illiberal, if not outright dictatorial, governments, were preparing to do. The debate took place in the Third Committee, whose official title, ironically enough, was the Committee on Social, Humanitarian and Cultural Affairs, but which occupied much of its time with assaults on colonialism, racism and now Zionism. Somalia had introduced no fewer than seven amendments tying Zionism to racism, but at the last minute these were concentrated in a single resolution. It stated baldly that "Zionism is a form of racism and racial discrimination."

Piero Vinci of Italy, representing the European Community as a whole, immediately objected and stated that the Europeans would oppose.[33] But procedural efforts by the United States and by Costa Rica failed to block the resolution as inadmissible, and on October 16 the final debate began.

Sierra Leone[34] and Zambia moved to postpone consideration of the resolution for a year, but the vote went against by 68 to 45, with 16 abstentions. Leonard Garment spoke before the vote, and so sat in the United States seat in the front row. Behind him sat Moynihan and the others who had worked on his speech. Garment warned that the UN was getting ready to "make a massive attack on the moral realities of the world." Under the guise of attacking racism, the resolution would endorse one of the oldest and most virulent forms of racism, anti-Semitism. That would be "an obscene act." Such acts do not go unnoticed, and they have consequences. "At risk today," he said, "is the moral authority which is the United Nations' only ultimate claim for the support of our peoples. This risk is as reckless as it is unnecessary." The United States moved to adjourn without a vote, but that move failed by 65 votes to 40, with 21 abstaining.

That was when Chaim Herzog made his great speech, and Pat Moynihan embraced him. He could, however, count, and it was plain that the votes were stacked against him. He went to work in two directions. One was to emphasize, however he could, that the nations who had voted for the Somalian resolution were by and large dictatorships, while those who had voted with the United States against it were by and large democratic. He called them "the decent countries," and said, "If you had to pick your company in the world, you couldn't pick better." He focused hard on getting as many African votes as possible, which was difficult. Some African countries were dependent on the Arab world for oil. Many were Muslim, or had substantial Muslim populations. The other tactic was to counterattack. Chile was being attacked by a UN working party, which had confirmed the existence of torture centers in that country. Moynihan called Paul Hofmann of the *New York Times* and told him, on background, that the Chilean vote on Zionism had been bought. "U.S. Aide Charges Chile sold U.N. Vote to Arabs" was the front-page headline.[35]

World opinion was, if anything, quicker to understand what was at stake than public opinion in the United States. In Moscow, Andrei Sakharov said that if the resolution was adopted "it can only contribute to anti-Semitic tendencies in many countries, by giving them the appearance of international legality." There were furious denunciations of it in London and across Europe. In Washington, Jacob Javits and Richard Stone in the Senate and the majority leader, "Tip" O'Neill, in the House introduced resolutions condemning what the Non-Aligned Nations were trying to do.[36] Chaim Herzog went before the Conference of Presidents of Major American Jewish Organizations and chided them for letting Israel down, though in truth Israel itself was preoccupied with other matters. "We were facing the severest attack on the Jewish people since Hitler," Chaim Herzog wrote in his memoirs, "yet the silence of the Jewish community was deafening. 'Where are your bloody Jews?' Pat Moynihan asked in his usual abrupt manner."[37]

Once again, attempts were made to head off the juggernaut that was rolling unstoppably toward the isolation and defeat of Israel and her friends. It fell to Belgium this time as the spokesman of the member countries of the European Community to move to postpone. The vote was no, by 67 to 55, with 15 abstentions and five absentees. As Moynihan pointed out later, if the abstainers had voted with the minority, the resolution would have failed. Again, Herzog spoke, eloquently and with passion. He began by noting that the resolution had come forward on the thirty-seventh anniversary of Kristallnacht, the night on which Nazi storm troopers smashed the windows of Jewish-owned businesses all over Germany, burned synagogues and made bonfires of the Jewish holy texts. That night, he said, led to the crematoria and the gas chambers. As he finished, he made a gesture of great symbolic importance. Forty years earlier, his father had publicly torn up the British White Paper limiting Jewish immigration to Palestine. Now the son tore up the draft resolution. But it passed anyway, this time by 72 votes to 35 with 32 abstentions, and three absent.[38] One of the Israeli delegates, Judge Hadassa Bin Ito, said that what she found so shocking was not the defeat, but the atmosphere. "The hatred was crawling on the floor," she said.[39]

Moynihan had waited until after the vote to deliver the speech of his life.[40] He began, as he was to end, with a lapidary sentence written by Podhoretz. "The United States rises to declare before the General Assembly of the UN, and before the world, that it does not acknowledge, it will not abide by, it will never acquiesce in this infamous act."

A great evil had been loosed upon the world. Sanction had been given to the abomination of anti-Semitism, and the General Assembly had granted symbolic amnesty to the murderers of the six million European Jews. "As this day will live in infamy," he said, "it behooves those who sought to avert it to declare their thoughts so that historians will know that we fought here, that we were not small in number — not this time — and that while we lost, we fought with full knowledge of what indeed would *be* lost."

He said that the resolution was "a political lie of a variety well known to the twentieth century and scarcely exceeded in all that annal of untruth and outrage. The lie is that Zionism is a form of racism. The overwhelming truth is that it is not." He went on to dissect the concepts of racism and Zionism. The very ideas that Jews were a "race," he pointed out, was invented not by Jews but by those who hated them, the nineteenth-century anti-Semites. What was at stake was not merely the legitimacy of the State of Israel. Today, he said, the United Nations had drained the word *racism* of its meaning. Tomorrow it might do the same with words like *national self-determination*. Many small nations could be in danger if the language of human rights, the only language by which the small can be defended, was no longer believed. "If we destroy the words that were given to us by past centuries" — he moved into his peroration — "we will not have words to replace them, for philosophy today has no such words. But there are those of us who have not forsaken those older words, still so new to much of the world. Not forsaken them now, not here, not anywhere, not ever." And he repeated the words with which he had begun. "The United States declares that it does not acknowledge, it will not abide by, it will never acquiesce in this infamous act."

On balance, the speech was well received. The Anti-Defamation League of B'nai B'rith reported that for the first time in its monitoring of the fifty major U.S. papers there was unanimity in condemnation of the resolution. It was the same in Congress. In the Senate, a resolution against the resolution had been unanimously adopted even before the UN vote; in the House, all but one member cosponsored a similar resolution. Now the thing had been done. The very day after the vote, the Senate and the House adopted identical resolutions opposing any participation by the U.S. government in the Decade against Racism and Racial Discrimination.

The whole idea of appointing the author of "The United States in Opposition" to the UN in the first place was to signal a new, robustly unapologetic style of diplomacy in the face of the alliance between a newly assertive Soviet Union and a newly clamorous Third World. That was what Pat Moynihan and Henry Kissinger had cooked up together. The trouble for Moynihan came when it began to look as if Henry Kissinger had joined those who thought he had gone too far. And Moynihan, in a state of mixed rage and exaltation after the Zionism debate, interpreted what happened as a deliberate and sneaky operation by Kissinger to undermine him. In one particular, it is likely that he saw more movement in the undergrowth than was really there, as we shall see. But as to the essence of the matter, his suspicion that Kissinger had decided to move covertly against him, it is likely that he was not wrong.

Two days after the vote, Henry Kissinger gave a press conference in Pittsburgh, at which he said that linking Zionism with racism "smacked of some practices that it would be better for mankind to forget," but he also warned against swinging to the opposite extreme by forgetting the benefits that the UN — "with all its failings" — could bring to the United States.[41]

Kissinger was then asked whether he would associate himself with the remarks made by Ambassador Moynihan about General Amin — remarks made six weeks earlier. He replied with one of those barbed jokes on which his reputation for wit depended. "Ambassador Moynihan makes so many remarks in the course of a day that it is not easy to keep up with all of them." Kissinger explained that he shared Moynihan's displeasure with Amin, "though I might express myself in a more restrained manner, given the differences in our temperaments." And then he mentioned Moynihan's slip, saying that he did not associate himself with identifying Amin with the OAU. Silently, the blade had gone in. Moynihan says too much. Moynihan's temperament is unrestrained. Moynihan makes mistakes. He is not, in a word, diplomatic. Then Kissinger was asked about something Moynihan had said on television that morning, to the effect that the countries who pushed through the Zionism resolution would suffer for it. "Was he speaking of the afterlife, or did he have something concrete in mind?" And Kissinger said he would be seeing Ambassador Moynihan later that day, and would find out exactly what he had in mind.[42]

That day Moynihan spoke in the Third Committee on behalf of a resolution calling for an amnesty for all political prisoners. Resolutions singling out Chile and South Africa had already passed the committee. He quoted the poet Stephen Spender, who had written that when he went to Spain during the civil war he realized that unless he cared about children murdered by either side, he didn't care about murdered children. "Unless we care about political prisoners everywhere," said Moynihan, "we don't really care about them anywhere." And he added that, as bad as things might be in Chile and South Africa, they might be worse in some of the countries whose governments had sponsored the resolutions condemning those two.

Kissinger, of course, was perfectly aware of the U.S. resolution, and when they met, at a White House dinner for the president of the

European Community, Gaston Thorn, nothing was said publicly. Or privately. After dinner, Kissinger took Moynihan back to his old office in the West Wing, even though he had recently ceased to be national security adviser as well as secretary of state. Moynihan says, "There was not a word to suggest any differences."[43] In its next edition, however, *Newsweek* reported that at this very meeting "Kissinger raked Moynihan over the coals . . . for his behavior at the UN. . . . The Zionism resolution made it easier to attack the concept of a secular Jewish state and thus furnished the first new philosophical framework for anti-Semitism since World War II."[44] (That was what Moynihan had been saying.) But, *Newsweek* went on, and Moynihan was bound to think the magazine reflected Kissinger's thinking, the dispute could do profound damage both to the UN and to the search for peace in the Middle East.

"Some Western diplomats complained that Moynihan's outspoken performance only aggravated the problem. Moynihan insisted that he had acted properly and that low-keyed opposition to the resolution would have been appeasement. 'Did I make a crisis out of this obscene resolution?' stormed the ambassador. 'Damn right I did!' "

The article then went on to blame Moynihan for the resolution's passage. It cited "many UN delegates and several experienced American diplomatists" as believing that Moynihan's "linkage of Amin and the OAU had cost him African votes on the deferral issue — perhaps enough to have won." His language, in any case, was intemperate.

Then came the intended deathstroke: Moynihan also seemed to be at odds with his boss. The ambassador insisted that he and Secretary Kissinger " 'are very old and close friends' [something of a diplomatic exaggeration] — and continue to be." But two highly placed sources in Washington asserted that Moynihan had angered Kissinger with his independent efforts to stir up Congressional reaction to the Zionism resolution. Kissinger "really took Pat to the woodshed," said one of *Newsweek*'s sources.

Moynihan claims to know that that story was written in Washington and not in New York. Given the way Washington journalism works, it seems very likely that *Newsweek*'s primary source was indeed the secretary of state himself, though it would not have been hard to find others in the White House or the State Department to corroborate his judgment. Kissinger explained in an interview[45] that his *modus operandi* with reporters was to spend so much time with them that he didn't have to brief them on tactical details, because they would understand what his policy was and guess right about his tactics. It is difficult, at this distance in time, to sort out exactly who said what to whom. Kissinger himself asked Moynihan, the day after the Newsweek piece appeared, how the people at the magazine could have been so stupid as to say that he had taken him to the woodshed when their conversation had been so friendly. But in one respect, the story was certainly accurate. Many UN delegates did indeed think that Moynihan's confrontational style had cost African votes. But it was the adverse opinion of one particular delegate that convinced Moynihan that Kissinger was indeed setting him up in an elaborate ambush.

Ivor Richard, Her Britannic Majesty's ambassador to the United Nations, was not a professional diplomat but a successful commercial lawyer and Labour member of Parliament. The son of a mining engineer from the Welsh coalfield, where Labour politics were in his day both a religion and an excellent career, Richard is a large man with a powerful grip and a robust manner. On November 17, he delivered a speech to the United Nations association, made public two days later, in which he made plain his disagreement with Moynihan's style. Indeed he dared to mock it. In a passage of his speech that Moynihan did not quote he compared the U.S. ambassador's diplomatic style to that of King Lear:

> I will do such things, —
> What they are yet I know not, — but they shall be
> The terrors of the earth.

The Zionism resolution, he said, was not being received in Europe with the same furor as in New York. "How much of the fury was self-induced and how much was deeply felt and spontaneous indignation," he said, "I find it difficult to judge — not being a New Yorker."[46] In Britain, he said, the resolution was treated first with contempt, and after closer analysis as showing that the alliance between the Arabs and the Africans on which an "automatic majority" at the UN had depended was not as strong as had been assumed. "This is not due to any lesser feeling on our part about the issue of anti-Semitism. It is more due to the fact that we have managed to avoid reacting to the vote in purely ideological and emotional terms." And he went on to argue that the UN was a "place to extend British influence and defend

British interests," not "a forum in which to argue my own particular brand of political theology" or a "confrontational arena." In a self-deprecating reference to his own powerful but unathletic frame, he added, "Whatever else the place is," he said, "it is not the OK Corral, and I am hardly Wyatt Earp."

Moynihan's first response, he says, was to assume that Richard had expressed his own thoughts, and he put out a brief statement to the effect that he knew that these were Richard's views, he had every right to state them, and they were the best of friends. The two ambassadors later met at the Soviet mission. Moynihan records[47] that Richard came up and said that Moynihan's brief statement was being taken to mean that he, Moynihan, thought that Richard's speech did not represent British policy. That evening, they met again, this time for dinner at the residence of the shah of Iran's ambassador. Moynihan's account is that he went up to Richard and said, "Ivor, there are people in the Department of State who are saying that your speech represents formal policy."

"Quite right," Moynihan quotes Richard as saying.

"Once Richard went out of his way to impress on me that his speech was official," Moynihan wrote in his account,[48] he "had no choice but to assume Kissinger was behind it." Indeed he went on to say that "large events followed from this, including, it could be argued, the outcome of the 1976 presidential election."

This is cryptic, to say the least. Moynihan's friend from the Nixon White House, William Safire, embroidered the theory. Kissinger had spent two days, from November 15 to 17, in Rambouillet, near Paris, at an economic summit where the British foreign secretary, James Callaghan, was also present. Safire insinuated that at a private breakfast meeting and in other talks Kissinger had suggested to Callaghan that he order Richard to attack Moynihan. Safire turned official denials inside out. With "uncharacteristic vehemence,"[49] Safire sneered, British and American spokesmen insisted that not a single word had been mentioned about British dissatisfaction with Moynihan's performance at the UN. "That's curious," Safire went on. Immediately afterward, Ivor Richard — "a Labor party politician anxious to follow Mr. Callaghan up the ladder" — delivered an "oblique but savage personal attack on America's ambassador": the Richard speech, that is, in Safire's version, which Moynihan believed, if indeed he did not propose it to Safire, was given on the orders of Jim Callaghan, and ultimately at the behest of Henry Kissinger.

Ivor Richard's account, not surprisingly, is different.[50] When I went to see him in 1998, shortly before he was retired from his post as the Labour party's Leader of the House of Lords, I put it to him that Moynihan thought that his difficulties with him were part of his difficulties with Henry Kissinger. "Yes, well," he said, "that was balls." I asked whether it was true that Kissinger put Callaghan, the British foreign secretary of the time, up to getting him to make the speech. "That is rubbish," said the noble lord. "Absolute nonsense. Jim knew nothing about the speech. The only comment I had, after the row had been rumbling on for a month, was a rather gentle telegram saying, 'I seem to be reading a lot about you,' and that was about all." Richard told me he wrote the speech himself in his office on Third Avenue, with no input from London whatever.

He also gave a significantly different account of the exchange at the Iranian embassy. "Pat came up," Richard remembers, "and said, 'It's only your view, isn't it?' And I thought, 'I'm not going to let him get off the hook as easily as that.' So I said, 'What a British ambassador says is the policy of Her Majesty's government.'" It is easy to see the origin of the cross-purposes. Moynihan wanted to nail down whether an infuriating speech, which he took as a personal attack, was part of a political plot against him by his own boss. Richard thought the American ambassador was trying to diminish his freedom of action and thus his importance and, perhaps foolishly, stood on his dignity. Obliquely, in his book, Moynihan goes halfway to withdrawing the charges he made. Two years later, he wrote that he now knew more "without understanding the event any better." He continued, "Kissinger did not think he inspired the attack, and certainly he did not request it. Callaghan evidently did not know it was coming, and was infuriated by it." It never seemed to occur to him that Richard might be a politician-ambassador like himself, also given to expressing his views bluntly, only holding, on this occasion, very different ones.

Henry Kissinger dismisses absolutely the theory that he inspired Richard's speech. "I would say to the British foreign secretary," he replied with incredulity in his rising inflection, "will you get your UN ambassador to attack my UN ambassador!"[51] He says that until the Richard affair, "I was not conscious that I was in conflict with Pat on philosophical grounds." Moynihan's tactics, he concedes, irritated him. "I could have killed off the Zionism resolution in the normal way. By paying off a few Latin American governments. Enmesh it. He seemed to *want* a confrontation."

Certainly the speech rankled with Moynihan. For one thing, for about the only time in his life, the account of Richard's speech is full of gratuitous Anglophobia, such as the comment that "Britain had made rather a speciality of failure in those years."[52] After all, Moynihan was saying that the same could be said of the United States. Equally uncharacteristically, he also made a broad hint that Richard was motivated by anti-Semitism.[53] Richard responded calmly to that, when I put it to him, as one might expect of someone who has been a lifelong member of the Labour party, with its strong Jewish support and long record of opposition to anti-Semitism. He did not have to defend himself against that charge, he said. Richard said he was surprised that Moynihan was so annoyed. He said he thought that by House of Commons standards his speech had been rather gentle.

Curiously, though, the main point Richard was making was not dissimilar from the one Moynihan was making. The Zionism resolution did show that the Third World coalition was weaker than the West feared. Richard said that was a reason for not upsetting potential recruits among its members. Moynihan insisted he had done as well as was possible, and better than he would have done by not treading on any toes. Such evidence as is available to support a counterfactual proportion suggests that he was right. Certainly both the Non-Aligned leadership and the United States took it for granted that the Zionism resolution would pass. Specifically, did Moynihan's San Francisco slip, when he said it was "no accident" that Idi Amin was president of the OAU, lose African votes? Did it make African delegates, or their instructing governments, think Moynihan was anti-African? That proposition, raised though not adopted by *Newsweek,* must be rated dubious. On the key vote, to postpone, thirteen sub-Saharan African countries voted with the United States, three abstained and three were absent. Only one of these had a significant Muslim population. Twenty-one sub-Saharan countries voted not to postpone, and of those nine had substantial Muslim populations. So Moynihan was able to say, and did say to *Newsweek,* that if you took non-Muslim, sub-Saharan African countries, eighteen sided with the United States, and only twelve were against. The usual massive vote against Israel did not appear. So at the level of technical nose counting, it was not the case that Moynihan's style cost Israel votes. Certainly the Israelis did not think so.

The larger question is whether Moynihan was right or wrong to speak up as he did for American interests and to express what he thought were the feelings of ordinary Americans. Some foreigners, not all of them necessarily anti-American, were undoubtedly made nervous by what felt to them like Uncle Sam throwing his weight around. But in the context of the middle 1970s, it was more a case of Uncle Sam, having had sand kicked into his face for some time by every bully on the beach, finally getting up and showing that he was not, as Richard Nixon put it, a "pitiful helpless giant."

The question of whether Ivor Richard gave his speech on his account, as he insists, or as the second-order cat's-paw of Henry Kissinger, as Pat Moynihan believed, at least for a while, is no longer perhaps of any great importance,[54] except in two respects. For one thing, Moynihan's response suggests what an angry mood he was in at the time, how troubled by what he saw as bad leadership, bad diplomacy and bad decisions that had humiliated the United States, and by the widespread perception in the world that the Soviet Union, under Brezhnev, was winning the Cold War. He himself was already convinced, and had begun to say, that it was the Soviet Union that was on the road to disintegration. He was also infuriated, as he says in his book,[55] by the failure of the British and other social democrats to react as he did to Soviet manipulation of the Third World.

Far more important, the Richard speech, and Moynihan's interpretation of it as a deliberate attempt to undercut him by Secretary Kissinger, set up the endgame that was to lead to his resignation from his job at the UN.

Four days after the speech, he told Liz at breakfast that he would be resigning at noon and suggested she might want to come to the press conference. He called the White House and the Department of State with this news. Richard Cheney, the White House chief of staff, said he couldn't resign without telling the president. Kissinger said the same. The press conference was canceled, and Moynihan agreed to see the president on Monday. Over the weekend, he went up, the trunk of his limousine full of Guinness, to see the Harvard-Yale football game. His friend Jim Wilson said he should not give up, or the country would lose "the most hopeful and popular turn in foreign policy in a decade, possibly a generation." This, Moynihan maintained in his account of these events, was something he had not noticed: that his robust diplomatic style was a hit with press and public opinion alike.

So, on Monday, November 24, Moynihan and Leonard Garment flew to Washington.[56] Garment had come equipped with a list

prepared by Suzanne Weaver of instances where the State Department (not Kissinger; the tactic was to avoid personal conflict with
him) had hampered or negated initiatives, particularly human rights
initiatives, favored by Moynihan. The president met Moynihan alone,
by the fireside, with Kissinger waiting outside and getting more and
more frustrated. The days were gone when Kissinger could get whatever he wanted from Richard Nixon merely by threatening to resign.
And then President Ford had insisted that he give up the national security adviser job, which in defiance of all precedent he had combined with the secretaryship since 1972.

Ford's White House staff had no reason for love of or loyalty to
Kissinger. And Moynihan was very aware of their disillusion. Once
Suzanne Weaver had hand-carried some important papers down to
one of them, Jim Connors, who said to her, "Now that Moynihan is
here, Kissinger is the sixth smartest person in the White House."[57] On
another occasion, Moynihan asked Connors why the Republicans did
not support their presidents. Connors replied that it had nothing to
do with the Republican party, but was a trait of the current secretary
of state.[58] "What matters," reported CBS's Daniel Schorr, presumably after briefings from those same staffers, "is that the White House
desperately wants to keep Dr. Moynihan, and that Dr. Kissinger was
perceived as a problem."[59] Like an aging champion, Kissinger might
still win a few more eliminators on points. But he no longer floated
like a butterfly or stung like a bee. Exasperated with everyone, he was
exhausted and embittered by his long virtuoso performance, and
now his star was in decline.

Moynihan understood that he must not appear to be seeking a victory over this still dangerous opponent. He began by withdrawing his
resignation and agreeing to carry on at the UN. Ford told him, in the
manner of a kindly father with squabbling teenage sons, that they all
had to get on together. Then Kissinger was asked in. His face was a
study. To quote Moynihan, "He assured me of his complete support,
I assured him of mine; the President assured us both." Garment, who
had also been waiting outside, grasped the importance of winning the
public relations battle. "Smile," he barked to Moynihan as they approached a phalanx of photographers and cameramen, "as if your life
depended on it." And so the news coverage was framed by the message "Moynihan wins!"[60]

They did not, however, live happily together ever afterward.
Three days later, James Reston, in his column in the *New York Times,*

wrote that Moynihan had been given "a phoney vote of confidence" by Ford and Kissinger. It was a theme to which he would return. By late January, Ronald Reagan, now getting ready to challenge the incumbent Republican president from the Right, was citing Moynihan with approval in his speeches. On January 27, Moynihan met with the president again.[61]

Moynihan recorded an unusually detailed account of his conversation with President Ford. They spoke of a number of issues, one of them Angola. Moynihan said that he knew all about the covert actions because he read the newspapers. Ford said the United States was winning there. Moynihan said he did not believe this. "I had sat in that room and in the Cabinet room over too many years hearing people tell that us we were winning in some jungle war." Ford said the problem was that congressmen simply wanted to vote against covert actions in Angola so that their record would be clear. Moynihan replied, "Mr. President, you want to attack Congressmen, I want to attack Russians."

Moynihan told Ford that his leave of absence from Harvard expired that week, and while his professorship in the Government Department meant more to him than anything except his family, he would give up his professorship and stay on in the administration through the primaries and the convention so as not to hurt Ford politically. He said he had told Kissinger that he would stay on. When Ford's national security adviser, Brent Scowcroft, left the room, Moynihan said there really wasn't any other point in his staying on, as he was completely cut out of policy. Ford did not disagree.

As Moynihan left the Oval Office, he was handed a note asking him to call Leslie Gelb, then a reporter with the *New York Times*'s Washington bureau. Gelb was calling to say he had gotten hold of a long year-end telegram of Moynihan's, called "The Blocs Are Breaking Up." It was not particularly controversial. Indeed, it had been widely circulated inside the government. But its thesis, that in spite of appearances the West was winning the Cold War, directly contradicted Henry Kissinger's growing philosophical pessimism. When it was published in the *Times,* it served as the catalyst for another column from Reston. Moynihan's "idea of confronting the UN was not only defensible but long overdue." But it also told the ambassador what he already more than suspected: that Ford and Kissinger "support him in public but deplore him in private." Having put him in the job, Reston went on, "they can neither tame nor repudiate him."

Moynihan's friend, the journalist Theodore H. White, called him to say, "You know you have to go!" He did not need telling. He sent in a letter of resignation to Ford, and this time he called the dean of Harvard College, Henry Rosovsky, and told him that he had sent his letter of resignation to the president. Rosovsky said that he was deeply disappointed. Moynihan said he was too, but it had become impossible for him to stay at the UN. "Oh," said the dean, "you mean *that* president!"

Four days later, in a friendly letter,[62] Moynihan told Kissinger that he was leaving to go back to Harvard, and added, "It has been an honor to serve you." But the United States, by rotation, would be the president of the UN Security Council in February. If the president would like, he said, it turned out that he could get permission from Harvard to stay for the month, and he would do so. So it was not until the end of February that he received a final handsome *envoi* from Henry Kissinger. "THERE IS ONLY ONE PAT MOYNIHAN," Kissinger wrote. "THROUGHOUT OUR MANY YEARS OF ASSOCIATION I HAVE ALWAYS ENJOYED, AND BENEFITTED FROM, YOUR CREATIVITY, DYNAMISM, HUMANITY AND WIT. I HOPE WE MAY COLLABORATE AGAIN IN THE FUTURE."[63]

The expiry of his leave from Harvard was something more than an accidental irritation as Moynihan saw it. "Next to great wealth," he wrote in his book[64] "a chair in the Harvard Department of Government was possibly the most important security a man could have in Washington." (James Q. Wilson told me that Moynihan always worried more about tenure and security than was reasonable; he could never quite realize how well known and how widely admired he was, and therefore how many options were open to him.) His dilemma, as he saw it at the beginning of 1976, was that the only way he could go on working for Ford and Kissinger at the UN was by giving up the Harvard chair, but that the moment he did so the balance of his relationship with Kissinger would change. "I would no longer be an equal. . . . I would have no real alternative to the job I held as his gift, or such at least would have to be his view. He knew that; and I knew it; and he knew that I knew. He would not be able to help himself."[65]

That certainly came close to the scorpion-and-frog view of Kissinger's character. But then Moynihan added, as if in an afterthought, "He was a friend, and I think sometimes hated what he did. He was a good man in a bad time." But before that, he added something else. "As if almost to acknowledge what would come," Moynihan wrote of Kissinger, "he said he thought I should run for the Senate." Kissinger says he does not believe that Moynihan sat down and planned to be "the victim of Kissinger." But, he says, "I had no reason to force him out. He had every conceivable reason to go."[66]

Henry Kissinger was hardly the only one to have been struck by the thought that his departing subordinate might become a senator. On January 27, the same day Moynihan saw the president, Ben Wattenberg wrote him a letter. Wattenberg was a journalist who shared Moynihan's dismay at what had happened to the Democratic party. He had made something of a name with a book he had coauthored with the pollster Richard Scammon in 1969, *The Real Majority*. He was working with Richard Nixon's former speechwriter Richard J. Whalen on another book, about multinational corporations, and he asked for Moynihan's help in setting up some interviews. "If you have some time to talk next week," he wrote, he would like to come in and discuss "multinational corporations, the role of American economic power in the world equation, and even more about something more immediate — the Senate race."

History does sometimes bestow on its favorites the satisfaction of revenge. By early December 1991, the alliance between the Soviet Union, the Arabs and the Africans was no more of a threat to the United States than Napoleon. The Soviet Union would cease to exist later that month. Such once hostile Arab states as Egypt, Syria and Saudi Arabia had joined a coalition led by the United States to throw Saddam Hussein's Iraqi Republican Guards out of Kuwait and looked to the United States to defend them against Saddam's retaliation. Israel, to be sure, was still threatened, but Israel was a more assured and formidable protagonist. And Daniel Patrick Moynihan was a ranking Democratic member of the United States Senate's Committee on Foreign Relations.

At a meeting in Jerusalem in February 1990, the doughty American human rights activist and lawyer Morris Abram suggested that the Human Rights Commission of the United Nations "call upon the General Assembly to erase the lie that taints the organization just as surely as the segregation of my youth tainted the American Democracy." This has been called "the opening of a U.S. campaign to rescind the 1975 resolution equating Zionism with racism."[67] In early 1990, the subcommittee of the Senate Foreign Relations Committee on Near East and South Asian Affairs, chaired by Senator Moynihan, held public hearings on Senate Joint Resolution 246, introduced by his Democratic colleague Senator Rudy Boschwitz of Minnesota, which called on the members of the UN to repeal Resolution 3379.

Assistant Secretary of State John Bolton, for the Bush administration, gave testimony that annoyed Moynihan, who wanted to see more action. "The West imposed no consequences of any kind," Moynihan charged, "on those nations that associated themselves with this filthy proposition of the Soviet Union." He said the United States should cut off aid to countries that supported the resolution, and asked how many of them there were. Bolton said a clear majority of the seventy-two countries that voted for the resolution received U.S. aid at the time and probably still did. "Did we ever tell one country, just one country," Moynihan asked, "that you are getting American money, and you are not getting any more until you change your mind?" And he told Bolton that the message he wanted the State Department to take back was "We don't like that resolution one damn bit. We feel it is a residue of a Stalinist, totalitarian Soviet Union . . . and they lost."

In 1990, the State Department dragged its feet, and so did many of America's allies, even some that, like Britain, had voted against the resolution in 1975. Some, like Margaret Thatcher, thought repeal of the amendment should be made conditional on Israel accepting the peace process. But the European Community, as it then was, committed itself to act for repeal. In mid-September 1991, relations between the United States and Israel deteriorated after President Bush sharply criticized the pro-Israel lobby that was pushing for $10 billion in loan guarantees. But on September 23, Bush reversed himself and called in his address to the General Assembly for repeal. The next day, the new Soviet foreign minister, Boris Pankin, called on the UN to "leave behind the legacy of the ice age, like the obnoxious resolution equating Zionism with racism."[68] At long last the United States began not just to lobby, but to twist arms. Bush ordered ambassadors to warn their host governments that failure to vote for repealing the resolution would damage their relations with the United States.

On December 16, 1991, without fanfare, the General Assembly of the United Nations, by virtue of Resolution 46/86, "decides to revoke the determination contained in its Resolution 3379 of 10 November 1975."

II

To the Senate

THE 1976 CAMPAIGN

> In any discussion of our nation's social distress
> or international posture, the mind and voice of
> Pat Moynihan promise unique contributions.
>
> — *New York Times,* September 10, 1976

O N OCTOBER 26, 1975, after the vote on the Zionism resolution in the Third Committee and before the vote in the General Assembly, Moynihan appeared on *Face the Nation.* At the end of the show, one interviewer said, "As you know there is a lot of talk that you are running for political office, specifically the Senate from New York State."[1]

The ambassador cut in quickly and answered emphatically.

Can I just speak right quickly to that? It is not so. It might very much please some of the people in the UN who see us as enemies to think that this is — that it is so, to explain positions we are taking on matters of principle as in fact having some squalid personal ambition. I am not. I would consider it a dishonorable thing, this charge having been made, I would consider it dishonorable to leave this post and run for any office, and I would hope that it would be understood that if I do, the people, the voters to whom I would present myself in such circumstances, would consider me as having said in advance I am a man of no personal honor to have done so.

That sounded like a Sherman declaration. Yet just over a year later Daniel Patrick Moynihan was elected to the United States Senate from New York. Under the circumstances, there was indeed nothing dishonorable about either his campaigning or his election. After all, he had left the UN mission some two months before he threw his

Irish fishing hat into the ring. But it is worth pausing for a moment over the evolution of what was, after all, one of the two or three most significant political decisions of Moynihan's life.

Moynihan's statement on *Face the Nation* was not an unfortunate improvisation under the pressure of a television studio. It was a memorized answer to a planted question.[2] Moynihan had asked the television reporter George Herman to ask it because he thought the imputation that he was using the UN job as a springboard was not only insulting to his honor but also damaging to his effectiveness. Indeed in his book *A Dangerous Place,* he wrote that when he first heard the suggestion that he was running for office he assumed that it was Soviet disinformation.[3] It was hardly necessary to posit anything so conspiratorial. There had been rumors for months that he was running for office. Ivor Richard remarked that he had taken Moynihan's political aspirations for granted ever since Moynihan arrived at the UN.[4] Many journalists had put similar suspicions in print. Even the sympathetic Paul Hofmann, after the Idi Amin speech, recorded that "one American said, 'What is Pat Moynihan running for?' "[5]

Moynihan denies that he was doing anything of the kind.[6] And when he left the United Nations, he duly headed back to Harvard and took up his teaching. Ben Wattenberg, however, was not the only person to suggest that he run for the Senate. In February, before he had even gone back to Cambridge, Richard Eaton, a young upstate lawyer, wrote him a letter asking him to run, then created a Moynihan for Senator committee and drafted an advertisement that ran in the *Oneonta Star.*[7] Two professional politicians, Joe Crangle, a former New York State Democratic chairman, and Chester Straub, a former New York State senator, approached Moynihan and asked him to run.[8] He would not do so immediately, but the very real interest in his candidacy could never have been far from his mind. His first entry into electoral politics since 1965 would not be on his own behalf but for Scoop Jackson's presidency instead. There again, it was Ben Wattenberg who made the first move.

Politics had darkened between 1965 and 1976. The nation had lived through the traumas of assassinations, riots, war, defeat, and Watergate, and Moynihan had lived through them more intensely than most people. The spirit of politics was sourer, the rhetoric harsher, and Moynihan had not been untouched by this darker new mood. He believed that much that was good in American life was being lost, or was under threat, both at home and abroad. Just as the reception of the Moynihan Report set him adrift from the liberal wing of the Democratic party, so the treatment he felt he had received from Henry Kissinger moved him alongside a group of people, most of them to be sure still nominally Democrats, who had definitively severed their ties with liberalism. Many of them were New Yorkers, furious at what they saw happening to their city. Some were academics, shocked by the departure of civility from the campus. Not a few were from the ranks of labor, dismayed by the new lack of respect for the established union leadership, and shocked by the McGovern tendency in their party. They were obsessed by a sense that the liberals had betrayed a trust in relation to the aggressive posture of the Soviet Union and the future of Israel, subjects they saw as twin aspects of the same threat. In the spring of 1976, Moynihan felt close to these people, and many of them hailed him as a new champion. Ben Wattenberg says, "He had left the UN in a blaze of glory" and that he had "the charisma of common sense."[9]

It was precisely at the point when he was retreating from the United Nations with a new defiance, and a new confidence in his own powers, that the letter from Wattenberg arrived. It pointed to a path ahead, a not so random walk back into domestic politics.

Wattenberg was heavily involved in Jackson's presidential bid. They were focusing hard on the New York primary on April 15. They decided to by-pass New Hampshire, but they could not duck Massachusetts: it was "the belly of the beast." Wattenberg was dispatched to get a specific endorsement from Moynihan, but all Moynihan would say was that the candidate was "the sort of man we need." The suspicion in the Jackson ranks, even at this early date, was that this was Liz's work, that she did not feel comfortable with the conservatism of Wattenberg and his friends. They had already paid for a full-page ad in the *Boston Globe,* to carry endorsements from a bunch of heavyweight Harvard intellectuals, among them Nathan Glazer, Richard Pipes and Oscar Handlin.

Wattenberg was thrilled when he succeeded in persuading Moynihan to run as a delegate in the Bronx. Better still, he persuaded Moynihan to speak for Jackson in Massachusetts before that state's primary: In the spring of 1976, when Moynihan was at Yale as a Chubb fellow after leaving the UN, Ben Wattenberg had got hold of a little private plane, and he and Moynihan campaigned briefly in the Bay State. Prior to the campaign, Jackson and Moynihan had never met. Their first meeting, in the height of the campaigns in New York and Massachusetts, took place in the back seat of a car, as Moynihan rode with Jackson out to the Newark airport from Manhattan. When Jackson won Massachusetts, it looked as though his candidacy was about to take off.

Again, Wattenberg showed up in a private plane lent by one of Senator Jackson's corporate friends, and whisked Moynihan off on a madcap campaign trip around Florida, accompanied by Theodore H. White and by R. W. Apple, Jr., of the *New York Times*. Many jokes were enjoyed and many libations poured. But the serious business of the trip was Moynihan's speeches to Jewish groups at Temple Emanu-El in Miami Beach and in Tampa and Fort Lauderdale. A couple of weeks later, he was out in Wisconsin, speaking for Jackson in Milwaukee and at airport press conferences across the state.[10] And in early April, he campaigned for Jackson and, perhaps, a little bit for himself in upstate New York. James Perry, of the *National Observer*, who went along in Wattenberg's Beechcraft for a day, has left a vivid picture of the professor-turned-campaigner.[11] At Broome County Airport, he urged reporters to read an article in the latest *New Republic* about the recent Communist party congress in Washington. "I'm sorry," he said and laughed. "Not Washington. Not yet. No. It was in Moscow."

In Rochester, he was asked "Why are you here?" and replied without shame, "Because Monroe County matters!" At a country club near Buffalo he quoted Reinhold Niebuhr: "Power without morality is tyranny, but morality without power is futility." A waitress in Albany thought it was Moynihan, not Jackson, who should be running for president.

These were agreeable wanderings, more like vacation trips in congenial company than a campaign; a pleasant way to reenter the world of American politics. Scoop Jackson won in New York, and there was talk that if he went all the way, he would make Pat Moynihan his secretary of state.[12] But he didn't go all the way. On April 27, Jimmy Carter, whose campaign was gathering momentum, beat him in Pennsylvania. Jackson had recently married, and he had no private money. On May 1, he withdrew from the race, saying frankly that he was not a wealthy man.[13]

All spring, in the intervals between these hectic campaign dashes, Moynihan continued to teach at Harvard. He knew that he was back in politics, though. Scoop Jackson had called after Pennsylvania to inform Moynihan that he was pulling out of the race for the Democratic nomination. "The same people who got me in as a delegate [for Jackson, from the Bronx]," Moynihan said later, "wanted me to run [for Senate in New York]."

On May 3, he spoke at the traditional Associated Press luncheon at the American Society of Newspaper Editors convention in New York, and picked up the theme he had drummed out at the UN, the theme of the Jackson people. In thunderous tones, he denounced "pervasive repetition of what has become the central theme of the last third of the twentieth century, which is that what is wrong with the world is America. Well, it isn't. . . . We do not see the United States as evil or even as disgraced."[14]

Then came those June days, as he remembered them. He had gone back up to Harvard to correct term papers. "Suzi Weaver and I sat around with piles of papers. Would I go to the farm? Or to New York? It was a very close call." While he was hesitating, two of the nine trustees of Ohio State voted against him being given an honorary doctorate of law. One, the only black trustee, had accused Moynihan of being a racist. Called for comment by the New York Times, Moynihan replied testily that he didn't need another honorary degree, he had twenty-five already.[15]

On June 10, he came off the fence. He took the decision that was to channel the next twenty-four years of his life. He went to the Biltmore Hotel, across the street from Grand Central Station, and announced that he was running for senator. He almost blew the whole campaign at the very start. There was a press conference, with a dozen TV cameras. "Could you move," Pat said, "so that the real journalists can see?"[16] The New York Times reported that "Daniel P. Moynihan announced his candidature for United States Senator from New York yesterday, putting on display his considerable support in labor circles." He also explained at length the statement he made last year that it would be "dishonorable" for him to run for office. "The case for my running is first of all that I can be elected," he said.[17] No doubt that was true. But before that could happen he had to get through a savagely contested primary campaign, and he only just made it.

It was by no means an ordinary year in the politics either of the city or of the nation. It was only in the previous year that the depth of New York's financial problems had become apparent. The combination of long-term structural decline, as both manufacturing and head offices moved out of the city, with the short-term impact of the oil price rise, was compounded by the very rise in the cost of welfare that Moynihan had predicted. By 1975, the city's plight was plain for all to see. The banker Felix Rohatyn was trying to put together a rescue package. The federal loan guarantee that proved the key element in that package was not in place until 1977. Only the federal government, in the short term, could help; and the federal government was neither in a position nor the mood. "Ford to City," ran the classic headline in the *Daily News,* "Drop Dead!"[18]

National politics were in an equally turbulent state. It had been nearly two years since Richard Nixon departed in disgrace. Gerald Ford, greeted with affection and relief, lost much of his political authority when he issued Nixon a blanket pardon. Jimmy Carter had appeared out of Georgia and was running surprisingly strongly. But he had little to do with Moynihan's politics, or with the dire problems of New York City. Nor did Moynihan expect, or get, any help from New York Governor Hugh Carey or New York City Mayor Abraham Beame. In the early stages of the campaign, in fact, the governor went out of his way to make it plain that he did not favor Moynihan.

Moynihan's natural allies were his neoconservative friends from the Jackson campaign and from Social Democrats USA, two overlapping groups. Many labor people, like Albert Shanker of the American Federation of Teachers and Al Barkan, chair of the political committee of the AFL-CIO, fell into both categories. Back in November, the Social Democrats had given Moynihan a reception and a silver julep cup. Carl Gershman, the Social Democrats' president, said wittily (in view of the candidate's known liking for a drink), that it would do nicely for keeping pens and pencils.[19] A motley group of friends and supporters showed up, including Midge Decter and Irving Kristol, who would not even then have described himself as a social democrat. Speeches were made by Bayard Rustin, one of the true heroes of the civil rights movement, who was close to labor in New York, and by Lane Kirkland, newly president of the AFL-CIO.

The second group that rallied round the nascent Moynihan campaign were pols. They were not, in the main, professional politicians of the old school, but rising lawyers and politicians like Joe Crangle, already a powerful figure in Buffalo, and his protégé Meyer "Sandy" Frucher from New York City. There were younger enthusiasts like Richard Eaton from Binghamton and Tim Russert, also from Buffalo.[20] Crangle was a former state Democratic chairman and a man with a national reputation at the time. Penn Kemble, a former Jackson staffer who moved over to the Moynihan campaign, recalls the mood. After 1974, there was a feeling among his friends that the Republicans were incompetent, and that the Democrats had a great chance if they could heal their divisions. For them, after the Zionism fight, Moynihan was their champion. But they also felt that he understood their instincts about social issues. "We saw him as a man who would hew to the center," Kemble recalls.[21]

Suzanne Garment quit her job as Moynihan's teaching assistant and took charge of the issues side of the campaign, which would help to ensure a strong but flexible neoconservative line in the positions the candidate took. Finance was largely in the hands of Richard Ravitch, a wealthy New York construction man. Leonard Garment played a big part. "Ravitch would spin his Rolodex," says Dick Eaton, "Garment would talk to the guy, and then they would put Moynihan on."[22] Another important figure on the financial side of the campaign was the Moynihans' personal adviser and friend John Westergaard, a Wall Street financial consultant who has remained an important part of the Moynihan political entourage; incidentally, Westergaard lives on West 42nd Street, a few yards from where Moynihan's bar and grill used to be.

There were four other candidates for the nomination: Paul O'Dwyer, who had a walk-on part in the 1965 city election; Ramsey Clark, a former U.S. attorney general in the Johnson administration who had moved quite far to the Left on many issues; a successful construction executive called Abraham Hirschfeld; and Congresswoman Bella Abzug. Of Hirschfeld, even the *New York Times* said he would be "better off sticking to building."[23] Clark never made much of a mark. But O'Dwyer, a Catholic and a liberal, was theoretically a strong claimant for many of the votes Moynihan would have to win. It was at the point when it became plain that Moynihan would in fact receive many of those votes that he emerged as the strongest opponent to Bella Abzug. She was all that Pat Moynihan most disliked in New York politics and even more what Liz Moynihan disliked. In 1976, she was in her third term in Congress and had made a reputation for herself as an outspoken leftist and feminist. The adjective *flamboyant* was attached to her almost as stock epithets were given to Homer's heroes; it was her trademark always to wear a large hat. She was loud, rude and proud of it.

Before the primary contest could reach its remarkably bitter final round, however, there was a crisis within the Moynihan camp. Elizabeth Moynihan, for the first time in Pat's political career, emerged as a formidable operator in her own right. Liz had been critical of the way Sandy Frucher, Pat's campaign manager, did his job. Among other things, she suspected Frucher of diverting money raised for Pat to support other Democratic candidates.[24] At a tense meeting at campaign headquarters, Liz Moynihan emerged as the victor and became the campaign manager. She has subsequently retained this job for all her husband's elections.

On September 1, the *New York Times* and other papers in the state carried a full-page advertisement laying out "where Pat Moynihan stands on the family, the city, the state and the nation."[25] The advertisement sounded one of the leading themes of the candidate's whole career, before and after: "Families are the key to the success or failure of society as a whole." Within a few days, however, the campaign had become a ferocious war of words. Bella Abzug showed no reluctance to resort to name-calling. She and her supporters made much of the "benign neglect" memo. Kenneth B. Clark, a sociologist whose work had contributed to the victory in the landmark 1954 *Brown* decision by the Supreme Court, weighed in for Abzug. In the midst of the furor over the Moynihan Report nearly a decade earlier, Clark had defended Pat against charges of racism, saying, "If Pat Moynihan is a racist, so am I." Now he said that the "benign neglect" memo was anti-black and called Moynihan a "liar" when he denied it.[26]

A few days later the campaign turned even nastier. On September 5, as Moynihan was campaigning on the Lower East Side, a young man shouted, "Fascist pig!" and smashed a banana cream pie into the candidate's face. The young man was immediately arrested, and Moynihan declined to press charges. But afterward, visibly shaken, he admitted, "It scared the hell out of me." In an age of political assassinations, he explained, "it was a violent act." And it was only one of several unpleasant incidents. On September 2, someone else had shouted "Fascist pig!" at the candidate at a rally in Rockefeller Center. Sandy Frucher reported a string of abusive phone calls at headquarters, and even a telephoned bomb threat.[27]

The turning point, not only of the primary, but arguably of Moynihan's entire career, came when he was campaigning in the Bronx. At about 10:00 at night, one of his aides came and told him that the *New York Times* had endorsed him.[28] The campaign for the Senate had been undistinguished, the editorial began. The candidates had few real differences of philosophy; instead they invited the voters to choose on the basis of personality. "Very well," said the *Times*. "We choose Daniel Patrick Moynihan, that rambunctious child of the sidewalks of New York, profound student and teacher of social affairs, aggressive debater, outrageous flatterer, shrewd adviser — indeed manipulator — of Presidents, accomplished diplomat and heartfelt friend of the poor — poor people, poor cities, poor regions such as ours."

> Mr. Moynihan should be able to sweep all the votes west of Mr. Buckley's left pinkie, were it not for his unfortunate — and undeserved — unpopularity among black citizens.
>
> He has been berated for a slur upon Negro culture in his contention a decade ago that slavery, racism and poverty had injured the structure of the black family. Even if he were wrong, his purpose in urging President Johnson to help the blacks was just, indeed noble. He was further misunderstood while he worked to reform our disgraceful welfare system in President Nixon's White House, because he loosely counseled "benign neglect" of racial rhetoric.
>
> . . . The wounds cut so deep that he has at times yielded to self-pity. We suspect that the confidence of the electorate, white and black, would finally heal that hurt and unleash his immense talents.
>
> In any discussion of our nation's social distress or international posture, the mind and voice of Pat Moynihan promise unique contributions . . . So he tried to butter up Mr. Nixon once too often and some embarrassing praise haunts him now. And he defended Israel against hypocrisy at the United Nations with such zeal that he was forced to demonstrate sincerity by vowing not to seek the nomination that he is seeking. These were excesses of a passionate public servant whose motives and intellect we nonetheless admire. Mr. Moynihan's talents and temperament clearly would add spice as well as distinction to the Senate, and they would serve us well.[29]

Moynihan had always taken a lot of notice of what the *New York Times* had to say. He has always kept in close contact with the paper's reporters and writers. During his time at the United Nations, however, he had a falling out with John Oakes, the editorial director and as such the chief editorial writer. Oakes, a descendant of the Adolph Ochs who founded the paper, was an urbane, internationalist liberal. He saw Moynihan's style at the United Nations as uncouth, populist and suspect of being racist. Oakes saw his own role in politics as a kind of noblesse oblige; Moynihan, for some years, had seen Oakes in a far less favorable light. The editorial page under his rule, Moynihan said, gave off a "universalist, even deracinated air," the mark of "German Reform Judaism of that particular branch that so flourished in and has so influenced the city of [New York]."[30] In short, there was no love lost between the editorial page editor and the senatorial candidate. So what occasioned this dramatic change of mind: Why had the *New York Times* endorsed Daniel P. Moynihan?

In fact, there was no such change of mind on Oakes's part. Oakes duly wrote an editorial, highly critical of Moynihan, and endorsing Bella Abzug. But for one of the very few times in its history, the publisher of the *New York Times*, Arthur Hays "Punch" Sulzberger, intervened to overrule his cousin and colleague, an exceptional event. It was not due so much to any obvious enthusiasm for Moynihan on the part of Sulzberger, though he did believe Moynihan would make a good senator. Rather, Sulzberger felt that it was time for the paper to reposition itself. The *Times* had come to be seen as predictably liberal while the country and the city were shifting to the Right. The *Times* could not afford to be left on the beach — it was time to catch a new wind. Pat Moynihan was the beneficiary of this shift.

It was a significant moment for the *Times*. As the great foreign correspondent Harrison Salisbury wrote in his history of the paper, it was "an event so shattering, so lacking in the amenities with which the *Times'* decisions were normally cloaked, that it produced from editorial editor John Oakes a violent outburst, deep permanent wounds and a published disclaimer (but even his disclaimer, Oakes bitterly noted, 'was cut to mute the force of . . . protest).' "[31]

Punch Sulzberger had never imposed his choice of a candidate on the paper or on his cousin.[32] Still, he was the publisher, and he had always taken it for granted that in the last analysis he would have the final word if he chose to insist on it. In many ways he was too conservative to feel entirely happy with Bella Abzug. Sulzberger was in attendance at one of Moynihan's ambassadorial parties at the Waldorf Towers when Moynihan said he was thinking of running for the Senate: "Of course, I would never get any support from the *New York Times*." Said the publisher, "Well, you never know. Why don't you try?"[33]

Sulzberger and Oakes argued in a friendly way about the endorsement until Oakes went away for his month's vacation on Martha's Vineyard. Before he left, he pointed out to Sulzberger that there was no need for an endorsement while he was away. Sulzberger responded, "Well, if you don't want to do it, I'll try my hand at putting something down on paper." He drafted an editorial, and Sydney Gruson, the publisher's assistant and himself a senior editor, took it to Max Frankel. Frankel, who was due to take over from Oakes four months later as the *Times's* editorial page editor, recalls that he warmly approved of the endorsement of Moynihan, but strongly disliked the writing.[34]

"Good," said Gruson. "That means you can rewrite it for us." Gruson explained to Frankel that while Oakes and most of his board of editorial writers wanted to endorse Abzug, the publisher had decided to overrule his editorial page editor. "I've rarely seen him so determined," Gruson said of Sulzberger. Frankel speculates that this determination may have been hardened by a sharp fall in the value of the New York Times Company's stock in addition to a profile of Sulzberger in *Business Week,* accusing him of being antibusiness.

Whatever the reason, Frankel reluctantly agreed to rewrite the editorial, though he insisted that his own role must be kept secret. What he produced was the candid but unapologetic endorsement just quoted. It was, Frankel commented in his memoirs, the first editorial he ever wrote for the *Times,* and the last that had "an immediate, demonstrable effect on events." Even if the *Times* had stayed neutral, he guesses, Abzug would have won the primary. Punch Sulzberger's need to position himself a little further to the Right and his decision to overrule Oakes and endorse Moynihan were not the least important of the "random walks" that influenced Moynihan's career.

Oakes was sufficiently worried while on vacation on Martha's Vineyard that he called his assistant, Fred Hechinger, and asked him to draft a memo detailing the reasons why Moynihan should not be endorsed. The day Oakes was getting ready to leave the Vineyard and return to New York, however, Hechinger called to say that he had been given Frankel's editorial with instructions to run it the next day. Oakes telephoned Sulzberger and protested. He pleaded with him not to run the Moynihan endorsement until he could get back to New York. No, said the publisher, it would have to run the next day, Friday, because the election was the following Tuesday; any later would be too late. Oakes was extremely upset; more so, he said later, than ever before in his thirty years on the paper. He suggested that Sulzberger publish the article over his own name. No, said the publisher. Then, said Oakes, he must be allowed to publish a disclaimer. On the ferry from Martha's Vineyard, he wrote a stormy letter making the case against Moynihan and for Abzug. Sulzberger refused to publish it in full. All Oakes was allowed in the end was a curt three-line letter. It read:

> As the editor of the editorial page of *The New York Times* I must express disagreement with the endorsement in today's editorial columns of Mr. Moynihan over other candidates in the New York Democratic primary contest for the U.S. Senate.
>
> John B. Oakes
> Sept. 10, 1976[35]

Within days Moynihan was proudly reciting his endorsement by the *Times* and by the *New York Daily News* at every stop.[36] There is little doubt that the *Times* endorsement, in particular, did have a great influence on the outcome of the race. It was pleasant, too, that Jacqueline Kennedy Onassis gave Moynihan her own endorsement and $1,000 the day after the *Times* editorial appeared.[37]

On September 12, with the vote only two days away, there was another debate. The candidates were all asked who they would support for Senate majority leader. Three of the five said they would support Hubert Humphrey. Moynihan said, in effect, that he would use the election of the majority leader to bargain for a place on the Senate Finance Committee. Years later he explained what he had in mind. Each of the candidates was asked which committee they would go out for. Ramsey Clark said Foreign Relations. Paul O'Dwyer said he had always been a friend of the workingman and would take Labor. Bella Abzug said she wanted to be on Health. But Moynihan plumped for Finance because that was where the money was: more of the federal budget goes through the Finance Committee than any other.

On the last day before the election, both Moynihan and Abzug campaigned in the garment district, "symbolic," as the *New York Times* said, "of their strong bid for Jewish voters." Jews, after all, would provide 40 percent of the votes. On election day, Moynihan beat Abzug by fewer than ten thousand votes, or less than one percent of the electorate. It was, the *Times* recorded, "one of the closest state-wide primaries in recent years."[38] The final result was: Moynihan, 327,478; Abzug, 317,905.

Moynihan ran slightly ahead of Abzug in the city and the suburbs and also upstate. But Mrs. Abzug made the race close by an unexpectedly strong run upstate.

By late October, the general election was in full swing. Moynihan faced the incumbent Republican, James L. Buckley, who rejoiced in the Conservative party's endorsement as well as that of the Republicans. Buckley, a successful Manhattan lawyer, was the brother of William F. Buckley, Jr., the conservative founder and editor of *National Review*. Bill Buckley and Moynihan had been on friendly terms since Buckley defended *Beyond the Melting Pot* against charges of racism. Moynihan concluded that he had been treated with a higher level of intellectual honesty in *National Review* than in liberal publications.[39] As wits, celebrities and sticklers for intellectual coherence and literary grace, Bill Buckley and Moynihan had a lot in common. So, by extension, there was far less personal needle in the race against Jim Buckley than against Bella Abzug. On the other hand, there was a genuine intellectual and ideological gulf. Jim Buckley, far more than his mercurial brother, was an unrepentant, predictable conservative, and whatever else he was, Moynihan was not that.

At last, Governor Carey called on regular Democrats to close ranks and support Moynihan against what he called the "doctrine of falsehood" offered by Buckley. But both Percy Sutton, the Manhattan borough president, and David Dinkins, city clerk and future mayor, two of the most powerful black Democrats in New York, refused to forgive Moynihan for his supposed slights. "The black community," said Dinkins, "wants some signal from Mr. Moynihan, some specific reference to black problems, a direct appeal, a walk in the black community." Moynihan had in fact scheduled a walk in the South Bronx, then at its most desolate and dangerous, but had to cancel it to appear in court. Jim Buckley was trying to stop Moynihan's name from appearing on the ballot as a candidate from the Liberal party (unique to New York) as well as being listed as a Democrat. The court found against Moynihan, but the ruling had little palpable effect.

On October 24, with the vote little over a week away, Moynihan campaigned among mainly conservative working-class voters in Queens and the Bronx. Buckley had said that Moynihan would cost every voter $3,000 a head. Moynihan threw the charge back, saying the truth was that it was Buckley who had voted for higher income taxes, and both men went on repeating charge and countercharge from every platform and street corner they could find. Speaking to an

International Ladies Garment Workers audience, largely Jewish, Moynihan tossed back another conservative slogan, saying federal government "is there to be used when it can help," that we should be getting the government "off our backs and on to our side."[40] Buckley, who publicized a meeting with Cardinal Cooke, persisted in calling Moynihan "Professor," and accused him of wanting the government to spend what it did not have. Moynihan retaliated by repeatedly calling Buckley a "millionaire extremist."

By the end of the penultimate week before election day Moynihan was 4 to 6 points ahead, according to a *New York Times* poll, based on interviewing done a week to ten days earlier. But Moynihan needed one more statewide advertising blitz, and he was desperately trying to borrow the money as a personal loan. He was already $146,000 in debt from the primary campaign; he had borrowed another $50,000 since the primaries; and he was expected to take out another $50,000 loan for a last-minute push in the closing days.

The substance of the contest was about economics, and in particular about the parlous condition of New York State. Here Moynihan had his antagonist's head in a lock, for the fact was that Buckley was not a man to run to the federal government for help, yet only the federal government could help New York on a scale that matched its problems.

"If you are so effective," Moynihan kept on asking in different ways, "then how come New York is in so much trouble?"[41] Buckley couldn't hide the fact that he didn't know what he would do, Moynihan summarized the campaign later. "That was how I got elected."

Moynihan made only the fourth deck of the *New York Times* front page headline. It read:

CARTER VICTOR IN TIGHT RACE
FORD LOSES NY STATE
DEMOCRATS RETAIN CONGRESS
Moynihan Defeats Buckley for New York Senate Seat

Moynihan ran ahead of Jimmy Carter in Catholic and also in Jewish neighborhoods, but less well in black ones. In the end, the analysts found, the race had ended up as a straight-liberal-Democrat-versus-conservative-Republican contest. And that led to a rather decisive result: Daniel Patrick Moynihan, 2,913,200; James L. Buckley, 2,517,292.

"New York was on the ballot," Moynihan told a jostling crowd at his headquarters. "And New York won."[42] And he added a phrase that showed, to anyone with ears to hear, how far he was from a doctrinaire conservative. "It's time," he said, "we made some claims on the national government."

The senator-elect, however, was nowhere to be seen in the celebrating throng of supporters. His wife insisted that he had gone off to Harvard to teach his class. It was true. The next morning, on no sleep, he duly met forty students taking Social Science 115 for the last time. He had missed only two classes in the whole campaign.

Two days later, at a press conference, he was in a tense mood, and not inclined to let the reporters get away with anything. A TV reporter asked about welfare. "It's not something for the simple-minded," Moynihan snapped. Another reporter raised the matter of his "flamboyance" (that word again) at the UN. "I got their attention," he said, and his staff applauded. "They," presumably, were the diplomatic representatives of the Non-Aligned Nations. Now the ex-ambassador and ex-professor would have to get the attention of a Russian nesting doll of new audiences. There would be a national audience for whatever the junior senator from New York wanted to say. Then there was quote-Washington-unquote, the few thousand judges of political horseflesh and political stock-pickers, unctuously courteous on the surface and mercilessly cynical underneath, who could determine a senator's reputation and therefore his effectiveness in the nation's capital. And, smallest and hardest of all audiences to win over, perhaps, the good opinion of the other ninety-nine senators. At last, as Moynihan's model, Disraeli, had put it, he had climbed to the top of the greasy pole.[43] Now the trick would be to stay there, and to make good use of the elevated position it afforded.

BOOK III

12

A Democrat Again

FIRST TERM, 1977–1982

> The rising hope of those stern unbending Tories.
> — Thomas, Lord Macaulay, "Essay on Gladstone"

P AT MOYNIHAN entered the Senate in January 1977 as a member and to some extent the protégé of an identifiable group. He was the candidate of the Democratic Right, in an election in which every other candidate was a liberal of one stripe or another. Few could forget that while he had always protected his status as a Democrat, he had worked for seven years in Republican administrations. Although much of his support came from within the labor movement, that support tended to come from the more conservative ranks. And while he owed his election to no single person, unless it was to the publisher of the *New York Times*, he was closely identified as a supporter of Scoop Jackson. Outside strictly partisan politics, his closest friends were of what was to be called the neoconservative persuasion. Paraphrasing Macaulay's description of the young Gladstone, later to be the great leader of the Victorian liberals, Moynihan in 1977 seemed to be the rising hope of the stern, unbending neocons.

Six years later, whether or not his real political beliefs or attitudes had altered, the way he was perceived was utterly different. By 1982, and indeed earlier, he was being seen as one of the clearest-sighted and most determined critics of the Reagan administration's policies at home and abroad. He was seen also as a staunch, albeit centrist, Democrat.

Many factors explain this transformation. For one thing, the Reagan administration was not the Ford administration, nor did much continuity exist between their programs or styles. "When circumstances change," said John Maynard Keynes, "I change my opinion. What do you do?"[1] Moynihan came quite quickly to the view that Reaganomics was a dangerous fraud. Whether the president understood what they were doing, Moynihan concluded, people in his administration were deliberately starving the government of revenue so as to make inevitable deep cuts in social expenditure. In foreign policy, while Moynihan remained a bitter critic of the Soviet Union, he also came to the conclusion that its strength was greatly exaggerated. He believed that it was indeed evil, but also economically weak, ethnically riven and not dangerous.[2] He also believed that the greatest danger to America came not from the Soviet Union but from exaggerating its power. By 1982, Moynihan had moved back into a position that was hard to distinguish from the traditional mainstream of the Democratic party from Roosevelt to Johnson. And, whereas in 1976 his primary margin of victory was as thin as India paper, six years later he carried New York with the biggest majority of any contested statewide election in modern American history to date.

It is, above all, New York that explains the evolution, apparent and real, of Moynihan's politics. Now he was no longer an officeholder in a federal administration: he was "the gentleman from New York." Not only did he depend for his political survival on the volatile, hypercritical electors of the Empire State; they depended on him. The financial plight of New York City, and of the state's other cities, notably Buffalo, would have been the most urgent job for any new senator. In political terms, too, it was vital. Moynihan believed that he won the election when his Republican-Conservative opponent, James Buckley, conveyed the impression that it would not matter very much if the city went bankrupt. Moynihan understood that it would matter a great deal: if nothing else, maintenance on every bridge, highway and public hospital in the state would stop. Buckley seemed to think it would be a salutary lesson for New Yorkers. Once elected, Moynihan was not a free agent, able to follow where logic or loyalties led, like his intellectual friends. He was the representative of a great and troubled state, and the representative of the New York State Democratic party.[3] It, too, depended on him, and he — until he could demonstrate his own vote-winning power — on it.

By 1977, the House and Senate had begun to change decisively. The amendments to the Federal Campaign Finance Act of 1971 in 1973,

1974 and 1976;[4] the abolition of the seniority system;[5] the steady replacement of the old conservative Democrats in the South by conservative Republicans and the Watergate crisis: all these developments
had begun to change the culture of the Congress before Pat Moynihan arrived there. Even so, Moynihan reminisces, "When I first came
here it was a different world."[6] There were still patrician Republicans
there, men with trust funds and strong tennis games whose families
had sent them east to Yale or Princeton to follow their fathers and
grandfathers. "There are few of them left," Moynihan told me one
afternoon, with a mixture of regret and satisfaction, on the little un-
derground railroad that takes senators from their offices to the floor
of the Senate Chamber, "and none arriving." The place was a club,
and predominantly a Democratic club. There were sixty-one Democrats in the Senate. They congregated on the floor and in three or
four local bars. You could listen to old Warren Magnuson,[7] "Maggie," telling stories about playing poker with FDR. The president
would sign checks on the National Bank of Poughkeepsie for his
losses, Maggie would tell all comers, in the certain knowledge that
they would never be cashed.

There were debates then, says Moynihan. It was the Senate. People listened to what was said, and sometimes changed their mind as a
result. This has all disappeared with television: both the proliferating
channels of cable, satellite and off-air TV and the Senate's own closed-
circuit feeds enable a senator to write letters or discuss policy with his
staff, one eye always on the screen in the corner of his office, ready to
dash for the little railroad if a vote is upcoming. The weekly Sunday-
morning political TV shows, such as Moynihan's beloved *Meet the
Press*,[8] are now just a handful among dozens of outlets. Now, says
Moynihan with wry amazement, the shows start at 8:30 in the morning, and that's where the news is made. In all this welter of information and misinformation, he adds, "We aren't governing properly."[9]

Moynihan decided before he ever got to Washington on the first
objective of his Senate strategy. He was determined to get on the Finance Committee. That was where the money was. The Appropriations Committee is a big committee, so big that the bills are written
in the subcommittees. But Finance has more power. And to get on it
was not as difficult as one might think. All the other senators had
their committee assignments, and a convention had grown up that
each could have a seat on only one A committee, now called Super A
committees: the A committees were Finance, Armed Services, Foreign

Relations and Appropriations. Besides, because of the United Nations, Moynihan was something of a celebrity. Even so, the decision would be taken by just two men: Robert Byrd of West Virginia, who was a candidate to be the majority leader, and Russell Long of Louisiana, chair of the Finance Committee. Moynihan had had a difficult relationship with Long ever since Long played a pivotal role in the death of the Family Assistance Plan. Moynihan's strong desire to serve on the very committee that, seven years previously, had axed one of his greatest personal initiatives might demonstrate that, amid the sense of betrayal, he had learned a valuable lesson about where the power lay in Congress.

Moynihan faced a tense choice. Both Byrd and Hubert Humphrey counted on his vote for majority leader. Humphrey, by virtue of his status as the leading liberal in the Senate and because of old relationships in the Johnson administration and Americans for Democratic Action, thought he had a claim to it. Some even maintain that Moynihan promised Humphrey his vote,[10] though he denies it. But Humphrey was already mortally sick. And Scoop Jackson wanted Moynihan to vote for Byrd. That in the end was decisive. Byrd was elected majority leader. And Moynihan went on to the Finance Committee. At first, the *New York Times* reported,[11] he was not too proud to find out how Russell Long planned to vote before deciding his own position. But that did not last. Well before the end of his first term, he was charting his own distinctive position on welfare, tax reform and other Finance Committee issues.

His other committee assignment could also be considered powerful: Public Works, now renamed Environment and Public Works. In earlier times, it had been a key political committee because it handed out "pork" in the shape of internal improvements: bridges, canals, docks and post offices. For a man interested in principles of federal architecture, there was no better position in the Senate from which to exert influence. The committee also had jurisdiction over some issues of great interest to the newly powerful environmental movement, although that aspect did not really interest Moynihan. "I made a conscious decision not to stress the environment," he remembers.[12] It was spoken for: other members of the Senate and the House, especially those from the Western states, could be counted on to press a whole range of environmental issues. Moynihan was skeptical. Characteristically, he suspected many environmental campaigns of being class-based, where the issues were more important to moneyed vacationers or to intellectual crusaders than to working people. Acid rain, for example, he dismissed as "a gentleman's issue, a trout fisherman's issue." Even so, Moynihan was not reluctant to help where help was welcome. When a scientist at Cornell had revealed that acid rain killed fish in the Adirondacks by releasing aluminum into streams running through granite, Moynihan got a bill passed for a ten-year study. Even without being personally overwhelmed by the issues, Moynihan soon discovered that the Environment and Public Works Committee had clout of its own.

The plight of New York City was to have been Moynihan's top priority in his maiden months, but first there was an issue that fiercely engaged the Jackson people who had helped to elect him. It involved President Carter's nomination of Paul Warnke as head of the Arms Control and Disarmament Agency and chief arms control negotiator with the Soviet Union. Warnke was a well-known liberal lawyer in Washington, where he was a partner of the famous Clark Clifford. But he had incurred the deep suspicion of members of the Jackson camp and, especially, that of Paul Nitze. Nitze was a lifelong public servant in the realms of foreign policy and defense: as secretary of the navy under Kennedy, as deputy defense secretary under Johnson and, throughout the Nixon administration, as the United States representative to the Strategic Arms Limitation Talks (SALT) — essentially the same position that Warnke had been nominated for. Nitze had disagreed with Warnke about Vietnam, and considered that Warnke had opposed almost every effort to modernize or improve U.S. strategic systems.[13]

In the 1950s and 1960s, most Democrats were "hawks" in foreign policy. After the Vietnam War began, Scoop Jackson began to feel increasingly isolated from his Democratic colleagues. In particular, he felt a deep antipathy to Senator J. William Fulbright, a Democrat from Arkansas, the chairman of the Senate Foreign Relations Committee. Jackson was asked by Richard Nixon to serve as his secretary of defense but turned the offer down. Jackson fought for one weapons system after another, benefiting the large defense contractors and military installations in his state. He thought that the day the supersonic transport was turned down was "the day American civilization died."[14] But his beliefs about defense were not solely rooted to the demographics of his state. Jackson believed that the Nixon-Kissinger policy of détente was a disaster, that the Democratic party was abandoning American interests and that the Soviet Union, under Brezhnev, was taking advantage of the weakness of American will. Jackson and his aides were also sharply alert to the threat to Israel.

The hearings for Paul Warnke's nomination began on February 8, when Moynihan had been in the Senate for just over a month. They soon took the form of a bitter personal duel between the nominee and his nemesis, Paul Nitze. Warnke sought to play down remarks that might seem to portray him as uncaring about national defense; Nitze remorselessly hunted him down with references to his own earlier positions. In the end, to the disappointment of some of his own staff and to the disillusion of Scoop Jackson,[15] Moynihan voted both ways on the Warnke nomination: for his nomination as head of the Arms Control and Disarmament Agency, but against his nomination as arms control negotiator. But he also, in one of his first floor speeches, made as ringing a declaration of his anti-Communist faith as Jackson or any of his circle could have wished. He crossed swords with Senator Frank Church, of Idaho, a leading liberal and critic of the Vietnam War. Church taxed him with believing that the Soviet leaders were irrational. "I don't think they are mad," Moynihan replied. "I think them to be evil and sane."

Even so, as time went by, the neoconservatives on Moynihan's staff detected signs that his anti-Communist fervor was burning lower. Some of them were bitterly disappointed. Others saw his movement as inevitable. He himself put it bluntly in an interview. Referring to the several people who had come from Jackson's presidential campaign and Senate office and worked on Moynihan's Senate campaign and in his Senate office, Moynihan commented: "The people who got me this job, wonderful people, came on my staff, they weren't much interested in what government could do. It was the Soviet Union that preoccupied them." That was the triangulation for them, he put it to me: "the Soviet Union, Israel, black anti-Semitism in the United States."[16]

Moynihan was moving to the view that the danger of the Soviet Union had been exaggerated, that it was a "spent force."[17] He says this view was reinforced by the access to classified information that he had as a member of the Senate Intelligence Oversight Committee.[18] By now, Moynihan wrote in 1998, "I was convinced that the Soviet Union, despite whatever grisly ventures it might undertake in

Angola or for that matter Nicaragua, was really in terminal decline."[19] Moreover, however unpalatable aspects of the Carter administration's attitude to foreign affairs might be, Moynihan observed that they were "recovering from the Democratic funk over defense matters, which followed the Vietnam War."

In 1979, Moynihan wrote in *Newsweek* that the Soviet Union might not last out the twentieth century. The article demonstrated a prescience that was the result of an analysis of the facts at hand but in hindsight looks slightly eerie. Moynihan predicted that the Soviet Union's ethnic tensions would not only be its downfall, but would lead to a new kind of tension. To underscore this, Moynihan added a warning that the breakup of the Soviet Union would be a time of exceptional danger.[20]

Moynihan was sounding a lot more like a traditional Democrat — Harry Truman or Lyndon Johnson — and noticeably less like Paul Nitze or Richard Perle, or even Scoop Jackson. The progression was marked. By the time of the 1980 Democratic National Convention, he used his speech to push the party line on defense at the time. Moynihan taxed the Republicans with dishonesty for accusing the Democrats of favoring "unilateral disarmament." The United States must be strong; American's military strength, indeed, must be "unsurpassed." But if "the world is a dangerous place . . . nothing is safer than freedom."

One of Moynihan's first significant actions in the Senate was to cosponsor a St. Patrick's Day statement. He and his fellow signatories, House Speaker Thomas P. "Tip" O'Neill and Senator Edward Kennedy, both from Massachusetts, and Governor Hugh Carey of New York, were all prominent Irish American politicians. Over the years of working together on the issue of U.S. involvement in Ireland, the group came to be known by many as the "Four Horsemen." The St. Patrick's Day statement was much resented by tabloid newspapers in Britain who saw it as interfering in Northern Ireland. But, in fact, it was an unprecedently strong call by American politicians of Irish descent to their fellow Irish Americans *not* to support the Irish Republican Army. Moynihan maintains that the prime mover was Governor Carey. "We appeal," the statement read, "to all those organizations engaged in violence to renounce their campaigns of death and destruction and return to the path of life and peace. And we appeal as well to our fellow Americans to embrace this goal of peace, and to renounce any action that promotes the current violence or provides support or encouragement for organizations engaged in violence."[21] It was by no means an encouragement to the IRA; rather it was a coded message to the Irish Americans who were clandestinely providing IRA funding.

The statement did not pass unnoticed by Irish American supporters of the Republican cause. Shortly after the St. Patrick's Day statement was issued, Senator Moynihan was invited to the annual dinner of the Friendly Sons of St. Patrick (a long-standing affair, with roots going back to the eighteenth century — dating back, to coin a phrase, beyond the melting pot.) Moynihan went to the dinner, the first Irishman from New York in the Senate for generations. He wore white tie and tails and sat next to the cardinal. When he got to the dais, he told a few jokes and then launched into the rights and wrongs of violence and civil subversion. At length, as he recalls it, "Another gent in white tie in the audience called out 'Bullshit!' " The cardinal insisted that the senator finish his speech. But the evening was a disaster, and the senator has never been asked back.[22]

This is perhaps an appropriate place to deal with Moynihan's attitude to Ireland in general, which is marked, as he puts it himself, by "a certain vagary" and is "too familiar for rigor."[23] He is of course Irish by descent on his father's side. He was brought up to some extent in an Irish environment in New York City. Although he has been an Anglophile since his time in London, even there his closest friends, the Golloglys, were Irish Catholics, originally from Belfast. He has many Irish friends and has always been proud of Irish culture and achievements. But he admits to special ambivalence where the Irish Republican Army and its political manifestation, Sinn Féin, are concerned.

It is all the more startling therefore to realize that he could easily have grown up as a member of the IRA. "I have a vague memory," he wrote me, "of being inducted into an IRA auxiliary in the back of a bar in Rockaway Beach in the 1930s."[24] Over the cash register hung that fine old tableau, beloved of Republicans, called "Who Fears to Speak of Easter Week?" The men in the room, he recalls, were on their one-week vacation from working on the subways and in the sewers, drinking beer most of the day, and the women were on the beach, turning their children to roast them red. In that environment, among cousins of his father's, he picked up what he calls "the usual lore," and he credits this early indoctrination with turning his mind toward his lifelong curiosity about ethnicity.

After he wrote the Irish chapter for *Beyond the Melting Pot* and his article "When the Irish Ran New York," he thought little about Irish affairs until the Troubles broke out again in Derry in 1969. His sympathies from the start were with John Hume, who has remained a close friend ever since, and his moderate, predominantly Catholic, Social Democratic and Labour party. Hume continues to maintain that the St. Patrick's Day statement and the subsequent creation of the Friends of Ireland were "turning points" in the campaign to negotiate a peaceful settlement to the conflict in Northern Ireland. He says that his most prized possession is a signed photograph of the Four Horsemen, sent to him by Moynihan.

Moynihan's position is that there is no denying the legitimacy of what Hume and the SDLP sought. So why would the Provisional IRA not follow or even join them? "The answer, of course," he says, "is that they were Marxists," and as such believed that the worse things got in Northern Ireland, the better for them. He also recalls that Egypt's President Mubarak, after returning from a visit to Libya, told him that Colonel Qaddafy was boasting that he was no longer sending money and explosives to the Irish.[25]

Each year the Four Horsemen repeated the St. Patrick's Day statement. In 1981, at the time of the IRA's hunger strikes, no fewer than twenty-four governors, senators and congressmen, including the original four, signed a joint statement calling for an end to "the fear and the terrorism and the bigotry" in Northern Ireland and asking the Reagan administration to find a way to promote a peaceful settlement. The group also announced the creation of the Friends of Ireland, which Senator Kennedy said hoped "to facilitate greater understanding of the positive role America can play resolving this tragic conflict."[26] The Friends of Ireland, the announcement went on, would seek the unification of the six counties with the Republic, but specified that that goal could be reached only "with the consent of a majority of the people of Northern Ireland," in other words, with the Protestants. In early August, when the death of two hunger strikers, Kevin Lynch and Kieran Doherty, heated Republican sentiment both in Ireland and in the United States to the boiling point, the group issued a new statement calling on the British government to compromise and on the Reagan administration to "play an active role in ending the current deadly impasse."[27] Moynihan played a leading part in these measured moves.

The senator fully shared the desire of moderate Irish nationalists for a negotiated end to the conflict and for the ultimate unification of North and South. But he had little sympathy with the Provisional IRA or its Sinn Féin colleagues, which he regarded as tarnished by its links both with Marxism and fascism. (He points out, as few American Irishmen do, that Eamon De Valera signed the condolence book in the German embassy in Dublin on the death of Adolf Hitler.) And he suspects the Dublin governments in the 1970s and 1980s of being happy enough to have IRA violence deflected to killing Protestants in the North rather than carrying on their armed feuds in the South.[28]

Moynihan understood from the very start of his Senate career that he must deliver goodies to New York. But he also understood that the goodies would need to be something more than the traditional tidbits of congressional pork. He is sensitive to the idea that, in contrast to Alfonse D'Amato, once known as "Senator Pothole," he has not been effective at delivering financial advantages to New York. "The first real bill I passed of any consequence," he said recently, "was for the federal government to take over the nuclear reprocessing plant at West Valley, New York . . . We have spent $1.2 billion. That's a big pothole!"[29] He claims that he saved New York State even more, $10.3 billion, by helping to secure tax exemption for the bonds of the Long Island Power Authority, floated to pay for its nuclear plant at Shoreham. But that money did not come through until the 1990s.

More immediately, Moynihan tackled the problems of New York City. On April 12, 1978, jointly with New York's other senator, the Republican Jacob K. Javits, he sponsored a bill authorizing the secretary of the treasury to guarantee the city's obligations to a maximum of $2 billion, and thereafter lobbied tirelessly for the bill.[30] On August 8, it passed the House and the Conference Committee and was signed by President Carter. In 1979, Moynihan also sponsored a bill by which the federal government would pay a bigger share of welfare and Medicare costs for big cities like New York, worth $600 million a year for New York State, and at least $200 million a year for the city.

The long-term solutions to New York's problems, however, as he well understood, would have to be macroeconomic. In the campaign, he had said that New York was not getting its share of federal revenues. James Buckley argued that it got back more than it spent.

Moynihan received a postcard from a Professor Erik Johnsen of Plattsburgh[31] saying that federal accounting grossly exaggerated New York's receipts. For example, New York was recorded as receiving 51 percent of interest on the federal debt and — even more absurdly — 44 percent of foreign aid, simply because those proportions of federal expenditure were paid through the big New York "money center" banks.

Johnsen's note triggered a typical Moynihan initiative, which he called the FISC project. From early on in his term, Moynihan formed the habit of writing a regular letter to his constituents. In April 1979, he sat down and wrote a double-length letter on the achievement of the Ninety-fifth Congress and of course about his own contribution to those achievements.[32] In it he wrote that "in past years Washington has collected more money in taxes from New York's residents and businesses than it has returned to the state in federal expenditures." But, he added proudly, "We have recently begun to restore the balance: in fiscal 1977, federal spending in New York increased by $7.7 billion, the largest increase obtained by any state."

The letter lists some of the actions that the new senator had taken to help the state's economy. In the process, it offers an intriguing glimpse at the small change of legislative work, the pothole side of the business. A trade adjustment loan for the Trifline Trouser Company in New York City. Money for a new public park in Utica. Workshops to show local officials how to apply for federal grants. Money for the Chemung County Historical Society. The navy's promise to buy more planes from Grumman Corporation on Long Island. A Conrail spur south of Rochester to help General Foods. Quick approval for a new interchange on I-684 to persuade the Nestlé Corporation to keep its U.S. headquarters in New York State. Pressure on the White House to declare nine rural New York counties disaster areas so as to qualify for help after the great snowstorm of 1977. Twenty years later a senator with a passion for architecture spoke with pride of his part in saving Louis Sullivan's great Prudential Building in Buffalo from demolition.[33]

Then there were more strategic federal investments: meeting the federal government conditions for beginning work on the Westway, a third water tunnel for New York City, federal help for the Winter Olympics at Lake Placid, money for a light rail system in Buffalo and progress on the southern-tier expressway. Less tangible but more important were macroeconomic shifts: legislation to stop the proposed tripling of energy rates upstate, to protect New York industries from unfair foreign competition (legislators usually see foreign competition to industries in their state as unfair!), reductions in corporate tax rates, tax incentives for employers who take people off the welfare rolls and help for parochial and other private schools, which educate far more children in New York than in any other state.

All these activities helped the New York State economy. More visible was Moynihan's role in passing the federal loan. He had a good relationship with Senator William Proxmire, the Wisconsin Democrat, and was able to persuade him to move the bill through his subcommittee, even though Proxmire himself felt obliged to vote against it for political reasons back home. More important still was the FISC project, an attempt, and in the long run a fairly successful one, to change the way people thought about New York and its economy. For decades, most Americans had thought of New York as golden Babylon, home of Wall Street and of fabulous wealth, of Whitneys and Rockefellers and Vanderbilts, of robber barons and the Four Hundred. Moynihan set out to teach people that New York was also home to some of the poorest people and the hardest-pressed communities in the country: welfare mothers in Harlem and Brooklyn, but also marginal dairy farming upstate and rust belt industries from Buffalo to the Battery. The number of Fortune 500 corporations whose headquarters were in New York City, spilling wealth to employees, contractors, suppliers and customers alike, had fallen from half of the total to just eight in thirty years.[34]

In another "Letter to New Yorkers" in 1981, Moynihan told the story of his effort to change minds on the subject of New York's financial relationship with the federal government.[35] The 1976 federal outlays showed that New York enjoyed a comfortable surplus in its balance with the federal government. Enter Professor Erik Johnsen and his postcard. Excitedly, Moynihan and his staff redid the accounts, stripping out half a dozen items that attributed to New York State money that simply passed through Wall Street on its way to somewhere else. On this new basis, federal taxes collected in New York State came to $33.7 billion, federal outlays in New York State to only $25.7 billion. What was even more surprising was that this deficit applied not just to New York but to all of the Northeastern and Midwestern states with mature industrial economies; in fact New York had the smallest ratio of imbalance between taxes and receipts, smaller than New Jersey, Pennsylvania, Ohio, Indiana, Illinois and Michigan.

The FISC investigation turned up another powerful argument. Not only was the balance between tax receipts and expenditures unfair to New York and other mature industrial states; so too was the "mix" of federal expenditures.[36] A high proportion of the money received by New York was what Moynihan called "soft" money: Medicaid payments and welfare payments. Other states in other regions got a far higher proportion of "hard" money, such as defense contracts and water projects.

On the basis of the first few years of these studies, Moynihan formulated a bold conclusion. "Any trend in the federal budget to hold down or cut back spending on social programs will have a disproportionate effect on a state or region such as ours. So will any trend in the federal budget to maintain or increase defense spending." That argument alone would provide a persuasive answer to the question why Pat Moynihan, as a senator from New York, would reject important segments of the neoconservative creed. To cut back on social spending and increase defense expenditure was not good for his constituents.

There is, of course, another dimension to the argument. Other New York senators, notably the two Republicans Jacob Javits and Alfonse D'Amato, were not moved by the argument because they had not uncovered the facts that made it. Moynihan spotted the implications of Professor Johnsen's postcard because he was already alert to the probability that New York was being shortchanged. He followed the argument to its conclusion because he was concerned about New York's economic crisis, but also because he was concerned about the consequences of economic policies for individual New Yorkers, and especially for less well off and positively poor New Yorkers. If a liberal is one who is concerned about social justice and equality, and a conservative thinks other values more important, then Pat Moynihan was not so very much of a conservative even at the time when the neoconservatives still saw him as their leader.

From the start, the relations between the new Democratic president and the newly elected Democratic senator from New York were not good. Before Moynihan had been in the Senate a year, the *New York Times* was reporting that (unspecified) people in Washington were already asking whether he was positioning himself for a run for the presidency in 1980 if Carter should stumble. Not surprisingly, the Carter people responded sharply. One of them, who agreed to be quoted by the *New York Times,* but declined to be named, spoke in harsh terms:

> Moynihan is an arrogant man. His methods and style rankle. The president is annoyed. Moynihan has teed everyone off here because of his style that he knows the answer to everything and because he goes public, figuring that criticism can move the president. If he'd call up and say he'd like to come over and talk about welfare reform and more economic help for New York, it might be different. But he has worn out his welcome with demands and he has to crow about everything he does.[37]

By 1978, Moynihan was comprehensively disillusioned with Jimmy Carter. He was appalled by the way the new administration completely cut out Scoop Jackson and all his followers from any role in defense or foreign policy. (It particularly rankled that the only diplomatic appointment that could be found for any of them was as ambassador to Micronesia!)[38] He was not impressed with Carter's appointees either, and from time to time would subject those who came before his welfare subcommittee of the Finance Committee to interrogations that verged on the brutal.

By 1979, Moynihan was sufficiently in despair about Carter's prospects in the 1980 presidential election that he does seem to have given some thought to the idea of running for president himself. Asked whether he ever thought seriously of making the race, both Moynihan and his wife responded at first with flat denials. Moynihan subsequently conceded that there was a time when he thought about the idea but it was never a serious possibility. It is quite true that he never took any of the specific steps he would have had to take if he were really contemplating a run. He did not register a fund-raising committee with the Federal Election Commission, for example. Nor did he discuss getting into the race in specific terms with anyone so far as I know.

There is, however, some reason to believe that at times in 1978 and 1979 he did think quite a lot about running for president,[39] but that he was deterred by a number of concrete political problems and perhaps also by one or more psychological and personal considerations.

Politically, it is always difficult to run against an incumbent president of one's own party. However unpopular and indeed at times almost overwhelmed Jimmy Carter might have seemed, for a Democrat to run against him could easily be put down to mere ambition and castigated as disloyalty. Then there was the looming bulk of the Hamlet of Hyannisport, Senator Edward Kennedy. Any Democratic insurgency against Carter would turn first to Kennedy, and if Kennedy did decide to enter the race the resources of prestige and money he could deploy might make a Moynihan campaign look trivial by comparison. Finally, in his first term Moynihan was not secure in his own base. He was always afraid that New York City liberals would seek revenge for his narrow defeat of Bella Abzug by running a Jewish woman against him, perhaps Elizabeth Holtzman, an attractive congresswoman with liberal credentials.

The question of whether Moynihan ever considered running for president is not just a matter of idle curiosity. It became one of the causes of a strain between him and his enthusiastic young neoconservative staffers and some of their elders. In 1978, Ben Wattenberg told Moynihan, "You ought to run for president." He and his friends, Wattenberg says, were looking for him to be the younger Scoop.[40] Elliott Abrams, who became the senator's administrative assistant when he went to Washington, actually toyed with an even more daring project than a campaign for the Democratic nomination. Abrams prepared a memo arguing Moynihan's credentials as a candidate for vice president on the Reagan ticket. The memo was sent to John Sears, then Reagan's campaign manager.[41]

However seriously or unseriously Moynihan himself took the possibility of a presidential run, and, after all, the ambitious young senators to whom such a possibility never occurs are few indeed, several of his neoconservative aides and friends did hope that he would run. Penn Kemble makes no bones about it. He and others who had worked for Scoop Jackson knew that Jackson had entered the race twice, in 1972 and 1976, and that he could not and would not try again. They rejected Carter essentially because they saw him as a weak president in dealing with foreign affairs. "We hoped Moynihan would run in the primaries,"[42] Kemble says. But two things that happened in the late 1970s persuaded him that it was not a feasible option. One was the fact that Kennedy got into the race, or at least far enough into it to leave no room for a Moynihan campaign. And the other was the awkwardness of a direct challenge to a sitting president. Then, too, New York politics bulked large in his mind.

Norman Podhoretz has recently admitted that he, too, hoped Moynihan would run for president, and that it was his failure to do so that freed him to vote for Ronald Reagan. In his memoir *Ex-Friends,* he wrote:

> I had hoped that my old and close friend Daniel P. Moynihan, whose election to the U.S. Senate from New York in 1976 I had done my share behind the scenes to make possible, would assume the leadership of the Jackson Democrats and run for president in 1980. But when it became dishearteningly clear that he had no such intention and that he was in fact moving for political reasons of his own in the other direction, down the drain went the last traces of my resistance to the lessons I had drawn from Vietnam.[43]

There are stories of rows, shouting, even, at a dinner party, between these old and close friends, suggestions that Podhoretz and his wife, Midge Decter, attacked Liz Moynihan for standing in the way of her husband's run for president. Moynihan says simply, "We didn't split up. We drifted apart."[44] He cited as an example of the way their views had diverged an article that Podhoretz wrote arguing that the United States ought to fight for Israel.[45]

Moynihan's daughter, Maura, confirms that Norman Podhoretz and Decter, whom she calls "the Pods," and of whom she speaks with affection, wanted their friend to run. "There were often heated debates," she remembers, "when Midge and Norman kept badgering Dad to run for president, which they did often in those days, but Dad never wanted to run anyway."[46]

There were personal as well as political reasons for not running. First, Moynihan has always been a cautious person. The flamboyance of his manner conceals careful calculation of probabilities. His experience of life's unpredictability in childhood, the early lessons that the world is a dangerous place, may have made him hesitate to risk the certainty of a seat in the Senate, something he valued very much, for the hazard of a long shot at the presidency in what looked like a conservative year.

He responded in those terms when questioned about whether he wanted to run for the presidency in late 1977. "The idea that I'm running for President is insane," he said. "I want President Carter to be a two-term President. I have absolutely no interest in the Presidency.

I'd like to stay in the Senate long enough to have some consequence. What I'd really like to do, if I could, would be to serve four terms."

Several of his friends, however, have suggested to me another personal factor: alcohol. They believe that he did not run for president at least in part because he (and his wife) were aware that he might be betrayed, even humiliated, by talk of his drinking. This is a convenient point at which to address a topic on which little has been written but much said.

Pat Moynihan has always liked a drink. His father was a drinking man, after all, and his mother ran a bar. His friends in London recall the consumption of oceans of gin, beer and whiskey. Recently he has given up drinking hard liquor and often drinks Tio Pepe, a dry sherry, before dinner and wine with it. (His staff call Tio Pepe "the Mexican ambassador," as in "The senator's with the Mexican ambassador.") Earlier, he sometimes drank Scotch before dinner, and brandy afterward.

There are only two important questions about drink and Daniel Patrick Moynihan. The first is whether alcohol has affected his performance as a politician or as a public servant. My own view is that it has not. He has by common consent an unusually strong head, and while I have often observed that wine or other forms of alcohol make him even better company than usual, I have never seen him, as the phrase goes, the worse for wear. In particular, I have never seen him lose his temper or lose control under the influence of alcohol.

The second question is whether the perception that he drinks too much has damaged him. This is harder to answer with confidence. There are those who say that they have seen him behave embarrassingly under the influence of alcohol. One former staffer says that in the 1970s and 1980s, Moynihan was drinking much more heavily than now, and that he sometimes arrived late for work as a result. Others claim to have seen him staggering. I can only say that I have not, after observing him on a large number of occasions over thirty-five years. His workload is formidable by any standard. He is a poor sleeper, and his vast reading often takes place at night, which might explain his not getting to his office as early as some other senators. In addition, the world around him has changed its attitude to alcohol, but he has not. While the "New Puritanism" has changed the drinking habits of many politicians and journalists, Moynihan has stuck to the customs of his generation.

There is no doubt that his wife has been protective of him in this as in other respects. She points out that he has physical characteristics, including a slight speech impediment, which can make his words sound slurred, and a foot condition called peripheral neuropathy, which can sometimes make him seem to stumble. She herself told me a story of how a reporter from a major newspaper was assigned to question her husband about his drinking habits. The senator suggested he talk to his wife. The reporter telephoned Liz and went to see her.

"Young man," she said, "my husband comes home from work, and he works very hard. He has a cocktail, and half a bottle of claret." (There have been occasions when the consumption was greater than that, but never mind.) "And the thing I think you ought to be looking into is this: unlike many of his colleagues, he has been coming home to have a drink with the same woman for the last thirty-some years!"

Without wishing to dismiss altogether the possible effects on his career of the perception that he drinks too much, which is certainly widely held, my own judgment inclines to that attributed to Abraham Lincoln. When they told him Grant drank too much whiskey, he is reputed to have said, "Go and find out what kind of whiskey he drinks, and give a barrel of it to some of my other generals!"

Moynihan took to the Senate instantly, but there were details that took some getting used to. He was annoyed to find himself running some of the most costly offices on Capitol Hill. He had difficulty for some time in making full use of the large staff allocated to a senator from a big-population state like New York. His files are full of slightly plaintive notes. In December 1977, for example, he was mortified to discover that he had missed a meeting of the board of the Hirshhorn Museum and Sculpture Garden, a cherished interest. He pointed out crossly in a memo to his staff that even when he was in India he would fly back in order not to miss a meeting.[47] "When large changes of plan . . . occur," he wrote, "the task of the Administrative Assistant is to think about the small changes that follow from the large one." He also complained that when he scribbled notes for the staff, no one bothered to type them and distribute them. Quite apart from these minor irritations, early signs of what was to be until recently a chronic difficulty in retaining staff, Moynihan was drifting apart from some of his key aides.

From 1977 to 1980, Moynihan shared the views of his neoconservative friends more than he disagreed with them, particularly on foreign affairs and on what he and they both saw as the liberal excesses of the Carter administration. For example, in a commencement address at Baruch College in June of his first year in the Senate, he sharply attacked Jimmy Carter for including the Soviet Union among the world's rich nations and enlisting it in a struggle to help the poor nations. He accused the president of "trying to divert our attention from the central political struggle of our time — that between democracy and totalitarian communism."

By his stand against the "Zionism is racism" resolution at the United Nations, Moynihan had earned what turned out to be lasting gratitude and trust from New York's Jewish community. It was mildly embarrassing that when senators were asked to declare their income from outside speaking engagements, Moynihan came easily first, with honoraria of $165,393 for 1976, the year before he joined the Senate. (The next highest earner, Senator Herman Talmadge of Georgia, trailed far behind with only $25,000.) At least $70,000 of these fees came from Jewish groups. It would be ridiculous to suggest that this income motivated him to take a stance in any way different from what he would have taken, indeed did take, before this sudden affluence. But he did continue to take positions fiercely defensive of Israel. For example, when the United Nations, under Soviet influence, held what Moynihan regarded as a "propaganda festival, scurrilous in its treatment of democratic Israel, and extravagantly favorable in its portrayal of the Palestine Liberation Organization," he recruited twenty-six senators to call upon the president to withhold the American share of the production costs of a UN film that took this line.

In general, his neoconservative staffers applauded his foreign policy positions. They were less enthusiastic about some of his domestic positions, but men like Penn Kemble still felt he was a "paladin."[48] One issue he devoted a good deal of time and energy to in his first term was the attempt to provide a tax credit for private schools, essentially meaning religious schools, so long as they were nondiscriminatory. The bill passed the House and the Senate Finance Committee, but was turned down by the Senate at large. More controversial was Moynihan's vehement reaction to a federal policy that would have required New York City to assign teachers on the basis of race. With considerable hyperbole, he said that "such practices evoke one image in our lifetime above all others: the sorting out of human beings for the death camps of Nazi Germany . . . the Congress has not enacted Nuremberg laws, and the executive branch had better think again before enforcing them."[49]

One cause of division between Moynihan and his neoconservative staff was the fact they were drifting toward the Republicans. In the event, Finn, Horner and Abrams all joined the Reagan administration. They had not fully understood how much their boss remained, not just a Democrat, but, as he told the *New York Times,* "a liberal Democrat."[50] As the time for reelection came, too, Moynihan turned more and more to Tim Russert and to Liz, both birthright Democrats and utterly immune to the charms of Reaganism.

After Ronald Reagan's victory in 1980, the gap between the senator and the neoconservatives widened sharply. From very early on in the Reagan administration, Moynihan became one of its sharpest critics. His first salvo across the new administration's bows was fired in a speech to the Economic Club of New York on March 5, 1981. What he found curious, he said, was "the degree to which conservatives seem to have displaced liberals as starry-eyed advocates of exotic and newfangled economic doctrines."[51]

Reagan was not noted for his grasp of any but the grandest outlines of economic thinking. He was, however, advised by conservative economists of the highest reputation, men like Milton Friedman, Alan Greenspan, Arthur Burns and Martin Anderson. But his campaign, and his administration, had also come under the influence of a set of economic publicists and promoters who offered doctrines that Moynihan once described as bearing the same relation to conservatism that anarchism does to liberalism.[52] One that was beginning to pass out of fashion even as the Reagan administration settled into Washington, was monetarism, in the sense of the doctrine that held that the level of economic activity was set solely by the money supply. The second, known as supply-side economics, took in its extreme version the absurd form of arguing that tax cuts would actually increase tax revenues. Such doctrines influenced, among others, the Moynihans' former Cambridge baby-sitter, David Stockman, who, after serving briefly in the House of Representatives, had become President Reagan's budget director.

Moynihan became convinced that Stockman was playing a deep and dangerous game. In September 1980, as Reagan's presidential campaign was getting under way, the candidate was persuaded by his advisers, who included Alan Greenspan, that within two years the federal budget would be in surplus, and therefore that substantial tax cuts would be both safe and beneficial. Between the beginning of the fall campaign and the spring of 1981, the economic climate changed for the worse. So when the administration pressed for a tax cut, combined with increased military expenditure, yet did not demonstrate the political courage it would take to make comparable cuts in domestic expenditure, ballooning deficits became inevitable. Moynihan came to believe that this result was not wholly accidental: that the administration in general and David Stockman in particular had deliberately created a huge federal deficit so as to make deep cuts in social expenditure unavoidable. Fairly early, Moynihan has said, he cottoned on to what he believes was Stockman's deficit strategy: to use the deficit to force the political system to dismantle big government.[53] No one believed him, he added ruefully. "Mind, Mr. Stockman has now written that that was indeed his strategy, and so far as I can see no one believes him either."

The Gridiron Club dinner is a Washington ritual. It is a huge white-tie affair, attended by more than a thousand men and women. It is hosted by the leading journalists in the capital, before whom politicians, including by tradition the president himself, come to be teased in a more or less good-natured vein as in the manner of an old-fashioned roast. There are usually two speakers, one Democrat and one Republican, and in the spring of 1981 the Gridiron invited Pat Moynihan to make the Democratic speech and David Stockman to reply for the Republicans.

Moynihan did not spare his former friend and protégé. He began by teasing the president, who was present, reminding him of his past as a Democrat and a member of the liberal group Americans for Democratic Action and calling him a mole. "But who would have dreamed you'd make it all the way to the White House . . . and institute the basic plan to destroy the Republican party from within." And then he turned to Stockman.

> Dave was everything you could dream of in a mole. Corn-fed and cow-licked, he was the best boob bait for conservatives ever to come out of the Middle West. The only trouble was he couldn't stop talking about the Viet Cong and American imperialism and the immorality of the Vietnam war. So we installed him on the top floor of our house and got him into the Harvard Divinity School. There he was taught, of course, that there is no such thing as morality.[54]

"I have never known a man," Moynihan went on, fixing Stockman in his sights, "capable of such sustained self-hypnotic ideological fervor. One day he arrives at Harvard preaching the infallibility of Ho Chi Minh. Next thing you know, he turns up in Washington proclaiming the immutability of the Laffer Curve."[55]

Moynihan braved the Zeitgeist by ending with an encomium to government; a free government, he said, is indeed the most precious of human institutions. "We" — that is, we Democrats — "believe in American government, and we fully expect that those who now denigrate it, and even despise it, will sooner or later find themselves turning to it in necessity, even desperation."

Two days later, leaving another Washington hotel, Ronald Reagan was shot by a young man, John Hinckley, for obscure reasons.[56] Taken to George Washington University Hospital, Reagan quipped about his rather serious wound with such debonair charm that he became for a while politically unassailable. Just as the assassination of John F. Kennedy had put Lyndon B. Johnson in a position to pass one of the boldest and most ambitious programs of legislation in American history, so now Reagan became the beneficiary of his own attempted assassination. In the next few weeks, he was able to pass a remarkable set of conservative proposals, and in particular to push through his big tax cut. Just when Moynihan seemed to be moving into position for a sustained and damaging attack on Reaganomics, the random act of a deranged young man made it hard to attack a president who had suddenly become immensely popular.

As early as May, though, Moynihan was back on the warpath. The administration — "political sorts in the Department of Health and Human Services," in Moynihan's informed opinion — sent to Congress proposals for sharp reductions in social security benefits. As the ranking member of the Finance Committee's subcommittee on social security, this was Moynihan's ball and his opportunity. He took it. The Senate voted 96 to 0 to reject the administration's proposal.

The president did not give up. He decided to take the issue to the country by means of a nationally televised speech. Time was booked for July 27, and Moynihan was chosen to reply on behalf of the Democrats. At the last moment, the president was persuaded by his staff that it would be politically disastrous to cut social security benefits for the thirty-five million retired but politically vocal Americans. He switched his tactics and announced tax cuts instead.

The Reagan administration, Moynihan told the television audience, was taking "a tax bill we can afford and turning it into a great barbecue that we can't afford." Some victories, he said, come too dear. Having given the usual breaks to "those with the foresight to own oil wells," the administration threw in the kitchen stove, in the shape of tax credits for wood-burning stoves. A tax cut for individuals was long overdue. The Congress was proposing one. Let it pass, and get on with the business of government. A tax cut, yes. But not a huge tax cut, intended not to restore wealth to the pockets of individual Americans, but to break the government and take away its ability to help people in need.

Six weeks later, he tried to hammer the same argument home to the Business Council of New York State.[57] The tax cut, he kept repeating, was just too big. It would create budget deficits so large that they would "shred" the "social compact of a half century concerning the role of government in abetting the health, education and welfare of our people." His audience, he said later, thought he was crazy. But what was undeniable was that he had parted company definitively with the neoconservative tendency as far as domestic policy was concerned. He was now speaking unambiguously as a Democrat, and indeed as a New Deal Democrat, willing to make adjustments and corrections to the public finances, but only within the limits of a commitment to the role of government in advancing the people's interests.

On April 24, 1982, in a New York hotel ballroom, Moynihan announced his candidacy for reelection. A thousand people, the *New York Times* reported, "listened in engrossed silence as Senator Daniel Patrick Moynihan delivered a nine-page treatise on the merits of American government and the principles of the founding fathers. Along the way, the Senator found reason to touch on nuclear war, the Middle East, the Atlantic alliance and Argentina."

Already, at the end of his first term, Moynihan was being extravagantly praised for the breadth and originality of his thinking, but criticized for being a lone wolf who was not good at building legislative coalitions and who failed to follow through and garner enough support to get his legislation passed. In an interview with Jane Perlez of the *New York Times*, he half acknowledged the truth of these criticisms. He was asked how he reconciled the roles of the diligent legislator who represents his constituents' interests with that of the national leader. There was no conflict, Moynihan answered. "The

Senators are representatives of states in the American constitutional system. They are also United States Senators. There are two things to be done, and they are."

The *Times* acknowledged Moynihan's effectiveness as a lobbyist for the financial rescue of New York City, suggesting that his persistence "was a crucial factor in persuading reluctant legislators to pass Federal loan guarantees." It drew attention to the difficulty he had making up his mind on the Reagan tax cut, and indeed to the speed with which he switched from voting for the cut to calling in his Business Council speech for a "mid-course correction."

The interview gave several examples of Moynihan's ability to choose a position that enabled him, apparently effortlessly, to please both sides on contentious issues. He was praised by the president of the American Stock Exchange as "very supportive," for example, and the president of the American Business Conference was delighted with his role in reducing the top rate of capital gains tax. Yet he was also admired for helping Senator Bob Dole to ban an arcane tax loophole known as the "butterfly straddle." He managed a straddle of his own on the most dangerous issue of all, abortion. He wrote an article for the Catholic magazine *Sign* saying that he thought abortion was a sin, but that people would have to make their own judgments about it. His aide Tim Russert claimed that he had voted more consistently in favor of Medicaid financing for abortion even than Senator Edward Kennedy, and the executive director of the National Abortion Rights Action League, while saying that both senators had the same voting record, said that Moynihan was "a very, very good friend. We rely on him very heavily."[58]

Moynihan acknowledged to the *Times* interviewer that there might be some validity to criticisms that he was not an effective builder of legislative coalitions, then added, "Give me a chance. I've only been here five years."

He was, however, in a good position to remedy this lack. Because Moynihan had been haunted by the fear that the New York liberals would punish him for beating Bella Abzug, and in such an ill-tempered campaign, by putting a strong, liberal Jewish woman up against him, he made a great effort to invoke the help of Governor Hugh Carey to persuade the Liberal party not to endorse Abzug. His support for tuition tax credits for the parents of children at parochial and private schools cost him the support of Judy Bardache of the American Federation of Teachers, a strong member of his 1976 election team. But by 1982, Moynihan had touched all the bases, from support for Israel through environmental issues like acid rain and nuclear waste to social security, so skillfully that he was no longer seriously vulnerable on the Left. In the public perception, he had successfully negotiated the transition from neoconservative politician to classic mainstream Democrat — which is what he maintains he has been all along.

His campaign arrangements were unorthodox but effective. Although Moynihan can seem old-fashioned, with his bow ties and his polysyllabic utterances, in one important sense he was from the moment of his arrival in the Senate a thoroughly modern politician. He had completely understood that politics in the late twentieth century takes place in the media. "He knows how to use the press and the airwaves better than any other politician," says his long-time political ally Dick Eaton.[59] Aided by Tim Russert, Liz was getting ready to swing into action for a campaign that was frugal but devastatingly effective. One of Elizabeth Moynihan's trademarks as a campaign manager was her belief that the best way to beat opponents was to discourage them from running in the first place. By spending limited resources on early campaign ads, she faked the Republicans into believing that Moynihan had raised more money than was in fact the case.

In the end, the Republicans came up with a comparatively lackluster candidate, Florence Sullivan. Moynihan won with 3.2 million votes to Sullivan's 1.7 million, or with just under two-thirds of the vote. It was, as I have noted, the biggest margin of victory in any statewide election in American history up to that time. By way of comparison, as strong a candidate as Mario Cuomo, running for governor, got 50.9 percent of the same electorate. Whatever the pundits might say, Moynihan's contention that he could take the high road and still serve his constituents in ways that earned their trust had paid off impressively.

13

Falling Out with Reagan

SECOND TERM, 1983–1989

> There was a very nearly successful assault on the
> constitutional system.
>
> — Daniel Patrick Moynihan, 1997, on the Iran-contra crisis[1]

W HEN PAT MOYNIHAN returned to the Senate in triumph
in January 1983, the Washington world was not the same
one in which he had taken his seat in 1977. Then, Jimmy
Carter and his men were trying to come to terms with a city they
never either liked or understood. "We came to Washington as outsid-
ers," Jimmy Carter complained ruefully in his memoirs, "and we never
appreciably changed this status."[2] All the powers in Washington —
Congress, media, lobbyists, the "permanent government" and the
mysterious social influences known in shorthand as Georgetown —
had carefully observed this Southerner, this small-town hick, this
peanut farmer, who dared to campaign against the "mess in Washington." They were horrified by what they saw, and they decided he
should not succeed. They prevailed, and he did not.

Then came Ronald Reagan. He too was an outsider. He too campaigned against the mess in Washington. The difference was that he
was working with the grain of the new politics, floating on the rising
tide of a new conservative mood in the country. He had few ideas,
but they were big ones. They were the ideas the country had been
waiting for, even if he didn't understand the details and didn't much
care about them. He thought people wanted lower taxes, wanted
government "off their backs." He wanted to stand up to the Soviet
Union, which he called the "evil empire," not to negotiate détente
with it. Like Carter, he wanted the country to be stronger, to be re-

spected in the world. But where Carter came across as a pessimist, a prude and a scold, Reagan's image was gracious, his tone upbeat. Where Carter proposed to treat energy shortages as "the moral equivalent of war" and called like a Baptist preacher for the nation to acknowledge its sins and pray for forgiveness, Reagan understood that Americans wanted to put a decade of bad news behind them. He persuaded people that it was "morning in America"; that was what they wanted to hear.

Instinctively, Moynihan found Reagan, the cheerful Midwestern extrovert with an alcoholic Irish father, more sympathetic than Jimmy Carter, the patrician bluenose evangelical from the Protestant South. Temperamentally, Pat Moynihan shared Reagan's deep faith in America. For years he had been insisting that things were not as bad as the liberals were saying, or rather that the things that were bad were different from the things that so concerned the liberals. Politically and intellectually, though, he could not accept Reagan's shallow optimism or the insouciant way he would wrap simplistic conservative nostrums in cloudy Fourth of July rhetoric. Moynihan's second term on Capitol Hill was the time when he emerged as one of Ronald Reagan's most determined opponents. His conviction that the administration was using the budget process to destroy the New Deal welfare system led him to break with his former neoconservative associates in his first term.[3] It would be foreign policy that fueled his opposition to the Reagan administration in the second. Specifically, it was Nicaragua.

Nicaragua began to emerge as an issue in Moynihan's first term. By 1980, it was plain that the Sandinistas, as Moynihan put it, had betrayed the revolution in that unhappy country,[4] where the dictator dynasty of the Somozas had been installed with American help in the 1930s and maintained in power there ever since. The Sandinistas had started as an alliance of all the anti-Somoza forces in the country. But by early 1980, the two moderate members of the five-strong ruling Sandinista junta, Violeta Barrios de Chamorro and Alfonso Robelo, had quit in disgust at the procommunist line taken by the remaining three members, especially by Daniel Ortega, who seemed to sympathizers and enemies alike to be emerging as the "Nicaraguan Castro." Even during the 1980 campaign, Ronald Reagan had made no secret of his concern at what was happening in Central America. The Republican platform that year virtually called for the overthrow of the Sandinistas.[5] Once in the White House, Reagan chose as his director of Central Intelligence William Casey. Casey was a New York politician, lawyer and investor who had earned a legendary reputation as an agent runner in Europe during World War II for the Office of Strategic Services, the predecessor of the modern CIA. Casey was a notoriously strident anticommunist, and he lost little time in seeking authority for covert action to use the "contras" (Spanish for the "antis") to overthrow the Sandinistas. The CIA chose to support the Federated Democratic Resistance, the more right-wing of the two rival contra groups. By November 1981, President Reagan had signed National Security Decision Directive 17, authorizing covert support for the contras. Yet a few days later, the administration asserted that the United States meant only to interdict the flow of arms from Nicaragua into El Salvador. Even if the involvement was discovered, its true purpose would remain concealed — the overthrow of a foreign government by the support of opposition forces.

At first, the training of the contras was to have been left to the Argentine military junta, but the government of General Leopoldo Fortunato Galtieri in Buenos Aires collapsed after it was defeated by Britain in the Falklands War. The CIA took over the support of the contras. By late 1982, however, there were reports in the U.S. press that the CIA's real aim was not merely stanching the supply of arms to El Salvador, but overthrowing the Sandinista government in Nicaragua. The chairman of the House Select Committee on Intelligence, Edward P. Boland of Massachusetts, was outraged by the revelations. He sponsored an amendment, which came to be known as "Boland I," which prohibited the CIA and the Pentagon from using appropriated funds to overthrow the government of Nicaragua. President Reagan accepted Boland I and said his administration did not seek to overthrow the Sandinistas, only to stop the flow of weapons into neighboring countries. In 1983, the CIA, having spent its previous appropriation, asked the Defense Department for another secret $28 million worth of equipment, including aircraft and patrol boats. This request was of course illegal; equipment bought with funds authorized and appropriated by Congress for one purpose were being diverted clandestinely to another. And so there began a conflict between the Reagan administration and Congress. The Democrats on Capitol Hill tried to keep the administration's Central American adventures on short rations. Casey and his associates, apparently convinced that the future of freedom on earth would be decided in

Nicaragua, sought ever more desperately for other sources, even if the money came from foreign governments or was diverted from arms sales to Iran. The CIA's covert activities in Central America finally disillusioned Pat Moynihan with the administration's conduct of foreign policy and indeed with the CIA's covert activity in general.[6]

Moynihan had been a member of the Select Committee on Intelligence since he first became a member of the Senate, brought in with the help of Scoop Jackson and Senator Daniel Inouye of Hawaii. He was strongly out of sympathy with the campaign mounted by some ex-CIA whistle-blowers like Philip Agee and John Stockwell, which had led to the exposure of many undercover agents and allegedly to the death of at least one. Indeed, in 1980, he ran into liberal flak for introducing, with Senate colleagues from both parties, the Intelligence Reform Act of 1980. "Simply put," wrote the *Washington Post*'s Pentagon correspondent, George Lardner, Jr., in *The Nation,* "the proposal amounts to an official secrets act."[7] Abetted by Moynihan, Lardner charged, the Carter administration seemed to want to give the CIA, now confronted with the Afghan war and the Iranian revolution, "a freer hand for covert actions, in a harking back to the 'good old days' " of the 1950s and 1960s. Moynihan himself said the legislation was only a modest start on "the reconstruction of our intelligence community." He was embarrassed when his staff admitted at a press conference that the legislation had been at least in part written in the agency's offices in Langley, Virginia.[8] Among other things it would have excluded most CIA files from the Freedom of Information Act and imposed sentences of up to a year in jail and fines of $5,000 on journalists, and ten years imprisonment and $50,000 fines on former CIA employees if they intended "to impair or impede the foreign intelligence activities of the United States." There was clearly a need to protect legitimate intelligence-gathering activities from whistle-blowers and enemy agents. But there is nevertheless a noticeable contrast between the tone of this Moynihan-sponsored legislation and the libertarian position he was later to take in his book *Secrecy*. The difference is no doubt in part explained by the reckless behavior and arrogant style of William Casey and others in the Reagan administration.

By the end of 1983, Moynihan was already suspicious of what the CIA was up to in Central America, aided and abetted by the hotheads on the White House National Security Council staff. In December, he paid his only visit to Nicaragua, accompanied by a CIA official called Clare George, whom Moynihan respected.[9] They paid a visit to

Commandant Tomás Borge, who worked on the top floor of the new ministry of the interior. Because the power was off, they had to climb nine flights of stairs. After an hour of dialectical disputation with the *comandante,* who was flanked by indignant middle-class lady supporters of the revolution, dressed in smart little black dresses and pearls, the senator and his escort were asked to lunch. They were taken to the restaurant at the farmers' market in the Barrio Sandino. It turned out to be a Potemkin sort of place. The visitors were offered goulash. They said they would prefer rice and beans, the food of the poor in Central America. The commandant set out to impress his visitors by his sympathetic response to a staged procession of protests. The effect was spoiled by the arrival of a messenger: there were no beans to be had.

From Managua, Moynihan and George went to El Salvador. Moynihan asked to see the rector, Ignacio Ellacuria, and the vice rector, Ignacio Martín-Baro, of Central American University. Both were Basque Jesuits, and Martín-Baro was a former pupil of Moynihan's friend James Coleman. Moynihan pressed them about the administration's contention that the rebels in El Salvador were being supplied with arms by the Sandinistas.

"Were the Sandinistas shipping arms to the Salvadoran insurgents?" Moynihan asked.

"No," said Ellacuria.

"But they had been?"

"True," replied the Jesuit.

"Then why no longer?" asked Moynihan.

"Because you are doing it now."[10]

The United States shipped millions of dollars' worth of equipment to the government forces, and the rebels could steal, or buy, enough of them not to need help from the Sandinistas. Both Ellacuria and Martín-Baro, Moynihan learned in 1989, along with four other priests, their cook, and the cook's fifteen-year-old daughter, were murdered by government forces armed by the United States.

Moynihan went back to Washington convinced that the story the Reagan administration was putting out, that the Sandinistas, armed and encouraged by Cuba, were stirring up revolution all over Central America, was nonsense.

Bill Casey and the gung ho enthusiasts in the CIA and on the National Security Council's staff in the White House, like Duane "Dewey" Clarridge and Lieutenant Colonel Oliver North, had wanted for some time to cut the Nicaraguan regime off from supplies of oil and other imports. In January 1984, they got Reagan to agree to let them mine three Nicaraguan harbors.[11] The mines had little effect on the tankers and their crews, though they did kill two innocent fishermen, but the impact on Capitol Hill was explosive.

The intelligence community was obliged by law to inform the Senate and House Intelligence Oversight Committees in advance of what it was doing. These briefings, according to the Intelligence Reform Act of 1980, must be "full," "current" and "prior." Apparently, the House committee, briefed on January 31, asked the right questions and learned that the harbors were being mined. But the Senate committee, briefed at length on March 8 and March 13, was left in ignorance. The only reference to the mining was a single, disingenuous sentence: "Magnetic mines have been placed in the Pacific harbor of Corinto," this weasel-sentence ran, "and the Atlantic harbor of El Bluff as well as the oil terminal of Puerto Sandino." But, as Theodore Draper points out in his book *A Very Thin Line,* the Sandinistas had claimed to have laid the mines, and there was nothing in Casey's sentence to contradict their claim and implicate the CIA. Later attempts were made to suggest that the reason why the Republican chairman of the Senate committee, Barry Goldwater, and Moynihan did not correctly interpret the CIA's veiled admission was that they were drunk at the time; there is not the slightest evidence to support this.[12]

Goldwater exploded in wrath. "All this past weekend," he wrote, "I've been trying to figure out how I can most easily tell you my feelings about the discovery of the President having approved mining some of the harbors of Central America. It gets down to one little, simple phrase. I am pissed off!"[13]

He explained that he had been personally embarrassed because he had assured a member of his committee that the president had not authorized the mining, only to learn that he had done so two months earlier in writing. "Bill," protested Goldwater in a letter to Casey, "this is no way to run a railroad. This is an act violating international law. It is an act of war. For the life of me, I don't see how we are going to explain it. . . . I don't like this. I don't like it one bit from the President or from you. I don't need a lot of lengthy explanations. The deed has been done and, in the future, if anything like this happens, I'm going to raise one hell of a fuss about it in public."[14]

The style may have been Barry Goldwater's. But the missive, Moynihan claimed later, was "in effect a joint letter."[15] He added that while the phrase "an act of war" was the chairman's, the judgment that the mining violated international law was his own.

That letter went off on April 9, and Chairman Goldwater left for a tour of Asia. On April 12, the president's national security adviser, Robert McFarlane, a former marine colonel, gave a speech at the Naval Academy in Annapolis in which he said he could not account for Senator Goldwater saying he was kept ignorant about the mining because "every important detail of United States secret warfare in El Salvador and Nicaragua, including the mining, was shared in full by the proper oversight committees." McFarlane, as Moynihan saw it, was calling his chairman a liar. And his chairman was away. It was, Moynihan said, "my watch." He was so angry that he did something highly unusual: on April 15, he resigned as vice chairman of the Intelligence Committee.

Moynihan told Theodore Draper that "Casey lied" to Robert McFarlane, "as to so many others." Faced with the anger of his senatorial overseers, Casey stepped back and apologized to the committee and its chair. Moynihan withdrew his resignation.

The committee was not content to leave things like that. They insisted that they must be informed in advance of significant planned operations. What was significant? Moynihan came up with a definition. Anything significant enough to tell the president about should be significant enough to tell the Senate about too. So on June 6 an agreement was drawn up which came to be known as the "Casey Accords." Casey promised to inform the committee of any presidential findings, and to keep it in touch with the progress of any covert operations.

In retrospect, this was an important stage in the process whereby Congress began to reestablish control over the intelligence community, which had grown up in the Cold War years with a sense that what was done for the president in the name of national security was no business of the rubes on Capitol Hill. It also marked a stage in Pat Moynihan's disillusion with the agency. He had not been impressed by the quality of its work as observed from Delhi. He was even less an admirer of its reporting of events in the Soviet Union. The mining of Corinto set him on the path to his book on secrecy and to his present position, that the agency should be closed down and its functions given to others less tainted by past attitudes and past failures. In retrospect, his judgment is even more severe than that. He saw Director

Casey's actions, and the acquiescence of the Reagan administration, as having the potential to lead to real disaster.

These for him were "the first acts of deception that gradually mutated into a policy of deceit" and led to the Iran-contra crisis. "In the history of the American Republic," he said, "I do not believe there has ever been so massive a hemorrhaging of trust and integrity. The very processes of American government were put in harm's way by a conspiracy of faithless or witless men: sometimes both."[16]

Central America was not the only issue, not even the only foreign policy issue, on which Moynihan found himself more and more at odds with the Reagan administration. "The administration," he wrote in 1988, "Soviet-obsessed, was missing more important things in the world."[17]

The first time Moynihan was troubled by the willingness of the Reagan administration to act in breach of international law when supposed communist influence was detected was in 1983, in the small Caribbean island state of Grenada. The senator had as it happened been visited in his office on Capitol Hill on June 8 of that year by Maurice Bishop, the Marxist leader of something called the New Jewel Movement, which had taken power in Grenada in 1979.[18] Bishop, "a pleasant enough type on first meeting," exchanged only generalities, until it occurred to Moynihan that Bishop thought he was being recorded. He volunteered to walk with him the two blocks to Union Station. On the way, Bishop complained that he was afraid of being overthrown by the CIA. The senator told him he should worry more about the KGB. Bishop was murdered on October 19; President Reagan ordered the invasion of Grenada on October 25. Moynihan went into the Senate press gallery to offer his opinion that this was a breach of both the United Nations charter and of the charter of the Organization of American States. He was shocked by the prevailing indifference in Washington to the idea that international law or the opinion of the international community mattered. The columnist George Will, for example, of whom Moynihan had a generally high opinion, wrote "it is bad enough we pay for the United Nations; surely we do not have to pay attention to it." Moynihan wrote later[19] that this action was "clearly a violation of the UN Charter."

The Nicaragua and Grenada episodes startled Moynihan. They moved him a long way from the analysis of international affairs he had made at the time he was writing "The United States in Opposition" or representing the United States at the UN. They also completed his break with the neoconservative allies who had helped bring him to the Senate. He came to believe that it was dangerous, as well as wrong, for the United States to act in breach of international law, even more wrong and more dangerous to think that international law was unimportant. He criticized UN Ambassador Jeane Kirkpatrick for saying that "the legalistic approach to international affairs" could not deal with Communist aggression and subversion.

In part, Moynihan was arguing that neoconservative spokesmen were predicating their "realism" on the idea that international communism was "winning," when in fact it was losing. Most of all he just felt that the United States was *better* than that. "There is clear evidence," he wrote in the concluding passage of his 1990 book, *On the Law of Nations,* "that the United States is moving away from its long-established concern for and advocacy of international legal norms of state behavior." This was not a matter of conservatism versus liberalism. Rather it reflected relative power. Weak nations hope that strong nations will be law-abiding. "We were once weak; later powerful." It is, he went on, "a fearfully dangerous thing, *the* thing most to be feared, to hold that some laws bind the President but others do not." The United States, he ended, had long championed international law. This was "a legacy not to be frittered away by forgetfulness of our own past, or by frustration with the behavior of others."[20]

In a series of actions and remarks as he moved from his first term into his second, Moynihan demonstrated his move away from the orthodox anticommunism that had been a defining characteristic of the early part of his first term. He became active in criticizing what he saw as the high-handed national security policy of the Reagan administration in Congress. He campaigned against the MX missile. He reiterated his 1979 *Newsweek* piece, exploring how the Soviet Union was internally weak and could collapse of its own accord. Invited to lecture at West Point, he told the cadets about the Sino-Soviet split. But perhaps his most original theme was that the Soviet Union might be as bad as, or worse than, the conventional wisdom held; but it was not as strong as it looked. What Moynihan does not always emphasize when he, justifiably, takes credit for prescience in this regard, is that at the time he thought the collapse of the Soviet Union might be bad news for the United States and the West. Soviet leaders might try, he feared, "to reverse the decline at home and preserve national unity" by seizing the Middle East and its oil.

A year into his second term, Moynihan gave a commencement address at New York University in which he dissented even more clearly from the anticommunism of the administration and his former neoconservative companions (many of them working for Reagan at the time). He began by returning to the MX missile. By deploying it in vulnerable Minuteman silos, he argued, the administration would commit the United States to a first-strike strategy. This would not only be perilous. It would be immoral. Moynihan evoked the Eisenhower administration and its Cold War polity. Moynihan claimed that the MX program would mark a departure from what McGeorge Bundy had described as "the fundamental rule [of] the Eisenhower administration: The object of any new strategic system is to deter, and to deter safely it must be able to survive."[21]

Then he shifted to a more optimistic tone. The strategy of the United States after World War II was to work for the emergence of a world community of like-minded, democratic nations. That had now happened. Of course it meant that the United States had to take more notice of what other nations thought than before. But this was a sign, not of failure but of success.

"The truth is," he went on, "the Soviet idea is spent . . . it summons no loyalty. History is moving away from it with astounding speed . . . it is as if the whole Marxist-Leninist ethos is hurtling off into a black hole in the universe." There were real problems in the world: the danger of nuclear war, the way the world monetary system was draining money from the poor to the rich countries, the culture of terror. But his conclusion was upbeat. "Our grand strategy should be to wait out the Soviet Union; its time is passing. Let us resolve to be here, our old selves, with an ever-surging font of ideas. When the time comes, it will be clear that in the end freedom did prevail."

Five years before the fall of the Berlin Wall, seven years before the dissolution of the Soviet Union, Moynihan was already looking further ahead. He was anticipating the growing fear of terrorism, reaffirming the concern with ethnicity he had felt since his visit to Yugoslavia in 1965, warning against the dangers of economic and financial globalism. But above all, he was asserting his lasting faith in American political ideals and his conviction that they could and must be shared with any other nations that wanted to make the experiment.

Throughout his career, Moynihan has had two overwhelming concerns. The first had been a foreign policy issue. It can be summed up as his continuing solicitude for the safety and the dignity of the United States. That took the form of robust anticommunism, tempered by the insistence that the government should not take anticommunism to the point of abandoning common sense. That was why, for example, he thought that those who predicted that the Sandinistas would one day march on Harlingen, Texas, had either lost their reason, or more probably were motivated by some unacknowledged political interest of their own.

In domestic politics, his concern has been broadly with what might be called public finance. That included welfare, both as a proper concern of a compassionate government and as a possible source of serious waste and social damage. But it has been wider than that. Moynihan has also been constantly preoccupied with tax policy and with social security because without sound public finance the government could be forced into giving up functions that he passionately believed it ought to undertake. Of these, proper provisions for poor children and for the elderly were among the most important.

Rob Shapiro, who joined Moynihan's staff from the National Bureau of Economic Research in 1981 and worked with him in various capacities until 1986, says that the senator saw very early that the deficit would sharply curtail future progressive policies. "If you had wanted to come up with a strategy to permanently hamstring liberals or the Congress," Shapiro says, "you would have wanted to create the biggest possible deficits on the federal budget."[22]

Long before the end of President Reagan's first term, Moynihan was not alone in seeing that the 1981 tax cut had gone too far. At the same time, there were calls from conservatives and liberals alike for a thorough reform of a tax code now encrusted with loopholes and special favors to various interests.[23] Representative Jack Kemp, a New York Republican, and Senator William V. Roth, a Republican from Delaware, had proposed a simplification of the tax code at low rates as early as 1977.[24] In 1982, two Democrats, Moynihan's friend and ally Senator Bill Bradley of New Jersey and Congressman Richard A. Gephardt of Missouri, also came out for a simplification of the tax code at low rates to remove some of the distortions introduced into the economy by tax considerations. In January 1984, President Reagan himself called for Congress to simplify the tax code, and in 1984 Jack Kemp and Senator Bob Kasten of Wisconsin proposed a flat tax.[25] In November of that year, Donald Regan, the Treasury secretary, proposed a new tax code with only three rates of income tax. This plan, known as "Treasury I," would also remove many tax breaks, such as accelerated depreciation for plant, which were being widely abused by "tax shelters."

A rare political climate surrounded the tax issue. Conservative Republicans who believed in cutting taxes for supply-side reasons, but wanted to limit the resulting revenue loss by eliminating some of the grosser loopholes, found themselves in alliance with liberal Democrats, who wanted greater fairness between rich and poor, but also wanted to protect the government's revenue so that it could be used for domestic programs. This unusual truce was dramatized in January 1985 when Senators Bradley and Kasten and Congressmen Gephardt and Kemp actually appeared together at a joint press conference to introduce their bills.

That same month Treasury Secretary Donald Regan and White House Chief of Staff James A. Baker III swapped jobs. On May 28, 1985, Baker came out with his own version of tax reform, dubbed "Treasury II." By eliminating a number of tax loopholes, it alienated many powerful interest groups and was close to defeat in the House on several occasions. But Chairman Dan Rostenkowski of the House Ways and Means Committee worked with the administration and kept the bill alive. Only after the president made one of his rare visits to Capitol Hill to lobby for his bill did the House finally pass it.

All the while, as pressures for tax reform mounted in many quarters, and powerful interests dug in to fight the process, the federal deficit mounted. The 1981 tax act alone cost $433 billion in lost revenues in just its first five years; by 1988, the lost revenues from that source (only three-quarters offset by increases elsewhere) had passed the trillion-dollar mark.[26] In spite of the desperate, at least partially unconstitutional, expedient of the Gramm-Rudman-Hollings Amendment in 1985, which mandated automatic cuts in federal spending on all but a few programs, the deficit was $212 billion in 1985 and $221 billion in 1986, an all-time record each year. (Moynihan was one of twenty-four senators to vote against Gramm-Rudman, in part because he thought it would dismantle the president's defense program and so cause the failure of the arms control talks, in part because he doubted whether it was constitutional.) Overall, the federal deficit had almost doubled in Reagan's first five years in the White House and would rise from under $1 trillion when he took office to $2.6 trillion when he left office in 1989.

So at the beginning of 1986, a tax bill had arrived at the Senate Finance Committee's door with many of the characteristics of a parcel bomb: it was complex, unpredictable and dangerous. Tax reform was obviously necessary. It also looked virtually impossible.

On January 4, 1986, Moynihan revealed his own ideas in characteristically rambunctious style in one of his letters to his constituents.[27] The letter was illustrated with a nineteenth-century steel engraving of cracksmen at work robbing a bank vault, and it bore the headline "The $28 Billion Heist: A Mystery." He began, "It was an inside job and no doubt about it, $28,219,000,000 in bonds missing from the Social Security Trust Funds."

Ever since Labor Day 1985, he went on to explain, there had been rumors in Washington that the Treasury was cashing in social security bonds to pay for the government's general expenses. Congress had created a fiscal crisis by refusing to raise the Treasury's debt ceiling. Normally, when the government receives social security contributions, it buys Treasury bonds. But that increases the national debt, and for the previous three years Congress had forbidden the government that course of action. So in 1985, the Treasury went one step further. It started cashing bonds held in the social security trust funds. In August 1985, the trust funds held $37 billion in Treasury bonds. By November this sum was down to $9 billion. "If you want to be lurid," Moynihan wrote later, "money held in trust literally for widows and orphans was used to pay for — what? — B-1 bombers."[28] Nothing like it had happened since social security's inception fifty years earlier. By law, the government was obliged to inform the congressional committees with oversight responsibility, and also the two public trustees of the funds, one a Democrat, one a Republican. On November 7, in his capacity as the ranking Democrat on the Social Security Subcommittee of the Finance Committee, Moynihan succeeded in getting a Treasury official to admit that the secretary of the Treasury had acted "in violation of the Social Security Act," though the official in question, the comptroller general, hastily added that the secretary did not act "unreasonably given the extraordinary situation in which he was operating." Moynihan agreed that Treasury Secretary Baker had been justified in what he had done; for the United States to default on its loans, which it would otherwise have been obliged to do, would have created "a world disaster."

Before Congress went home for the holidays, however, the subcommittee demanded that the government repay the sums taken out of the trust funds, and the Treasury confirmed that it had done so. The social security trust funds were safe. It was now the government of the United States that faced bankruptcy. The budget would have to be balanced, and although Moynihan realized he would make no friends by saying so, the only way to balance the budget without damaging the nation was to increase revenues.

Joe Gale, now a judge of the U.S. tax court, was Moynihan's key tax expert. Earlier, Moynihan had taken an interest in specific tax issues, especially tuition tax credits for parents with children in private and parochial schools. Now, says Gale, his boss became involved in a major effort to reform the tax code as a whole.[29] Most knowledgeable observers, says Gale, would call the 1986 act one of the two or three most significant pieces of tax legislation since the passage of the original income tax in 1916.

Initially, however, Gale points out, Moynihan was quite skeptical of the growing movement for tax reform. In general, he was in favor of using the tax code for reasons of social policy. He has always been in favor of child allowances, and of the government, through the tax code, helping the nonprofit sector. But a number of factors helped to change his mind. The tax bill illustrates better than perhaps any other legislative battle the blend of idealistic and pragmatic considerations typical of Moynihan's legislative calculations.

As a New York senator, he first wanted to protect state and local revenue. Second, as a former Harvard professor, he wanted to protect the nonprofit sector (though he was quite prepared to give Harvard a hard time where he thought it was being greedy), believing it an important American tradition that the great educational and cultural institutions, foundations, art museums, orchestras and private hospitals and private universities are free from government control. Third, as a mainstream Democrat, he wanted to close loopholes for fat cats. And, finally, as always, he wanted to be part of a Big Idea.

He calculated that he would be more likely to achieve his goals if he worked with the Republican chairman of the Finance Committee, Senator Robert Packwood of Oregon, than by working against him. He also wanted to be part of a historic tax reform. Moynihan also understands that in a two-party government, if you want to go for big change you must build a bipartisan consensus, or whatever you do will simply be undone the next time the other party is in power.

Over the next months, Moynihan's respect for Bob Packwood grew until he became probably Moynihan's closest friend in the Senate up to that time. When in late 1992 the story broke that Packwood had been accused of sexual harassment by several female staffers, and even more when in 1995 Bob Dole, as the Republican majority leader, let it be known that he could no longer defend Packwood, Moynihan was deeply saddened.

Packwood's original proposals followed the general lines of those sent up by President Reagan. The idea was to lower tax rates both for individuals and for corporations, while maintaining the level of federal revenues by removing a number of exemptions. In addition, the president and the House proposed to increase business taxes, so as to reduce the level of individual taxation still further.

Moynihan had no illusions about the Finance Committee, which looks after some of the biggest and most demanding special interest groups in America: oil and gas, timber, mining, sugar, farming, housing and foreign trade among them. So as the committee began to amend the Packwood bill, the interests chipped steadily away at proposals to remove their various exemptions and loopholes. "On the day we voted the depreciable life of an oil refinery to be five years," Moynihan wrote, only partly in jest, "something told us our immortal souls were in danger."[30] An oil refinery is good for at least fifteen years, and often much longer. To allow oil companies to write them off over five, taking deductions against the income tax liability at three times or more the rate justified by real economic costs, was truly sinful.

Packwood had prepared a 221-page draft bill. Amendment by amendment, the committee voted to put back favors to one special interest after another. On Friday morning, April 25, Moynihan and Senator Dave Durenberger, a Republican from Minnesota, had put together the votes to strike out Packwood's proposal to end the deductibility of state and local taxes against federal tax liability. To Moynihan, this was not just a financial interest; it was a constitutional issue. It was wrong, he and Durenberger argued, for the federal government to invade the tax base of states and their component parts. Packwood privately did not disagree with them. But he realized that if this amendment went through it would be followed by dozens more. His tax bill was in ruins. So he banged his gavel and announced that there would be no more votes that day. Tax reform seemed to be dead.

Packwood, as Moynihan tells the story, summoned his chief of staff, Bill Diefenderfer, "a bulldog of a man with a sea captain's beard and a bos'n's girth,"[31] and together they departed to a tavern called the Irish Times, across the street from Union Station and a gentle walk from the Capitol. Over a pitcher of beer, they decided to scrap their ruined bill and to come back with a dramatic new proposal: to go for broke. What, after all, did they have to lose, given that they had already to all intents and purposes lost their carefully constructed bill? Moynihan was one of a "core group" of six senators, three Republicans, three Democrats, invited to meet early the next morning in Packwood's office. The others were two moderate Republicans, John Chafee of Rhode Island and John Danforth of Missouri, and two Democrats, both, like Moynihan, from northeastern states that had suffered from decades of assiduous manipulation of the Finance Committee by southwestern and western energy and mining interests: Bill Bradley of New Jersey and George Mitchell of Maine. The conspirators, for that is what they were, had two things going for them. The administration wanted, indeed given the debt crisis, needed, a tax bill, and a fairly radical one at that. And the press was distracted by the disaster at the Soviet nuclear power plant at Chernobyl in Ukraine.

Packwood put two basic decisions to the core group, which accepted both of them. The first was to adopt Bill Bradley's drastic proposal, to eliminate all the gradations in the income tax code and replace them with just two rates of tax: 15 percent for those with incomes up to $42,500, and 27 percent for all higher incomes. This simplification would go along with sharp cutbacks in all the usual deductions, except for an increase in the personal exemption, which would once again make children a factor, and except for mortgage payments.

The second decision was based on an idea that Moynihan had introduced himself three years previously. It depended on drawing a distinction between "active" and "passive" income. Active income meant "real" income, from salary, fees, interest or dividends. "Passive" income meant notional income from capital gains or losses. The point was to hit at tax shelters, investments deliberately made in order to incur notional losses so as to reduce liability for income tax.

Moynihan was given this idea by a New York tax lawyer, Donald Schapiro. He had originally intended it to be part of a proposal that even the wealthiest must pay at least a minimum amount of tax. But

David Brockway, the chief of staff to the Joint Committee on Taxation, which serves both Senate Finance and House Ways and Means, reported that tax shelters were now being abused on such a grand scale, by comparatively modest professionals as well as by the super-rich, that to apply Schapiro's ban on most tax shelters would save the federal government a staggering amount. So Moynihan proposed that the committee put at the head of the new code a provision that passive losses could not be set against income. So there would be no point in even starting tax shelters. The senators asked how much that would save. The next morning Brockway ran the computer and came back with the answer: $50 billion. That represented one-third of what the administration had sought to raise in taxes on the corporate sector. A horrified *Wall Street Journal* reported that "the effect would be to nearly wipe out tax shelters that are a major force in financing commercial real estate development, oil and gas drilling and certain agricultural activities, such as cattle feeding."[32]

On May 4, a Sunday, the core group finished drafting its bill. The full committee met on Monday morning and by Wednesday, May 7, the committee had agreed on a bill. The oil and mining interests managed to salvage some of their privileges. But in essence the bill worked out by the core group passed, by 20 votes to none. "Whatever our state or regional interests," Moynihan put it, "we all knew something radical had to be done and there would never be a better time to do it."

On June 24 the bill sailed through the full Senate by 97 votes to 3.[33] But that was not the end of the story. Where important legislation as passed by one chamber of Congress differs significantly from similar legislation passed by the other, the measures go to a conference committee, sometimes called "the third house of Congress," for resolution. When the conference has hammered out a compromise it goes back to the two houses, to be passed or rejected by a single vote.

On July 17, the conference committee met in the dignified hearing room of Ways and Means in the Longworth House office building on Independence Avenue. Bob Packwood vowed to close the loopholes on the "princes of privilege," and the very powerful chair of the House Ways and Means Committee, Congressman Dan Rostenkowski of Chicago, maintained that it was time that bank tellers stopped paying more tax than banks. Moynihan mused in his diary of the events that he wasn't sure that the tax bill should be compromised in a conference committee, but there was no alternative because the president had said the only bill he would sign was one that came out of conference.

Rostenkowski opened with a crafty move, "learned in Chicago politics," Moynihan guessed. He accepted the Senate's proposal of just two rates of income tax, 15 percent and 27 percent. But, as Rosty well knew, the conference could not simply accept the Senate bill because the numbers came out wrong. The joint committee on taxation said that, given new, less optimistic economic forecasts, the Senate bill would leave the government $21 billion short over five years.

"Everyone is entitled to his own opinion," Moynihan noted, "but not his own facts." So the joint committee's staff provides both sides with the same facts. "Mind-numbing labors are performed by youth," he added, "who after suitable servitude are sent forth to affluence, knowing more about the tax code than any save their predecessors." It is true that a place in a good Washington law firm awaits those blessed souls who have passed this grueling apprenticeship.[34]

On July 25, it was time to start writing a bill. David Brockway passed out a single sheet of paper with twenty-three issues that had to be resolved if there was to be a comprehensive revision of the tax code. Number 23 was the one Moynihan himself had proposed, and Brockway had made so attractive by running the computer and showing that it could save $50 billion. Moynihan the social scientist added a characteristic comment for the enlightenment of Moynihan the politician: "Data is said to be the plural of anecdote. To wit, $50 billion."

He was still sure he would lose, as he had when he proposed eliminating passive losses in 1983, 1984 and 1985. But not now. "Take out the passive losses provision, and there is no bill." Both the House conferees and the senators agreed that it must stay.

The tax bill fight brought out Moynihan's populist side. He noted with surprise that, according to the Democratic staff of the Joint Economic Committee, the top half of one percent of the U.S. population owns thirty-five percent of the wealth. He noted with indignation that, according to the study, black, female-headed households with incomes under $10,000 have an average net worth of $88.

Meanwhile the bill was running into trouble. The deputy Treasury secretary, Richard Darman, came before the conference and explained that there would be no dramatic tax cuts for voters. "This is a reform bill, not a tax cut. . . . Glum news for people who run for office," commented Moynihan.

By July 28, the bargaining began. Maybe there wouldn't be a tax bill, said the House conferees. Fine, said the senator, "more or less by prearrangement." Things were getting nasty. The Senate Republicans thought the bill would be bad for business. The House Democrats were sore because they thought they were doing what the White House wanted for once, and now they found that if there was to be reform Ronald Reagan would get most of the credit, with a little for Bill Bradley and nothing for them. There were threats of a filibuster.

For nine days, the conference did not meet. When it did convene again, on August 5, the mood was calmer. There would be some kind of tax reform, everyone was beginning to realize, but there wouldn't be much glory in it. On August 8, the senators drifted in and out of the committee room, voting on a supposedly final proposal, line by line. Most of them had a dozen other things to do, so they let staff members vote for them. "I can't imagine another country in which this would happen so easily, and seem so unexceptional," says Moynihan. Lobbyists for the banking industry, predicting "debits, damnation and default," were proven to be exaggerating. The next day the mood was sunny; the conferees broke into laughter as they dealt with savings plans for pastors and the depreciation of "horses over 12 years old."

On August 12, the computer was showing the two bills almost too far out of reach for compromise. The conference voted for the two chairmen to work out a bill, like two medieval armies agreeing to stand or fall by the fate of their champions. Moynihan bumped into Packwood in the Senate chamber and told him about a conversation he had had that morning on the phone with his friend the Berkeley political scientist Aaron Wildavsky, who had just published a history of taxation. "When things that are perfectly legal are regarded as morally tainted," said the professor, "you've got to stop." Packwood stopped, thought and looked up. "That's all I've been about since the beginning," he said.

Packwood would now have to abandon some friends. The main compromise he made was to let the tax rate for the higher income bracket float up 1 point, to 28 percent. But now there must be compromises of one kind or another, because there must be a bill. "We have all but ceased to govern," said Moynihan, sententiously but not untruthfully. "We must now do so."

All Friday the two champions, Packwood for the Senate and Rostenkowski for the House, met and negotiated in H-208, a small room just off the House floor in the Capitol building. By 3:00 in the morning they were both still fresh, but the staff had hit a wall of exhaustion so that they could barely stutter out the numbers, and it was now the middle-aged chairmen who were helping the young lions. "Rosty fresh as the morning soon to break," Moynihan wrote. "Packwood still in a jacket, utterly composed."

On Saturday morning, the senators met for a caucus, with an eighty-three-page agreement in front of them, dated August 16, 1986. That evening, at 9:35 P.M., the signature sheets slid along the polished surface of the dais in the Longworth building. The tax reform bill was on its way to Ronald Reagan, who would have no alternative but to sign it.

It was, said Packwood, the greatest opportunity for Americans in half a century. Russell Long said it was the best revenue bill that had passed in as many years. About 85 percent of all individuals would henceforth pay tax at 15 percent. Wealthy Americans would not be able to avoid tax through shelter schemes. Six million poor people would be removed from the tax rolls, and New Yorkers would send $1.5 billion less to the Treasury every year. Most important of all, as Moynihan saw the summer's work, it had gone a long way to restoring fairness and integrity to the tax system.

"I am not one of those who say Pat Moynihan is ineffective as a legislator," said Bob Packwood in an interview. "He never flinched."[35]

Tax, social security and welfare. Those have all been on Moynihan's "permanent agenda." In 1988, as he prepared to run for a third term in the Senate, it was welfare's turn to come to the top of the deck. In his 1986 State of the Union message, President Reagan announced that he intended to make welfare reform one of his priorities. Presidents Nixon and Carter before him had tried and failed to reform welfare. In mid-1987, Moynihan had welfare on his mind.

He agreed with Professor Samuel Preston of the University of Pennsylvania who told the Population Association of America that an "earthquake" had shuddered through the American family. The divorce rate in the United States was the highest in the world, and so was the rate of teenage pregnancy. Young Americans were half again as likely to be poor as the population as a whole, and children had replaced the old as the poorest group in society. Honest scholars legitimately asked whether existing welfare programs made things worse.

"Not especially honest ideologues have insisted that the answer was yes."[36] The federal government's commitment to welfare had waned. The burden of reforming an overloaded Aid to Families with Dependent Children (AFDC) program fell to the states. So it was governors who took up the cause of welfare reform: Governor Dukakis in Massachusetts, Governor Deukmejian in California, Governor Kean in New Jersey, Governor Cuomo in New York, Governor Clinton in Arkansas. The National Governors Association made welfare reform their priority issue for 1987. President Reagan took up the issue, and so did Senator Moynihan. His approach reflected long-held beliefs. "Welfare" — that is, AFDC as established by Title IV of the Social Security Act of 1935 — could not be reformed. It could only be replaced. And what replaced it must include a reliable system of child support. So he wanted to see a universal system of child support whereby any man who fathered a child must contribute to its support through the social security system. Mothers must be helped to get education and be given transitional help with child care and health care, so that they could work and earn income. Assistance should top up family income, not replace it. "In 1988," Moynihan reminisced a decade later, "we said, 'Welfare is not a permanent condition.' We said, 'Lady, you have to help yourself. This is not good for you, and it is not good for your child. We will help you, but you have to help yourself.' "[37]

In 1987 the House passed its welfare bill, HR-1720. In July, Moynihan introduced his bill, which, like the House bill, included mandatory education, training and work requirements, but cost less than the House bill because it did not raise welfare payments. Thanks to pressure from governors, on April 20 the Finance Committee approved a slightly amended bill. On June 16, it passed the Senate by 93 votes to 3, and on September 27 the conference approved a compromise with the House version, which the president duly signed on October 13, only a couple of weeks before the presidential election. Moynihan, *Congressional Quarterly* commented, was "the key player."[38] Many Democrats were far from happy about the bill. Some liberals even privately called it "slavefare," and Gus Hawkins of California, the African American chairman of the House Education and Labor Committee, called the work requirement "absurd and unrealistic." But the majority in both parties paid tribute to Moynihan. Bob Packwood said, "There's no guarantee that this bill will resolve the crisis facing our welfare system. But there's one certainty, and that's that the present system does not work and cannot work. And but for Pat Moynihan, we would not be trying to fix it at all."

There was never much doubt about Moynihan's reelection. Liz Moynihan had run the 1982 campaign out of the front bedroom in her house on Capitol Hill, though with a team of helpers in New York. The campaign in 1976, she says, was chaotic and amateurish, but by 1982 she had developed a campaigning style all her own. She had three basic rules, which were quite explicit.

"Rule 1: *Never do anything for a negative reason.* Never run a negative ad. Never make a political charge. Never a slur." Moynihan himself makes the point that because he usually ran against weak candidates, he could stick to these self-denying ordinances. But he also believes that the voters noticed that everyone else was in the mud, and he wasn't.

"Rule 2: *Never use 'soft money,'* that is, money not dedicated to a named candidate, which would therefore escape the rules and regulations limiting direct campaign contributions." From time to time well-wishers would offer money to a Committee for Upstate New York, or the like. Liz would simply say, "No thanks." Incidentally, the senator knew little or nothing of the campaign finances. It was, for example, news to him that soft money had been offered, and that his wife had turned it down.

"Rule 3: *Keep the staff small.*" Liz's theory was that most of the bad news about a campaign comes out of the candidate's own headquarters. When the group is close and compact, that doesn't happen. At any rate, it never happened to the Moynihans. In 1988, the staff at 500 Fifth Avenue was never larger than eleven people, plus Liz herself. Each day, to stiffen up the sinews, summon up the blood, one aide, Ted Zukowski, would change the Number of Days to Election on a small blackboard that greeted people as they entered the three-room suite.

Compared to many modern campaigns, with armies of volunteers, consultants, pollsters, space buyers, press handlers, spin doctors, accountants, phone bank operators and the like, Moynihan campaigns were Spartan. That does not mean the staff were casual or that there was anything accidental about their success. Most modern campaigns are heavy on "media," meaning paid political advertisements, with all the polling, analysis and professional ad production that implies. Moynihan had always put the major emphasis in his campaigns on unpaid media. Many of his staff noticed, sometimes with amusement, how much effort he devoted to cultivating the *New York Times*. And Steve Weisman, a *Times* reporter turned editorial writer who covered Moynihan and then became a personal friend, says, "He really does care a great deal about what the *New York Times* thinks." Weisman points out that Moynihan has had a close relationship over the years with several key people at the *Times,* including Max Frankel and Joseph Lelyveld, successive editors, and Howell Raines, the editorial page editor.[39] He pays close attention to how the *Times* covers him, noting such details as whether its report of one of his speeches was placed above or below the fold. Although he also maintains contact with other New York papers, notably the *New York Daily News,* the *New York Post, Newsday* and influential papers upstate, he knows that the *Times* is crucial because as well as reaching its own influential readers, it also influences other media. Similarly, he pays a good deal of attention to television. He prefers the talk-show format, particularly NBC's *Meet the Press,* because it enables him to develop his often unfamiliar and quite subtle ideas in a way he cannot do in sound bites on the evening news.

Liz herself is a formidable campaigner, shrewd and implacable. Her basic strategy was to knock out the strong candidates early. There were two reasons for this. One was that while the Moynihan campaign could raise a certain amount of money ($1.6 million by March 1988 and a further $3.1 million between March and December 1988), it could not hope to raise the sort of money that was being spent in statewide races like the California Senate race in 1986, when $23 million was spent, or even the Democratic primary in much smaller New Jersey, where Frank Lautenberg and Pete Dawkins spent over $7 million each in 1988.

Secondly, the senator was heavily involved in Washington as chairman of the Social Security and Family Policy Subcommittee of Senate Finance. His campaign manager had to do without his presence at first. She started work on March 17, 1987 — St. Patrick's Day — with fund-raising. She set up the Moynihan Committee office at 500 Fifth Avenue on August 1, 466 days before the election, and regards the next six months as the most critical of the campaign. Although no Republican candidate had declared, several potentially powerful candidates were either making plans to run or were rumored to be doing so. One was Ronald Lauder, then the U.S. ambassador to Austria, heir to the Estée Lauder cosmetics fortune and a major Republican fund-raiser. Another was Dr. Henry Kissinger, and a third, perhaps the most formidable, was United States Attorney Rudolph Giuliani.

The early-attack strategy was also rooted in an understanding on the part of both Moynihans that in a crucial respect the conventional wisdom about New York politics was out of date. The traditional view was that because upstate was rock-solid Republican, with the partial and occasional exception of Erie County (Buffalo), everything depended on heavily Democratic New York City. Living as they did for part of the year in upstate Delaware County, Pat and Liz understood that this was no longer axiomatic. Given the seven million people in New York City, it was possible for Averell Harriman to win the governorship in 1954 by winning just five counties. But the Moynihans realized that the landscape was changing. Moynihan carried fourteen counties in 1976, and fifty in 1982. In 1986, Governor Mario Cuomo won fifty-seven, and his attorney general, Robert Abrams, won sixty. The strategy therefore was to demonstrate great strength in New York City first. Then potential opponents would do their own private polling, discover how strong Moynihan was upstate in comparison with traditional Democratic candidates and bow out.

With this purpose, Liz Moynihan again decided to commit a sizeable share of her limited resources to an early ad campaign, known at 500 Fifth Avenue as the "Winter Offensive." She identified two issues, targeting Giuliani in particular: social security and Giuliani's strong suit, crime. The senator wrote the script for the thirty-second TV spots himself, beginning in January. The plan was to knock Giuliani out by the end of the first week in February.

Liz had personally sized up the most dangerous opponent the previous summer. There was already much talk of him running against Moynihan when he was chosen as the grand marshal of the Columbus Day parade in New York. ("Thank you, Mario!" Moynihan comments, because it was Democratic Governor Cuomo who chose a Republican for this prominence.)[40] As the parade formed on Fifth Avenue, Giuliani was there in his top hat and sash. So too was a gray-haired lady with her head covered with a kerchief. As she says, no one ever pays any attention to gray-haired ladies in kerchiefs. After half an hour's close observation, the elderly woman turned to the young man with her, a campaign staffer, and said, "We can take him!" And so she could. On February 8, two days behind schedule, Giuliani announced he was withdrawing from the race. So did Ronald Lauder,

Representative Jack Kemp and Dr. Kissinger, among others — and twenty-nine possible Republican candidates in all.

Liz and her eleven disciples did their work to such effect that the senator was reelected for a third term by an even higher margin than for the second. In 1982, he had broken the New York State record for the biggest margin of victory in a Senate race. In 1988, his margin of victory was the greatest ever achieved in any state, breaking a California record set in 1980.[41]

And with 68.3 percent of the vote cast, he had won the highest percentage of any candidate for senator. It was, furthermore, a broad-based victory. Moynihan carried sixty-one of New York's sixty-two counties.[42] He even carried rural Dutchess County, tribal home of the Hyde Park Roosevelts, something Franklin D. Roosevelt himself never achieved in four presidential races. Moynihan's appeal, moreover, was widespread both in terms of ethnic groups and social class. In NBC exit polls, he won 75 percent of the votes of those with less than a high school diploma, and 79 percent of those with more than a first college degree; he won 91 percent of the Jewish vote, and 94 percent of the African American vote.

He was understandably elated by the scope of his victory. It vindicated his broad political strategy of seeking to appeal to all groups. But, as he himself conceded by implication in his book *Miles to Go*,[43] this high-water mark of the old Democratic politics of the Big Tent was also its last hurrah. A new, more sharply divided style of politics was on its way, both in New York City and in the nation, thanks to a new style of politician, exemplified by Representative Newt Gingrich, Republican of Georgia, in one arena, and by the Reverend Al Sharpton in another.

14

Money and Power

> The long twilight struggle is ending; we appear to
> have prevailed.
>
> — Daniel Patrick Moynihan, *On the Law of Nations*

SIXTY-TWO YEARS OLD when he returned to Washington after his unprecedented victory, Moynihan was at the height of his powers. Indeed, in the subsequent six years he performed as a writer, as a legislator and as a politician at as high a level as ever in his life. In 1989, the Reagan administration, which he first feared and later came to despise, was gone. The new president, George Bush, he could truthfully describe as a good friend for the longest while; Barbara Bush was to become Liz Moynihan's closest friend among political wives in Washington.

The children were grown up now, but the family was a close one, and Maura in particular brought in a series of her friends so that Pat and Liz kept in touch with the younger generation. Several of Maura's friends, in succession, came to play an important part in the senator's professional life. Mandy Grunwald was his media adviser before working for both Bill and Hillary Clinton; Lawrence O'Donnell was chief of staff of the Finance Committee at the time of the health care bill in 1993 and 1994.

Private life was pleasanter than ever. In 1990, Liz managed to buy two adjacent apartments on the top floor of a new building on Pennsylvania Avenue and convert them into an exceedingly agreeable apartment, not enormous, but comfortable, convenient and not without a certain sense of high style.

In the 1980s, visiting the Waddington Gallery in Dublin, where over the years Moynihan had picked up a dozen or so sketches and watercolors by Jack B. Yeats, the painter brother of William Butler Yeats, the dealer showed him one of Yeats's most important oils, *The Overcoat*. It is a picture of a boy who stares a trifle sulkily out from the street of an impoverished nineteenth-century Irish town, perhaps not so very different from the one that the young John Cornelius Moynihan left a hundred years earlier. Would the senator like it? Of course he would, but there was no way he could afford it. Not so, said the dealer. Over the years, there had been growing appreciation of Yeats's work, and prices had risen accordingly. If the senator would care to send him the smaller works he had acquired, the gallery would be happy to sell him *The Overcoat*, and there might even be a check for a balance as well. In the end, the boy came to live in the apartment on Pennsylvania Avenue and with him came a five-figure check into the bargain.

Then there was the farm. Liz had succeeded in buying a second farm, the Banner place, so that now they had close to a thousand acres, all the land up to the horizon most of the way around. They had added a bedroom, bathroom and closets for themselves, between the house and the old porch, so that the porch kept its view over the pond. The poplars had grown up, draining the little swamp, and Liz had converted the big barn and put in a swimming pool. It was disrupted by groundhogs who dug tunnels under the concrete and whom Liz pursued grimly.

Pat was writing as gracefully and as originally as ever. Most summers he would retreat to the farm, immure himself in the little white schoolhouse three hundred yards up the road for six weeks or so and come out with a powerful tract, or at the very least a collection of essays, tied together by an introduction in which reminiscence was blended with polemic. In 1989, as it happened, he brought together some ideas that had been maturing in the cellars of his mind since the Vietnam War about the importance of international law.[1] The book, *On the Law of Nations,* is a reflection on the dangers of American presidents acting in the world on impulse; one reviewer called it "a cry of alarm . . . deeply reasoned, informed by our finest traditions and imbued with moral fervor." In 1991, Moynihan wrote the Cyril Foster lecture, given at Oxford University that November, and later considerably expanded as a book.[2] Once again, he met head on an issue of the greatest possible importance and topicality, the ethnic divisions he had been studying all his life, and which were now flaring into conflict and atrocity in the former Yugoslavia. Yet now his books, even though they were from many points of view better books, were not getting the attention from publishers, reviewers and consumers that his earlier, passionate and partisan tracts like *Maximum Feasible Misunderstanding* and *A Dangerous Place* had reaped.

The irony was that the new internationalist thrust of his thinking drove him to vote against the Gulf War in the early 1990s. He has said that this vote was the one he most regretted casting. At the very moment when his predictions about the course of international politics were being borne out by the discrediting of Marxism, the collapse of the Soviet Union and the rush among its former clients to adopt the American ideals their governments had once derided, he was in danger of losing touch with a new American mood toward the outside world. It was at once indifferent and triumphalist, and showed itself almost as much among his Democratic allies as among his Republican opponents.

As a legislator, his reputation was higher and his opportunities greater than ever. And in the third term he was to play a leading, sometimes a starring role in a number of congressional dramas. He was in the thick of the fight over the Bush budget of 1990 and the Clinton budget of 1993. He successfully crafted what many Washington judges consider his most accomplished legislative achievement, "Ice Tea," or the Intermodal Surface Transportation Efficiency Act of 1991. Almost for the first time, he played his way like a grandmaster through the interlocking complexities of transportation theory, policy and sectional interest; yet the battle has had to be largely fought all over again. If its long-term effects on American society, and in particular on the balance between city, suburb and outback, will be felt for decades, it has hardly received its due as a major legislative landmark.

In 1992, in an academic lecture at Yale, he coined one of the phrases that will become part of his permanent intellectual legacy. He suggested that the key to understanding many problems in modern American society was our tendency to "define deviancy down." Few scholars and virtually no politicians could match his grasp of the way social theory, social policy and social reality interact in their impact on troubled neighborhoods and damaged lives. Yet on two of the biggest issues of the term, on health care and on welfare "reform" (which he correctly pointed out is in too many cases a cynical euphemism for welfare abolition), he found himself so out of touch with the way the new tides of thought were moving that he was forced to the margin of legislative action.

As for politics, he began the term, as we have seen, on as high a peak as he could have hoped, backed by absolutely the largest majority in American political history. By the end of the third term, that massive consensus in New York had been badly chipped, not so much by a relatively successful primary challenge from Al Sharpton, as by Moynihan's own discomfort with the new politics of individual self-interest and group aggression.

But the New York arena should not be exaggerated. After all, he beat Sharpton three-to-one in the primary and was never in a moment's danger in the general election. What was more frustrating — as he was well aware — was that the winds of national politics, which seemed for a while to be blowing him into an absolutely central position in Washington, suddenly began to veer in ways that were unpredictable and not at all helpful for the course he had set.

In November 1992, Governor Bill Clinton was elected president. He had been a Moynihan ally on welfare issues in the past and he was a moderate Democrat of a kind that Moynihan might have been expected to welcome. That December, Moynihan sent his thoughts to the president-elect in a memo detailing a new adventure. Moynihan's travels took him, a senior senator, aged sixty-five, under fire in one of the most dangerous spots on earth, Sarajevo, then under siege by the Serbs in the vicious, multisided civil war that had broken out in the former Yugoslavia. So far as can be judged, Clinton took little or no notice of this extraordinary document,[3] though he did appoint Moynihan's companion, Peter Galbraith, a staffer with the Senate Foreign Relations Committee and a son of the Moynihans' old friend John Kenneth Galbraith, as U.S. ambassador to Croatia.

Moynihan began with what he called some Indiana Jones "atmospherics." He described how he had persuaded the base commander at the great U.S. Rhein-Main base near Frankfurt to whisk him onto a C-12 that was already taxiing down the runway, bound for Sarajevo. The city was being besieged by the Bosnian Serbs with clandestine support from the rump government of the former Yugoslavia in Serbia. United Nations forces drawn mostly from France, Ukraine and Egypt protected the city. The naïve rationale behind this ramshackle arrangement was that the French would get on with the Roman Catholic Croats, the Ukrainians with the Orthodox Christian Serbs and the Egyptians with the Bosnian Muslims. Life in the Balkans, however, is even more complicated than it appears to officials of the United Nations in New York.

As the plane left Austrian air space on its flight south, the pilot, a West Virginia Air National Guard officer, received a radio message saying that U.S. senators were not allowed into Sarajevo. Moynihan told the pilot to signal back that if the crew could take the risk, so could he. Then word came back that the Sarajevo airport was closed. "This was a lie," Moynihan bluntly reported to the commander in chief. When the plane landed at Zagreb, they were told that Sarajevo was open, and two C-130s had just taken off. So the next morning, to the fury of the U.S.-European command, Senator Moynihan flew into Sarajevo on a Canadian air force C-130 and flew back on the following Wednesday on a British Royal Air Force Hercules. Moynihan and Galbraith landed in what he called, accurately,

> the most intense urban warfare environment in the world just now. AK 47s chattering. Dash for the sandbags, insinuated into a Ukrainian armored personnel carrier, set out across no man's land. . . . An Egyptian APC, considerably more user-friendly, to the presidency [i.e., to the headquarters of the Bosnian President Alija Izetbegovic, a Muslim]. Television as you are greeted by President Izetbegovic. Back to HQ. Briefing. Artillery getting heavy now. Whiskey. A good meal in the mess. (Morillon, the commander, is a Legionnaire. They have a thing about dining well under fire.) To bed, shells landing 300 yards away.[4]

Taking care to remind Clinton that he had been in Sarajevo forty years earlier, Moynihan proceeded to deliver a dazzling essay on one of his favorite themes: ethnicity. Characteristically, too, he insisted that Americans were not wholly innocent bystanders at a witches' Sabbath of primitive violence, but had been deeply involved in the intellectual and political processes that had led to the Bosnian mess. "How did all this happen?" he asked, and answered his question with the thought that "there is a sense, I suppose, in which nothing very much has happened." What he meant was that "the twentieth century began in August 1914" when an Austrian archduke was murdered by a Serb, Gavrilo Prinzip, in Sarajevo, in the cause of Greater Serbia. For decades, that cause was kept on hold, and in the meantime "largely at the behest of the United States, the international order had proclaimed the principle of self-determination." What, then, of the self-determination of those Serbs who lived in Bosnia-Herzegovina? Hitler, Moynihan pointed out, appealed to the very same argument, and cited Woodrow Wilson chapter and verse, when he invaded Czechoslovakia, making World War II inevitable. Ideology obscured, "perhaps especially for Americans," the importance of ethnicity and the way it had been responsible for most of the conflicts of the twentieth century.

Whereupon he launched into a diatribe against the conventional wisdom, to him the worst folly, of the foreign policy and national security establishment that had led President Bush and his secretary of state, James Baker, to ignore the strength of the ethnic forces tearing Yugoslavia and also the Soviet Union apart. This, he contended, unintentionally sent a signal to the Serbs that the United States would not stand in their way as they collected outlying Serb populations into a Greater Serbia. He beseeched the new president not to rely on the CIA. "It is brain dead," wrote the former member of the Intelligence Oversight Committee, "and should be honorably interred."[5]

Moynihan made dire forecasts about how serious the crisis in the former Yugoslavia could become. "At minimum," he predicted, "it will be a human disaster." He reported predictions that fifty thousand, or perhaps five or even ten times as many, would starve to death. The Muslim population of Bosnia might be "systematically extirpated. Genocide." There could be "something like a European war in this region." So what was to be done? The Bush administration had left Clinton with too few options. It would have been good to send a message to the Serbs that "ethnic cleansing" was not worthwhile by bombing every bridge in Belgrade in one raid. As it was, all the United States could do was to see that food got in. Then, presciently, Moynihan looked farther afield than Bosnia, at the Balkans as a whole. His closing plea was that Bill Clinton and the people he brought into government should "try to absorb and to come to terms with the forces of hate in the world." He could do worse than send every new assistant secretary to Slano, near Dubrovnik, which had been occupied by Montenegrin Serb territorials.

"There is nothing left there but the handwriting on the wall." The phrase echoed what the British journalist had said to him when he visited East Berlin in 1951. "In roman letters, so that the Croatians would be sure to understand, the graffiti declared that there will be more to come. One soldier named Marko was concerned that his message go beyond the borders of Croatia, and so scrawled in English letters to wit: YOU ASK FOR IT. I find the slight illiteracy in the English wonderfully evocative. Not 'you asked for it' and now you have got it. Past tense. But rather, your very existence constitutes grounds for retaliation against you. Unto the end of time."[6]

A couple of months earlier, in September 1992, on the death of Senator Quentin Burdick of South Dakota, Moynihan had reached his first chair, of the Committee on the Environment and Public Works. And in January, he finally climbed to the top of the greasy pole and took over as chairman of the Senate Finance Committee, one of the four great chairmanships on the Senate side, which strong men plot and wait for, and the one he had picked out when he first arrived on Capitol Hill as the proper target for a New York senator's ambitions.

A *Time* magazine journalist supposed this post made him "one of the ten most powerful people in Washington." Moynihan knew better. The Republicans had picked up one Senate seat in 1992. That meant that there were eleven Democrats on the Finance Committee, against nine Republicans. Every Democrat would have to vote with the chairman if he was to prevail, so in effect every Democratic senator had a veto.[7] This was not a recipe for strong chairmanship, as exercised by the legendary "whales" of old;[8] and in fact, in his two brief years as chairman, he was often prevented from playing the positive role he would have preferred.

Above all, there was the shattering blow of defeat for the Democratic party in 1994, just when it had recaptured the White House and might have reasonably expected to look forward to a period when governmental power in Washington was not divided between one party in the White House and another in control of both houses of Congress. In his memoir of those years, *Miles to Go,* Moynihan freely admits that he never saw the storm clouds of the "Gingrich revolution" coming up out of the sea. He compared it to the collapse of the Soviet Union, which he *had* anticipated: "I had expected the Soviet implosion; the Congressional debacle of 1994 came as a complete surprise."[9]

In 1919, Lietenant Colonel Dwight D. Eisenhower was given an important peacetime assignment.[10] He was to take a convoy of army trucks from Fort Meade, near Washington, D.C., to the Presidio in San Francisco, to see how well the nation's roads could replace the railroads in a national emergency.[11] The answer was: not well. Young Eisenhower and his men found that it took two months, at an average speed of under seven miles an hour, to cross the continent. The experience left him with a lifelong interest in the role of highways in national defense. In 1956, as president, Eisenhower was finally able to fulfill his youthful dream. After working with a group of young congressmen led by Jim Wright of Texas, later Speaker of the House, Eisenhower signed legislation to establish a forty-four-thousand-mile Interstate and Defense Highway System.

That, Eisenhower told his aide Bryce Harlow, was the most important domestic achievement of his administration. It has also been described as the biggest rip-off in history. The cost, originally budgeted at $27 billion, eventually came to $128 billion. It was supposed to be finished in thirteen years; the last links in the system, the Anderson Freeway in Los Angeles and the Big Dig in Boston, are still not complete at the time of writing, more than thirty years later. The ribbons of concrete, gently curving from coast to coast across farmlands, mountains, forests and prairie, have moved the imagination almost as deeply as the transcontinental railroads, inspiring a whole genre of "road movies." But those same divided highways, as Pat Moynihan has come to see it, have themselves been a cause of division, between town and country, city and suburb, section and section, class and class. If in the rural South and West the economic and social impact of the Interstate System has been largely and in some cases overwhelmingly beneficial, freeing farm families from the oppression of distance, the impact on the cities of the Northeast and the Middle West has been very different. For one thing, the interstate highways have been a prime mover, subsidized by federal funding at 90 percent, driving the exodus to the suburbs. They have had catastrophic effects on the cities, dividing and literally overshadowing neighborhoods, killing the economic activity that once sprang up around railroad hubs, shifting industry out to suburban and rural sites.

Moynihan took an interest in the impact of the Interstate System on towns and cities as early as 1960, when it was only beginning to be built. As a young aide to Governor Harriman, he observed what happened when the highway struck the middle-sized cities of New York State, and he put his conclusions into one of his first important articles for *The Reporter*.[12] "The program is doing about what was to be expected," he wrote, "throwing up a Chinese wall across Wilmington, driving educational institutions out of downtown Louisville, plowing through the center of Reno. When the interstate runs into a place like Newburgh, New York, the wreckage is something to see."

Moynihan's former chief of staff, Roy Kienitz, who also worked for him on the staff of the Environment and Public Works Committee,[13] says of the senator,"Finally, the interstates were all but done. He happened to be in the right place at the right time. But he was able to do great work because he had ideas of his own, and he looked around and asked other people for their ideas."

The massive highway lobby, which the Interstate System had largely brought into existence, had no intention of letting the goose that had laid so many golden eggs die. Starting in 1989, the lobbies, among them the Highway Builders Association, the truckers, AAA and the state transportation departments, especially of the Southern and Western states, started pushing for a new and even grander project: a National Highway System, three times the size of the existing Interstate System, drawing into it every kind of feeder road, all to be paid for by simple block grants.

They persuaded the Bush administration to go along with them. President Bush's transportation secretary, Samuel K. Skinner, was respected on Capitol Hill. On February 13, 1991, the president, with Skinner at his side in the executive office building auditorium, rolled out the administration's five-year highway plan. It would cost $105 billion and focus on connecting the existing Interstate System into a National Highway System of 155,000 miles of road.

The Environment and Public Works Committee had jurisdiction in the Senate, and jurisdiction in the House was split among seven committees. But Senator Quentin Burdick, the chairman, was eighty-six and in poor health. His staff did a deal with Moynihan's. So long as South Dakota, Burdick's home state, got its money, they would not object.[14] And Moynihan's response was trenchant. "I said, 'We built the interstate system, you're not going to build another one!' "[15] Left to themselves, the highway lobby would pour concrete until there were forty-four lanes stretching across the continent. And in the meantime, highways, and the lack of public transport they had created, were strangling great cities like New York.

Kienitz and the rest of the staff understood that in New York the easy thing to say was that you should take the highway money, of which New York would get 2 percent, and put it into a formula for developing mass transit, of which New York might get 20 percent. "But in the Senate," he went on, "New York has just two votes. So you can forget that." Strategically, Moynihan had to separate the debate about who got what share of the money from the more important debate, as he saw it, about what the money was used for. He had to defeat the administration's bill by trumping it with another that not only kept up the level of expenditure on transportation infrastructure, but shifted the emphasis from simply pouring concrete for more and more roads into mass transit for cities, and at the same time looked at new and radical ways of tackling the problems of congestion and pollution.

The prevailing view was that Moynihan was an impressive figure, but a bit cranky on the subject of transportation, an amateur who would soon succumb to the pressures of one of the best-organized clusters of lobbies in the country. He proved them wrong. "We worked weekends for four months," says Roy Kienitz. "We held hearings in Fort Lauderdale; Billings, Montana; Albany; Los Angeles; Reno; and Idaho Falls," not coincidentally the hometown of Senator Steve Symms, Republican of Idaho, a key member of Moynihan's committee. "We produced a bill in April. We had it out of committee in May, and on the floor by June."

The timetable was indeed swift. The House passed its version on July 25, and the Senate approved the Moynihan bill, S-1204, on June 19 by 91 votes to 7. But the real battle was still to come. As *Congressional Quarterly* put it, Moynihan's colleagues did not challenge his radical vision for the future. Instead, a more traditional battle occurred over formulas that allocated highway funds to states.

Indeed. For the past forty years, the empty states, led by Alaska and Montana, had gotten back far more from the Highway Trust Fund than they put in. (In the case of Alaska, almost eight times more!) But another dozen states, including California, Texas and Florida, three of the four most populous, regularly contributed more than they got back. There was nothing scandalous about this. The whole point of the Interstate System was to link Fort Meade and the Presidio, New York, Texas and California, and to do that meant building highways across big, half-empty states. "Any federal activity, by definition," said Moynihan, "is unequal in impact. Is life fair?"

Perhaps not. But the practical point was that, once the Moynihan bill opened up the federal compromises made over the years, a cat fight over resources was inevitable. Moynihan understood this very well. What he was trying to do was to buy the support of the big, populous donor states and at the same time achieve two long-held personal goals: to shift the nation's transportation policy away from its overwhelming dependency on the automobile; and in the process to help the economies of urban states in general and the New York region in particular.

The House had less radical ideas. In March, it produced a proposal that would endorse President Bush's concept of a National Highway System, but hang onto it hundreds of special road projects dear to the hearts of individual congressmen. These were first called "demonstration projects," slightly more than one for every member of the House. Then House Public Works Committee Chairman Robert A. Roe, a New Jersey Democrat, came up with an even more inspiring name for them: "congressional projects of national significance." Transportation Secretary Samuel Skinner was scathing. What the House proposed was "paving the country with pork."

All of this was to be paid for by a 5-cent gasoline tax increase. But by August, it was clear that the votes were not there for a higher gas tax. After the recess, in October, the House produced a revised bill without the tax hike. Eventually a compromise was hammered out: not a 5-cent increase, but 2.5 cents. This debate took place in an atmosphere of sulfurous political name-calling. Chairman Roe called his opponents "princes of darkness." Republican conservatives who were later to play a leading role in the Gingrich regime in the House, like Tom DeLay and Dick Armey of Texas, worked up a head of steam against Democratic pork-barreling.

It was not until November 7 that the House and Senate versions of these highway and mass transit bills reached the conference. It was a huge group: twenty-six from the Senate and no fewer than sixty-six from the House. State governments were getting restive; some were on the brink of running out of spending authority. The Bush administration kept threatening to veto the bill. But there was a growing perception that the economy needed the public spending contained in it. No one perhaps was a Keynesian anymore. But congressmen hated the idea of giving up on billions of dollars of federal spending in their states.

In the end, there was something for everyone.[16] The Bush administration got a National Highway System. The congressmen got their money, $151 billion of it. States and cities got more freedom and flexibility than they had ever had before to spend the money where and how they wanted. Donor states, in particular, got an agreement that every state should get back a minimum of 90 percent of what it paid into the Highway Trust Fund.

Moynihan was happy to see everyone else happy. For he got what he really wanted. "This is the first transportation legislation of the post-Interstate era," he could say. "It marks the transition from system building to system performance."

It also marked a massive shift of resources into mass transit. Not only did the legislation allocate the formidable sum of $31 billion for mass transit; it allowed states to spend half, and with the approval of the Transportation Department up to 100 percent of their *highway* money too on mass transit.

There were other touches that were pure Moynihan, reflecting the social scientist as legislator. There was a handy $700 million for a pet interest of the senator's, "mag. lev.," for magnetic levitation, a technology for suspending trains fractionally above their "rails" to avoid friction. There was money for experiments in "intelligent vehicle and highway systems." Moynihan even achieved a personal wish by getting the federal government to reimburse the state of New York for the billions it spent in the 1940s and 1950s on the New York Thruway, largely completed before the 1956 act made federal funding available.

Most important of all, perhaps, and this constituted the sharpest break with the approach of most House members, Moynihan had understood the outlines of economic bargaining on an altogether larger scale than the traditional congressional scrapping over air force bases, interstate exchanges, post offices and the like. This was, perhaps, "sectional pork." It was not that Moynihan was above pushing for specific projects for New York. But he was playing a bigger game. He was trying to tilt the continent backward, so that resources that had been so lavishly poured out to the West and the Southwest might flow back into the Northeast.

He was certainly not above fighting for big projects for New York in the old-fashioned way. He was determined to build a new federal courthouse in Brooklyn to replace the late-nineteenth-century structure, which had become dilapidated and quite inadequate for the ceaseless throng of lawyers, litigants and witnesses. The jurisdiction of the eastern district of New York included both Kennedy and La Guardia airports and run-down inner-city neighborhoods with some of the highest drug caseloads in the country. Already in 1989, the

Judicial Conference of the United States, headed by Chief Justice Rehnquist, declared the first ever "judicial space emergency" in Brooklyn; juries were meeting in closets, and files were stacked in hallways.[17] Moynihan and his fellow senator from New York, Alfonse D'Amato, wrote to the administrator of the General Services administration, asking what he planned to do. He came back with a plan to lease the Brooklyn post office at Cadman Plaza, a handsome nineteenth-century stone building and, while preserving its facade, reconstruct it entirely as a courthouse.

Nothing happened for a while, so Moynihan wrote again. The GSA asked Moynihan's staff to offer an amendment to authorize the project. At the time, the transportation bill was still in conference. So Moynihan's staff, he said, asked the House staff if there would be any objection to a no-cost amendment authorization being tacked on to the big bill. There was no objection, so language was inserted into the conference report, authorizing the Brooklyn courthouse.

At this point, things went horribly wrong. All government expenditure has to be first authorized, then appropriated. Moynihan understood that the money was authorized along with the transportation bill, and he told the Senate that he and the GSA both intended to appropriate money for the project as required in the next year. It was estimated that the courthouse would cost the not inconsiderable sum of $457 million. But then it went to the Bush administration's Office of Management and Budget, which ruled that the cost would have to be "scored" against the transportation bill. In effect, OMB was saying, "OK, you tried to run this past us as highway spending. Very well, we will treat it that way, and see whether you like it!" Worse, it was scored at almost $1 billion, more than twice the estimated cost. Indeed the Congressional Budget Office scored it at the astronomic figure of $3.5 billion, which might have made it the most expensive building ever built. The senator insisted that he only meant to authorize the money for the new courthouse, but in effect, by attaching the funding money to the highway bill, he was sidestepping the appropriations process. The Office of Management and Budget wouldn't wear that, and a months-long struggle began.

It was, as Moynihan put it, a "Kafkaesque" situation.[18] Because the senator had attached the courthouse funding to the transportation bill, OMB — with a certain bureaucratic logic — chose to cost the courthouse as if it were a highway, which just happened to make it almost three times more expensive at $1 billion. That in turn put the whole highway budget over the spending ceiling, so OMB cut the highway bill's budgetary authority by $1.2 million. It was calculated that this cut would cost the economy fifty thousand lost jobs building highways!

Tempers rose. The suggestion by another Republican senator, Kit Bond of Missouri, that Moynihan had cost his state $18 million in highway funding, led to what the *Washington Post* described as an "off the floor confrontation."[19] Republicans insisted that Moynihan had "slipped" the funding into the highway bill. Moynihan insisted the language had been drafted primarily by the GSA. The GSA denied it. On June 18, after three unsuccessful tries, Moynihan gave up.[20] "So be it," he said. "I have gotten the message."[21]

Finally, on July 28, to most people's surprise, the House suspended its rules and passed the Senate's bill anyway. The Bush administration indignantly denounced Moynihan for pork-barrel politics. Many in Washington thought he had been caught out in a deft parliamentary maneuver that went wrong. He insisted his staff had only been trying to help the GSA. Whatever happened, he got his courthouse, and so did Brooklyn.

An architectural ambition on a far grander scale than anything in Cadman Plaza was the Pennsylvania Avenue project in Washington. Moynihan remained committed to it, as he had been since 1963. I once teased him for having, like the emperor Augustus, found Rome a city of brick, and left it a city of marble. Surely, he shot back, it was more like the case of the prince regent's architect John Nash, of whom it was said: "London hath a new master / Found it brick, left it plaster."[22]

Over the years his interest in Pennsylvania Avenue, and in clothing the federal government in fitting and beautiful buildings, did not diminish — it deepened and expanded. This project was very personal. Moynihan has written, and written with feeling and perception, about architecture.[23] In a paper given at a meeting of the American Institute of Architects in 1969, and later republished under the title "Architecture in a Time of Trouble," Moynihan spelled out why he thought great public buildings were not an indulgence, but an essential element in a democratic society.[24] There had been, he said, a "steady deterioration in the quality of public buildings and spaces," which amounted to "a decline in the symbols of public unity and common purpose." The point was, he emphasized: "Good or bad architecture is not an option. It is a fundamental sign of the competence of government as will be found. Men who build bad buildings are bad governors. A people that persists in electing such men is opting for bad government."[25]

Robert A. Peck was trained as a lawyer, but he had studied architecture and written about it when he went to work for Moynihan. In 1981, he approached Moynihan and suggested that "it is time we do something about Union Station."[26] The senator "didn't bat an eyelid," and together they began the slow process of getting Congress to come through with the money to rehabilitate and refit Daniel Burnham's magnificent station building, begun in 1901. "This government began as an architectural fantasy," Peck says, and Moynihan had always understood the link between good building and what Moynihan called — in his "Guiding Principles for Federal Architecture" — the "dignity, enterprise, vigor and stability of the Federal government."[27]

In 1970, Jacqueline Kennedy Onassis wrote in her breathless style from Glyfada, Athens, thanking Moynihan for sending her a copy of his book on the Pennsylvania Avenue development: "I often wondered what had happened to the hopes for Pennsylvania Avenue. I dreaded they had just fizzled away — it makes me so happy to know they are in your domain — If anyone can make them materialize — it will be you."[28]

Seventeen years later, Pennsylvania Avenue was still his domain, as chairman of the Senate Environment and Public Works Committee, and he was able to send Mrs. Onassis a note telling her that the Senate had passed the Federal Triangle Development Act. Ten years further on still, the progress had been remarkable, as Moynihan reported in the *Washington Post*: "The Willard [hotel] is back. I. M. Pei's East Wing of the National Gallery is across the street from a magnificent Canadian embassy. The superb Navy Memorial at Eighth Street sets in place the flow of effects down from what is now the National Museum of American Art and the National Portrait Gallery."[29]

He was privately less happy about the FBI Building, a forbidding fortress in shuttered concrete, which he called "the biggest police station in the world."

Moynihan and Nathaniel Owings found major nineteenth-century buildings such as the Patent Office and the Pension Building all but abandoned in the 1960s. Moynihan transformed the latter into a fine National Building Museum by an act introduced in 1978. And Moynihan was chair of the body that commissioned the Thurgood Marshall

Building, designed by Edward Larrabee Barnes, on the east side of Union Station.[30]

Not so trouble-free was the most ambitious single project on the whole trajectory from the Treasury Building to the slopes of Capitol Hill, the International Trade and Cultural Center. It was Moynihan's characteristic inspiration to disarm Republican opposition to this enormous project by proposing that it be known as the Ronald Reagan Building.

Moynihan's 1987 bill, the one he told Jacqueline Onassis about, was not the beginning. In the early 1970s, a man called Kenneth R. Sparks, president of the Federal City Council, which is a civic group, not an elected body, wanted to build an international trade center in Washington. In 1986, he met the new administrator of the government's General Services Administration. Terence Golden, a former partner in the Dallas-based developer Trammell Crow, was shocked that the federal government was paying more than $300 million in rent every year to accommodate half the federal office workers in the Washington area. He and Sparks came up with the idea of building a massive trade center on the eleven-acre lot at 14th and Pennsylvania, the last unfinished part of the Federal Triangle, built between 1926 and 1937. They easily persuaded Moynihan to come in with them. The concept was original, at least for a federal project. The government would put no money up front. Instead it would pay the developer back over thirty years and would end by owning a billion dollars of real estate. Moreover, by putting the project in the hands of the Pennsylvania Avenue Development Corporation, the builders did not have to live by the sometimes restrictive rules imposed by the GSA.

Ten years later, the *Washington Post* reported on how the project had worked out. The building, not quite complete, would be second in size among federal buildings only to the Pentagon. At $818 million, it would be the most expensive federal building ever constructed. That would be 125 percent more than Congress was first told. The original concept of an international trade center was in doubt. Instead, the giant building would be occupied by government agencies like the Environmental Protection Agency, the Agency for International Development, the Customs Service and the Wilson Center. The legislation passed by Moynihan's subcommittee imposed few cost controls. Interviewed by reporters from the *Washington Post,* he was asked why the legislation failed to include such controls. He replied that he did not have "the slightest idea."[31] Some in the Reagan administration warned about the likelihood of cost overruns. "We screamed and hollered that this was a blank check," one anonymous source said. But these were the Reagan years, a time of business triumphalism. Many in the administration were contemptuous of chintzy governmental penny-pinching. That was not what they were used to in the corporate world. Like Moynihan, if for different reasons, they wanted the building to be monumental. And monumental, in every sense, it was.

Once, in Delhi in 1973, as Moynihan was turning the pages of a week-old Sunday edition of the *New York Times,* he found an article by the paper's architecture critic, Ada Louise Huxtable. With pleasure, he noticed that she found a kind word for "the leadership of such men as Daniel Patrick Moynihan, then Assistant Secretary . . ." The story jumped over the page, and there to his chagrin he saw that his old friend went on: " . . . of Labor and *éminence grise* of the Federal design program, before the days of benign neglect." He wrote angrily in his diary, "There it is again, snapping at me. An *éminence grise* at 35, an outcast at 46. I shall have no memorials, but any such would most likely be on the order of Benedict Arnold's boot on the monument of the Battle of Bennington."[32]

Not so. Even the cost overruns of the Reagan Building were forgiven. The international trade center survived. It was Senator Moynihan who was asked to give the address, tracing the fortunes of Jefferson's dream that "design activity and political thought are indivisible" at the building's dedication.[33] President Clinton came and joked that there were days when he drove by, week after week, and saw only a vast hole in the ground, and wondered whether the Moynihan hole would ever become the Reagan Building.[34]

The Reagan Building is one memorial, as solid as marble and stone could make it. The Brooklyn courthouse is another. So are the new Manhattan federal building and courthouse at Foley Square, the new federal building in Buffalo, the new Union Station and, last but by no means least, the projected new Pennsylvania Station in New York City. On May 20, 1999, President Clinton flew to New York to celebrate a $484-million plan to turn the General Post Office on Eighth Avenue into a new Pennsylvania Station. Mayor Rudolph Giuliani boycotted the event on the grounds that the project was both ill-conceived and too expensive. But President Clinton promised, paraphrasing the post office's famous inscription: "Neither snow nor rain, nor heat, nor gloom of night could have stopped Pat Moynihan" from creating the new station. There are books and ideas that Moynihan can take satisfaction in as monuments. But there will be monuments of the monumental kind, too.

In 1992, Kai Erikson, the chairman of the Sociology Department at Yale, invited Moynihan to speak at a conference on "Sociological Visions." Not long after his Yale talk, Moynihan was invited by his old friend James S. Coleman, newly chosen president of the American Sociological Association, to give an address at his induction. The senator used the occasion to introduce his concept of "defining deviancy down."

He took off from an observation by Professor Erikson in a book about crime and criminals in colonial Massachusetts. The book set out to test the contention of Emile Durkheim, one of the historic founders of sociology, that "the number of deviant offenders a community can afford to recognize is likely to remain stable over time."[35] A community's capacity for handling deviance, Erikson suggested, can be roughly estimated by counting its prison cells and hospital beds, its policemen and psychiatrists, its courts and clinics.[36]

Moynihan suggested that over the past generation the amount of deviant behavior in American society had increased beyond the level the community could afford to recognize. And so he put forward his thesis. "Accordingly we have been redefining deviancy so as to exempt much conduct previously stigmatized, and also quietly raising the 'normal' level in categories where behavior is now abnormal by any earlier standard. This redefining has evoked fierce resistance from defenders of 'old' standards and accounts for much of the present cultural war such as proclaimed by many at the 1992 Republican National Convention."[37]

He proceeded, in the best academic manner, to subdivide the concept of redefinition that he had himself just introduced. There was "altruistic redefinition," he suggested, as when President Kennedy proposed that recently discovered tranquilizers made it possible to empty the mental hospitals. There was "opportunistic redefinition," where the nominal intent only was to do good, and "the true object is to do well." He pointed out that "a growth in deviancy makes possible a transfer of resources, including prestige, to those who control the deviant population," so that the controller adopts various strategies for redefining the behavior involved, for example, family break-down, as "not all that deviant really."[38]

For his final category, "normalizing redefinition," he chose crime and violence as his examples. He quoted an article of his own: "From the wild Irish slums of the nineteenth-century Eastern seaboard to the riot-torn suburbs of Los Angeles, there is one unmistakable lesson in American history: a community that allows a large number of young men to grow up in broken families . . . asks for and gets chaos. Crime, violence, unrest, unrestrained lashing out at the whole social structure — that is not only to be expected, it is very near to inevitable."[39]

He added a litany of mayhem. Los Angeles, his friend James Q. Wilson pointed out, has a Valentine's Day massacre every weekend. Torture was treated as routine in newspaper reports. The number of deaths from firearms in Texas had recently overtaken the number of deaths from automobile accidents. One out of every three black men in the United States in their twenties was under the supervision of the criminal justice system, and there would soon be more people in the country in prison than in four-year colleges.[40]

Not for the first time in his life, Moynihan had struck a chord that resonated in many minds. On the street and in school, in politics and in marriages, behavior that had once been seen as deeply disgraceful, as dooming its perpetrators to exclusion from decent society, was now redefined as normal, or at least tolerable.

The response to this thesis was remarkable at the time, and it has spread and deepened ever since. But when President Clinton was accused of perjuring himself over his relationship with the White House intern Monica Lewinsky, suddenly everyone was repeating what Jack Newfield, in the *New York Post* on March 16, 1998, called Moynihan's era-defining phrase, "defining deviancy down."

Cardinals and editorial writers seized on the alliteration. On May 1, 1998, the *Washington Times* reported that Cardinal John O'Connor, on CNN's Evans and Novak show, had said that President Clinton could "exercise enormous leadership" on partial-birth abortion. "I think that's a perfect example of Senator Moynihan's defining deviancy down," he added. By August 6, 1998, George Will was writing of the president that "surely there are Democrats of probity who are unwilling to ratify by passivity any more of his defining political deviancy down."

It was not long before the three D's were being borrowed by plain citizens well beyond the Washington Beltway. On August 13, W. Phillip Sullins of Oxnard, California, wrote in a letter to the *Ventura County Star:* "we have seen many examples of what Sen. Daniel Patrick Moynihan called defining deviancy down over the past 40 years." Two days later and a continent away, Jeff Topps, of Washingtonville, New York, wrote to the *New York Times*, "So this is what we've come to . . . Defining deviancy down has reached its nadir." By the end of the year Moynihan could write: "This can't go on indefinitely, but defining deviancy down really has found a conceptual place in the way we think about things."[41]

When, in January 1993, Moynihan finally became chairman of the Senate Finance Committee, it was typical of the way Congress had been working that some of his first tasks involved simply getting extensions so that the government did not run out of money. He was proud of his ability to rush through an extension to the Emergency Unemployment Compensation Act, which passed the committee on February 24 and the full Senate on March 3. At the beginning of April, it was time to rush through yet another extension to the debt ceiling. On April 2, the committee passed out a bill to increase the legal limit from $4,145 trillion to $4,370 trillion. Congress, Moynihan notes, can act in a matter of hours when there is a true majority.

Next, Moynihan turned to what he called "an affair of the heart,"[42] the establishment of a World Trade Organization. He had worked on trade legislation since his days in the Department of Labor in 1962. Now there was an opportunity to modernize the international machinery for resolving trade disputes and at the same time to maintain the momentum of pressure for freer trade. The Roosevelt administration's plan for international relations in the aftermath of World War II involved not two international organizations, the World Bank and the International Monetary Fund, but three. There was to have been a World Trade Organization, to see that never again would narrow-minded legislators do to the world economy what the notorious Smoot-Hawley Tariff of 1930 had done. But in 1947, the Senate Finance Committee turned that down. Instead, the world's trade was regulated, and slowly nudged into more liberated ways, by the General Agreement on Tariffs and Trade, based in Geneva. The trading nations met and negotiated in a series of cumbersome sessions, each stretching over several years: the Tokyo Round, the Kennedy Round and finally the Uruguay Round.

Even as recently as the Kennedy Round in the 1960s, trade negotiations involved tangible things like steel, automobiles, cotton textiles. Now they dealt with imponderables such as "non-tariff barriers" (the habit of the Germans, for example, of saying that only beer brewed in their way counted as beer, or the fact that the United States had technical standards different from those of other countries), intellectual property rights, financial services like banking and insurance. Such issues were genuinely complex. Because they involved cultural attitudes and deeply ingrained national folkways, they were all the harder to resolve. Because the United States saw itself as noncompetitive with Asian and some European producers (although it was in fact emerging from that noncompetitive period), the Clinton administration had vowed to be more "aggressive" in pushing for a more level trading field.[43] That might or might not be fair, but it did not necessarily make negotiations with the recipients of this new aggressiveness any easier. The United States decided to press to replace the GATT with a new World Trade Organization. Moynihan saw himself as lucky to be in a position to put right the mistake of his own committee forty-six years earlier.

As far back as 1981, Moynihan had pointed out the dangers of the Reagan administration's willingness to run huge deficits. In September of that year, he told the Business Council, "the only way to balance the budget without damaging the nation is to increase revenues." When he became chairman of the Finance Committee, he favored a deficit-reduction package, two-thirds of it made up of tax increases, one-third from budget cuts. President Clinton had talked about a tax cut for the middle class in his election campaign, but by the time he was inaugurated it was plain that the country needed a massive reduction in the deficit, and Clinton put forward a plan for a reduction of $500 billion over five years, roughly half from tax increases, half from budget cuts. The Senate Finance Committee passed this bill by 11 votes to 9, with all the Republicans voting against, on June 1. It passed the full Senate by just 51 to 50, with Vice President Al Gore casting the deciding vote. But the decisive vote was on reconciliation — the bill that would reconcile the president's deficit-reduction ambitions with the tax bills actually passed by Congress. Working with Senator George

Mitchell of Maine, the Senate majority leader, and with House leaders, Moynihan was heavily involved in the effort to put together a bill that could pass both chambers. The whole process was agonizingly close. All spring the main fight was over the president's energy tax proposal. It was not until August 2 that Mitchell, Speaker Thomas S. Foley of Washington and Majority Leader Richard Gephardt of Missouri were able to announce a bill. It accepted the loss of the energy tax, and made up for it by increasing taxes on those earning more than $140,000 (for individuals) and $180,000 (for couples). In the end, the House voted 218 to 216 for the bill, which meant victory by a single vote; but it had been desperately close, with the votes swinging both ways until the very last moment.

The administration, and Moynihan, knew it was going to be at least as close in the Senate. They knew they needed one more vote than they had gotten the first time around, because Senator David Boren of Oklahoma had changed his position. So the key vote was that of Senator Bob Kerrey of Nebraska, a close friend of the Moynihans. Kerrey, who had won the Congressional Medal of Honor as a Navy Seal in Vietnam, had run against Clinton in the presidential primaries, and relations were strained. He had called for budget cuts in his campaign, and now that he was up for reelection in Nebraska he wanted to keep his name associated with the idea. So he came up with a strange proposal. Instead of the reconciliation bill, he wanted a special session of Congress to cut the deficit. Clinton went jogging with Kerrey. No good. The president's aide David Gergen worked on him. So did the president himself in the White House residence, out of sight of reporters.

The decisive conversation, however, seems to have been with Liz Moynihan.[44] She was busy in the barn, maybe thirty yards from the back door of the farmhouse, painting an oil drum to turn it into Thomas the Tank Engine for her small grandson, Michael Patrick.[45] She had put the phone out on a long wire and it was halfway between farm and barn that she had the crucial conversation with Bob Kerrey. She successfully made the case to him that if he defeated a bill of such immense significance to a Democratic president, one to which that president had so publicly and unreservedly committed himself, he would never be forgiven by Democrats, and could say goodbye to presidential ambitions. In the end, Kerrey agreed. The Moynihans were ecstatic. They had saved their friend from what they saw as a damaging mistake. They had saved the president's legislation. And they had vindicated the hard work of the new chairman of the Senate Finance Committee. All, however, was not to remain sweetness and light between the senator and the White House for long.

Health care reform was to be the major domestic achievement of the first Clinton administration, second in importance in the president's mind only to economic management, which he had made the centerpiece of his election campaign. His approach was characteristic. Clinton and his wife were convinced that the nation's health care system was in crisis, that escalating costs were out of control and that it was intolerable that tens of millions of Americans had either no health insurance or inadequate coverage. But as a new-style, centrist Democrat, eager to bid for the middle ground of politics, the president rejected the various plans for universal, government-provided health care, extending the principle of Medicare and Medicaid. Congressional reformers such as Senator Edward Kennedy and the two John Dingells, father and son, had made these proposals for decades. Instead, as the policy-wonk president, instinctively fascinated by the most complicated details of legislative proposals, Clinton wanted to put together a program that would meet every objection, from the politicians, the health care professionals and, so far as possible, from the trillion-dollar health care industry. And, convinced that the intellectual prowess of the Oxford- and Yale Law–educated Friends of Bill could unravel knots that defeated lesser mortals, the president and especially Hillary Rodham Clinton set out to put together a program that would be all things to all men and women. Hillary Clinton was out in front on this project to a degree unprecedented among presidential wives. And the major responsibility for this task, on which the administration's political fortunes depended to an almost alarming degree, had been entrusted not to officials of the executive branch of government, but to a Friend of Bill called Ira Magaziner, a consultant in the health care industry.

The politics of a major health care reform in 1993 were intensely complicated, more so apparently than Magaziner and Hillary Clinton understood, though the bill they produced was complex enough, and long enough, at over 1,300 pages. The health care and health insurance industry, immensely wealthy and skillfully organized to lobby against any attempt to curb its profits or its power, had succeeded for decades in blocking any serious reform. The Republican party was coming more and more under the influence of intransigent conservatives like the Republican freshmen in the House, led by Representative Newt Gingrich of Georgia. The Republicans generally were not keen to seem to be blocking reform of so sensitive an issue for their constituents. On the other hand, they were acutely sensitive to the clout of the health industry lobbies. And they were aware of the growing strength of the idea that government, as a corollary of the general feeling that it had too much power over people's lives, had no business interfering in health care.

This dilemma was particularly acute for the Republican minority leader in the Senate, Bob Dole of Kansas. Dole, it was understood, wanted to help craft a moderate but significant health care reform bill. But he was loath to do anything that might hurt his chances of being nominated as the Republican presidential candidate for 1996. The Senate majority leader, George Mitchell of Maine, was equally keen to bring out a historic health care reform bill. But he was privately doubtful about whether anything like the president's bill could be passed.

This broken field presented very delicate political problems for the new chairman of the Senate Finance Committee. Pat Moynihan's handling of the health care reform issue was enigmatic. One of those anonymous wits who were altogether too prone in the Clinton White House to say clever things to reporters was asked by *Newsweek* at the height of the health fight whether Moynihan was brilliant or a crackpot; he replied: "I have to choose?"

Certainly many people found Moynihan's course through the political obstacles puzzling. Only after the whole health care reform project had collapsed in a heap did it seem that Moynihan's handling of the issue might have been rather more rational than it appeared to many at the time. Indeed the thought occurred to some that he might have seen deeper into the political realities than his critics imagined.

One element in the situation was the relationship between Moynihan and President Clinton, and in particular that between Liz Moynihan and Hillary Rodham Clinton. Although Moynihan had been quite approving of the contribution Governor Clinton had made on welfare reform, he was on the whole unimpressed by the way the new administration went about its task. In general, Moynihan, for a loyal Democrat, has not been conspicuous for the warmth in which he has held national Democratic leaders. His view of Jimmy Carter was not flattering, and the same could be said of his view of Clinton. The relationship was not helped by the fact that another of those witty aides, asked by a reporter from *Time* magazine what the Clinton administration would do about Moynihan as chairman of the Finance Committee, said, "We'll roll right over him if we have to." It was not just that Moynihan was annoyed. The remark convinced him that the president was surrounded by people who did not understand how Washington worked, how Congress worked or the real relationship between a president and Congress.

The Clintons were keen to make up for this bad start. "We tried everything with Pat," a "top White House strategist" has said:

> We had Liz and Pat and Hillary and Bill dinners. We had Liz and Pat and Hillary and Bill movies. The president went to Moynihan's December 1993 fund-raiser and practically prostrated himself. But there was one perceived insult after another. And nothing made up for it. We even let him claim he'd picked the first Supreme Court Justice and ran the confirmation process out of his office. Nothing could defuse it. And Lawrence [O'Donnell] had minimal respect for anyone at the White House. I think he kept working Pat up.[46]

Lawrence O'Donnell, Jr., was Moynihan's chief aide on the Finance Committee. Moynihan praised him lavishly: he had, the senator said, the "combination of intellect and brawn that only someone out of the street corners of Irish Dorchester by way of Harvard College could conceive, much less carry off."[47] The intellect and the brawn were generally conceded, but not as universally admired. O'Donnell was good at mastering the complex numbers and even more complex political equations in the Finance Committee; he was less good at getting on with people. One veteran reporter who had covered Moynihan since 1973 said of O'Donnell, "He is an amazingly arrogant man."

He cut an unusual figure among Senate aides, with his motorbike and his mane of graying hair. His bluntness, laced with profanity, on the subject of major political players was also unusual on Capitol Hill, still culturally very much a Southern place, where rancorous feuds and vicious infighting are traditionally veiled in old-world courtesy and polysyllabic periphrasis. He hit a jackpot with a book and screenplay, *Deadly Force*,[48] on the strength of which he acquired a house in Los Angeles and what seemed to Washingtonians a California manner. He was married to the actress Kathryn Harrold, and in order to be with her when she was working in New York, he — most unusual of all — lived in New York and traveled down to Washington on the shuttle. This arrangement led to his departure, it being decided that a chief of staff should live in Washington.[49]

Liz Moynihan did not get on well with Hillary Clinton at first. Early in 1993, Mrs. Clinton invited her to lunch in the White House, just the two of them in the Blue Room in the residence, but the meeting was not a success. As to dinner, Hillary Rodham Clinton called up and asked both Moynihans to dinner. "There were just the four of us," Liz recalls. There was a good deal of inconsequential chatter, brought to an end by Liz saying in her blunt way to the president, "Ask him about the budget!"[50] There were, she says, no movies. She was annoyed that Mrs. Clinton told the *Newsweek* journalist Eleanor Clift that they had discussed health care. The two words were never mentioned, she insists.[51]

The Moynihans invited Mrs. Clinton to lunch in their Pennsylvania Avenue apartment, to meet Professor William J. Baumol of New York University, a friend of theirs who had propounded the theory that Moynihan called "Baumol's disease." He meant that the cost of labor-intensive social programs must inevitably rise out of control.[52] Moynihan liked to point out that the cost of Medicaid doubled in the eight years of the Reagan administration, then doubled again in the eight years of the Bush administration. "Assuming geometric progression, sir," he liked to ask visitors in his best mock-professorial manner, "what day is the day on which we reach the point when Medicaid doubles in a single day?" He would then delightedly answer that the cost would double in the course of the single day December 29, 1996, less than two months after the next presidential election. Baumol duly assured the First Lady that, while health care reform was a fine thing, "The one thing you mustn't say is that you're going to stop the rise in costs." Mrs. Clinton did not agree.

The chemistry between Mrs. Clinton and Mrs. Moynihan was still not good.[53] It was in part perhaps a matter of generations. Elizabeth Moynihan is an extremely able woman. She is a talented sculptor. She has published a number of books about Mughal India. She has made study trips all over central Asia, and has made significant discoveries in Mughal history. She has been awarded a doctorate for her work by New York University. At the same time, she has run four of the most successful Senate campaigns in history, with a minimum of fuss and expense. But she did not go to college. Middle-class women of her background in her generation did not usually do so. Mrs. Clinton, a generation younger, exudes the new, confident feminism of the sort of women who took it for granted that they would go to college, go on to graduate school and that their law degrees would guarantee them financial rewards and career opportunities. It was built into their different backgrounds that Mrs. Clinton would underestimate Mrs. Moynihan, and Mrs. Moynihan would think that Mrs. Clinton was patronizing her. Later, the atmosphere changed somewhat. But in 1993 and 1994, Liz Moynihan was deeply suspicious of the First Lady.

Another anecdote illustrates the yawning gap between their ways of thinking.[54] When she knew she was going to India, Hillary Clinton asked Liz Moynihan whom she should see. Liz said that whatever else she did, she must go and see her friend Ela Bhatt, a friend of Liz's who has done remarkable work with poor women in Ahmedabad. The meeting was arranged, and Mrs. Bhatt formally invited Mrs. Clinton, who formally accepted. For a woman struggling to operate a program in an Indian city, this opportunity was clearly unique. But then Mrs. Clinton started to back off. She wanted to go to see the glamorous Benazir Bhutto in Islamabad, the capital of Pakistan, instead. It was all about the United Nations conference on women in Beijing, Liz suspected. "She wanted to pose as an expert on Third World women." In the end, Mrs. Clinton did go to Ahmedabad, and sent a note to Liz saying it was the best part of the trip. But by then the damage had been done.

All spring and summer of the Clinton administration's first year in office, Ira Magaziner and his armies of dedicated policy wonks, whipped on by Mrs. Clinton, labored over the giant health care reform bill. But it wasn't until the fall that the political battle began to heat up. In September, the Health Insurance Association of America launched its deadly "Harry and Louise" ad campaign. A pleasant couple, average Americans, as anyone could see, played by Harry Johnson and Louise Caire Clark, whose real first names found their way into the script, debated health insurance.

"The government may force us to pick from a few health care plans designed by government bureaucrats," said the announcer.

"Having choices we don't like is no choice at all," says Louise.

"They choose," says Harry.

"We lose," says Louise.

The campaign was deadly — so much so that the White House panicked. Mrs. Clinton launched a violent diatribe over which the *New York Times* ran the headline "Hillary Clinton Accuses Insurers of Lying about Health Proposal."[55]

The president was due to present his plan in a major address on September 21, though a 239-page draft was of course widely leaked for several days before his speech to a joint session of Congress. On September 19, to everyone's surprise and to the White House's dismay, Moynihan went on his favorite talk show, *Meet the Press,* and launched into a contemptuous attack on the legislation. He called the Clinton administration's plan to finance its health care reform a "fantasy," and said he preferred the alternative proposed by the Republican congressional leadership. And he said the administration's belief that it could slow the projected rate of growth in the cost of Medicare by one-half after years of double-digit growth "is to have lost touch with reality." His charges were all the more damaging because in fact the administration was not yet in a position to give its own detailed figures; it would be months before the Office of Management and Budget could come up with defensible estimates.

The Clintons planned to raise $105 billion of the estimated $700 billion cost of their proposals over five years by raising taxes on tobacco. At the beginning of November, Moynihan upped the ante again by proposing a steep increase in the taxation of handgun ammunition, and hinted that he would in effect hold the Clinton health care reform bill hostage unless it included a higher ammunition tax. For good measure, he suggested a 10,000 percent tax increase on particularly destructive types of ammunition.

He reckoned that this tax might raise $200 million, but he did not see it as a revenue-raising measure so much as an attempt to drive the most murderous weapons off the streets. The effect of this idea might be to entangle the Clinton proposals in the congressional thickets of the gun lobby. But to be fair, Moynihan had long put considerable effort into a personal campaign against handguns and especially so-called "cop-killer" ammunition. "Guns don't kill people," was one of his mantras, "bullets do." When the former Finance Chairman Lloyd Bentsen came before the committee, Moynihan made the point that, to judge by the evening television news, one of the major health care problems facing the country was gunshot wounds. He was particularly outraged by advertisements for a type of hollow-tipped "dum-dum" ammunition called "Black Talon." Angrily, he read out an advertisement claiming that it expanded "to expose razor-sharp reinforced jacket petals" that "cut tissues in the wake of the penetrating core . . . very nasty; very effective; a real improvement in handgun ammo."

Moynihan also used the hearings to develop his case that the welfare crisis and the soaring rate of illegitimacy constituted a far more serious health care emergency than the lack of coverage and rising costs that inspired the Clinton proposals. He began the hearing by noting that 30 percent of all current births now were to unmarried women, 71 percent in Detroit, 66 percent in Washington and 45.2 percent in New York. What did all of this have to do with health care reform, he was asked by reporter Adam Clymer of the *New York Times* after the first day's hearing. "I don't want another vast social program," Moynihan replied, "that makes no difference to the fact that our cities are becoming unlivable."

He was using the hearings not only to test the Clinton administration's plans for health care reform, but also to draw attention to a number of his own long-term concerns. One was handguns and cop-killer bullets in particular. Another, of course, was welfare and the need for reform of the system. More broadly, he wanted to make his point that crime, illegitimacy and health care itself were all parts of a larger social crisis.

In January, he went on the attack even more aggressively. At a lunch with the editorial writers of the *New York Post,* Moynihan dismissed the administration's whole health care reform plan as "boob bait for bubbas,"[56] populist stuff for the populist *Post,* with a concession to New York contempt for Arkansas thrown in. He acknowledged he ought never to have said it.[57] More seriously, a few days later, he went on *Meet the Press* again. Asked by the *Washington Post*'s veteran political writer David Broder what he meant by his "boob bait" remark, he answered, "We don't have a health care crisis in this country. We do have a welfare crisis."[58] Moynihan explained that he thought Clinton was reneging on his campaign promise to reform welfare, and hinted that he might hold the health care bill hostage to make the president and in particular the White House staff take welfare more seriously.[59]

That was not all. In that same January 9 *Meet the Press* appearance, Moynihan criticized the president for dragging his feet on Bosnia. He urged him to appoint an independent counsel and make his papers relating to the Whitewater scandal public. He sounded altogether unsympathetic to the administration's projects and priorities. Moynihan was annoyed by the way the administration had underrated him and his ideas. But he had also looked ahead and was taking a different view of the political realities.

Five congressional committees had jurisdiction over the health care issue, and there were more than half a dozen different positions on it, several of them in the Senate and even within the Finance Committee alone. Senator Kennedy, whose Labor and Human Resources Committee was also holding hearings on health care, and who had himself three times attempted to introduce national health insurance, wanted more, not less government involvement in health care than did the Clintons. His influential chief aide, Nick Littlefield, had something close to contempt for Moynihan's lack of commitment to the issue. On the Finance Committee, Senator Jay Rockefeller, Democrat of West Virginia, was a strong ally of the Clintons. Senator Dole was caught between his general wish to see Congress tackle the escalating costs and inadequate coverage of the existing health care system, and his need to keep conservative backing for his presidential ambitions. Republican Senator John Chafee of Rhode Island was generally a close ally of Moynihan's, but he did not share Moynihan's dismissive attitude to the need for health care. A bipartisan group of senators led by John Breaux of Louisiana favored a compromise bill. And even this list by no means exhausts the complexities of the situation. The Democratic leadership, represented by Senator George Mitchell of Maine, the Democratic majority leader in the Senate and his anointed successor, Senator Tom Daschle of South Dakota, were impatient with Moynihan. They were keen to push ahead and get a bill passed that would consolidate the Democrats' claim to have made health care their issue over the decades.

There were an infinity of different positions on the details and technicalities of the various rival bills that were being canvassed. But one major strategic disagreement divided the Democrats. Could a health care bill be passed without substantial bipartisan support? George Mitchell, like the administration, acknowledged that some Republican votes would be needed. But Moynihan thought that the Republicans as a group would oppose anything that the Democrats could accept, even to the extent of filibustering it. If that was so, Moynihan calculated, then the sooner Democrats worked with moderate Republicans to put together a bill that could win sixty votes and so defeat a filibuster, the better. The Clintons, Kennedy and the Democratic leadership all thought it was folly to start to compromise before battle was joined. Yet Moynihan thought that was the only hope of getting a bill. And of course he was intent on getting as many other good things as possible, among them a ban on cop-killer bullets and a speedup of welfare reform, out of the advantage his position as Finance Committee chairman gave him.

There was even a suggestion in the press in early February, attributed to White House sources, that he and Senator Kennedy had joined up to push the White House into ignoring the representations of the State Department and of its own ambassador in London, Raymond Seitz, in order to give a visa to Gerry Adams, leader of Sinn Féin, the political wing of the Irish Republican Army. That was totally to misunderstand Moynihan's position on the Northern Ireland issue. However much he might understand the historic case for Irish nationalism, he had no sympathy for the IRA, and a good deal for the British government, pressed by terrorism. He might be Irish, he let it be known, but he was not that Irish. His aide Lawrence O'Donnell was emphatic. "The Senator was intemperate enough to say he may hold health care reform hostage for welfare reform this year," he was quoted as saying, "but he is not going to hold either one hostage for Gerry Adams."

In early March, the ranking Republican on the Finance Committee, John Chafee, welcomed his colleagues to Annapolis, where they tried to hammer out a common Republican position, something that Chafee, as a realist, knew would be impossible. The sticking point for Bob Dole, as for many of his party colleagues, was the idea of a "mandate." Even to ask every citizen to be responsible for arranging his or her own health insurance, as every driver is mandated to buy auto insurance, stuck in many Republicans' craws as an unwarrantable interference with personal freedom. The idea of employers being mandated to arrange coverage for their employees was even more unwelcome.

These divisions were even more apparent when the whole Finance Committee went into "retreat" in Leesburg, Virginia, on April 15. It was obvious that the Democrats were at least as badly divided as the Republicans, and that the chairman himself was, to say the least, unenthusiastic about legislation of the kind the president was proposing. Senator Mitchell openly challenged Moynihan's commitment to getting out a bill. Back in Washington, the markup began behind closed doors, while Moynihan continued to hold hearings.

One day in May, there was the hint of a dramatic solution. As the hearing broke up, Bob Dole passed Moynihan a note. The chairman took it out of sight of the public, the lobbyists and the reporters, who were leaving the room, and opened it.

"Is it time for the Moynihan-Dole bill?" he read.

This was the moment Moynihan had been waiting for.[60] All along, he had envisioned a bipartisan proposal that would be certain of reaching the 60 votes needed to break a filibuster. Now Dole seemed to be justifying that assessment. The probable Republican presidential candidate had just offered him the chance of sending a Democratic president into the race with a bill he could campaign on. More immediately, Dole offered Moynihan the chance of taking back control of his own committee. He was so excited that after first handing the note to Lawrence O'Donnell, he saw its historic potentialities and asked O'Donnell to hand it back.

That was, however, the high-water mark of Dole's willingness to compromise on health care reform. He was coming under increasing pressure from the Republican Right, and by early June he threatened to kill any bill with an employer mandate in it. In early June, Senator Kennedy's Labor Committee voted out a bill, and numerous senators of every persuasion were running around trying with varying degrees of desperation to find a compromise. On June 14, Moynihan and Senator Bob Packwood went to see the president. Packwood was blunt, both with Clinton and with the reporters who clustered around when they emerged from the White House. "At the moment," he said, "all plans are dead. There is not a majority for any single plan."[61] Moynihan agreed but was more tactful, promising to work on a bipartisan basis to write legislation that would provide universal coverage."[62]

In mid-June, as rumors circulated about the contents of the Moynihan bill, the *New York Times,* in an editorial, gave the chairman the benefit of a good deal of doubt.[63] From a policy point of view, the newspaper conceded, the Moynihan bill might be an unconvincing compromise. But politically it looked much better. "Viewed as a health care plan, the bill disappoints . . . In a word, odd. . . . But Mr. Moynihan was playing politics, not health economics. And his touch appears deft. He offered a bill that, despite differences, borrows heavily from the Clinton plan because he knew it would fail — proving once and for all that the President's plan cannot win and that horse-trading is essential."

In the last week of June, Dole came out with a bill of his own, and

Moynihan finally produced his bill. It was indeed an odd and in some respects unconvincing text. He introduced it with the Hippocratic oath: *"Primum non nocere,"* first, do no harm. It borrowed elements from many proposals, especially from the president's, as well as some pet ideas of his own. Insurance would be mandated only as a last resort, where a set of deadlines had passed. Guns and ammunition, as well as tobacco and alcohol, would be taxed to provide part of the cost of something less than universal coverage. And the bill provided ample funding for medical research. Cold-eyed reporters noted that much of this research was to take place in New York State.

> He is often accused of disdaining pork, but he is larding his bill with $40 billion in extra help for the crown jewels of New York's and the nation's medical establishment — academic medical centers — and revising the Federal matching formula for Medicaid to help New York in a way that would hurt so many other states it has virtually no chance of passing. Whatever the substantive effect of the draft, the political effect was to make Mr. Moynihan, more than ever, the man to see."[64]

"The one thing this plan does is belie the claim that Pat Moynihan is not a master politician," said Representative Charles E. Schumer,[65] a Brooklyn Democrat, now a senator, no political slouch himself.

Moynihan's performance puzzled some, infuriated others, left others again with the uneasy feeling — by no means incompatible with fury — that he might, just possibly, have been a little bit right all along.

Somewhere between puzzlement and fury was Robin Toner of the *New York Times.*[66] "Privately," she wrote,

> some who are committed to health care restructuring wonder why Mr. Moynihan took so many of his doubts and second thoughts about the Clinton health initiative to the Sunday morning talk shows. Some wonder why he did not use his time to make a more forceful case for reform and universal coverage in general . . . Mr. Moynihan's critics wonder whether he did not cede too much power to the Republicans, waiting for a bipartisan agreement while the Senate Republicans, as a group, moved further and further right.

By July, the president himself, in a speech in Boston, admitted that his bill was in dire trouble. In August, Moynihan infuriated the majority leader, George Mitchell, by suggesting publicly on CBS's *Face the Nation* that the Senate ought to go home and come back after Labor

Day to see if a health care bill could be hammered out against the deadline pressure of the midterm elections.

What no one understood, least of all Moynihan himself, was that those elections would utterly transform the face of American politics. Campaigning for his conservative "Contract with America," Newt Gingrich of Georgia stormed back to Washington at the head of a devout brigade of ideological conservatives.

In retrospect, it looks as if Gingrich himself misunderstood the cause of his own success. He and his allies interpreted their victory as the final conquest of the nation by the conservative ideas that had first triumphed under Ronald Reagan in 1980; indeed many of them thought they were leapfrogging Reagan into a new and purer era of conservative victory.

The reality was that for every convert to pure ideological conservatism, there were hundreds who were tired of endless stories about Washington shenanigans. Some comparatively trivial allegations about congressmen helping themselves to cheap loans from the so-called congressional bank were the last straw that broke the camel's back. Years of sordid stories about dishonest congressmen, drunken congressmen, lecherous congressmen, had persuaded half the country that Washington inside the Beltway was a way station on the road from Sodom to Babylon. When the dust had settled, it was clear that Gingrich and his friends had miscalculated. Gingrich's arrogance and the House Republican freshmen's habit of speaking only to the converted ditched Bob Dole's campaign for the presidency in 1996, and sent Bill Clinton back to the White House. Further efforts by the conservative enthusiasts to disgrace him led to troubles for him and for them. But in the fall of 1994, it was clear that all assumptions must be reassessed, and all bets were off.

To Moynihan himself, "the congressional debacle of 1994 came as a complete surprise."[67] In retrospect, it is plain that Bill and Hillary Clinton utterly misunderstood the situation. Looking about them in early 1992 for a policy banner with which to rally moderate Democrats, Reagan Democrats and Middle America generally, they had decided to campaign on those economic issues that George Bush had underestimated and misunderstood as well. Once in the White House, they felt the need for some cause less self-interested than "it's the economy, stupid." In the pure spirit of policy wonkery, with little or no sense of the politics of the issue, or the politics of the time, they allowed their experts to give birth to a bill that was monstrous. It was too long to sell, too technical to understand and too plump with the jargon of the insurance industry to inspire anyone.

In theory, and in the eyes of idealists, Pat Moynihan, newly arrived as chairman of the Finance Committee, was the man to broker a bill that could marry Ira Magaziner's ponderous expertise with the traditional populist ideals of the Democratic party's base in labor, and so appeal to a new constituency of middle-class Americans, aghast at the rising cost of health care. In practice, that was not what Americans wanted, and the political constellations were totally in the wrong aspect. The Democrats controlled the Finance Committee only by 11 votes to 9, and each faction was divided. It was not only that the key Republican player, Bob Dole, was taking his eyes off the health care ball because he had to protect his campaign from sniping from the Right. The simple truth was that Moynihan didn't like the White House bill, didn't control his own committee and had to adopt a strategy of damage limitation, for health care legislation, for the Democrats and for himself. *Primum non nocere*, indeed. First and foremost he had to emerge from the barbed wire with no serious wounds.

There was something more. Health care was not Pat Moynihan's issue. He admitted that at the beginning of the hearings he knew little about it. The hearings were partly a graduate seminar for a chairman who had so often given seminars to his own staff on those issues he had made his own. He suspected the Clintons of pulling health care out as a "crisis" for the sake of the political capital that could be made by solving it. He really was more concerned with other issues — welfare, social security, crime, the governance of society, and, yes, race — than with the intricacies of this health care insurance plan or that. And now, back in New York, he was confronted once again with the racial politics that had twice before been his nemesis.

Moynihan gradually woke up to the fact that he would have to deal with a more or less serious challenge from Al Sharpton. Politically and in every other way, both Pat and Liz Moynihan would have loved to ignore the man. Moynihan made a point of calling him the Reverend *Alfred* Sharpton; it made him sound less genuine as a tribune of the people. But in 1994, it was no longer possible to deny that the man was a serious, if limited, political threat. At the very least, there was the possibility that he would strip away some of those African American voters who had contributed substantially to Moynihan's huge majorities in the past.

In 1992, Sharpton, already known as a street leader and demagogue in black neighborhoods, decided to run for the Senate, He emerged only third out of four in the Democratic primary. In July 1994, Sharpton announced that he would run against Moynihan again. "People are not hearing anything but theories and 'I wish it was 50 years ago' from the Senator," he told Gabe Pressman, on Channel 4, WNBC-TV's *News Forum*. "People should vote their interests," Sharpton said, "and Mr. Moynihan has not addressed those."

Sharpton announced that he had received far more than the fifteen thousand signatures required by state law to get on the ballot for the September 13 primary, and on July 15 Senator Moynihan's campaign announced that he would not challenge Sharpton's figuring. Sharpton also asserted that his support went far outside the boundaries of the African American community. Whether or not this claim had much substance, it was clear Sharpton now posed a more serious threat than in the two years previously. He collected endorsements from a number of black and Hispanic politicians. Moynihan declined the challenge and stayed for the most part in Washington, campaigning intensively only for the last week or two before the election. He ran brief television spots about his accomplishments while Sharpton ranged the streets of black and Hispanic neighborhoods, denouncing Moynihan for his alleged indifference to welfare mothers. Moynihan insisted that the Democratic state convention not give Sharpton the 25 percent of its votes that would have been needed to put Sharpton on the ballot, and it did not.

Annoying Sharpton might be, and stronger than in the past. But Moynihan survived the Democratic primary easily enough and went into a one-sided contest in the general election with Bernadette Castro, a fifty-year-old former executive of the family convertible-sofa business and a formidable fund-raiser for conservative Republican candidates. Financially, the candidates were well matched. Ms. Castro raised about $500,000 and planned to spend about $1.2 million of her own money. She called herself a "Christine Todd Whitman Republican," after the moderate governor of New Jersey, and said she supported a woman's right to abortion and Medicaid financing for poor women. The Moynihan campaign called the senator "New York's Moynihan." Castro, attempting to cash in on the recurrent anti-Washington feeling, spent $1 million on television advertisements depicting her opponent as "Washington's Moynihan."

The result, while not as overwhelming a victory for Moynihan as in 1988 or even in 1982, was decisive enough. A last-minute Republican surge swelled Castro's vote, as part of the national trend that gave control of Congress to the Republicans, and Moynihan's vote was sharply reduced. He carried New York City easily, with 75 percent of the vote to Castro's 21 percent, but in the suburbs he won only by 49 percent to 48 percent, and the two candidates split the upstate vote evenly. Overall, Moynihan won by 55 percent to 42 percent.

15

The Legislator as Magnifico

> Today Saint Patrick is 1,612 years old, and Senator Pat is
> 70 years old. Saint Pat was, perhaps, the Church's greatest
> missionary; after all, he subdued the Irish. Senator Pat is
> also a missionary, and he has brought to his task many of
> the same qualities as his illustrious predecessor . . .
>
> — James Q. Wilson, after-dinner remarks at the conclusion
> of the Moynihan Seminar and Celebration, Woodrow
> Wilson Center, March 17, 1997

O N MARCH 16, 1997, the senior senator from New York received a somewhat puzzling letter from the vice president of
the United States. "Daniel," it began, unpromisingly, "I was
very pleased to learn about the recent birth of your twins."[1]

On it plunged. "Tipper joins me in sending our warmest con-
gratulations and best wishes to you. We know that everyone close to
you shares the excitement of the new additions to your family." It
ended with the vice president's expression of his hopes for "a happy
and successful life for you and your new babies." Red faces for Al
Gore, champion within the Clinton administration of technological
innovation and administrative efficiency, and for those on his staff
who failed to catch this early April Fool as it floated out of the com-
puterized good will bank. For what the senator was celebrating that
March 16 was not the arrival of twins — it was, after all, almost forty
years since the birth of the Moynihans' last child — but that biblical
milestone, his seventieth birthday.

A year later, Robert Byrd of West Virginia, the man who was
perhaps, in the opinion of their brethren, Moynihan's chief rival in
the Senate for eloquence and personal authority, found words for a

more appropriate tribute from the greatest writers of English poetry and English prose, respectively.[2] From Shakespeare's *Henry VI,* he quoted, "He was a scholar, and a ripe and good one, exceeding wise, fair-spoken and persuading." And from Edmund Burke, he drew the observation that "a king may make a nobleman, but he cannot make a gentleman." Elections, Senator Byrd went on, can make a senator, but they can never make a gentleman. In an age of road rage, rap music and "television that makes a man blush while changing channels," there were few gentlemen to point to, but Senator Moynihan was one, and "an intellectual leader, a sage and a prophet for the Senate and for the Nation" into the bargain.

On St. Patrick's Day, the day after his seventieth birthday, Moynihan's friends gathered for a daylong seminar and celebration at the Woodrow Wilson Center and a dinner in the red sandstone Gothic castle of the Smithsonian Institution on the Washington Mall. The organizer was Charles Blitzer, the Yale historian who had been one of the Moynihans' closest friends since 1970, when they worked together to set up the center, of which Blitzer was the director. (Blitzer, who died early in 1999, owned a home on the Moynihans' property in upstate New York.) The day was devoted to a dozen papers about different aspects of Moynihan's interests and achievements by friends and colleagues from every phase and stage of his life. They included academics such as Blitzer, Seymour Martin Lipset, Nathan Glazer and Michael Barone; his Senate colleague Bill Bradley of New Jersey; former staffers such as Richard K. Eaton of the New York law firm Stroock, Stroock and Lavan, Suzanne Garment of the American Enterprise Institute, Stephen Hess of the Brookings Institution, Robert A. Peck, now head of the federal government's Public Buildings Service and Tim Russert of NBC's *Meet the Press;* former students and graduate teaching assistants such as the epidemiologist Nicholas Eberstadt and Robert Katzmann, now a federal judge. The gathering was an impressive roster of people of talent and influence who had been affected by Moynihan in their careers, and who formed a sort of intellectual praetorian guard to defend his ideas and protect him from his enemies to the left and right.[3]

Their tributes came from many directions and many disciplines; they extolled many dimensions of the senator's work and many stages of his life. Most succinctly, Charles Blitzer focused on three characteristics that have been emphasized again and again in this book. First was Moynihan's "almost uncanny ability to fix upon issues that are not yet widely noticed or discussed," like the crises in the African American family and in welfare, and many more. Second, he underlined Moynihan's consistency. While he was often criticized for having abandoned or betrayed one cause or another, Blitzer maintained that Moynihan had always in his long career sought the best data. If they supported his position, he would eloquently proclaim the fact; but if the data were insufficient he would counsel caution; and if the data did not support his previous belief, he would follow the data. And the third and most unappreciated characteristic of his way of thinking was his ability "to transform the very nature of a familiar, even somewhat shopworn debate by looking at a problem in a new way."

Each of these points made by Blitzer was illustrated in other papers read at the seminar. Nicholas Eberstadt, for example, took Blitzer's third point further by examining Moynihan's record as a student of epidemiology. The focus of this branch of public health and medical studies is not on individuals but on groups. Eberstadt showed how Moynihan's approach to three issues of continuing interest since his days in Albany — traffic safety, crime and drugs — had in each case been shaped by the insights and techniques of epidemiology. But he also quoted Moynihan's warning: "Epidemiologists have powerful insights that can contribute to lessening the medical trauma, but they must be wary of normalizing the social pathology that leads to such trauma."[4]

Nathan Glazer traced the way Moynihan's conviction of the importance of ethnicity had evolved through his career since they co-wrote *Beyond the Melting Pot*. He had moved from an interest in the role of ethnic traditions and rivalry in domestic politics, to the discovery of the stubborn resistance of ethnic sentiment inside the totalitarian communist regimes, to his more recent emphasis on the primacy of ethnicity as a cause of conflict in the world since the fall of the Soviet Union. Glazer pointed out that his coauthor, as a practicing politician, had chosen in recent years to avoid domestic ethnic divisions, and to make his main contribution in the study of the problems raised by ethnicity in international relations. "What Pat has done has been to leave aside the most controversial issues of race as a legislator, such as affirmative action for civil rights, and has attempted rather to heal our division through the advocacy of social policies targeted to categories defined by misfortune, not by race or ethnicity."[5]

That other formidable social scientist, Seymour Martin Lipset, addressed himself to the first of Blitzer's characteristics, Moynihan's "almost uncanny" prescience. He examined how Moynihan came to find himself isolated in his thinking about each of the great public policy issues of his life, starting with "the Negro Family," then the Family Assistance Plan and the Clinton health care reform bill, but also in declining to join his neoconservative friends in moving further to the Right. He suggested that the reason Moynihan had proved so prescient in each of these crises of his intellectual and political career was because he knew from the start that there is no first cause, either in politics or in social science. Then Lipset corrected himself. For Moynihan, the first cause was the family.

> Pat knew about the family all along. And those who do not know about it, whether they are liberals or conservatives, whether they think genes determine where people wind up or do not believe genes have much effect on intelligence or learning, are wrong. What Pat teaches is that not only are there no utopias, there are no solutions, not in the state or in the completely uncontrolled market. There are only approximations, only the continuing struggle for decency, for morality, for equality of opportunity and for respect.[6]

Stephen Hess, Moynihan's deputy in the Nixon White House, described the mixture of high ambition and low cunning that made his boss such an effective operator in the federal bureaucracy under Kennedy, Johnson and Nixon. He was never an executive in the sense of a manager. Rather, Hess wrote, Moynihan is a man of political ideas. "Some are his own, some he borrows, some are cosmic, others more modest"; he was "our generation's greatest spotter of ideas that might make our society somehow better." Bill Bradley of New Jersey, one of Moynihan's closest friends in the Senate, defined the New Yorker's strategy in the simplest terms: "He reached across the aisle. He would place himself in the center, where power rested." Most eloquent of all, Michael Barone, of the *Reader's Digest* and coauthor of the invaluable *Almanac of American Politics*, paid Moynihan the supreme tribute. Moynihan's career, he wrote, was the disciplined product of an original thinker whose ideas dazzle and a political operator whose skills are hidden like strong walls overpainted with a Renaissance fresco. He was, said Barone, "the nation's best thinker among politicians since Lincoln, and its best politician among thinkers since Jefferson."

High praise, where until a few short years before praise of any kind was rare enough. Suddenly, near the midpoint of his fourth term in the Senate, Moynihan found himself the focus of that special kind of admiration that overcomes disagreement and even occasional exasperation. Colleagues, who not only did not understand half of what he was saying and would have disagreed profoundly if they had seen where his arguments were headed, nevertheless seemed to feel a sense of pride that such a learned and eloquent legislator was among them. To walk through the corridors of the Capitol with him was to see that he had acquired something more than mere celebrity, something close to affection. Biological age and longevity in the Senate had something to do with it, but there was more to it than that. The gentleman from New York had become a legend, a monument, a Grand Old Man.

Once when I was interviewing one of Moynihan's former aides, a neoconservative who has moved in a very different direction from Moynihan's path, but who retains great respect for his former boss, he suddenly said, "You know, it's a pretty damn good life in the Senate. You have long vacations. You stay in embassies when you travel. You have a staff of bright young people working for you."

It is indeed a good life. At the most basic level, senators are not in need. It is true that many of them, as lawyers, could make more money outside the Senate than in it. But senators do earn $160,000 a year, which is not poverty, even in late-twentieth-century Washington. Both Pat and Liz Moynihan sometimes talk as if penury stared them in the face, and it is true that they are not rich people as Washington, let alone New York or Los Angeles, counts rich. But in the present a senator can count on numerous pleasures and perquisites, and in the future a four-term senator who has been in the government service, more on than off, for over a third of a century, can expect a pension of well into six figures. And late in 1998, Moynihan learned that he had been given the Heinz Prize, carrying with it a cash award of $250,000. That meant, he said, a trust fund for Michael Patrick and Zora, his two grandchildren.

Indeed, to spend time with the senior senator from New York is to observe the progress of the legislator as magnifico. Any member of the United States Senate is treated with great respect. Above all, senators are helped through the long days and demanding schedules of contemporary politics with generous quantities of that scarcest of commodities in the modern world: attentive and skilled personal service. The size of senatorial staffs varies according to a formula that is proportionate to the population of the state. In addition, a senior senator controls staff related to his committee assignments. The staff for Senator Moynihan's personal office, defined as "noncommittee" staff, has remained constant at about fifty full-time people for the last ten years or so.[7] His total annual personal office budget comes to roughly $2.6 million, of which about $2.3 million is for payroll. Rent, heat, employee benefits, printing and other expenses are defrayed directly by the Senate. But in addition, the senator has full control over the minority staff of the Finance Committee. There are seventeen of them, and the total annual budget under this head comes to an additional $750,000, so that the Moynihan staff comes to about sixty-seven people, and the operating budget, not counting costs paid by the Senate directly, is $3.375 million.[8]

Moynihan no longer drives. His habit of paying more attention to conversation than to the traffic alarmed Liz and she finally persuaded her husband to give up the wheel. Instead, an aide drives him around Washington. A senator, like the CEO of a major corporation, is spared many of the irritating details of daily life and travel. If he goes abroad, he can not only stay in embassies if he wants to; he can fly on government planes in many circumstances if he is on official business. The best tables in restaurants and special attention from maitre d's are minor lubricants of the legislative day.

In his later years in the Senate, Moynihan traveled a great deal. Peter Galbraith was on the staff of the Senate Foreign Relations Committee and undertook the role of Moynihan's dragoman on a series of three-week foreign trips.[9] In February 1989, Galbraith and Moynihan went together to India and Pakistan, where Benazir Bhutto, a friend of Galbraith's at Oxford and Harvard, had just become prime minister. In January 1990, they visited Morocco and Egypt before the senator went on to visit Israel alone. In November 1992, they went together to Sarajevo (see Chapter 14).

Galbraith's Moynihan imitation is almost as practiced as Tim Russert's. One of his more memorable turns is a description of Moynihan as a member of a high-powered congressional delegation to the king of Saudi Arabia's palace at Riyadh in September 1990. The senior senator from New York gave his dozen or so colleagues, including Chairman Claiborne Pell of the Foreign Relations Committee and Congressmen Richard Gephardt and Robert Michel, the benefits of his considerable architectural knowledge. Moynihan pointed out those parts of the royal palace that were inspired respectively by Versailles, Buckingham Palace or the great monuments of the Islamic world, a roof copied from Dulles Airport or a wall in the Moroccan manner. Finally, as the legislators were ushered into the throne room itself, they were confronted with a painting, banal at best, of a Swiss mountain scene, featuring a mountaineer in lederhosen blowing into an alpenhorn. "I'm not a wealthy man," pronounced the senator in a voice that would itself have carried across a sizeable Alpine valley, "but now I can tell my friends I've got one painting in my living room better than anything the king of Saudi Arabia has."

The Moynihans do not own an apartment in New York; instead, thanks to the proprietor, a suite is kept available for them at the Hotel Carlyle in the most elegant neighborhood of Manhattan's Upper East Side. Besides his suite of offices in the Russell Senate Office Building in Washington and his "hideaway" room in the Capitol itself, Moynihan has offices, staffed by Senate employees, in three locations in New York State: a staff of ten in Manhattan, including several case officers; two in Buffalo; and two in Oneonta, where the senator's office exists not to keep an ear to the ground on political opinion, but to service Moynihan when he's at the farm. Every day when they are in residence there, an aide drives over to Pindars Corners, bringing a large pile of mail, including publications of every kind.

A senator like Moynihan, who insists on being well informed and who speaks often and in great detail on a number of different subjects, can draw on the superb resources of the Congressional Research Service, the Library of Congress and the Congressional Budget Office, as well as on his own and his committees' staff. Moynihan himself is no slave to modern technology. He types many of his own speeches, articles and letters on an elderly Smith-Corona electric typewriter, which perches on a small table close to his desk in his Senate office. (Another similar machine lives in the schoolhouse at Pindars Corners.) It was not until late in 1998 that his staff persuaded first his wife, then him, to use e-mail. But Senate offices have access to the latest in information technology, and Moynihan's staff are in a position to find out the most obscure information on a vast range of subjects in a remarkably short time. He is quite likely to ask staffers to come up with anything from government data on social problems to public health and welfare statistics to literary references. Moynihan has an unusually retentive and accurate memory, but he also likes to check his references like a scholar. He reads prodigiously, and the machinery of his office keeps him supplied with a rich diet of information and comment.

His main office is on the fourth floor of the Senate office building, a Beaux Arts structure with echoing marble corridors and overcrowded, high-ceilinged offices. His own room is a museum, filled with books and personal objects. There is a fireplace, an Early American desk, two wing chairs and a red carpet. It is decorated with paintings on loan from the Smithsonian's National Museum of American Art. Its single most noticeable feature is a more than life-size statue of a Revolutionary War soldier by his son Tim. (Timothy P. Moynihan has exhibited life-size sculptured caricatures of American presidents at the Vorpal Gallery in New York and in San Francisco.) Because of his seniority — by the later years of his fourth term, he was seventeenth in length of service in the Senate — Moynihan also had the right to a small hideaway office in the Capitol itself. Bookshelves line one wall, and there is room for a comfortable sofa and the senator's easy chair. Here, after the sun has sunk below the yardarm, he entertains guests between roll call votes with Tio Pepe dry sherry from a small fridge in the bathroom, where once it might have been hard liquor. The office is decorated with hundreds of books, a few good nineteenth-century oil paintings and prints, and a few mementoes, such as a street sign from East Berlin. A closed-circuit TV screen keeps him in touch with what is happening in the chamber, just as it does in his main office.

The Senate is for Pat Moynihan what the White House was for Theodore Roosevelt: a bully pulpit. Increasingly, in his fourth term, Moynihan used it as just that. The Democrats had lost control of the Senate, and instead of being chairman of the Environment and Public Works and Finance committees, he found himself in the comparatively powerless role of ranking minority member. More and more, he used his lofty perch in the Senate, not for detailed legislative negotiation, but as a watchtower from which he could fulfill what Walter Bagehot, the nineteenth-century editor of *The Economist,* said were the duties of a constitutional monarch: to warn, to encourage and to advise. Specifically, he used the prestige and the visibility of the office to draw the attention of members of Congress, and of those sectors of the wider public who focus on the public agenda, to issues which he thought needed to be addressed. Sometimes he did this with a speech in the Senate chamber. More often, he used a television talk show, a television interview or an op-ed piece in the *New York*

Times or elsewhere. But the orchestral forces from which he could draw the right combination of instrumentation to move the public to scorn or rage, to promote a complicated idea or demolish what struck him as false reasoning grew richer as the years of experience (and frustration) went on. To sell the idea that the consumer price index ought to be revised, for example, he set up what was in effect a private commission of inquiry. To attack what he saw as the excessive cult of secrecy in Washington, as we shall see, he used a congressional ad hoc committee that he himself contrived to have established. For other issues, he took advantage of the steady stream of invitations to speak at every kind of conference, college commencement or other gathering. At times, he would simply write an article and send it to whatever he thought was the most suitable and effective outlet, most often the op-ed page editor of the *Washington Post* (his old friend Meg Greenfield in her lifetime) or of the *New York Times* (Howell Raines, with whom he was also on friendly terms). On one memorable occasion, he used the *New York Review of Books,* to which he sent his diatribe against welfare reform, "Congress Builds a Coffin."

By the fourth term, he had refined his technique, like that of the maestro of a great symphony orchestra, now bringing out the emotional tones of the oboes, now calling forth intimidating volumes of sound from massed strings, or summoning up the strident brass of moral indignation. More than any other senator in modern times, he relied for his effects not so much on political manipulation of his senatorial brethren — though he took care to cultivate courteous, not to say courtly relations with them — as on commanding attention for his ideas in a three-ring circus, with one tent in political Washington, one in New York and one in the intellectual community. He was, in his last term, less a legislative craftsman than a prophet, an outside operator, battering on the external walls of the Congress with the trumpets of his indignation, rather than an insider, moving legislation from within.

In large part, of course, this was the result of the Republican victories in the 1994 midterm elections and the Democrats' loss of control of the Senate and the House. Moynihan found himself not a centrist resisting the ambitious health care reform plans of a more or less liberal Democrat in the White House, but as a mainstream Democrat in the brave new world of Newt Gingrich and the new Senate majority leader, Trent Lott of Mississippi. Lott's office is immediately around the corner from Moynihan's, but with him no hail-fellow-well-met greetings were exchanged as they had been with such comparatively moderate Republicans as Bob Dole of Kansas, Bob Packwood of Oregon, Bill Roth of Delaware or John Chafee of Rhode Island. The new Republicans had an ideology, and they had an agenda. High on the latter were two issues close to Moynihan's permanent agenda: social security and welfare. By no means did Moynihan share their ideas on either.

To understand Moynihan's position on social security in the late 1990s, it is necessary to go back fifteen years to one of the periodic crises that have threatened the social security system and in particular the benefits a graying population has expected to get from it. In 1981, the Reagan administration, confronted with one of these waves of nervousness about the system's future, proposed benefit cuts. Moynihan, as a member of the Finance Committee's social security subcommittee, proposed an increase in payroll taxes as an alternative.[10] In the end, the administration set up a presidential commission, chaired by Alan Greenspan, and with a professional actuary, Robert Myers, who had served the social security system for more than twenty years, as its staff director. Moynihan was a member, and so was Bob Dole from the Senate, together with Barber Conable, Republican of New York, and Claude Pepper, Democrat of Florida, from the House. The deadline for rescuing the system was said to be some time in the middle of 1983, and by the end of 1982 the commission, for all its experienced members and its dedicated efforts, had not come up with an answer.

On January 3, 1983, Senator Dole published an article on the op-ed page of the *New York Times,* rejecting the idea that Republicans in Congress were not giving President Reagan the support he needed. Social security was a case in point, Dole wrote. Through a combination of "relatively modest steps," he said, "the system can be saved," and when it was, the president and the Republican party would deserve much of the credit.[11] That day Moynihan was sworn in for his second term in the Senate. He had read the article in the morning's *Times,* and went up to Dole on the Senate floor and asked him, if he really thought that, "Why not try one last time?"[12] Dole did think it was worth it. As Moynihan put it, "a year of listening to Myers had altered a lifetime of Republican dogma."

Moynihan and Dole met the next day. The day after that, they roped in Barber Conable, ranking minority member of the House Committee on Ways and Means. By January 15, only thirteen days after the first exchange between Moynihan and Dole, agreement was reached at Blair House, and the social security system was "saved." It was in fact Conable who had created a somewhat artificial crisis, by refusing to support the Medicare loan in 1982 until Congress agreed to a fixed term for the necessary borrowing. That meant that in the summer of 1983, social security checks would be delayed. Given the pressure of that deadline, it was possible to bring together the interest groups involved. Tax increases alone could not bridge the gap between social security entitlements and revenues. Nor could the benefit cuts the Reagan administration wanted. But by putting together a package that could be presented to labor as a tax increase, and to business as a benefit cut, it was possible to allow liberals and conservatives both to claim that the other side had given in, and so to arrive at a compromise that found $168 billion to rescue social security.[13] Three weeks after the commission restarted negotiations, it had bolted that compromise into place. And only eight weeks after that, Congress had done its work and President Reagan had signed the resulting bill.

That was in 1983. By 1998, social security was in trouble again. The new, Gingrich wave of conservative Republicans, elected in 1994, did not share the enthusiasm of moderate Republicans like Conable for social security. The whole ideological foundations of American politics had shifted to the Right.[14] The search was for ways of getting government out of responsibility for social programs, especially for expensive programs that benefited unmarried mothers. Many of the so-called baby boom generation, eligible for social security benefits in the second decade of the twenty-first century, had come to wonder whether they would ever receive a worthwhile amount of money. Those who had been able to save and invest in the stock market, conversely, had seen their money grow, sometimes dramatically. State provision was out of favor, private pensions a far more attractive prospect. "As the 1990s arrived, and the long stock market boom," Moynihan wrote, "the call for privatization of Social Security all but drowned out the more traditional views."[15]

In common usage, "social security" meant the old-age pension introduced by the Roosevelt administration as part of the New Deal. But Title IV-A of the Social Security Act of 1935 also replaced the widows' pension with Aid to Families with Dependent Children (AFDC). Over a third of the century, from the time of "Moynihan's scissors" in the middle 1960s, to the age of the Contract with America in the mid-1990s, AFDC had ceased to be a help for workingmen's widows, mainly white. It had come to be seen as a provision for women, many of them never married and all of them single mothers, who were in truth about half African American and were perceived by many white taxpayers as being overwhelmingly so.

There was a broad consensus that "welfare," in this sense, must be reformed. It might or might not encourage single-parent families. It was certainly seen as encouraging dependence on government help. And it was undeniably expensive. Because the cost fell largely on the states, governors in particular were motivated to reform the system with various ingenious "workfare" schemes, by which welfare would be made conditional on the recipient's making a serious search for work. One of the most enthusiastic of these governors was the young and brainy Bill Clinton of Arkansas, who worked closely with Senator Moynihan on welfare reform.

In October 1991, presidential candidate Clinton opened his campaign for the Democratic nomination at Georgetown University by promising to "end welfare as we know it." When the Clinton administration arrived in Washington in early 1993 it was, in Moynihan's half-scornful words, "sparkling with . . . enthusiasms." The senator was particularly contemptuous of something called "family preservation," which he scathingly described as "a dollop of social services and a press release for some subcommittee chairman." After hearing the then chairman of the new administration's Council of Economic Advisers, Dr. Laura D'Andrea Tyson, discussing this proposal at a meeting of the Democratic Policy Committee, he recited in scholarly detail the evidence that there was no reason to believe that anything like the administration's proposed family preservation program would work. With the most withering sarcasm, he wrote to the economist that he had been "repeatedly impressed by the number of members of the Clinton administration who have assured me with great vigor that something or other is known in an area of social policy which, to the best of my understanding, is not known at all."

Ideological certainty easily degenerates into an insistence upon ignorance. The great strength of political conservatives at this time (and for a generation) is that they are open to the thought that matters are complex. Liberals have got into a reflexive pattern of denying this. I had hoped twelve years in the wilderness might have changed this; it may be it has only reinforced it. If this is so, [the] current revival of liberalism will be brief and inconsequential.[16]

It was not until June 21 that the Clinton administration sent the Work and Responsibility Act to Congress. By that time it was competing with Newt Gingrich's Contract with America, which promised that within a hundred days Congress would be asked to vote on ten bills, one of which defined welfare reform with the sentence "The government should encourage people to work, not to have children out of wedlock." Moynihan later cited numerous passages to show that by 1994 and 1995 conservatives were talking of welfare reform as if it were a form of child abuse, whereas liberals had given up daring to defend it.

The distinction Moynihan insisted on, however, which many of his critics apparently found hard to draw, was between reforming the welfare system, which he had wanted to do for years, and abolishing it. By 1995, he found himself all but isolated. As early as March of that year, the new, Republican-controlled House passed HR-4, the Personal Responsibility Act, which abolished AFDC. The Senate called the House bill the Work Opportunity Act, and passed it on September 19. But Minority Leader Tom Daschle offered an amended Family Self-Sufficiency Act. That, too, abolished AFDC. It failed, 45 to 54. The next day, Moynihan introduced his own bill, and lost 41 to 56, with five Democrats voting against. An administration official, on condition of anonymity, told the *New York Times* that AFDC was "the bone that the Clinton White House can throw to the hounds at the door, the people who want to make radical changes in the welfare state."[17]

Moynihan was angry that the White House, as he put it later, would not talk to him; instead it talked about him. On September 14, he expressed on the Senate floor his sense of how the destruction of AFDC marked a shift in the public philosophy of the whole country. "I had no idea," he said, sounding almost like King Lear in his dismay at the passing of old loyalties, "how profoundly what used to be known as liberalism was shaken by the last election. No president, Republican or Democrat, in history, or sixty years' history, would dream of agreeing to the repeal of Title IV-A of Social Security. I cannot understand how this could be happening. It has never happened before." And he added, almost in desperation, "Are there no serious persons in the administration who can say, 'Stop, stop right now! No, we won't have this'?"

There were no such serious persons. Moynihan carried on almost alone. At the House-Senate Conference Committee in the Ways and

Means Committee Room in the Longworth Building, as he put it himself later, "I called and raised."[18] He went on, "Just how many millions of infants we will put to the sword is not yet clear. There is dickering to do. In April, the Department of Health and Human Services reported that when fully implemented the time limits in the House bill would cut off benefits for 4,800,000 children. . . . Those involved will take this disgrace to their graves. The children alone are innocent."[19]

By 1996, the new wave of radical Republican conservatives passed legislation repealing Title IV-A. But Democrats, as well as Republicans, voted for what the *New York Times* called "a comprehensive welfare bill that would reverse six decades of social policy, eliminating the Federal guarantee of cash assistance for the nation's poorest children."[20] The intellectual climate had changed so that, as a writer in the *New York Times* noted in 1997, "Reformers are no longer the people who want to adjust the programs to strengthen them; they are the ones who want to gut or abolish them. In today's political lexicon, welfare reform often means the end of welfare."[21] Passage of the 1996 welfare "reform" bill, a classic demonstration of this linguistic shift, became certain after President Clinton, admitting weakly that it had "serious flaws," announced that he would vote for it nonetheless.

In the 1992 election campaign, when Clinton again promised to "end welfare as we know it," he said he wanted to "empower people with the education, training and child care they need" to escape from dependency. And as a guarantee of his commitment, he promised to increase welfare spending by $10 billion. Four years later, on July 31, 1996, he stood at a lectern in the White House and admitted the complete failure of his conception of welfare reform by agreeing that he would sign the Republican bill that cut $55 billion from welfare spending over the following six years. But it was not only Republicans who voted for the bill: twenty-five Democrats voted with the Republicans, and only twenty-one against. One of those, of course, was Moynihan, who had just denounced the bill in a short but passionate speech. "I continue to hope for the best," he began, "even if I fear for the worst." The Urban Institute, he pointed out, predicted that 3.5 million children would be dropped from the welfare rolls by 2001, and nearly 5 million by 2005. More than a million children, the Urban Institute calculated, would drop below the poverty line as a result of passage.

Characteristically, he blamed liberals, "to the extent that liberals can be said to think at all." He reserved his fiercest scorn not for his conservative opponents, but for the Clinton administration. "The current batch in the White House," he said, "now busily assuring us they were against this all along, are simply lying, albeit they probably don't know they are lying. They have only the flimsiest grasp of social reality, thinking all things doable and equally undoable. As for example the horror of this legislation." On August 1, he spoke to the *New York Times*'s R. W. Apple, Jr. "I don't want to sound apocalyptic," he warned, "but the effect on New York City could be something approaching an Apocalypse."[22]

"If you think things can't be worse," he said, "just you wait until there are a third of a million children in the streets. That's what you are talking about — children on grates, because there's no money in the states and cities to care for them." The welfare crisis could be solved, but it would take decades. In the meantime, "Our only hope is to save the children."

On September 14, 1995, he denounced the welfare bill, and blamed liberals, the advocacy groups, and the White House. On December 12, he said, "We have fashioned our own coffin. There will be no flowers." Millions of children would be "put to the sword." The passion, almost violent, of these outbursts puzzled many. They seemed disproportionate, and out of step with Moynihan's often demonstrated willingness to "reform" welfare. Critics asked whether he had given up on welfare reform.[23]

In reality, this language expressed both a shrewd sense of contemporary political realities, and an unfeigned sense of outrage at an affront to his most deep-seated personal experiences and beliefs. In the speech that was published with the emotive headline "Congress Builds a Coffin," there spoke not only the politician trying to shame backsliders into joining his opposition to what he saw as a terrible bill, but also the policy analyst, long concerned with the welfare issue — not to mention the boy whose mother in the worst days was kept going only by welfare, the Catholic moralist committed to the salvation of the family and the Christian humanist moved by the supreme imperative of saving the children. Those who were surprised by the vehemence of the senator's response had simply not been paying attention to what he had been saying for more than three decades: reform welfare, by all means, but not by destroying it.

If in the welfare debates Moynihan had seemed to revert to the mainstream liberal instincts of the Johnson administration and its War on Poverty, his next major contribution to thinking about social security was, at least on the surface, very different. Before that, however, he had demonstrated several times his gift for inserting a new idea into public debate at just the right time and in just the right way.

Back in 1981, the economist Robert Gordon of Northwestern University, in an article in *The Public Interest*,[24] had suggested that the consumer price index (CPI) seriously overstated the rate of inflation in the United States, and also explained some of the potential consequences of this error. They were not trivial. For two decades, political scientists and politicians alike had wrestled with the paradox that while innovations and technology appeared to be transforming American productivity and indeed every other aspect of American life, according to official figures real income, after stripping out inflation and taxes, had actually fallen by 13 percent between 1973 and 1995. If the government had overestimated inflation by about 1 percentage point — that is, by about 50 percent — the apparent paradox would disappear. So too would the federal budget deficit that had loomed over national politics since the beginning of the Reagan years. Many, many other weighty consequences would flow from such an apparently small error.

In October 1994, that doughty Washington warrior, Alice Rivlin, previously head of the Congressional Budget Office and now President Clinton's head of the Office of Management and Budget, handed out a paper at a White House strategy meeting cautiously marked "for handout and retrieval in meeting." It listed as one of a number of "big choices" reducing the CPI by 0.5 percent as a "technical reform"; Rivlin estimated that the CPI might overestimate inflation by 0.4 to 1.5 percentage points.[25] Early in 1995, Senator Bob Packwood, chairman of the Senate Finance Committee, and his friend Senator Moynihan, as a result of the midterm elections reduced to ranking minority member, began a series of hearings on the problem. There can be no doubt that the initiative came from Moynihan. He had been aware of the problem for years. When he was nominally responsible for the Bureau of Labor Statistics as assistant secretary of labor, he had avoided being drawn into a controversy with the economist Oskar Morgenstern, who had written an article in *Fortune* magazine calling into question the wisdom of basing policy on numbers like the CPI, calculated to unreliably precise decimal places.

A series of distinguished economists and economic policymakers were asked by how much in their opinion the CPI overstated the rate of inflation. On March 13, Alan Greenspan, chairman of the Federal Reserve, gave it as his opinion that the overstatement was between 0.5 and 1.5 percentage points. Dr. Gordon calculated that it was a minimum of 1.7 percent. In a second hearing on April 6, Dr. Dale Jorgenson of Harvard said "around 1 percent," and Dr. Ariel Pakes of Yale said 0.8 of a percentage point. On June 6, the committee heard Dr. Michael Boskin of Stanford, who said the overstatement was at least 1 and perhaps 2 whole points. Altogether nine out of thirteen witnesses gave numerical estimates of the overstatement. On average, they estimated that the CPI overstated inflation by 1.1 percent.

On June 26, 1995, Packwood and Moynihan announced the appointment of a nonpartisan commission to look into the methodology by which the CPI was calculated and to advise Congress about whether it provided an accurate measure of the cost of living. The commission issued an interim report on September 15, 1995, called "Toward a More Accurate Measure of the Cost of Living." The commission acknowledged that the CPI was the best measure currently available, but said it was not a true cost of living index. Indeed, this deficiency had been recognized by the Bureau of Labor Statistics for years. Changes in the CPI had substantially overstated the actual rate of price inflation, recently by about 1.5 percent. The commission found it probable that this bias had continued for at least a couple of decades. The Bureau of Labor Statistics goes to great lengths to measure the consumer price index. It checks seventy-one thousand different prices at twenty-two thousand different outlets. But it does not catch up with all the changes in the patterns of American consumption. In particular, it does not measure the ways in which new products, new processes and new lifestyles force down the real cost of actually living. For example, if prices in downtown department stores are too high, shoppers will switch to suburban malls or convenience stores. The CPI does not fully reflect this fall in the real cost of living. It is the same with the substantial gains made by such technological innovations as e-mail or Internet shopping, or with improved technology in production or medicine.

As Moynihan reported to the Senate on October 23, 1995, Boskin and his colleagues pointed out that the upward bias in the CPI programmed into the federal budget an automatic annual increase in indexed benefits and a real cut in taxes. Tax and social security statutes made provision for benefits and taxes to be adjusted for changes in the cost of living. The law stipulated that these adjustments should be based on changes in the CPI, as if that index measured changes in the cost of living. But, as Moynihan pointed out, there was mounting evidence that changes in the CPI overstated the increase in the cost of living, so that the implementation of those statutes was being distorted. "The law," he repeated, "is being thwarted."

On December 5, 1996, the Boskin commission came out with its final report. It confirmed that the CPI had indeed overestimated inflation by 1.1 percent. By the year 2008, correcting that miscalculation would reduce the federal deficit by over $202 billion and reduce the accumulated national debt by $1.1 trillion.

The *Washington Post* responded with something close to glee. "Stagnant wages, lagging productivity, lackluster economic growth, a looming social security crisis — suddenly, all these anxieties looked like they could be made to disappear with the wave of a statistical magic wand."[26] "The Boskin report's larger significance," wrote Robert J. Samuelson of *Newsweek,* "is that it demolishes the theory that living standards have stagnated."[27] Economists greeted the Boskin commission's findings cautiously. Yes, the consensus held, the CPI did overestimate inflation, and that meant that the American economy, and individual Americans, had indeed been doing better than the previous measures suggested. But they had probably not been doing as well since the 1970s as they had done in the golden years of the 1950s and 1960s. Lawrence Katz of Harvard University, previously chief economist at the Labor Department, said there was little doubt that the CPI did overstate inflation by ignoring or undervaluing the improvement in the quality of new products, and therefore the incomes of average American families had indeed been rising. But Katz thought it was "logically inconceivable" that the upward bias of the CPI could have been as high as 1.1 percent for a long period.

If the economists were wary, the politicians were positively nervous. For if the CPI had been too high, then so had social security pensions, perhaps by as much as $300 billion. After ten years, $10,000 a year in pension would be worth not $13,497, as at the current rate of inflation, but only $12,190. That $1,300 or so less every year would translate into tens of millions of puzzled, angry social security recipients, all voters. A cut in the CPI, for most senior citizens, would look like a cut in social security. That was wrong, Moynihan insisted. "We would not be cutting anything. We are just getting accurate data by which to conform to law."[28]

The CPI was a typical Moynihan operation. It sprang from his long experience of Washington: who else on Capitol Hill in the late 1990s was aware of technical arguments about the consumer price index in the Bureau of Labor Statistics thirty years earlier? It reflected his training as a social scientist: his instinct was to ask, Where are the data? But not by any means would every social scientist have been able to see what the data meant in terms of public finance and politics. It was also characteristic of Moynihan to see the big choices implied by what looked, even to most economists, as a mere technical question. Above all, if the CPI did indeed exaggerate inflation over the past twenty years or so by something like 50 percent, then the accepted wisdom that saw U.S. incomes as more or less stagnant from the early 1970s to the 1990s would have to be corrected. If inflation was lower than we supposed, then the increase in living standards was higher.

So we were doing better than the liberals said we were doing. That had been another persistent theme with Moynihan since the late 1960s. In fact, a constant in his thinking has been a tension between a certain philosophical pessimism and his refusal to go in for *Schadenfreude*, to take pleasure in the tribulations of American society merely because they discomfited his opponents. All this was vintage Moynihan. But what was also all too typical was his failure to follow through in political and legislative terms. He had spotted a discrepancy, understood its meaning and its importance, educated the economists, the journalists and the politicians about what it meant: and then he had stood back, leaving it to others to act, or in this case not to act, on his undeniably original perception.

The president of the United States can veto a money bill as a whole, but he may not veto individual items in such a bill. For decades, various groups of reformers had proposed to endow the president with what came to be called a "line-item veto," so that he could strike out individual provisions in a money bill but still sign the bill as a whole into law. Supporters of the line-item veto focused particularly on the idea that it would enable the president to eliminate "pork," that is, payments out of the Treasury in favor of individual states, cities or interest groups. Opponents rejected the idea on the grounds that it would shift the constitutional balance of power between the president and Congress.

This somewhat arcane dispute became more acutely political when the Democratic-controlled Congress, in 1974, offended by President Nixon's custom of "impounding," that is, not spending, money appropriated by the Congress, passed the Impoundment Control Act.[29] In 1994, the House Republicans, led by Newt Gingrich, made the line-item veto, along with the Balanced Budget Act, the very first of their proposals in the Contract with America,[30] and in the midterm elections of that year the Republicans captured control of both houses of Congress. Sure enough, on March 27, 1996, the Senate passed the Line Item Veto Act by 69 to 31, and the next day the House passed an identical bill by 232 to 177.[31] As the voting suggests, the line-item veto was not supported by Republicans or conservatives only. Gingrich claimed that 80 percent of the American population were in favor of it, and many commentators endorsed it because of their eagerness to stamp out pork, especially in a time of menacingly large federal deficits. Moreover, President Clinton, who had enjoyed the right to a line-item veto when he was governor of Arkansas, was glad to sign the measure,[32] which duly became law on January 1, 1997.

Nevertheless, on the day the bill passed the Senate, Moynihan rose to denounce it, "in serene confidence" that the bill was "constitutionally doomed." And the day after it became law, Moynihan joined with the Senate minority leader, Robert C. Byrd, with Senator Carl Levin, Democrat of Michigan, and the Republican Senator Mark Hatfield of Oregon, and with two representatives, both Democrats, to file a complaint in federal court to challenge the line-item veto's constitutionality. They argued that the act "violates Article I of the Constitution" in that it "unconstitutionally expands the President's power."[33] The government, in the name of Moynihan's former aide Franklin Raines, now President Clinton's budget director, and of Treasury Secretary Robert Rubin, appealed their complaint, but on April 10, Judge Thomas P. Jackson in the federal district court denied their motion and granted summary judgment for Byrd, Moynihan and their fellow plaintiffs. The issue went to the Supreme Court, which reversed the district court's ruling and dismissed the complaint, on the grounds that the congressmen lacked standing to bring the suit because they had not demonstrated harm to themselves as a result of the line-item veto.

President Clinton wasted no time[34] in using his new power to "cancel" items in the budget, however, and it was not long before parties could be found who could indeed allege that they had been injured. On April 27, 1998, the Supreme Court heard an action brought against Clinton by New York City and also by the Snake River Farmers' Cooperative in Idaho and one of its individual members. The city had lost $2.6 billion, it argued, because the president had canceled a recoupment of taxes against Medicare providers, while the cooperative also lost a tax break that the president had canceled. On June 25, the Supreme Court found that the president's action violated the "presentment clause" of the Constitution, in other words the "single, finely wrought and exhaustively considered procedure"[35] laid down by the Framers for enactment of a law.[36] "There is no provision in the constitution that authorizes the President to enact, to amend or to repeal statutes," wrote Justice John Paul Stevens for the majority of the Court. President Clinton greeted the decision with ill grace. It was "a defeat for all Americans."[37] While some Republicans talked of introducing new legislation that would oblige the president to sign a separate bill for each of thousands of line items in the budget, others were beginning to cool on the whole project.[38] The idea, after all, had been to curb the wicked ways of Democratic legislators whose pork bills were signed into law by Democratic presidents. Republicans were less keen on giving additional power to Clinton or to a possible Democratic successor.

Moynihan and his frustrated fellow litigants were now ecstatic. They appeared at a press conference brandishing miniature copies of the Constitution.[39] "This is a great day for the United States, a great day for the Constitution of the United States," said Senator Byrd. "God save this honorable Court!" Moynihan followed with some hyperbole of his own. "In the history of Congress," he said, "we have never had an issue of such importance for the powers of the executive and legislative branches. Liberty has prevailed."[40]

Ever since his time on the Intelligence Committee, Moynihan had been getting more and more skeptical of the value of the all-pervasive secrecy that shrouded anything that could be said to bear on national security.

He himself has given a characteristically anecdotal account of how his attention was drawn to the subject. Early in January 1993, he has said, he paid a farewell call to his friend George Bush, then leaving the White House. As he was leaving the Oval Office, he ran into

Bush's chief of staff, James A. Baker, who asked him to wait in his office for a moment. Moynihan went to Baker's office, was served coffee, and waited. In a while, Baker came back with a small stack of what looked like magazines. He wanted to show the senator what had become of the president's daily intelligence brief, the *National Intelligence Daily*. In Moynihan's time in the White House, some twenty years earlier, it had been ten or a dozen pages long, with a plain cover, marked "Top Secret." Now Baker showed him half a dozen different daily summaries, from different intelligence agencies. Some had photographs on the cover, some were printed in color. Baker explained that he had to arrive in his office at dawn just to read them all and prepare a summary of the summaries for the president.[41]

That month, Moynihan introduced legislation calling for a bipartisan study of the damage that secrecy had done to the policymaking process in Washington. As a result, on April 30, President Clinton signed Public Law 103-236,[42] establishing the Commission on Protecting and Reducing Government Secrecy. The operation bore several Moynihan hallmarks. One was the title: to attack secrecy more effectively, he was prepared to suggest that he was protecting it. In the same spirit, he recruited the ultraconservative Senator Jesse Helms, chairman of the Senate Armed Services Committee, as a member of his commission. No point in opening a flank to conservatives who might say that Moynihan's secrecy commission was putting the republic or its armed services in danger. The vice chairman, Representative Larry Combest from Lubbock, Texas, was a "solidly conservative"[43] Republican who was on record as believing "we need more intelligence, not less." The committee did its work in a thorough manner. It held thirteen formal meetings. Members and their staff made seventy-five visits, to — among other institutions — the Central Intelligence Agency, the National Security Agency, the Federal Bureau of Investigation. It interviewed more than three hundred individuals, including some convicted spies in federal penitentiaries.

Moynihan's great advantage in getting such a carefully balanced commission to move in the direction he wanted lay in the obvious mania for overclassification that had gripped Washington since the late 1940s. By 1996, the National Security Oversight Office, the body that attempts to keep track of such matters in Washington, reported that though there had been an attempt to limit classification and a decrease in the number of government offices empowered to classify documents, the actual number of documents classified as secret had increased by 62 percent to 5,789,675. "Madness," said the senator.[44] Shelves were groaning with the weight of secret papers, and the cost of classifying, keeping and guarding this tide of paper was astronomical. Moynihan contrasted the cost of the national intelligence effort, given as $26 billion when it was finally disclosed in 1997,[45] with the intelligence communities' feeble record in finding out the truth about the world, and in particular its consistent exaggeration of Soviet economic achievement. A Senator Helms or a Congressman Combest might not agree with every detail of Moynihan's view on those matters. But he could certainly feel that the volume, and the cost, of classified documents was excessive and ought to be controlled.

As a result, the commission duly issued a unanimous report on March 3, 1997. "It is time," it began, "for a new way of thinking about secrecy." It concluded that the government was classifying far too many documents at an intolerable cost; that those secrets that it was vital to protect were actually less well kept because of the vast volume of unnecessarily classified material; and that public confidence in government was harmed because so much secrecy served only to protect not national security, but the careers and reputation of civil servants and politicians. The report also included an eighty-six-page essay, largely written by Moynihan, reviewing the history of secrecy in the United States. Its fundamental principle was that there should be a "balancing test," by which the government's wishes should be weighed against the public interest in the decision to classify, or declassify, a document. The White House opposed this innovation. But on January 19, 1999, the Government Secrecy Reform Act was reintroduced with Senators Moynihan and Helms, as well as Trent Lott and Tom Daschle, respectively the majority and minority leaders, and Susan Collins (Republican of Maine), Fred Thompson (Republican of Tennessee) and Charles Schumer (Democrat of New York) as sponsors.

Moynihan, however, had not finished with the issue of secrecy. While he was working on the report, he was asked to review a new edition of his friend Edward Shils's account of the McCarthy period, *The Torment of Secrecy*.[46] He became so intrigued by the issues involved that he decided to expand the commission's report into a book. He took as his starting point the work of two of the classic founders of sociology, Emile Durkheim and Max Weber. From Durkheim, he derived the idea that secrecy was a form of ritual, enhancing the power of its initiates. To Max Weber he owed the thought that secrecy was a form of regulation: with the difference that, usually, when the government imposes regulation, it tells the citizen what he may not do; in imposing secrecy it is telling him what he may not know. Shils had pointed out how damaging secrecy was in the physical sciences: there really were few secrets about how to build an atomic bomb. Without espionage to help them, Russian scientists might have taken longer to build an atomic bomb, but they would have built one, as they later built a thermonuclear bomb on their own.

Moynihan realized that the proposition applied even more to social science than to physics. The big questions for the intelligence community were about the wealth of Soviet society, its military and economic efficiency, and the likelihood or otherwise of its falling apart as a result of political or ethnic divisions. But he focused particularly on an episode that had recently come to light, and which, as he saw it, demonstrated more clearly than any other the dangers of excessive secrecy. This was the revelation, in 1996, of what were called "the Venona papers." Venona was the code name given to transcripts of radio traffic intercepts between Moscow and Soviet agents in the United States. These documents made it plain that a number of agents whose guilt had been vehemently denied by liberals, such as Julius Rosenberg, David Greenglass and Theodore Alvin Hall, were indeed Soviet spies. They also strongly suggested that the same was true of two high officials in the Roosevelt administration, Alger Hiss and Harry Dexter White.

Moynihan immediately saw the immense political significance of these revelations. They demolished both the liberal and the conservative view of what had occurred when, in the late 1940s, Soviet agents exposed the United States to a systematic campaign of penetration. (These included both professional intelligence officers who were Soviet citizens, and American citizens who had been persuaded for one reason or another to help them.) Venona certainly demolished the persistent liberal contention that the accusations brought against the atomic spies were false and motivated by the machinations of the political Right. But, Moynihan saw, they equally discomfited the conservative position. For decades, conservatives had maintained that the country had been rescued from the threat of Soviet espionage by the heroic investigative efforts of men like Richard Nixon, Whittaker Chambers and Senator Joseph R. McCarthy. But what if the government had known all along what was happening? What if the Truman government had made a clean breast, saying, "Yes, the Soviet Union is trying to acquire our secrets. It has sent spies to get them. We have caught some of them, and we will catch the others in time." Then, Moynihan argued, there would have been no McCarthyism, no "torment of secrecy." Perhaps, though he did not say so, there would have been no Nixon presidency, either.

He even argued that secrecy had extended to the president of the United States himself, and here, though there can be no certainty, it looks as if he pushed his argument too far. Moynihan based his argument that "President Truman was never told of the Venona decryptions" on a memorandum from an FBI agent, Howard B. Fletcher, to D. Milton Ladd, head of the FBI's security division, on October 18, 1949. The subject of the memo was a recent conference with General Carter W. Clarke, then chief of the army's security agency, about the dissemination of Venona material to the CIA. The memo described a difference between General Clarke and Admiral Earl E. Stone, head of the new Armed Forces Security Agency, soon to be renamed the National Security Agency. Clarke stated in the memo that he vehemently disagreed with Admiral Stone's view that the materials should be forwarded to the president and his director of Central Intelligence, Admiral Roscoe H. Hillenkoetter. Clarke and Stone took their disagreement to General Omar N. Bradley, then chairman of the Joint Chiefs of Staff. According to General Clarke, Bradley agreed with the stand Clarke had taken and stated that he would personally assume the responsibility of advising the president or anyone else in authority if the contents of any of this material so demanded.

Moynihan was quite right, of course, that there could scarcely have been any more graphic demonstration of excessive secrecy than a decision to conceal from the president himself decisive evidence about an espionage affair that poisoned American politics for almost a decade. Historians have already pointed out, however, that the Fletcher memo is slender evidence to support a conclusion that the president was never told about the content of the Venona decryptions. Bruce Craig, for example, author of *Treasonable Doubt*, an account[47] of the Harry Dexter White case,[48] states that documents posted on the FBI's Web site state that President Truman was aware of the identification of the agent code-named JURIST, mentioned in the Venona files, with White. Another contributor to the same on-line debate went further. Steven Aftergood pointed out in *Secrecy and Government*

Bulletin that Moynihan had gone a step beyond previous writers in claiming that the October 1949 FBI memo constituted "proof" that the FBI did not inform Truman of Venona.[49] For one thing, Bradley took responsibility for telling Truman if the contents of any of this material "so demanded," a formula that removed the onus from the FBI and put it upon Bradley himself. Second, J. Edgar Hoover himself noted on an October 16, 1950, memo from Ladd, "Wouldn't it be swell to send substance to Ad. Souers for information of the President." (Rear Admiral Sidney W. Souers was special consultant to President Truman.) And a subsequent memo to Hoover on February 28, 1951, reported that "we did furnish, in a carefully paraphrased form, the identification of Harry Dexter White on the basis of [redacted secret code name for what was subsequently called Venona] information to the White House under date of October 17, 1950."[50] The date suggests that Ladd acted promptly on Hoover's suggestion that it would be "swell" to tell Truman about Harry Dexter White, at least.

In view of the questions raised by these documents, there must be at least a possibility that Moynihan was hasty in concluding that President Truman was left in the dark about all the Venona transcripts.[51] But the issue of what Truman knew, and when he knew it, while important, and all the more so because Moynihan relied on it rhetorically both in his *Secrecy* book and also in speeches and other references to it, does not affect the importance of the book's general thrust. Here was a "Cold War liberal" unequivocally attacking the secrecy that had been such an important part of the Cold War mentality.

Moynihan reviewed the damaging consequences of secrecy. He pointed out that the government's prosecution of Daniel Ellsberg for releasing, and the *New York Times* and the *Washington Post* for publishing, the Pentagon Papers, a review by its Democratic predecessor of the history of American involvement in the Vietnam War, was wholly unnecessary. He quoted Erwin Griswold, the solicitor general of the United States at the time, to the effect that he had never seen any trace of a threat to the national security from the publication. "Indeed," he added, "I have never seen it even suggested there was such an actual threat."[52] Even more acidly, he denounced the threat to constitutional government made possible by secrecy in the Iran-contra affair in President Reagan's second term. He quoted with approval Theodore Draper, who wrote, "If ever the constitutional democracy of the United States is overthrown we now have a better idea of how this is likely to be done."

"We are not going to put an end to secrecy," Moynihan warned, "nor should we." Secrecy itself is at times necessary. But a *culture* of secrecy was something else, and had done the nation deep and grievous harm. Both East and West, he pointed out, "paid hideous costs for keeping matters of state closed to the people whom the states embodied." A case could be made, he ended, for saying that "secrecy is for losers, for people who do not know how important information really is."[53]

On his way to that ringing denunciation of the culture of secrecy, Moynihan examined how things had changed in the former Soviet Union. In several speeches and writings, he quoted from a "National Security Blueprint" published in 1997 by the Russian Federation, the largest of the Soviet Union's successor states.[54]

By early 1998, the European Union was actively considering applications by about a dozen states, most of them former members of the Warsaw Pact (the Soviet Union's equivalent to the North Atlantic Treaty Organization). At the same time, NATO itself was contemplating expansion to the East. At a summit meeting in Brussels in January 1994, NATO leaders reaffirmed that the alliance was open to new members, and by 1995 made public a study that stated that the end of the Cold War both created a need and constituted an opportunity for enlarging NATO. Enlargement, it found, would "contribute to enhanced stability and security for all countries in the Europe-Atlantic area in numerous ways."[55]

Moynihan did not agree. Nevertheless, the Clinton administration pressed forward. At a NATO summit in Madrid in July 1997, the Czech Republic, Poland and Hungary were invited to join NATO. At the same time, other arrangements, short of membership, including the so-called Partnership for Peace, were made with a total of twenty-seven countries in Eastern and Central Europe, among them Russia.[56] A NATO-Russia Permanent Joint Council was set up on which NATO and Russia both sat. Russia established a mission to NATO, and it soon became normal to see former antagonists in gray Russian uniforms sitting in on all but the most secret meetings at NATO headquarters.[57] At the Madrid summit, "accession protocols" were signed, admitting the three former Warsaw Pact countries to NATO. But these would have to be ratified by NATO member countries, including the United States. It was hoped that ratification would be complete by the Washington summit planned for the summer of 1999, which would also celebrate the fiftieth anniversary of NATO.

The Clinton administration was keen to pass NATO expansion. Not that there was any great concern in the country. Moynihan himself says he attends editorial board meetings all across the country and is amazed by how infrequently foreign issues come up. One can only speculate about why the administration was so eager. Almost certainly, official Washington saw the admission of key countries in Eastern Europe as preemptive of their admission to the Western European Union, an organization that was contemplating expanding its security role, and to which the United States and Canada did not belong. Making sure that Poland, Hungary and the Czech Republic were in NATO, therefore, would be a way of ensuring that American influence was not diluted in this way.

Moynihan thought that the Clinton administration's analysis missed the point. He made two main arguments. For one thing, it was forgetting that Russia and three of its former allies (Ukraine, Belarus and Kazakhstan) still had substantial numbers of nuclear weapons and their delivery systems. "We are not free of nuclear war," he said.[58] "The world is not a nuclear-free zone." Second, NATO expansion would encourage the feeling, always latent in Russia, that the West was encroaching and encircling. "This is not time to give the nationalists in Russia a boost." Moynihan cited his old friend George Kennan: "This is the worst mistake we have made in seventy years."

On April 30, 1998, Moynihan led the forlorn hope against expansion in the Senate. The senators rejected his amendment, which proposed to delay admission of Poland, Hungary and the Czech Republic until they became members of the European Union, by 83 to 17. Senators heard a passionate declaration of pride in her Polish heritage by Senator Barbara Mikulski of Maryland. If NATO did not enlarge, she said, it would remain, as the Czech president Vaclav Havel had said, "an alumni club for Cold War victors." Moynihan argued, to the contrary, that expansion would worsen tensions with a Russia that still possessed nuclear arms, but where democracy was fragile. Pushing NATO's frontier up against the borders of Russia meant "back to the hair trigger," he said. But he argued in vain; the Senate swept his warnings aside. In light of the Kosovo crisis and NATO's need for Russian mediation to end it, they now look uncannily prescient.

In one respect, the knowledge that he would not be running for the Senate in 2000 was a great help. By the fall of 1998, the House Republicans first turned consideration of the Starr Report on President Clinton's relationship with the White House intern Monica Lewinsky, and the way he may or may not have sought to cover it up, into a partisan issue. They then rammed it through the House of Representatives. Soon Moynihan would have to vote in the Senate trial on the Articles of Impeachment. Inevitably, as an acknowledged, if self-taught, constitutional expert, Moynihan's opinion would be canvassed by the media and sought by many of his colleagues. Not to be running in 2000 meant having no personal ax to grind and added to the expectancy with which Moynihan's opinion on the impeachment was awaited.

It was no secret that he had no great love for the president. He had watched the story, and the president's equivocations, unfold throughout 1998. In August, after Clinton's belated admission that "I did have a relationship with Ms. Lewinsky that was not appropriate. In fact it was wrong," Moynihan made plain his private opinion that "this is bad," that it was a serious matter for a president to lie to the country, whether or not he had technically committed perjury.[59] In September, before the special counsel's report was released, Moynihan called the Lewinsky affair "a crisis of the regime," and gave it as his opinion that perjury either in a civil deposition or before a grand jury could amount to an impeachable offense.[60] There was a rising sense, among those who knew the senator and thought they understood how his mind worked, that he was preparing a dramatic intervention of some kind.

One plausible theory was that his considerable contempt for Clinton would impel him not to denounce the president and call for his removal from office, but to "heap coals of burning fire on his head" by emerging very plainly as the man who saved the presidential bacon.

So a certain suspense built up as to where Moynihan would come down on impeachment. On August 19, two days after Clinton's admission of an inappropriate relationship, Moynihan was interviewed by Fred Dicker on WROM in Albany.[61] How did he view the president's speech? "I think the speech," he replied, "if you want to call four minutes a speech, was not adequate to its purpose." Why had the president attacked the special prosecutor? Clinton "had put an awful lot of people through terrible times in the last seven months and it was a time to just stand up, and say, 'I apologize.' He didn't say that." True, Moynihan went on to point out that the world was still a dangerous place. Saddam Hussein was defying United Nations inspectors in Iraq. Osama bin Laden was attacking U.S. embassies. There were nuclear weapons in the Indian subcontinent. There was famine in North Korea, and chaos in Russia. "Presidents have to survive," he said. "You cannot have a wounded executive. No matter what your personal feelings might be, you need a commander in chief."

This was the dilemma. For an American of the World War II generation, the president was, ought to be, the national leader, the commander in chief whose orders must be obeyed. Yet one of Moynihan's own presidents, Richard Nixon, had been forced to retire rather than face impeachment. Moynihan himself felt that Ronald Reagan came close to allowing a coup d'état in the shape of the defiance of Congress and the law in the Iran-contra affair. At the same time, for a Catholic husband, father and moralist of that same generation, surreptitious fellatio from the help, in the sacred precincts of the White House, was simply repellent. Equivocating, shuffling and lying about it, sworn or unsworn, was worse. So Moynihan was torn. The man's behavior deserved nothing but contempt. But the office must be defended even when the incumbent could not be honored.

Once, Moynihan seemed to be on the brink of coming out hard against Clinton. On September 3, Senator Joseph I. Lieberman, Democrat of Connecticut, a good friend of Moynihan's and an orthodox Jew with strong moral principles, called on Congress as a whole and the Senate in particular to do its duty. He was seconded by Senator Bob Kerrey of Nebraska. Moynihan rose and spoke in his most florid style. He thanked his two friends for bringing home the inadequacy of the president's response. We are all sinners, he went on, and added, "I am the oldest of the three of us, and therefore have sinned the most. Of that you may be sure." But a point of decision would come to the Congress . . .

"We take an oath to uphold the Constitution of the United States, uphold and defend the Constitution of the United States against all enemies, foreign and domestic — foreign and domestic, sir, which acknowledges that we can be our own worst enemies if we do not hew to our best standards, knowing that we are all imperfect but have an obligation to do our very best."

Then he quoted, from memory, one of the proudest and most classic pronouncements of English law, the judgment by which Lord Mansfield, in the *Somersett* case in 1772, effectively abolished slavery in England. "In an epic statement," Moynihan quoted, "Mansfield said, *'Fiat justitia, ruat Coelum,'* — 'Let justice be done, though the heavens fall.'" And then he glossed the great judge's thought. "If justice is done with sufficient regularity and moderation, the heavens need not fall. They might even rejoice in the nation that has shown a capacity for redemption and self-renewal."[62]

He was thinking, no doubt, of how the Senate might do its duty in an impeachment that had not yet arrived from the House. But he was also, no doubt, thinking beyond the immediate issue of the president's case to his own political principles.

The three speeches did not pass entirely unnoticed. "What these three have done," commented the *Wall Street Journal,* "is [to have] brought to this matter the *gravitas* it so clearly deserves."[63] And the *Washington Post*'s Meg Greenfield agreed. ". . . [T]he best and only hope for coming out of this with a shred of national dignity and honor," she wrote, "lies with taking the advice of Lieberman, Moynihan, Kerrey *et al.,* who stepped in . . . with a civil and civilized idea of what was needed." The problem, as the three senators had understood, was that while what the president had done might not merit dismissal from office, censure was not an attractive alternative, if only because the president's defenders were representing censure as tantamount to acquittal, or at least as the proverbial slap on the wrist.

By December 19, when the House passed Articles of Impeachment, Moynihan had changed his opinion. Or rather, where at first he had allowed his instinctive disdain for the way the president had behaved to prevail, now he emphasized the enduring constitutional implications of the case. By Christmas Eve, he was ready to go public. In a telephone interview with Richard L. Berke of the *New York Times,*[64] he made it clear that he still believed that the president should be censured, but warned that any attempt to force Clinton out of office "might very readily destabilize the presidency."

Reached by phone at his Washington apartment, Moynihan told

Berke he was in the middle of rereading the *Federalist Papers* in order
to prepare for the trial. "We are an indispensable nation," he said.
"And we have to protect the presidency as an institution." If not, he
said, "do not doubt that you could degrade the Republic very
quickly." Did he back censure? he was asked. "You obviously can
infer that," he replied. Was he moved by partisan loyalty or by concern for the presidency? He answered simply, "It's the institution."
What did he think of the idea, mooted by some, that the president
might be fined as part of a censure agreement? "Bad, bad, bad!" he
said. "Wrong, wrong, wrong!" Impeachment was not about punishment, which the courts could decide upon after the impeachment trial
was over. He expressed great annoyance at the fact that the president
had held a rally with two busloads of congressmen on the White
House's South Lawn after the impeachment vote in the House. "If
the rally was meant for the president's spirits," he said, "that's just
fine. If it was meant to influence the Senate, it was just wrong. We
take an oath. Our oath is to the Constitution, to uphold and defend
the Constitution."

The great question was, "Do these allegations rise to the level of
high crimes and misdemeanors?" For the Founding Fathers, Moynihan insisted, the list of high crimes and misdemeanors began with
treason and bribery. He implored the *Times*'s readers to pick up the
Constitution and read it. And when he was asked if he thought
the Republicans would lose politically by the way they had handled
the case, he snapped at his interviewer: "Oh, I don't know and I don't
care! This is a time to think of the Constitution."

After the *Times*, Moynihan turned to *Meet the Press*, with Tim
Russert in the chair as usual. There will be a trial, Russert said. But
what sort of trial? Would witnesses be heard? Would it run its course?

Moynihan was in an insouciant mood. Later in the show, perhaps
to goad the television evangelist Pat Robertson, a fellow guest, he
quoted Thersites, the low-life cynic in Shakespeare's *Troilus and Cres-
sida:* "Lechery, lechery, still wars and lechery./Nothing else holds
fashion."

Let the Senate decide, said Moynihan. But first, "We have got to
be thinking about the stability of the American presidency . . . We
could so easily mutate into a president-of-the-month . . . Impeachment is not a process involving punishment. It simply involves removal from office, and the president has no say."

It would be hard to imagine the routine removal of presidents by a congressional majority, but stranger things have occurred. Speakers become president. No one knows who is the commander in chief, who is the chief executive officer. And the whole stability of this nation, the senator argued, upon which the stability of the world rests, could be seriously and grievously undermined.[65]

Moynihan was emphasizing the international dimension of the dangers he foresaw from impeachment. He showed the reflexes of one who had grown up and spent most of a long career in the Cold War. There was a better argument on his side of the case. It was that, once impeachment became an easy or frequent affair, the separation and balancing of the executive and legislative powers that lie at the very heart of the American Constitution would be changed. The United States would cease to be what the Framers, and in particular James Madison, had in mind, namely a polity based on separated and balanced powers, and become instead a parliamentary democracy. At the critical moment, and in the critical place, that is on the floor of the Senate in the closing stages of the impeachment trial, Moynihan deployed this argument with decisive effect.

The trial was a tedious business, made worse by the insistence of the chief justice, William Rehnquist, who presided, that senators must remain in their places (difficult for Moynihan, as his back was giving him serious pain, which was worse when he sat down). Denied their usual fix of the oxygen of publicity, they defied the spirit of Rehnquist's rule by going on television and arguing vociferously about every detail of procedure and politics. An observant eyewitness[66] recorded the behavioral patterns of the senatorial fauna. Senator Joseph Biden scribbled a diary into a composition book. Ted Kennedy, sagging in a resigned heap, did not conceal his dismay at being compelled to take part. John Kerry fidgeted, Paul Sarbanes "guzzles water," Jesse Helms, "among others," dozed, and only Strom Thurmond, at ninety-six, was a model of upright attentiveness. What of Moynihan? He seemed to keep his papers at some distance, as if afraid of being "contaminated by their distasteful content." A look of "pursed-lipped bemusement" conveyed his view that there must be a "better way for him to end his career in the Senate." Certainly, the confinement of the trial and its minutiae, solemn but also tawdry in the extreme, not to mention the brooding political spite of the prosecutors and of some of the House "managers," made it an infuriating experience for Moynihan and for his fellow magnificoes. The day after the trial ended, he began a letter, "Free at last!"[67]

wryly echoing the peroration of Martin Luther King's great speech to the 1963 March on Washington.

Moynihan stuck it out for just over a month before making his long-awaited intervention. After the trial began on January 8, he had more time than usual for reading. Having read the Constitution and analyses of impeachment by the chief justice and the great legal scholar Charles L. Black, he went back to James Madison's diary of the constitutional convention and there found the key he was looking for in an explanation of how the words "high crimes and misdemeanors" came to be chosen as the definition of what would make a president impeachable. President Clinton's fate turned on this question. For it was not denied that he had done things, and said things, that were "inappropriate," indeed as he said himself, "wrong." They were perhaps crimes, or misdemeanors. The whole question was whether they were "high crimes and misdemeanors" within the meaning of the Constitution, acts, therefore, that demanded his dismissal from office. Where others wrangled about what the Constitution might mean, or ought to mean, Moynihan — characteristically — went back to look at the evidence as to what the men who wrote it thought it meant.

On February 10, he rose and told his brethren what he had found. The drafters of the American Constitution, he pointed out, derived from England and from the colonial governments "fully formed models of what a legislature should be, what a judiciary should do. But nowhere on earth was there a nation with an elected head of an executive branch of government." Few of them wanted another monarchy. "Yet given what Madison termed 'the fugitive and turbulent existence of ancient republics,' who would dare to suggest that a modern republic could hope for anything better?" Madison could, said Moynihan, because "study had produced new knowledge." This was a declaration of intellectual independence, he said, equal to anything asserted in 1776. Until then, political theory had sought to instill right thinking into a small class of rulers. But, Madison argued, "If men were angels, no government would be necessary." His revolutionary idea was that the deficiency of virtue could be replaced with the balancing of interests. That was why the powers of executive, legislative and judiciary must be separated and balanced.

Impeachment, as Madison saw it, was to be the device by which the Congress could counteract the "defect" — the lack, we would say — of "better motives" in a president. And impeachment, Moynihan pointed out, was very much in the minds of the men who met to frame the American Constitution in Philadelphia in 1787. For they knew Edmund Burke well. And in April 1786, it was Burke who stepped forward as the leader of the seven managers in the impeachment trial of Warren Hastings, the haughty governor general of Bengal, who arrogantly proclaimed that he was "astonished at his own moderation" when accused of stealing from an Indian queen jewels and other property worth the vast sum of six million pounds in the money of the eighteenth century. The Hastings trial went on for seven years and was reported regularly in the *Pennsylvania Gazette* and other colonial newspapers.

So when, on Saturday, September 8, 1787, the Constitutional Convention turned, for the only time, to the question of what ought to be the standard of crimes that would justify impeachment, the trial of Hastings was in everybody's mind. And here Moynihan, like the professor he had once been, led his colleagues through the debate that had taken place.[68]

The draft the Framers had in front of them referred only to "treason and bribery" as grounds for impeachment. Madison's notes say of the debate:

> The clause referring to the Senate, the trial of impeachments against the President, for Treason and bribery, was taken up.
>
> Col. MASON, Why is the provision restrained to Treason & bribery only? Treason as defined in the Constitution will not reach many great and dangerous offences. Hastings is not guilty of Treason. Attempts to subvert the Constitution may not be Treason as above defined. As bills of attainder which have saved the British Constitution are forbidden, it is the more necessary to extend the power of impeachments. He mov'd to add after "bribery" "or maladministration."
>
> Mr. GERRY seconded him.
>
> Mr. MADISON, So vague a term will be equivalent to a tenure during pleasure of the Senate ...
>
> Mr. Go'r [Gouverneur] MORRIS, An election of every four years will prevent maladministration.
>
> Col. MASON withdrew "maladministration" & substituted "other high crimes & misdemeanors against the state."[69]

The convention, Moynihan explained, later replaced the word *State* with *United States*. And on September 12, 1787, the Committee on Style — which had no authority to alter the substantive meaning of the text — deleted the words "against the United States." Thus, he concluded, like a man coming to the end of a logical proof, the Framers clearly intended that a president should be removed only for offenses "against the United States." He went on, "It may also be concluded that the addition of the words 'High Crimes and Misdemeanors' was intended to extend the impeachment power of Congress so as to reach 'great and dangerous offences,' in Madison's phrase."

So now he jumped forward 212 years to the question in everyone's mind. "The question now before the Senate," he reminded his colleagues, "is whether the acts that form the basis for the Articles of Impeachment against President Clinton rise to the level of 'high crimes and misdemeanors.' " Which is to say "great and dangerous offences against the United States." And now at last he revealed the conclusion to which historical study and political instinct alike had driven him. "Senators, do not take the imprudent risk that removing William Jefferson Clinton for low crimes will not in the end jeopardize the Constitution itself. Censure him by all means. He will be gone in less than two years. But do not let his misdeeds put in jeopardy the Constitution we are sworn to uphold and defend."[70]

A few days later, free at last, he was on *Meet the Press* yet again. He schmoozed — there is no other word for it — with Senator John McCain of Arizona, recently announced as a candidate for the Republican nomination. He handled questions, with urbanity and a pinch of malice, about whether Hillary Rodham Clinton would run for his Senate seat: Mrs. Clinton, he said, "will be my legacy . . . that magnificent young, bright, able Illinois-Arkansas enthusiasm to New York, which probably could use a little," which is as nice a way as anyone has ever found to say "carpetbagger." And then he offered some final, characteristic reflections on the sorry saga of Bill Clinton, Monica Lewinsky and Kenneth Starr. "The whole thing is over and our institutions are intact." Should the president be indicted? "Move on. I mean, I've had enough of everything, particularly Kenneth Starr. One thing we can do in this Congress is not extend the life of the independent counsel statute." And then the thrust, the reminder that inside the mellow elder statesman an old anger still sometimes burned: "It was a post-Watergate liberal notion and it was a disaster."

Years before he announced that he would not run for another term in 2000, in the picaresque fashion I've described in Chapter 1, Pat

Moynihan and his wife, Liz, had made up their minds that his fourth term would be the last. Whatever mental reservations or private regrets he might have had, Pat accepted that decision as one they had made together. His health was part of it. He walked slowly and awkwardly as a result of his peripheral neuropathy. Then, too, Liz wanted to see more of him. And she was determined that he should quit while he was ahead. She could not bear the thought of that superb political intelligence slowing and missing tricks until people first whispered, then said out loud, that he had lost it. Nor was winning reelection guaranteed. They were mulling these questions over at a time when Newt Gingrich was Speaker of the House, and in a world where Rudolph Giuliani was riding a crest of popularity, and even an Al Sharpton was a potentially serious threat.

Liz wanted Pat to have the rest and reputation he had earned abundantly, *otium cum dignitate*, ease with dignity. In the Senate of the late 1990s, lapped by the shark-filled waters of the media, that was not an option.

> O! let him pass; he hates him
> That would upon the rack of this tough world
> Stretch him out longer.

Speaking of racks, his back was beginning to hurt again. A stenosis of the lumbar vertebrae was what the specialists called it. Two vertebrae fused together, pinching a major nerve. The plain fact was that it hurt like hell. He had first injured his back when he fell into the hold of a freighter in Narragansett Bay in 1946. In London, it had been one, if only one, of the reasons he had gone to see the psychoanalyst Patrick de Maré. Ten years later, he had written to President Kennedy's physician, Dr. Janet Travell, with a slightly embarrassing story about falling off a political platform. It hadn't stopped him from swinging a powerful ax when splitting wood at the farm. But it was there, and now, in early 1999, it came back, worse than ever. It was worst of all when he had to sit for long periods of time, as he did during the Senate impeachment trial. There were visits to specialists, and there was talk of surgery. Once, in a private letter, he even called it "mortal."[71] It wasn't that. But it was miserable, and sometimes it made him wonder if life was worth living. Sometimes the faithful Tony Bullock had to go out and find a drugstore in midafternoon to get something to soothe the pain. In the end, in April 1999, surgery at Johns Hopkins University Hospital in Baltimore was successful, and he has made a satisfactory postoperative recovery, though with moments of difficulty and nausea, and he has lost some forty pounds. Yet most of the time, pain or no pain, Pat was cheerful, even if something of the old ebullience had gone. He still greeted old friends with hearty pleasure, and still read voraciously.

Like most politicians, he derived a good deal of satisfaction from discovering a fact or reading an article that vindicated a position he had been criticized for long ago. He loved to collect evidence that he had been right, and in particular that those who had called him racist had been wrong, about the Moynihan Report and about the breakdown of the family. He was particularly delighted when a conference at the Morehouse Research Institute and the Institute for American Values in Atlanta published a statement on "Father Absence in Black America" that echoed his ideas of 1965, though to be sure the paper did not mention him.[72] Still, it did recommend legislation "aimed at reversing the trend of father absence in our nation." That sounded suspiciously like "The Negro Family: The Case for National Action." The reception of the "benign neglect" phrase still rankled, and there was still pleasure in any evidence that he was "not so bad a man as that." Equally, he squirreled away references to that other, happier phrase he had bequeathed to the language, "defining deviancy down."

There were still two years to go and battles to fight. At the end of his political life, it was strange how he was called on again and again to revert to his "permanent agenda." There were the perennial concerns about public finance, about welfare, and especially about social security. Moynihan supported Senator Bob Kerrey's plan for allowing people to invest a part of their social security contributions in equities. The world was changing. But Pat was more impressed by an argument that was, if not actually populist, at least fully compatible with the mainstream Democrat he had become once again. If the rich man gets capital appreciation by investing in equities, he argued, why should not the workingman do the same?

The Moynihans looked forward, if that is the right way of putting it, to a time when life would be less magnificent than it had been for the legislator. Sooner or later, they felt, they would have to sell the farm; and dearly as they loved it, they were aware that it would not make their fortune. There would be no more visits to the suite at the Carlyle, either. Still, life would be more than comfortable. Almost certainly, they would stay in the three apartments Liz had knocked into one on Pennsylvania Avenue, and the odds were that Pat would have an office in the Woodrow Wilson Center in its new home in the Reagan Building.

From the balcony of the apartment, Pat would be able to survey the emblematic representations of his life's stages. Below and to the left was the navy monument, with its bleak granite map of the oceans and a bronze sailor with his duffel bag, waiting to go back on board. (There is a miniature cast of the sailor, sans duffel bag, on the balcony itself.) Below, at the monument, on a summer evening, an old navy man could snap to the salute as the band played "Anchors Aweigh" and let his mind go back to World War II and a young man working his way through "naval science" into graduate school and the full freedom of Cold War America.

If he looked further to the left, of course, he could see the wedding cake grandeur of the Capitol, where he had worked for almost a quarter of the century. (A block of granite from one of the Capitol's several refurbishments also stands on the balcony.) To the right, "America's Main Street" stretched away, strolling tourists separated by eight ribbons of traffic, past the Ronald Reagan Building, where perhaps, in a suitably marmoreal office, he would pitch his camp after he left the Senate. There in the dusty distance was the greenery surrounding the South Lawn of the White House. Between the two poles of the legislative and executive branches of government, symbols of the divided powers of the Founding Fathers' imagining, he had lived much of his adult life. Almost within a stone's toss was the corner office in the Labor Department where he had called in Paul Barton and Ellen Broderick and set them to work on the great inquiry that went so wrong, but still led to glory as well as misery in the end for its author.

Barely out of sight was the White House itself, where he had saluted the memory of what John Kennedy might have been, and witnessed what Richard Nixon became. And at the other pole of this grand symbolic landscape was the Russell Building, his home for nearly a quarter of his years of frustration and fulfillment.

Of course, when he stands on that balcony, small enough to be just slightly vertiginous, he must call up other imagined landscapes. Childhood memories of Indiana holidays. London, with the grand associations of parliamentary eloquence and its Palladian vistas, but also with the memories of friends and the frowsty coziness of a

Greenwich pub. Cambridge, Massachusetts, and the social sciences, with their elusive search for certainty in a world of politicized argument and ambition disguised as scholarship. Delhi, with its blast-furnace heat and its prompting of reflections on the United States in opposition. The farm, with its pond and the white wooden school-house with its cast-iron stove.

Above all, when the tall old gentleman in the tailored blue blazer with brass buttons allows his mind's eye to stray from the marble panorama of monumental Washington, it must most often drift up to Manhattan. If Washington has been for Moynihan the arena of great conflicts and the field of glory, New York was the layered palimpsest of struggle. There the child learned to be wary of the older boys who might steal the quarters he had earned by shining shoes. There the adolescent encountered the mysterious splendors and austere authority of the Roman Church, now as worldly as a monsignor with a talent for finance and administration, now Marian in its compassion. There the young man worked as a longshoreman, listened to jazz, met girls and sat in bars, incessantly talking, but sometimes also calculating and always dreaming. There as a child he lived in cold-water flats, as a student he slept above his mother's bar, in Hell's Kitchen at last; there he lived on the top floor of the Waldorf Towers and in a suite at the Carlyle. There, as an undiplomatic ambassador, he vehemently championed the minority against the majority; there, as a largely apolitical senator he preferred the world of ideas to the world of money and power. East Side, West Side, all around the town, for more than fifty years he had sought out those who had something to say, argued with them, and learned what they had to teach.

The sound of Liz, talking to Michael Patrick in the apartment, would remind him that in his adventures he had never been alone. Their closeness might have been hard for their children to penetrate, but here at last were Michael and Zora, the third generation, getting ready to push their boats out on the inshore beginnings of their voyages. Now at last he would be able to spend time with Liz as of right, and not steal it from the voracious demands of books and politics, staff, voters and endless reporters, including this one.

Down in Washington, after the trauma of the Kennedy assassination, he was deeply involved in the building of what Lyndon Johnson called the Great Society. The phrase is half forgotten now, as deeply out of mind and out of fashion as the rusty skates and broken wooden tennis rackets stored in a family attic. But to build *a* great society, a society that would be great in its ideals and its achievements, great in the determination with which it pursued its aims, great too in the generosity with which it helped the unfortunate at home and the impoverished abroad — that ambition was in the very air you breathed in the America of the postwar years, in FDR's New York, Harriman's Albany, the Washington of Kennedy and Johnson, and in the Cambridge of the 1960s.

Life and experience of the "tough world," the dangerous place, made Moynihan and many of his best friends skeptical of this shibboleth from the years of the liberal consensus, the Great Society. They came to associate the word *liberal* with the insincere and the pretentious.

He acquired a profound doubt about the central paradigm of liberal government: the assumption that social scientists should identify a need, devise a program of government action to meet that need and supervise the application of public money to the sore place through the ministrations of enlightened bureaucracy. He came to believe that the function of social science was not to propose action to government, but to monitor it. But, unlike many of his traveling companions and some of his closest friends, he never abandoned his faith in the capacity, and the duty, of government to make society better, and especially for the poor and their children.

He remains skeptical of the efficacy of political and government action. But this is not because of any ideological objection to government, still less a preference for private or corporate action. His skepticism is simply part of a pessimism, almost a melancholy, about the workings of the universe and its human inhabitants which is culturally, if not theologically, religious in nature, and is quite compatible with cheerfulness, even ebullience, about the actual workings of government.

With all his distrust of the politician's or the social scientist's ability to find magic, or even competent, solutions, he has never abandoned his faith in an American government that should exemplify — what were the words he used in *Guiding Principles for Federal Architecture?* — "dignity, enterprise, vigor and stability."

This has been his true permanent agenda, and will be his lasting epitaph. Pat Moynihan's friend James Q. Wilson said, and said truly, that he brought to his task "luminous intellect, personal conviction, deep historical knowledge, the eye of an artist and the pen of an angel, and above all an incorruptible devotion to the common good."

But the likelihood is that, after the dazzling speeches and elegant essays, the wit and the prophetic utterances, are largely forgotten, he will be remembered as the man who — in the face of a generation that thought it had abolished the need for government — had the lucidity and the courage to restate the enduring propositions of the American political creed. That tradition holds many riches, but above all a faith in the redemptive power of republican government.

Notes

ABBREVIATIONS
DPM   Daniel Patrick Moynihan
GH   Godfrey Hodgson

Preface and Acknowledgments

1. Godfrey Hodgson, *America in Our Time*, New York, Doubleday, 1976.
2. Godfrey Hodgson, *The World Turned Right Side Up*, Boston, Houghton Mifflin, 1996.

1. The Prophet: An Introduction

1. Tony Bullock, e-mail to GH, November 12, 1999.
2. DPM letter to GH, November 10, 1998.
3. The narrative that follows is based largely on the two sources cited above, i.e. Bullock's e-mail and DPM's letter.
4. Statement from the office of State Comptroller H. Carl McCall, November 6, 1998.
5. DPM letter to GH, November 10, 1998.
6. Michael Goodwin, "A Giant Still Walks Among Us," *New York Daily News*, July 29, 1998.
7. Deborah Orin, "He's Gentle Genius & Giant Among Pols," *New York Post*, November 7, 1998.
8. Statement by George E. Pataki, November 6, 1998.
9. Statement by Rudolph W. Giuliani, November 6, 1998.
10. Statement by Bob Kerrey, November 6, 1998.
11. Statement by Al Gore, November 6, 1998.
12. Statement from the White House, Office of the Press Secretary, Highfill, Arkansas, November 6, 1998.
13. DPM to GH, June 1965.
14. See Chapter 8.
15. DPM, "The United States in Opposition," *Commentary*, March 1975.
16. See, for example, his Phi Beta Kappa oration at Harvard in June 1967, at the

height of the youth insurgency, subsequently published as "Nirvana Now," *The American Scholar*, Autumn 1967.

17. See Chapter 7, pp. 154–55.
18. See Chapter 7, *passim*.
19. Elliott Abrams to GH, July 21, 1997. A former member of DPM's staff, Abrams was an assistant secretary of state in the Reagan administration and is now president of the Ethics in Public Policy Center in Washington, D.C.
20. Irving Kristol to GH, July 1997.
21. Marty Tolchin to GH, July 1997. Tolchin is founder and editor in chief of *The Hill*.
22. Robert Packwood to GH, 1999.
23. Robert Dole to GH, 1999.
24. Rob Shapiro to GH, 1997.
25. Charles de Gaulle, *Mémoires de Guerre*, Paris, Plon, vol. 1, 1954, p. 1.
26. John Kenneth Galbraith to GH, December 1997.

2. Growing Pains: New York and London

1. Michael Barone and Grant Ujifusa, *Almanac of American Politics*, Washington, D.C., *National Journal*, 1998, pp. 962–63.
2. Max Frankel, *The Times of My Life*, New York, Random House, 1999, p. 378 (quoted from the *New York Times*, September 10, 1976).
3. This account of DPM's great-grandfather and grandfather is taken from an obituary in the *Bluffton Evening Banner*, 1958: "J. C. Moynihan, 85, Dies at Hospital," Moynihan Papers, Library of Congress.
4. Douglas Schoen, *Pat: A Biography of Daniel Patrick Moynihan*, New York, Harper and Row, 1979, p. 4. For DPM's childhood and early adulthood, I have drawn heavily on Schoen, pp. 2–38, to which I acknowledge my debt.
5. Obituary of Margaret B. Phipps in *Louisville Courier-Journal*, Moynihan Papers, Library of Congress.
6. Richard Whalen, *The Founding Father: The Story of Joseph P. Kennedy*, New York, New American Library, 1964.
7. DPM commercial telegram to Nelle Simpson Smith, February 28, 1976, Moynihan Papers, Library of Congress.
8. "H. Allen Smith, Humorist, Dies; Wrote 'Low Man on Totem Pole,' " *New York Times*, February 26, 1976.
9. Schoen, op. cit., p. 10.
10. Quotations about the failed marriage on pp. 29 and 32 are from a personal letter from DPM to GH, January 25, 1998.
11. Ibid.
12. Ibid.
13. Interview with Elizabeth Moynihan. Interestingly, her father, also an Irish Catholic, also left her mother, and also remarried. One of Elizabeth Brennan Moynihan's half sisters became a nun.
14. Richard Meryman, who went with DPM on an adventure to Hungry Horse, Montana (see pp. 39–40), told me that when he split up with DPM in Chicago, he said he was going to find his father. "He sort of mumbled, but it was my clear understanding that he was going to look for his father."

15. Michael Moynihan letter to DPM, April 13, 1953.
16. Schoen, op. cit., p. 12.
17. Tim Crouse. See "Ruling Class Hero," *Rolling Stone*, August 12, 1976, p. 46.
18. Ibid.
19. DPM, *New York Post*, April 20, 1993.
20. DPM, "Letter to New Yorkers," November 15, 1990. See also ibid.
21. Schoen, op.cit., p. 14. Schoen says DPM did not need to take an exam, but DPM maintains that he can remember walking in to take the exam with his longshoreman's hook in his pocket. It's possible that he has confused two events.
22. Schoen, op. cit., p. 20.
23. DPM, "Letter to New Yorkers," November 15, 1990.
24. Moynihan Papers, Library of Congress.
25. Schoen, op. cit.
26. DPM, "New York as It Was," *New York Post*, April 20, 1993. Based on a speech to the Association for a Better New York, April 15, 1993.
27. Elizabeth Moynihan to GH, August 1997.
28. DPM, "Letter to New Yorkers," November 15, 1990.
29. Moynihan Papers, Library of Congress.
30. Schoen, op. cit.
31. Richard Meryman to GH, August 1997.
32. DPM letter to GH, January 25, 1998.
33. DPM's London journal, Moynihan Papers, Library of Congress.
34. Ibid.
35. This account is based on accounts by both DPM and Meryman.
36. DPM to GH.
37. DPM to GH, January 25, 1998.
38. Moynihan Papers, Library of Congress.
39. DPM to GH, August 1997.
40. Ann Bohm to GH, December 1997.
41. DPM's London journal, Moynihan Papers, Library of Congress.
42. Later Dr. de Maré became one of the leaders of the group therapy movement. In 1999, in his late nineties, he declined to comment on Moynihan's psychoanalysis, as was of course professionally correct: letter to GH.
43. "Pat was well off," said John Cole Cool, a Yale graduate who was a friend of DPM at the LSE. "He had $160 a month." It was $225 a month, remembers Sander Vanocur, also a close friend at LSE, and later a distinguished NBC correspondent.
44. One of Moynihan's friends, John Cool, told me that he acquired a professional library in London on his grant.
45. Signal from DPM to Third Naval District, February 20, 1952. Moynihan Papers, Library of Congress.
46. Ann Bohm to GH, 1998.
47. Ralf Dahrendorf, *LSE: A History of the London School of Economics and Political Science, 1895–1995*, Oxford, Oxford University Press, 1995, p. 11.
48. Ann Bohm to GH.
49. Dahrendorf, op. cit., p. 368.
50. Hayek returned to his native Austria in 1962.

51. Sander Vanocur to GH, December 1997.
52. Personal knowledge.
53. DPM to GH, December 1997.
54. It was she who married Joe Reisler and ended up as the wife of a corporate executive in Pittsburgh.
55. DPM's London journal, Moynihan Papers, Library of Congress, October 26, 1950.
56. DPM letter to GH, December 1997.
57. Ibid.
58. Moynihan Papers, Library of Congress.
59. DPM, "Letter to New Yorkers," November 15, 1990.
60. John Cole Cool to GH, August 1997.
61. DPM, "Letter to New Yorkers," June 17, 1994.
62. Ibid., November 15, 1990.
63. DPM letter to GH, October 28, 1997.
64. Moynihan Papers, Library of Congress.
65. Fenton went on to buy the apartment next to the Moynihans in Washington.
66. DPM's London journal, Moynihan Papers, Library of Congress.
67. Powell (1912–1998) was a tormented conservative ideologue of great intellectual earnestness. He had been a classics professor in Cambridge and Australia. He made a famous speech predicting "much blood" if black immigration into Britain continued, and was one of the pioneers of conservative economics in Britain.
68. Sander Vanocur to GH, December 1997.
69. John Cole Cool to GH, August 1997.

3. Chance Encounters, Random Walks: Harriman, Marriage and J. Edgar Hoover

1. DPM letter to GH, January 25, 1998.
2. Schoen, op. cit., pp. 49–50. DPM to GH, January 25, 1998.
3. Elizabeth Moynihan to GH, August 1997.
4. DPM, " 'Bosses' and 'Reformers,' " *Commentary*, 1961.
5. DPM, "When the Irish Ran New York," *The Reporter*, June 6, 1961. Later in the same article, Moynihan points out that on the night in 1897 when Tammany won one of its greatest victories by electing the first mayor of the consolidated city of New York, Boss Croker, John F. Carroll, Tim Sullivan, Charles Murphy and George Washington Plunkitt were a bitter disappointment to the waiters: "Here's the orders: Croker, vichy and bicarbonate of soda; Carroll, seltzer lemonade; Sullivan, apollinaris; Murphy, vichy; Plunkitt, ditto. Before midnight we were all in bed, and next mornin' we were all up bright and early attendin' to business."
6. John Westergaard to GH, August 1997.
7. Richard Sennett with Jonathan Cobb, *The Hidden Injuries of Class*, New York, Knopf, 1972.
8. DPM letter to GH, January 25, 1998.
9. DPM letter to GH.
10. Schoen, op. cit., p. 53.
11. Moynihan Papers, Library of Congress.

12. Philip M. Kaiser to GH, April 1998.
13. The following four paragraphs are based on interviews and correspondence with Elizabeth Moynihan, 1997–1998.
14. The following account owes much to Rudy Abramson, *Spanning the Century: The Life of W. Averell Harriman*, New York, 1992, especially pp. 516–69.
15. Ibid., p. 547.
16. Ibid., pp. 549–50. See also p. 65 in this chapter.
17. Ibid., p. 558.
18. Ibid., pp. 560–64.
19. Ibid., p. 563.
20. DeSapio was convicted on three counts of conspiring to bribe an official on December 5, 1969. On February 11, 1970, he was sentenced to two years in prison and fined $4,500 (*New York Times Index*).
21. DPM letter to GH, January 25, 1998.
22. Schoen, op. cit.
23. Elizabeth Moynihan to GH.
24. Moynihan Papers, Library of Congress, Box 21. The manuscript is labeled "Harriman 2nd Draft February 1962" and bears the return address 3016 Cortland Place, NW, Washington, D.C. It is organized in thirteen chapters and fills fourteen folders.
25. DPM to GH, 1997.
26. Moynihan Papers, Library of Congress.
27. DPM to GH, July 1997.
28. Schoen, op.cit., p. 60.
29. Charles McCarry, *Citizen Nader*, London, Jonathan Cape, 1972, p. 86.
30. DPM, "Letter to New Yorkers," October 23, 1992.
31. Meg Greenfield died after a long illness in early 1999.
32. DPM, "Epidemic on the Roads," *The Reporter*, April 30, 1959.
33. Ibid.
34. Schoen, op. cit., p. 55.
35. Harold A. Katz, "Liability of Automobile Manufacturers for Unsafe Design of Passenger Cars," *Harvard Law Review*, no. 69, 1956, pp. 863–73.
36. McCarry, op. cit., p. 20.
37. DPM, "The War Against the Automobile," *The Public Interest*, Spring 1966.
38. McCarry, op. cit.
39. Irving Kristol to GH, July 1997.
40. Abramson, op. cit., pp. 549–50.
41. What follows is based on a letter from Nathan Glazer to GH, September 21, 1997, and on an interview in December 1997.
42. "Ethnic Groups in America: From National Culture to Ideology," in Monroe Berger, ed., et al., *Freedom and Control in Modern Society*, New York, Van Nostrand Reinhold, 1954.
43. In fact DPM referred favorably to the Arensberg book in his article "When the Irish Ran New York," *The Reporter*, op. cit.
44. DPM letter to Nathan Glazer, March 22, 1962, Moynihan Papers, Library of Congress.
45. Moynihan Papers, Library of Congress, Box 26.

46. Nathan Glazer to GH, December 1997.
47. Nathan Glazer and DPM, *Beyond the Melting Pot,* Cambridge, Mass.: MIT Press, 1963, p. vi.
48. Moynihan Papers, Library of Congress, Box 21.
49. Schoen, op. cit., p. 65.
50. The correspondence about DPM's applications for federal jobs, including his application for HEW, Commerce, Labor and the Budget Bureau, is in Box 412 at the LBJ Library at the University of Texas. This box contains the folder on Moynihan from the office files of John Macy, director of the Civil Service Commission.
51. Sander Vanocur to GH, December 1998.
52. Schoen, op. cit., p. 67.
53. Sander Vanocur to GH, December 7, 1997.
54. DPM letter to Arthur Goldberg, September 5, 1964, Library of Congress, and DPM, "Secrecy as Government Regulation," *PS: Political Science & Politics,* June 1997.
55. Sander Vanocur to GH, December 7, 1997.
56. DPM, *Secrecy: The American Experience,* New Haven, Yale University Press, 1998, p. 216.
57. DPM letter to Richard Donahue, June 6, 1961.
58. Richard Donahue letter to DPM, June 7, 1961.
59. DPM, *PS: Political Science and Politics,* June 1997, p. 162.
60. James Q. Wilson to GH, April 16, 1998.

4. On the New Frontier: 1961–1965

1. Kennedy used the conceit in his acceptance speech at the Los Angeles Democratic Convention in 1960, but it was not original even then.
2. Georgetown was not, of course, named for George Washington. It was probably named for King George II; it was during his reign in 1751 that the inhabitants petitioned the Maryland Provisional Assembly to establish a town. Other historians, however, believe it may have been named either for George Beall, son of Ninian, or for George Gordon, owner of a piece of land called Knave's Disappointment, which he changed to Rock Creek Plantation.
3. Elizabeth Moynihan letter to GH, April 8, 1998.
4. Oneonta is in Otsego County, West Davenport across the line in neighboring Delaware County.
5. In that month he wrote to his former colleague James L. Sundquist, complaining that "a good year ago" he wrote to the agriculture committee in Albany "asking about soil bank situation of a farm I was thinking of buying in Otsego."
6. Later they bought the adjacent Banner farm, and now they have eight hundred acres and own their view.
7. Stephen Hess to GH, Summer 1997.
8. Moynihan Papers, Library of Congress, Boxes 24–26.
9. Ibid.
10. Robert Peck to GH, 1997.
11. "Report to the President by the Ad Hoc Committee on Federal Office Space," May 23, 1962, p. 15.

12. DPM talk on the occasion of publication of *Pennsylvania Avenue: America's Main Street,* by Carol M. Highsmith and Ted Lamphair, Washington, D.C., National Archives, January 19, 1989. The Walton sketch is in DPM's Senate office.

13. DPM letter to Lyndon Johnson, November 26, 1968, Library of Congress.

14. Jacqueline Kennedy letter to DPM, June 10, 1987, cited in DPM, *Washington Post,* November 23, 1987.

15. DPM, "One Third of a Nation," *The New Republic,* June 9, 1982, p. 19.

16. *Congressional Quarterly: Congress and the Nation,* September 20, 1962, vol. I, p. 618.

17. "One Third of a Nation: A Report on Young Men Found Unqualified for Military Service," Report of the President's Task Force on Manpower Conservation, January 1, 1964.

18. DPM private letter to Harry C. McPherson.

19. Dwight Macdonald, *The New Yorker,* 1962.

20. Michael Harrington, *The Other America,* New York, Penguin Books, 1963.

21. Ibid., pp. 1–2. "Tens of millions of Americans are . . . existing at levels beneath those necessary for human decency."

22. See also Robert Lampman, "The Low Income Population and Economic Growth," a study prepared for the Senate-House Joint Economic Committee, 1959; and "The Share of Top Wealth-Holders in National Wealth, 1922–1962," a publication of the National Bureau of Economic Research, Princeton, N.J., 1962. See also Marvin E. Gettleman and David Mermelstein, *The Great Society Reader: The Failure of American Liberalism,* New York, Random House / Vintage, 1967.

23. Richard A. Cloward and Lloyd E. Ohlin, *Delinquency and Opportunity: A Theory of Delinquent Gangs,* New York, Free Press, 1960.

24. U.S. Department of Health, Education and Welfare, "Report to the Congress on Juvenile Delinquency," Washington, D.C., Government Printing Office, 1960.

25. "A Proposal for the Prevention and Control of Delinquency by Expanding Opportunities," New York, Mobilization for Youth, Inc., 1961.

26. Albert K. Cohen, *Delinquent Boys: The Culture of the Gang,* New York, Free Press, 1963.

27. DPM interview on WTOP radio, Washington, D.C., November 23, 1963.

28. Ibid.

29. This account is based on DPM, *Coping: On the Practice of Government,* New York, Random House, 1973, pp. 5–7; see also *PS: Political Science & Politics,* June 1997, p. 161.

30. DPM, *Came the Revolution: Argument and the Reagan Era,* New York, Harcourt Brace Jovanovich, 1988, p. 9.

31. DPM, *Coping,* p. 5.

32. Ibid., p. 6.

33. It is still in Senator Moynihan's possession. See photo insert.

34. Charles Chiniquy, *Fifty Years in the Church of Rome,* London Protestant Literature Depository, 1886, p. 512.

35. DPM, *Maximum Feasible Misunderstanding,* New York, Free Press, 1969, p. 85.

36. Ibid., p. 82.

37. Ibid., p. 167. "The object of this essay has been to chronicle in brief the introduction of a social science idea into a government program."

38. This is persuasively argued in Gareth Davies, *From Opportunity to Entitlement: The Transformation and Decline of the Great Society*, Lawrence, University Press of Kansas, 1996, pp. 30–53. The following passage is especially indebted to three books: Alan Brinkley, *The End of Reform: New Deal Liberalism in Recession and War*, New York, 1995; Gareth Davies, op. cit.; Steve Fraser and Gary Gerstle (eds.), *The Rise and Fall of the New Deal Order*, Princeton, N.J., 1989.

39. E.g., Edwin Amenta and Theda Stocpol, "Redefining the New Deal: World War II and the Development of Social Provision in the United States," in Margaret Weir, Ann Shola Orloff and Theda Stocpol (eds.), *The Politics of Social Policy in the United States*, Princeton, N.J., Princeton University Press, pp. 81–92, cited in Gareth Davies, op. cit., p. 19. See also Brinkley, op. cit.

40. John Kenneth Galbraith, *American Capitalism: The Concept of Countervailing Power*, Boston, Houghton Mifflin, 1952, p. 1.

41. Gareth Davies, op. cit., p. 52.

42. DPM, *Maximum Feasible Participation*, pp. 102–5.

43. Frank Tannenbaum, *Slave and Citizen*, New York, Knopf, 1947.

44. Stanley Elkins, *Slavery*, Chicago, University of Chicago Press, 1959.

45. E.g., Nicholas Lemann, *The Promised Land*, New York, Knopf, 1991, p. 173, which attributes the Report to "complex career machinations."

46. Moynihan Papers, Library of Congress.

47. Nicholas Lemann, op. cit., p. 174.

48. DPM, "Case for National Action," p. 47.

49. DPM, "Social Goals and Indicators for American Society," *Annals of the American Academy of Political and Social Science*, May 1967.

50. I owe it to an astute suggestion by Gareth Davies, whose help in this and other instances I acknowledge with gratitude.

51. Harry C. McPherson, Jr., Oral History IV, 1.

52. LBJ Library, Box 149.

53. Commencement address at Howard University, June 4, 1965, "To Fulfill These Rights," Presidential Papers of the Presidents, Lyndon B. Johnson, Book II, no. 301, U.S. Government Printing Office, 1966.

54. Willard Wirtz to GH, August 1997.

5. The Dark Hour: The Election and the Report, 1965–1966

1. Including the Hodgsons.

2. Moynihan Papers, Library of Congress, Box 455.

3. Elizabeth Moynihan to GH, August 19, 1999.

4. In his encyclical *Ecclesiam Suam*, August 6, 1964, he did, however, make a tactful reference to "the children, worthy of our affection and respect, of the Hebrew people."

5. Moynihan Papers, Library of Congress, Box 26.

6. DPM, "Breakthrough at Ljubljana," *National Jewish Monthly*, September 1965.

7. Ibid.

8. *New York Times*, June 19, 1965, p. 13.

9. General William T. Sherman, on being offered the Republican presidential

nomination, is said to have retorted, "If nominated, I will not run, and if elected, I will not serve."

10. Moynihan Papers, Library of Congress, Box 26.
11. Robert Caro, *The Years of Lyndon Johnson*, New York, Knopf, 1981.
12. William Manchester, *The Death of a President*, New York, Harper and Row, 1967.
13. Jeff Shesol, *Mutual Contempt: Lyndon Johnson, Robert Kennedy and the Feud that Defined a Decade*, New York, W. W. Norton, 1997.
14. Jack Valenti was one source. Harry McPherson to GH, January 20, 1998.
15. Harry C. McPherson to GH, 1998.
16. Tom Wicker to GH.
17. In a 1998 interview, Professor Schlesinger did not deny that he was present at such a gathering, but said he had no recollection of it.
18. Harry McPherson letter to GH, January 20, 1998.
19. Mary McGrory, *Washington Star*, June 20, 1965.
20. Julius Duscha, *Washington Post*, June 22, 1965.
21. Willard Wirtz to GH, August 1997.
22. Moynihan Papers, Library of Congress, Box 61.
23. Harry McPherson note to President Johnson, July 8, 1965, LBJ Library.
24. Elizabeth Moynihan e-mail to GH, April 4, 1998.
25. Matt McCloskey, known to the Moynihan children as Uncle Matt, had been youth commissioner in the Harriman administration in Albany.
26. Harry McPherson letter to GH, January 20, 1998.
27. Harry McPherson memo to LBJ, June 24, 1965, from Mr. McPherson's personal papers.
28. LBJ Library, FG 160 1A.
29. One of McPherson's memos to Moyers on the subject makes it plain that this was not true. In at least one case, President Johnson did write to thank an outgoing assistant secretary for his services.
30. Lyndon Johnson handwritten note on Harry McPherson memo to Lyndon Johnson, Lyndon Johnson Papers, LBJ Library, September 29, 1965.
31. Jeff Shesol, op. cit.
32. In the LBJ Library, White House Central files, Box 617, is the text of a letter, October 7, 1965, from President Johnson to DPM thanking him for "the imagination and dedication you brought to your work." But it is a draft, written by McPherson, and I do not believe it was sent.
33. LBJ Library.
34. LBJ Library.
35. Quotation from William V. Shannon, *The Heir Apparent: Robert Kennedy and the Struggle for Power*, New York, Macmillan, 1967, p. 156.
36. *New York Times*, August 10, 1965.
37. Ibid.
38. *New York Times*, September 6, 1965.
39. Ibid.
40. Ibid.
41. GH personal recollection.
42. Elizabeth Moynihan to GH, July 1997.

43. DPM to GH, July 1997.
44. *New York Times,* July 26, 1965.
45. Moynihan Papers, Library of Congress, Box 25.
46. DPM letter to GH, May 12, 1997.
47. Rowland Evans and Robert D. Novak, "The Moynihan Report," *Wall Street Journal,* August 18, 1965.
48. Moynihan Report, p. 19.
49. Edward Wight Bakke, *Citizens Without Work,* New Haven, Yale University Press, 1940.
50. Harry McPherson letter to GH, January 20, 1998.
51. See Godfrey Hodgson, *America in Our Time,* New York, Doubleday, 1976, pp. 265ff.
52. Lee Rainwater and William L. Yancey, *The Moynihan Report and the Politics of Controversy,* Cambridge, Mass., MIT Press, 1987, p. 196.
53. Ibid., p. 248.
54. DPM letter to Harry McPherson, April 15, 1966, McPherson Office files, LBJ Library, Box 21.
55. Rainwater and Yancey, p. 402.
56. Ibid., p. 253.
57. Herbert Gans, *Commonweal,* October 15, 1965.
58. Rainwater and Yancey, p. 458.
59. Ibid., p. 467.
60. He wrote a book with this title. William Ryan, *Blaming the Victim,* New York, Pantheon, 1971.
61. DPM, "The President and the Negro: The Moment Lost," *Commentary,* February 1967.
62. Ibid.
63. *New York Times,* September 16, 1965.
64. DPM letter to GH, May 12, 1997.
65. Ibid., November 24, 1997.
66. Ibid., May 12, 1997.
67. Ibid.
68. DPM to Mrs. Reinhold Niebuhr, February 26, 1966, Moynihan Papers, Library of Congress.
69. DPM to Reinhold Niebuhr, December 9, 1965, Moynihan Papers, Library of Congress.
70. I haven't been able to identify the story. Nor have Professor Roy Foster, of Hertford College, Oxford, or his colleague Tom Paulin, both leading experts on twentieth-century Irish literature, or Professor Morris Harmon, of University College, Dublin, the editor of O'Faoláin's collected fiction. It seems possible that, as Professor Harmon suggested to me, O'Faoláin showed Moynihan, when both men were at Wesleyan, a story that has never been published, perhaps even a story O'Faoláin wrote specially for his unhappy friend.
71. DPM letter to GH, May 12, 1997.
72. DPM, "Op. Ed.," *New York Times,* May 28, 1976, p. A-25. See also Peter Steinfels, *The Neo-Conservatives: The Men Who Are Changing America's Politics,* New York, Simon and Schuster, 1979.

6. The Era of Bad Manners: From Harvard to Nixon

1. DPM, *Commentary,* February 1967.
2. See, e.g., Norman Podhoretz, *Making It,* New York, Random House, 1967.
3. The following account of the origins of *The Public Interest* is based on interviews with, among others, DPM, Irving Kristol, Nathan Glazer and Seymour Martin Lipset, as well as on the magazine itself and other printed sources.
4. DPM, "The Professionalization of Reform," *The Public Interest,* Fall 1965.
5. Ibid.
6. James Q. Wilson to GH, April 16, 1998.
7. Nathan Glazer, "On Being Deradicalized," *Commentary,* October 1971, pp. 74–80.
8. Seymour Martin Lipset to GH, July 1998.
9. James Q. Wilson to GH, April 16, 1998.
10. Ibid.
11. Elizabeth Moynihan to GH. She may have been more pleased than he was to be out of the harsh light of controversy and in a pleasant place like Wesleyan.
12. Ibid., May 1998.
13. *Wesleyan Argus,* October 19, 1965.
14. *Middletown Press,* no date, 1965.
15. DPM, *Commonweal* review of E. Franklin Frazier's "The Negro Family in the United States," April 1, 1966.
16. DPM, "The President and the Negro: The Moment Lost," *Commentary,* February 1967.
17. William Shakespeare, *Julius Caesar* (Act III, Scene ii).
18. DPM, "The President and the Negro: The Moment Lost," *Commentary,* February 1967.
19. Ibid.
20. Ibid.
21. James Q. Wilson to GH, April 16, 1998. See also Chapter 5.
22. Ibid.
23. Edward C. Banfield and James Q. Wilson, *City Politics,* Cambridge, Harvard University Press, 1963.
24. James Q. Wilson to GH, April 16, 1998.
25. Later president of the University of Pennsylvania.
26. Alan Altschuler to GH, December 1997.
27. Ibid.
28. Elizabeth Moynihan e-mail to GH, April 1998.
29. James Q. Wilson to GH, April 16, 1998.
30. DPM to GH, 1973.
31. Frederick C. Mosteller and Daniel P. Moynihan, eds., *On Equality of Educational Opportunity: Papers Deriving from the Harvard University Faculty Seminar on the Coleman Report,* New York, Random House, 1972, p. 4.
32. For the seminar and the arguments that grew out of it, see Godfrey Hodgson, "Do Schools Make a Difference?" *The Atlantic Monthly,* March 1973.
33. James Q. Wilson to GH, April 16, 1998.
34. Mosteller and Moynihan, op. cit.
35. DPM, "Equalizing Education," *The Public Interest,* Fall 1972.

36. "Nirvana Now" was first published in *The American Scholar,* Autumn 1967. It can also be found in DPM, *Coping,* New York, Random House, 1973, pp. 116–33.

37. Ibid., p. 133.

38. The text is conveniently to be found in DPM, *Coping,* New York, Random House, 1973, pp. 185–94. It was first published in the *New Leader,* October 9, 1967.

39. Melvin Laird, ed., *Republican Papers,* New York, Doubleday Anchor, 1968.

40. DPM to GH, Summer 1997.

41. Ibid.

42. The firm was originally Mudge Rose Guthrie and Alexander. When Nixon joined in 1963, it became Nixon Mudge Rose Guthrie and Alexander. When it merged with the municipal bond specialist firm run by John N. Mitchell, later Nixon's attorney general, it became Nixon Mudge Guthrie Alexander and Mitchell. See Leonard Garment, *Crazy Rhythm,* New York, Random House, 1997, p. 62.

43. To be precise, it was then called the Herman Herd. Ibid., p. 27.

44. Ibid., p. 68.

45. Ibid., p. 123.

46. Leonard Garment to GH, August 1997.

47. See Richard J. Whalen, *Catch the Falling Flag: A Republican's Challenge to His Party,* Boston, Houghton Mifflin, 1972.

48. Leonard Garment to GH, July 31, 1997.

49. Moynihan Papers, Library of Congress, Box 184.

50. Richard M. Nixon address to National Association of Manufacturers, December 8, 1967.

51. DPM to GH, July 1998.

52. DPM to Richard M. Nixon, October 24, 1968, Moynihan Papers, Library of Congress, Box 184.

53. Leonard Garment to GH, July 31, 1997.

54. DPM in Melvin Laird, op. cit., p. 139: "We have got to get more money directly into the hands of the poor. The best way to do this, or at least the best known way, is through a family (or children's) allowance."

7. Tory Men, Whig Measures: Working for Nixon in the White House

1. Richard A. Winter, Management Educators, letter, August 9, 1971, Moynihan Papers, Library of Congress, Box 184.

2. DPM letter to GH, July 2, 1998.

3. Moynihan Papers, Library of Congress, Box 220.

4. Ibid.

5. DPM letter to GH, July 2, 1998.

6. Ibid.

7. DPM to GH, July 1997.

8. Nixon Papers, National Archives, DPM to President-elect Nixon, undated.

9. DPM to Nixon, Nixon Papers, National Archives, President's Office Files, September 18, 1969.

10. DPM memo to H. R. Haldeman, Nixon Papers, National Archives, October 1, 1969.

11. Haldeman tapes, April 7, 1970. Haldeman notes Nixon as saying, "No one takes

the offensive, all just lie down (except Garment and Moynihan who are not really on our side)." Nixon then urged Haldeman to go and see the movie *Patton* to learn how to fire people up.

12. DPM to Richard Nixon, Nixon Papers, National Archives, Presidential Handwriting Files, November 25, 1969.

13. Ibid., May 9, 1970.

14. Ibid., April 15, 1969.

15. Ibid.

16. Stephen E. Ambrose, *Nixon: The Triumph of a Politician, 1962–72*, New York, Simon and Schuster, 1989.

17. DPM to Richard Nixon, Nixon Papers, National Archives, President's Office Files, Presidential Handwriting File 5, May 12, 1970.

18. *New York Times*, December 14, 1970.

19. DPM to Richard Nixon, Nixon Papers, National Archives, Presidential Handwriting Files, January 26, 1969.

20. A higher proportion of black Americans then went to college than of all young people in Britain, Moynihan pointed out.

21. DPM to GH, June 28, 1998.

22. Haldeman Diaries on CD-ROM, March 1, 1970.

23. DPM to GH, summer 1998.

24. There is some confusion about this quotation. In his book *The Politics of a Guaranteed Income*, Moynihan reports Nixon as having said "he had been reading a biography of Disraeli and Lord Randolph Churchill." In fact, though there is a good deal about Lord Randolph Churchill in the Blake biography of Disraeli, the phrase comes in a discussion in one of Disraeli's political novels. The words, correctly quoted as the epigraph to this chapter, "A sound conservative government, I understand: Tory men and Whig measures," come from the dialogue of the cynical party manager, Taper, in Disraeli's novel *Coningsby*. They were certainly intended ironically by Disraeli. Blake points out that, inverted, they could be the slogan of a sound liberal government.

25. DPM, *The Politics of a Guaranteed Income*, New York, Random House, 1974, p. 215.

26. DPM to Richard Nixon, Nixon Papers, National Archives, August 20, 1969.

27. Nixon Papers, National Archives, January 23, 1969.

28. Milton Friedman, "The Case for the Negative Income Tax," in Melvin Laird, ed., *Republican Papers*, New York, Doubleday Anchor, 1968, pp. 202–20.

29. Milton Friedman, *Capitalism and Freedom*, University of Chicago Press, 1962, p. 192.

30. The conference was held in March 1967. Arden House, the Harriman mansion, was donated, along with one thousand acres, to Columbia University.

31. Vincent Burke, *Nixon's Good Deed*, New York, Columbia University Press, 1974, p. 41; DPM, *The Politics of a Guaranteed Income*, p. 71.

32. DPM letter to GH, June 1998.

33. *Telos* is the Greek for "end" in the sense both of "conclusion" and "purpose."

34. Quoted in DPM, *The Politics of a Guaranteed Income*, pp. 77–78.

35. Ibid., p. 78.

36. *New York Times*, January 15, 1969.

37. Richard Nixon memo to John Mitchell, Robert Finch, Bryce Harlow and DPM, January 15, 1969, in Franklin D. Raines, "Presidential Policy Development: The

Genesis of the Family Assistance Program," Harvard University undergraduate thesis, p. 5.

38. DPM memo to Richard Nixon, February 1, 1969, Nixon Papers, National Archives.
39. Burke, op. cit., p. 62.
40. DPM, *The Politics of a Guaranteed Income*, p. 181.
41. After leaving the Nixon administration, Dr. Anderson moved to Stanford University.
42. DPM memo to Richard Nixon, January 31, 1969, in Raines, op. cit., pp. 20–21.
43. Raines, op. cit., p. 24, says it is not clear whether Nixon saw this memo.
44. Burke, op. cit., p. 3, Raines, op. cit., pp. 52–58.
45. DPM memo to Richard Nixon, Nixon Papers, National Archives, March 13, 1969.
46. Ibid., January 31, 1969.
47. Stephen E. Ambrose, *Nixon: The Triumph of a Politician*, New York, Simon and Schuster, 1989, p. 272.
48. Raines, a young African American staffer, had been a pupil of Moynihan's at Harvard and later was President Clinton's budget director and chief executive of the Federal Mortgage Agency ("Fanny Mae").
49. Nixon Papers, National Archives, January 31, 1969.
50. DPM to Richard Nixon, April 11, 1969, Nixon Papers, National Archives.
51. Haldeman Diaries, April 20, 1969.
52. Tom Wicker, *One of Us: Richard Nixon and the American Dream*, New York, Random House, 1995 edition, pp. 583–86, 626–31.
53. Haldeman tapes, April 24, 1969.
54. Raines, op. cit., p. 87.
55. Ibid., p. 92.
56. Haldeman Diaries, June 20, 1970.
57. Ibid., July 1, 1969.
58. Ibid., July 14, 1969.
59. Henry Kissinger, *White House Years*, Boston, Little, Brown, 1979, pp. 156–58.
60. Ibid., p. 156.
61. Haldeman Diaries, July 14, 1969.
62. DPM, *The Politics of a Guaranteed Income*, p. 214.
63. Ibid., p. 215.
64. Ibid., p. 216.
65. Public Papers of the Presidents, Richard M. Nixon, August 6, 1969.
66. Ibid.
67. Stephen E. Ambrose, *Nixon: The Triumph of a Politician: 1962–1972*, New York, Simon and Schuster, 1989, p. 294.
68. Haldeman tapes, November 1, 1969.
69. Kissinger, op. cit., p. 483.
70. Ambrose, op. cit., p. 338.
71. Kissinger, op. cit.
72. Ibid., p. 489.
73. Ibid., p. 495.
74. Ambrose, op. cit., p. 341, citing Seymour Hersh, *The Price of Power*, New York, Summit Books, 1983, pp. 187–88.

75. Ibid., p. 342.
76. Kissinger, op. cit., p. 498.
77. Ambrose, op. cit., p. 342.
78. DPM to GH, July 23, 1998.
79. Haldeman tapes, May 9, 1970.
80. DPM letter to Richard Nixon, August 3, 1970, Nixon Papers, National Archives.
81. Haldeman tapes, June 5, 1970.
82. DPM to GH, July 23, 1998.
83. DPM to GH, April 1999.
84. The following account is based on a letter from DPM to GH, June 20, 1998, and on an interview, July 23, 1998.
85. DPM to GH, July 23, 1998.
86. Haldeman tapes, November 21, 1970.
87. DPM letter to GH, June 20, 1998, and interview, July 23, 1998.
88. DPM letter to Richard Nixon, December 13, 1972, Nixon Papers, National Archives.
89. DPM, *The Politics of a Guaranteed Income*, p. 557.
90. Ibid., p. 542.

8. Watergate from Afar: Rethinking Nixon, America and the World

1. DPM letter to Richard Nixon, March 23, 1973.
2. Richard Nixon letter to DPM, June 5, 1973.
3. DPM diary, June 13, 1973.
4. He hinted something of the same to GH at the time, though oddly enough the individual he named was one untouched by the Watergate scandal.
5. DPM to Nathan Glazer, May 25, 1973.
6. DPM diary, March 1, 1974.
7. DPM to Nathan Glazer, May 25, 1973.
8. Blumenthal subsequently became attorney general of Connecticut.
9. DPM letter to Nathan Glazer, May 25, 1973.
10. Ibid.
11. DPM diary, June 28, 1973.
12. Charles Stewart Parnell, "the uncrowned king of Ireland," was the (Protestant but nationalist) leader of the Irish members in the House of Commons in the 1880s. Falsely accused of connivance in agrarian crime, he was disgraced as a result of his adultery with Kitty O'Shea, the wife of a colleague, and died at age forty-five in 1891.
13. DPM letter to Nathan Glazer, May 25, 1973.
14. DPM, July 14, 1974.
15. *Congressional Quarterly: Congress and the Nation*, vol. III, p. 486.
16. Charles W. Colson, previously an aide to Senator Leverett Saltonstall, a Massachusetts Republican, served as a White House aide from 1969 to 1973. He was best known for saying that he would "walk over my grandmother if necessary" to ensure Nixon's reelection. The Watergate conspirator E. Howard Hunt worked for him as a consultant. Colson later became a born-again Christian.
17. Presumably Howard Phillips, leader of the Conservative Caucus. Or possibly Kevin L. Phillips, author of *The Emerging Republican Majority*, 1969.

9. Proconsul: Ambassador to Delhi

1. DPM, *The Politics of a Guaranteed Income*, New York, Random House, 1974.
2. DPM letter to GH, June 20, 1998.
3. Statement by DPM in proceedings of the Third Committee, United Nations, October 7, 1971.
4. Ibid.
5. Moynihan Papers, Library of Congress.
6. Kissinger, *White House Years*, p. 867.
7. Henry Kissinger to GH, July 2, 1999.
8. Moynihan Papers, Library of Congress.
9. Kissinger, op. cit., pp. 842, 894, 917. Cf. Christopher Van Hollen, "The Tilt Policy Revisited: Nixon-Kissinger Geopolitics and South Asia," *Asian Survey*, vol. 20, April 1980, pp. 339–60.
10. DPM to GH, July 1998.
11. Henry Kissinger to DPM, January 2, 1973.
12. Chester Finn to GH, July 23, 1997.
13. Peter Galbraith to GH, April 1999.
14. DPM diary, Moynihan Papers, Library of Congress, November 2, 1974.
15. Ibid., January 1974.
16. DPM with Suzanne Weaver, *A Dangerous Place*, Boston, Little, Brown, 1978, pp. 40–41.
17. Ibid. See Howard Kohn's account in *Outside* magazine, San Francisco, in 1978, and a full account by Snanda K. Datta-Ray, *Illustrated Weekly of India*, June 4, 1978.
18. E. Howard Hunt, a long-time employee of the CIA and writer of spy novels, was involved in the Watergate break-in and other "White House horrors."
19. DPM diary, Moynihan Papers, Library of Congress, no date.
20. Ibid.
21. Rich Bland memo to DPM, June 4, 1998. Bland is on Moynihan's staff.
22. *Newsweek*, March 18, 1974.
23. Richard Nixon letter to Indira Gandhi, December 19, 1974.
24. Indira Gandhi letter to Richard Nixon, January 4, 1974.
25. Rich Bland to DPM, June 4, 1998; DPM diary, January 3, 1974, Moynihan Papers, Library of Congress.
26. Rich Bland to DPM, June 4, 1998.
27. DPM diary, Moynihan Papers, Library of Congress, no date. See also DPM to Lawrence Eagleburger, October 12, 1974.
28. DPM to GH, July 1998.
29. DPM diary, Moynihan Papers, Library of Congress, January 9, 1974.
30. DPM to Henry Kissinger, June 19, 1974.
31. Ibid., July 12, 1974.
32. By 1987, Moynihan had internalized this interesting anecdote. Admission to the "legendary" Indian Civil Service, as he now remembered it, was by way of a "gruelling oral examination." The cobra test was part of the examination.
33. DPM diary, Moynihan Papers, Library of Congress, January 9, 1974.
34. Henry Kissinger to GH, July 2, 1999.

35. DPM diary, Moynihan Papers, Library of Congress, October 24, 1974.
36. Ibid., undated [October 27, 1974].
37. DPM to Robert Christopher, Moynihan Papers, Library of Congress, undated.
38. DPM letters to McGeorge Bundy, November 8, 1974; Chester E. Finn, November 4, 1974; A. M. Rosenthal, *New York Times*, November 1, 1974; Cyrus Sulzberger, *New York Times*, November 29, 1974. Moynihan Papers, Library of Congress.
39. Richard Meryman, *Playboy*, March 1977.
40. Indira Gandhi letter to DPM, January 3, 1975.
41. DPM, "Letter to New Yorkers," 1984.
42. DPM letter to Robert Christopher, Moynihan Papers, Library of Congress, undated.
43. Paul Seabury letter to Norman Podhoretz, November 24, 1974, Moynihan Papers, Library of Congress.
44. Peter Willetts, *The Non-Aligned Movement: The Origins of a Third World Alliance*, London, F. Pinter, 1978.
45. Now the British Library.
46. Moynihan Papers, Library of Congress.
47. DPM, *A Dangerous Place*, pp. 40–41.
48. Draft marked "Author's original," dated January 26, 1975, Moynihan Papers, Library of Congress.

10. The Other End of 42nd Street: Ambassador at the United Nations and the Zionism Resolution

1. Proceedings of the Third Committee, United Nations documents, October 17, 1975.
2. Chaim Herzog, *Living History*, New York, Pantheon Books, 1996.
3. Ibid., p. 197; Leonard Garment, *Crazy Rhythm*, p. 311; DPM, *A Dangerous Place*, pp. 184–85.
4. I spent a few days staying with the Moynihans in their apartment in the Waldorf Towers and well remember Pat's mood of exaltation and controlled rage.
5. DPM to GH, 1975. In his book *A Dangerous Place*, p. 3, he attributes a milder version of this comparison to Kissinger's colleague, Dr. Helmut Sonnenfeld. But he told it to me the way I tell it here.
6. DPM diary, Moynihan Papers, Library of Congress.
7. Henry Kissinger, *White House Years*, pp. 341, 348.
8. Natan Sharansky, *Fear No Evil*, New York, Random House, 1988, pp. x–xxii.
9. Yohanan Manor, *To Right a Wrong*, New York, Shangold, 1997, p. 3.
10. Ibid, pp. xi–xxii.
11. Kissinger, op. cit., p. 1271; *Congressional Quarterly, Congress and the Nation*, vol. IV, p. 133.
12. William Bundy, *A Tangled Web: The Making of a Foreign Policy in the Nixon Presidency*, New York, Hill and Wang, 1998.
13. Henry Kissinger to GH, July 2, 1999.
14. DPM, *A Dangerous Place*, p. 93.
15. Ibid., p. 67.
16. Ibid., p. 60.

17. DPM letter to Gerald Ford, Moynihan Papers, Library of Congress, Box 337.
18. Garment, op. cit., p. 304.
19. Henry Kissinger speech in Milwaukee, July 14, 1975.
20. Suzanne Garment to GH, July 29, 1997.
21. Manor, op. cit., p. 14.
22. Barbara White memo, Moynihan Papers, Library of Congress, July 9, 1975.
23. DPM, *A Dangerous Place*, p. 96.
24. Ibid., p. 119.
25. Ibid., p. 55.
26. Ibid., pp. 55–56.
27. Ibid., p. 127.
28. Ibid., p. 162.
29. Ibid., p. 145.
30. Ibid., p. 146.
31. Ibid., pp. 166–68.
32. Ibid., p. 162.
33. Manor, op. cit., p. 19.
34. Coincidentally, Sierra Leone's ambassador, Edward Blyden, had been at Tufts with Moynihan and had become a friend of his.
35. DPM, *A Dangerous Place*, p. 187.
36. Ibid., p. 189.
37. Herzog, op. cit., pp. 196–97.
38. Manor, op. cit., p. 23.
39. Ibid.
40. DPM, *A Dangerous Place*, pp. 197–99, and in UN General Assembly, 1975, vol. II, pp. 795–97.
41. DPM, *A Dangerous Place*, p. 204.
42. Ibid., pp. 204–5.
43. Ibid., pp. 208–9.
44. *Newsweek*, November 1975.
45. Henry Kissinger to GH, July 2, 1999.
46. DPM, *A Dangerous Place*, p. 219.
47. Ibid., p. 215.
48. Ibid., p. 216.
49. Ibid., p. 219.
50. Lord Richard to GH, August 1998.
51. Henry Kissinger to GH, July 2, 1999.
52. DPM, *A Dangerous Place*, p. 28.
53. Ibid., p. 219.
54. According to Richard, the two men met at dinner with Henry Catto, the American ambassador in London during the Bush administration, and the evening passed pleasantly.
55. DPM, *A Dangerous Place*, pp. 229–30.
56. Ibid., pp. 222–23.
57. Suzanne Garment to GH, July 29, 1997.
58. Moynihan Papers, Library of Congress, January 27, 1976.
59. DPM, *A Dangerous Place*, p. 223.

60. Garment, *Crazy Rhythm*, p. 314.
61. Ibid., p. 315.
62. Moynihan Papers, Library of Congress.
63. Henry Kissinger telegram to DPM, Moynihan Papers, Library of Congress, February 27, 1976.
64. DPM, *A Dangerous Place*, p. 271.
65. Ibid., p. 272.
66. Henry Kissinger to GH, July 2, 1999.
67. Jewish Telegraph Agency, quoted in Manor, op. cit., pp. 239–41.
68. *New York Times*, September 14, 1991.

11. To the Senate: The 1976 Campaign

1. The following account is taken from DPM, *A Dangerous Place*, p. 212.
2. Ibid.
3. Ibid., p. 211.
4. Lord Richard to GH, August 1998.
5. *New York Times*, October 4, 1975.
6. DPM to GH, August 1997.
7. Richard Eaton to GH, July 1997.
8. Ibid.
9. Ben Wattenberg to GH, August 1998.
10. Moynihan Papers, Library of Congress.
11. James M. Perry, *National Observer*, April 17, 1976.
12. At a rally on Boston Common on Sunday, November 26, 1975, Jackson introduced Moynihan, then said, to warm applause, "Wouldn't he make a great secretary of state?" Bill Anderson, *Boston Globe*.
13. *New York Times*, May 2, 1976.
14. Ibid., May 4, 1976.
15. Ibid., June 8, 1976.
16. DPM to GH, July 1998.
17. *New York Times*, June 11, 1976.
18. *New York Daily News*, October 31, 1975.
19. DPM, *A Dangerous Place*, p. 228.
20. The following account of the 1976 election draws on interviews with, among others, DPM, Elizabeth Moynihan, Richard Eaton, Penn Kemble, Ben Wattenberg, Suzanne Garment, John Westergaard.
21. Penn Kemble to GH, August 1997.
22. Richard Eaton to GH, July 1997.
23. *New York Times*, September 10, 1976.
24. Elizabeth Moynihan to GH, July 31, 1997; John Westergaard to GH, August 6, 1997.
25. *New York Times*, September 1, 1976.
26. Ibid., September 11, 1976.
27. Ibid., September 6, 1976.
28. DPM to GH, July 1998.
29. *New York Times* editorial, September 10, 1976.
30. DPM, *A Dangerous Place*, p. 64.

31. Harrison E. Salisbury, *Without Fear or Favor: The New York Times and Its Times,* New York, Times Books, 1980, pp. 49–50.
32. The following account relies heavily on Salisbury's narrative, ibid., pp. 49–51. It is confirmed in general terms by DPM and by Max Frankel, *The Times of My Life and My Life with the Times,* Random House, 1999, pp. 377–79.
33. This exchange suggests that, in spite of his protestations, Moynihan was at least thinking of running for the Senate before he left the UN.
34. Frankel, op. cit., p. 377.
35. Ibid., p. 379.
36. Frank Lynn, *New York Times,* September 13, 1976.
37. *New York Times,* September 11, 1976, p. 45.
38. Ibid., September 18, 1976.
39. John B. Judis, *William F. Buckley, Jr.,* New York, Simon and Schuster, 1988, pp. 326–27.
40. *New York Times,* October 24, 1976.
41. DPM to GH, July 1988.
42. *New York Times,* November 3, 1976.
43. "Yes, I have climbed to the top of the greasy pole." W. F. Monypenny and G. E. Buckle, *The Life of Benjamin Disraeli,* vol. IV, p. 600.

12. A Democrat Again: First Term, 1977–1982

1. Although Keynes has often been quoted as saying this, his most authoritative biographer, Robert Skidelsky, told me he has been unable to trace it. Lord Skidelsky says there is much evidence that Keynes believed this, but he does not know where he said it.
2. DPM to GH, July 27, 1998.
3. Elliott Abrams to GH, September 14, 1998.
4. *Congressional Quarterly: Congress & the Nation,* vol. IV, pp. 985–1007.
5. See account in ibid., pp. 750–51.
6. DPM to GH, July 29, 1998.
7. Senator Warren G. Magnuson, a Washington Democrat, was a member of the House from 1937 to 1945 and of the Senate from 1945 to 1981.
8. Moynihan holds the record for the number of appearances on *Meet the Press,* with thirty-two at the time of this writing. His score may have been helped by the fact that the show's current host, Tim Russert, is a former staffer.
9. DPM to GH, July 29, 1998.
10. E.g., Charles Horner to GH, July 1997.
11. "Moynihan's Flamboyance and Quick Wit Draw Attention to Washington Freshman," *New York Times,* November 7, 1977.
12. DPM to GH, July 28, 1998.
13. Paul Nitze, *From Hiroshima to Glasnost,* London, Weidenfeld and Nicolson, 1989, p. 355.
14. Ibid.
15. Elliott Abrams and Charles Horner to GH, July 23 and 26, 1997.
16. DPM to GH, July 27, 1999.
17. Ibid.

18. Ibid.
19. DPM letter to GH, December 4, 1998.
20. *Newsweek*, November 19, 1979. Incidentally, Charles Horner told me that he "wrote" this *Newsweek* article, signed by Moynihan.
21. Moynihan Senate Papers, March 17, 1977; Gray Maxwell letter to GH, March 17, 1999.
22. DPM letter to GH, March 27, 1999.
23. Ibid.
24. Ibid.
25. Ibid.
26. *New York Times*, March 17, 1981.
27. Ibid., August 4, 1981.
28. DPM to GH, August 2, 1998.
29. Ibid., August 2, 1997.
30. The bill as finally passed (PL 95-339) was complex. Among other provisions it authorized the secretary of the treasury to issue federal loan guarantees to a total of $1.65 billion for fifteen years. *Congressional Quarterly: Congress & the Nation*, vol. IV, p. 280.
31. Professor Johnsen taught at the Technical Assistance Center at the State University College at Plattsburgh. See p. 288.
32. DPM, "Washington and New York," Letter to New Yorkers, Part I, April 1979.
33. DPM to GH, July 1998.
34. Ibid., August 2, 1997.
35. DPM, Letter to New Yorkers, September 4, 1981.
36. DPM, "Washington and New York," Letter to New Yorkers, Part I, April 1979.
37. *New York Times*, November 7, 1977.
38. DPM to GH, August 2, 1977.
39. The author recalls private discussion of this possibility with DPM and Elizabeth Moynihan in 1979.
40. Ben Wattenberg to GH, December 1998.
41. Elliott Abrams to GH, July 1997. Abrams was unable to locate the memo.
42. Penn Kemble to GH, August 13, 1997.
43. Norman Podhoretz, *Ex-Friends*, New York, Free Press, 1999, p. 101.
44. DPM to GH, July 27, 1997.
45. Norman Podhoretz, "Making the World Safe for Communism," *Commentary*, 1975.
46. Maura Moynihan e-mail to GH, July 1999.
47. DPM memo to staff, December 4, 1977.
48. Penn Kemble to GH, July 1997.
49. DPM quoted in Edward C. Burke, *New York Times*, November 7, 1977.
50. Ibid.
51. Speech to the Economic Club of New York, March 5, 1981. Reprinted in DPM, *Came the Revolution*, New York, Harcourt Brace Jovanovich, 1988, p. 16.
52. Speech to New York State Business Council, September 13, 1981, reprinted in *Came the Revolution*, op. cit., p. 31.
53. DPM, *Came the Revolution*, passim.
54. Ibid., p. 5.
55. The Laffer Curve was a curve drawn by Arthur Laffer (famously but mythically

on a paper napkin in a Washington restaurant) to demonstrate that the lower the tax rate, the more money that would be raised in taxation, an idea with immense appeal to high-bracket taxpayers.

56. Hinckley had apparently become obsessed by the actress Jodie Foster as a result of seeing her performance in the movie *Taxi Driver*.

57. Speech to the Business Council of New York State at Kiamesha Lake, New York, September 13, 1981. Reprinted in DPM, *Came the Revolution*, pp. 29–35.

58. Jane Perlez, *New York Times*, December 1982.

59. Richard Eaton to GH, July 1997.

13. Falling Out with Reagan: Second Term, 1983–1989

1. DPM to GH, August 3, 1997.

2. Jimmy Carter, *Keeping Faith*, New York, Collins, 1982, p. 127.

3. This realization came gradually. What he suspected in 1981, he felt sure of by 1983. "By the close of 1983 I knew that the early Reagan deficits had been deliberate, that there was a hidden agenda." DPM, *Came the Revolution*, p. 151.

4. "By 1981 it was plain that the Sandinistas, in the best Leninist fashion, had betrayed the revolution." DPM, *Came the Revolution*, p. 176. In the beginning, the Sandinistas, named for César Augusto Sandino, the rebel general defeated by the first Somoza with American help, were a broad nationalist movement, embracing liberal and Catholic intellectuals as well as apolitical peasants and socialist as well as Communist politicos. It was not long, however, before the influence of Communists and their fellow travelers was dominant. See Theodore Draper, *A Very Thin Line: The Iran Contra Affair*, Hill and Wang, New York, 1991; see also Jane Mayer and Doyle McManus, *Landslide: The Unmaking of the President, 1984–1988*, London, Collins, 1988.

5. "We will support the efforts of the Nicaraguan people to establish a free and independent government." Draper, op. cit., p. 16; see also Mayer and McManus, op. cit.

6. Draper, op. cit., pp. 16–18.

7. George Lardner, Jr., "Moynihan Unleashes the C.I.A.," *The Nation*, March 10, 1980.

8. Ibid., p. 176.

9. For a full account of this visit, see DPM, *Secrecy: The American Experience*, New Haven, Yale University Press, 1998, pp. 208–10. DPM provided details in an interview on August 3, 1997.

10. Dialogue from DPM, *Secrecy*, pp. 209–10. The last sentence, implying that the Jesuits identified with the Salvadoran rebels, comes from the August 3, 1997, interview.

11. Mayer and McManus, op. cit., p. 73.

12. Peter Rodman, *More Precious Than Peace: The Cold War and the Struggle for the Third World*, New York, Scribner, 1994.

13. The full text of Senator Goldwater's letter is in Draper, op. cit., pp. 20–21.

14. Ibid., p. 21.

15. DPM, *Came the Revolution*, Washington, D.C., Economic Policy Institute, 1996, pp. 178–79.

16. Ibid.

17. Ibid., p. 186.
18. For the Bishop meeting, I rely on DPM, *Loyalties,* New York, Harcourt Brace Jovanovich, 1984, pp. 93–96; DPM, *On the Law of Nations: A Historical and Personal Account of the Rise of International Law in Foreign Policy,* Cambridge, Mass., Harvard University Press, 1990, p. 128; DPM to GH, August 1998.
19. DPM, *On the Law of Nations,* p. 128.
20. DPM speech to Council on Foreign Relations, February 1979.
21. DPM, Commencement Address, New York University, May 24, 1984, printed in DPM, *Came the Revolution,* p. 189ff.
22. Rob Shapiro to GH, August 1997.
23. The following account of the background to the tax bill of 1986 is based on *Congressional Quarterly: Congress and the Nation,* vol. VII, pp. 33–107.
24. Ibid., vol. VI, p. 231.
25. Robert E. Hall and Alvin Rabushka, *The Flat Tax,* Stanford, Calif., Hoover Institution Press, 1995, p. 47. Hall and Rabushka first proposed the flat tax in an article in the *Wall Street Journal,* December 10, 1981.
26. *Congressional Quarterly: Congress and the Nation,* vol. VII, p. 78.
27. DPM, "Special Report to New York," Letter to New Yorkers, January 4, 1986, p. 1.
28. Ibid., p. 2.
29. Joe Gale to GH, August 14, 1997.
30. DPM, "Special Report to New York," Letter to New Yorkers, June 1, 1986, p. 2.
31. Ibid.
32. *Wall Street Journal,* May 2, 1986.
33. *Congressional Quarterly: Congress and the Nation,* vol. VII, p. 81.
34. I have had the privilege of being present when a Finance Committee staffer was being wooed by such a law firm.
35. Senator Bob Packwood to GH, April 1999.
36. DPM to GH, August 1997.
37. Ibid.
38. Moynihan, *Congressional Quarterly: Congress and the Nation,* vol. VII, p. 169; Hawkins, *Congressional Quarterly Almanac,* 100th Congress, 2nd Session, p. 364; Packwood, ibid.
39. Steve Weisman to GH, August 1997.
40. DPM letter to GH, January 31, 1999.
41. The following figures are taken from DPM, *Miles to Go: A Personal History of Social Policy,* Cambridge, Mass., Harvard University Press, 1996, pp. 2–3.
42. DPM blames himself, or rather Liz blames him, for losing the sixty-second county, Hamilton. The state was looking for a landfill to store the toxic chemicals dumped by General Electric in neighboring Washington County. There was difficulty about finding a suitable site, even some question of buying a farm from a widow for the purpose. Not to worry, said the senator, there are plenty of potential sites in Hamilton County. "OK, smart ass," said the campaign manager, "you just lost Hamilton County." She was right.
43. DPM, *Miles to Go,* pp. 25–26. "The seeming consensus of 1988 had dwindled at home, but in the rest of the nation it had quite disappeared."

14. Money and Power: Third Term, 1989–1994

1. DPM, *On the Law of Nations: A Historical and Personal Account of the Role of International Law in Foreign Policy*, Cambridge, Mass., Harvard University Press, 1990.
2. DPM, *Pandaemonium: Ethnicity in International Politics*, New York, Oxford University Press, 1993.
3. DPM memorandum to President-elect Clinton, November 28, 1992, datelined Zagreb.
4. Ibid., p. 4.
5. Ibid., p. 13.
6. Ibid., pp. 14–15.
7. DPM, *Miles to Go: A Personal History of Social Policy*, Cambridge, Mass., Harvard University Press, 1996, pp. 5–6.
8. Lyndon Johnson's term for chairmen such as Senator Richard B. Russell or Senator Robert Kerr of Oklahoma. See Harry C. McPherson, Jr., *A Political Education*, Boston, Atlantic, Little, Brown, 1972, p. 49.
9. DPM, *Miles to Go*, p. 2.
10. DPM, "Report from the Committee on Environment and Public Works, Together with Additional Views" to accompany S-1204, *Congressional Record*, June 4, 1991; DPM to GH, August 2, 1997.
11. Dwight D. Eisenhower, *At Ease: Stories I Tell My Friends*, New York, Doubleday, 1967, p. 157.
12. DPM, "New Roads and Urban Chaos," *The Reporter*, April 14, 1960.
13. Roy Kienitz to GH, August 1997.
14. Ibid.
15. DPM to GH, August 2, 1997.
16. The following details of the legislation are taken from the *Congressional Quarterly Almanac* for 1992, which published a detailed account of the legislation, "Highways, Mass Transit Funded," *1992 CQ Almanac*, pp. 137–51.
17. DPM speech on Senate floor, June 18, 1992.
18. Walter Pincus, "Bill Would Undo Courthouse Funding," *Washington Post*, March 19, 1992.
19. Ibid.
20. *Congressional Quarterly, Congress and the Nation*, vol. VIII, p. 438.
21. DPM speech on Senate floor, June 18, 1992.
22. DPM to GH, summer 1997.
23. See, for example, DPM's "Architecture in a Time of Trouble," *Journal of the American Institute of Architects*, 1969, and DPM, "Maria Regina Martyrum," *Atlantic Monthly*, May 1967, reprinted in DPM, *Coping*, pp. 243–47.
24. DPM, "Architecture in a Time of Trouble," *Journal of the American Institute of Architects*, September 1969, reprinted in DPM, *Coping*, pp. 233–42.
25. Ibid., p. 239.
26. Robert A. Peck to GH, August 1997.
27. DPM, "Report to the President by the Ad Hoc Committee on Federal Office Space," U.S. Government Printing Office, May 23, 1962, p. 13.
28. Jacqueline Kennedy Onassis to DPM, June 18, 1970, Moynihan Papers, Library of Congress.

29. DPM, "Not Bad for a Century's Work," *Washington Post*, November 23, 1997.
30. Ibid.
31. *Washington Post*, November 16, 1997.
32. DPM Delhi journal, March 18, 1974.
33. *Washington Post*, May 6, 1998.
34. Remarks by President Clinton at the Dedication of the Ronald Reagan Building and International Trade Center, May 5, 1998.
35. Kai T. Erikson, *Wayward Puritans: A Study of the Sociology of Deviance*, London, Collier Macmillan, 1966, citing Emile Durkheim, *The Rules of Sociological Method*, Paris, 1895. See DPM, *Miles to Go*, pp. 141–43.
36. The French writer Michel Foucault, in his *Histoire de la Folie à l'Age Classique*, Paris, Gallimard, 1976, showed that as leprosy disappeared from medieval Europe, leprosaria were converted into Bethlehem hospitals, or "bedlams," for the mentally ill, thus illustrating the thesis that society can accommodate only a certain number of deviants.
37. DPM, *Miles to Go*, op. cit., p. 144.
38. Ibid., p. 146.
39. Ibid.
40. Ibid., p. 156.
41. DPM letter to GH, December 8, 1999.
42. DPM, *Miles to Go*, p. 7.
43. In a 1993 interview, the new trade representative, Jeffrey Garten, used the word *aggressive* four or five times in a few minutes to describe the Clinton administration's policy.
44. DPM and Elizabeth Moynihan to GH. See also Elizabeth Drew, *On the Edge: The Clinton Presidency*, New York, Simon and Schuster, 1994, p. 271.
45. Son of Maura Moynihan, who had married John Avedon, son of the celebrated photographer Richard Avedon.
46. Johnson and Broder, *The System: The American Way of Politics at the Breaking Point*, Little, Brown, Boston, 1996, p. 355.
47. DPM, *Miles to Go*, p. 6.
48. Johnson and Broder, op. cit., pp. 265–66.
49. Marty Tolchin to GH, August 1997.
50. Elizabeth Moynihan to GH, August 1, 1997.
51. Ibid.
52. DPM and Elizabeth Moynihan to GH, August 1998. See also account in Johnson and Broder, op. cit., pp. 354–55.
53. It has improved since early 1999, when Mrs. Clinton, interested in running for Pat Moynihan's Senate seat, had the good sense to consult Elizabeth Moynihan several times on how to carry New York State.
54. Elizabeth Moynihan to GH, August 1, 1997.
55. Johnson and Broder, op. cit., p. 210.
56. DPM, *Miles to Go*, op. cit., p. 29.
57. Ibid.
58. Johnson and Broder, op. cit., p. 351.
59. Jason de Parle, *New York Times*, January 8, 1994; William Claiborne, *Washington Post*, January 10, 1994.

60. Johnson and Broder, op. cit., pp. 372–73, tell the anecdote well. Also DPM letter to GH, January 27, 1999.
61. Johnson and Broder, op. cit., p. 380.
62. *New York Times*, June 15, 1994.
63. Ibid., June 13, 1994.
64. Todd S. Purdum, *New York Times*, June 16, 1994.
65. Ibid. Elected as Moynihan's Senate colleague in 1998.
66. Robin Toner, *New York Times*, June 29, 1994.
67. DPM, *Miles to Go*, p. 2.

15. The Legislator as Magnifico: Fourth Term, 1995–2000

1. Al Gore letter to DPM, March 16, 1997, communicated by Moynihan staff.
2. *Congressional Record*, March 16, 1997, pp. S1966–1967.
3. The papers were collected in a Festschrift, edited by Robert A. Katzmann, and published as *Daniel Patrick Moynihan, The Intellectual in Public Life*, Washington and Baltimore, Woodrow Wilson Center Press and Johns Hopkins University Press, 1999.
4. DPM quoted by Eberstadt and published in ibid., p. 64.
5. Ibid., p. 23.
6. Ibid., p. 42.
7. Information from Senator Moynihan's chief of staff, Tony Bullock.
8. Numbers supplied by Senator Moynihan's office.
9. Peter Galbraith to GH, April 1999.
10. *Congressional Quarterly: Congress and the Nation*, vol. VI, 1981–1984, p. 646.
11. Robert Dole, "Reagan's Faithful Allies," *New York Times*, January 3, 1983, p. A19.
12. DPM's version of these events was given in the speech "Social Security Saved!" at the Institute of Politics, John F. Kennedy School of Government, Harvard University, March 16, 1998.
13. Paul C. Light (director of the Public Policy Program of the Pew Charitable Trusts), letter to DPM, January 16, 1998. See also Paul C. Light, *Still Artful Work: The Continuing Politics of Social Security Reform*, New York, McGraw Hill, 1995.
14. See, among many accounts, Martin Anderson, *Revolution*, New York, Harcourt Brace Jovanovich, 1988; Godfrey Hodgson, *The World Turned Right Side Up*, Boston, Houghton Mifflin, 1996.
15. DPM, "Social Security Saved!" op. cit.
16. DPM letter to Dr. Laura D'Andrea Tyson, quoted on Senate floor, December 12, 1993, and reprinted in "Congress Builds a Coffin," the *New York Review of Books*, January 1994.
17. *New York Times*, August 2, 1996.
18. DPM, *Miles to Go: A Personal History of Social Policy*, Cambridge, Mass., Harvard University Press, 1996, p. 41.
19. Ibid.
20. *New York Times*, August 2, 1996, p. 1.
21. Ibid., April 13, 1997.
22. R. W. Apple, Jr., "His Battle Now Lost, Moynihan Still Cries Out," *New York Times*, August 2, 1996.

23. Ibid.
24. Robert J. Gordon, "The Consumer Price Index: Measuring Inflation and Causing It," *The Public Interest*, 1981.
25. DPM, *Miles to Go*, p. 131.
26. Steven Pearlstein, "A Single Number Puts the Economy in a New Light," *Washington Post*, December 11, 1996.
27. Robert J. Samuelson, "Clinton and the CPI," March 24, 1997, *Newsweek*.
28. James K. Glassman, "A 1.1 Percent Solution," *Washington Post*, December 10, 1996.
29. Properly the Congressional Budget and Impoundment Control Act of 1974. See *Congressional Quarterly, Congress and the Nation*, vol. IV, 1973–76, pp. 71–81.
30. Ed Gillespie and Bob Schellhas (eds.), *Contract with America: The Bold Plan by Rep. Newt Gingrich, Rep. Dick Armey and the House Republicans to Change the Nation*, New York, Times Books, 1994, pp. 29–33.
31. 142 *Congressional Record*, S-2995; Idem H-2986.
32. Public Law 104–130, signed April 4, 1996.
33. Supreme Court, *Raines v. Byrd*, no. 96–1671, p. 2.
34. "Within two months." Supreme Court, *Clinton v. New York*, no. 97–1374, p. 1.
35. This was the language used by the Supreme Court in deciding *Chadha v. IRS*, the case in which the Court struck down the so-called "legislative veto."
36. Ibid.
37. Helen Dewar and Joan Biskupic, "Line Item Veto Struck Down; Backers Push for Alternative," *Washington Post*, June 26, 1998.
38. Ibid.
39. Robert Pear, "Justices, 6–3, Bar Veto of Line Items in Bills," *New York Times*, June 26, 1998, p. A1, continued with picture on p. A16.
40. Ibid.
41. DPM speech at Georgetown University, "Secrecy as Government Regulation," March 3, 1997.
42. Richard Gid Powers, introduction to DPM, *Secrecy*, New Haven, Conn., Yale University Press, 1998, p. 9.
43. Michael Barone and Grant Ujifusa, *Almanac of American Politics*, Washington, D.C., National Journal, 1998, p. 1382.
44. DPM, "Secrecy as Government Regulation," *PS: Political Science and Politics*, June 1997, p. 164.
45. DPM, *Secrecy*, op. cit., p. 76, quoting Tim Weiner, "For First Time, U.S. Discloses Spying Budget," *New York Times*, October 16, 1997.
46. Edward A. Shils, *The Torment of Secrecy: The Background and Consequences of American Security Policies*, Free Press, Glencoe, Ill., 1956, reissued with an introduction by Daniel P. Moynihan, Chicago, Ivan R. Dee, 1996.
47. Forthcoming at the time of writing, information from h-diplo@h-net.msu.edu, March 5, 1999.
48. Strictly speaking, White was not accused, as he died before his case was determined.
49. Steven Aftergood, "Moynihan, Venona and Truman," *Secrecy and Government Bulletin*, issue 77, March 1999.
50. Ibid.

51. The question of whether President Truman was in fact informed of the Venona material was the subject of a political exchange between Moynihan and Richard Perle, assistant secretary of defense in the Reagan administration. In the December 1998 edition of *Commentary*, Perle questioned Moynihan's assertion that Truman was not informed. In March 1999, *Secrecy and Government Bulletin* stated that "newly publiished FBI documents indicate that information derived from Venona was in fact provided to the Truman White House." Moynihan then wrote a letter to *Commentary* reiterating that "no evidence" showed that Truman was ever told about Venona. Perle wrote back to the magazine, citing the October 17, 1950, FBI memo as indicating that Venona material "was in fact provided to the Truman White House." However, according to a memorandum prepared for Senator Moynihan by his staff on June 10, 1999, the October 17 memo has never been found, even after a diligent search within both the FBI and CIA. And Robert Lamphere, responsible for liaison between the Venona team and the FBI, wrote to Moynihan on October 1998 confirming that "we never in the FBI briefed President Truman on the facts that [the Venona cryptographers] were decrypting the KGB messages." While Moynihan may have gone beyond what can be proven with absolute certainty in maintaining that Truman was definitely *not* informed, on balance it looks as though Moynihan's contention is correct.
52. Erwin N. Griswold, "Secrets Not Worth Keeping," *Washington Post*, February 15, 1989.
53. DPM, *Secrecy*, op. cit., p. 227.
54. For example, a commencement address at Middlebury College, May 24, 1998, and an article entitled "NATO Expansion and Nuclear War," vol. 10, nos. 7–8.
55. *NATO Handbook*, 1999, p. 82.
56. Ibid., p. 97.
57. Author's personal knowledge.
58. DPM to GH, July 29, 1998.
59. Ibid., August 1998.
60. See Jeffrey Toobin, "Pat 'n' Bill," *The New Yorker*, February 8, 1999.
61. Interview with DPM on the *Fred Dicker Show*, WROM-AM, Albany, New York, August 19, 1998.
62. *Congressional Record*, vol. 144, no. 115, September 3, 1998.
63. "More than Inappropriate: Review and Outlook," *Wall Street Journal*, September 4, 1998, p. A10.
64. *New York Times*, December 25, 1999.
65. DPM on *Meet the Press*, December 27, 1998.
66. Jeffrey Toobin, op. cit.
67. DPM letter to GH, February 1999.
68. *Congressional Record*, February 10, 1999.
69. James Madison, *Journal*, September 8, 1787.
70. *Congressional Record*, vol. 145, no. 26, February 12, 1999.
71. DPM letter to GH, April 1999.
72. Obie Clayton, Ron Mincy, David Blankenhorn, et al., "Turning the Corner on Father Absence in Black America," Morehouse Research Institute and the Institute for American Values, 1999.

Index